T0330273

Manufacturing

Modern Japanese

Literature

Asia-Pacific: Culture, Politics, and Society

EDITORS

Rey Chow, Michael Dutton, H. D. Harootunian,
and Rosalind Morris

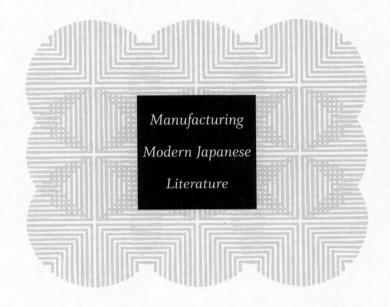

Manufacturing Modern Japanese Literature

PUBLISHING, PRIZES, AND THE

ASCRIPTION OF LITERARY VALUE

Edward Mack

Duke University Press   Durham and London   2010

© 2010 Duke University Press

All rights reserved

Printed in the United States of America on acid-free paper ∞

Designed by Heather Hensley

Typeset in Whitman by Keystone Typesetting, Inc.

Library of Congress Cataloging-in-Publication Data appear on
the last printed page of this book.

To Kasumi

CONTENTS

● ● ●

ACKNOWLEDGMENTS

● ● ●

There are too many people who have contributed to this manuscript for me to list them all, or the manifold ways they have helped me intellectually, emotionally, logistically, and materially. I am grateful to my colleagues and friends, from the beginning of my graduate experience through to my current position at the University of Washington, all of whom contributed to this project either directly or indirectly. I owe a particular debt to those individuals who have read through this manuscript, all or in part, for their patience and input: Tani Barlow, Davinder Bhowmik, Harold Bolitho, Rich Calichman, Albert Craig, Harry Harootunian, David Lurie, Atsuko Sakaki, Henry Smith, Scott Swaner, Alan Tansman, Richard Torrance, John Treat, the members of the Japanese History Seminar, and my anonymous readers. As a member of my dissertation committee, Andrew Gordon spent a great deal of time with this text, and helped me develop its original structure. In Japan, I have enjoyed the support of Asaoka Kunio, Asako Hiroshi, Sainowaki Kazuhide, Satō Toshio, Takahashi Noboru, Nakagawa Shigemi, and Rimbara Sumio, all of whom have been sources of invaluable advice, encouragement, and assistance. The manuscript has benefited directly from the labors of all these individuals, and indirectly from the efforts of many more.

I have enjoyed institutional and financial support at key points that made all the difference. These include a fellowship from Fulbright-IIE, which allowed me to spend a year doing my research at the University of Tokyo, and a Whiting Fellowship in the Humanities, which gave me the support I needed to complete my work. I have also received support from

Nihon University and Kobe University, both of which provided me periods of research in Japan; these stays were also made possible by the University of Washington, which has been generous in its allowances of support and time.

Finally, I would like to acknowledge the specific contributions of six individuals, each of whom made a crucial difference to my academic career and intellectual life. David Howell introduced me to the study of Japan and provided me with essential support at the earliest stages of my education. Paul Anderer showed me how fascinating the field could be and provided me with the opportunity to pursue it professionally. Dennis Washburn helped me first as a member of my dissertation committee and later as a colleague, providing direction, counsel, and support. Komori Yōichi taught me an extraordinary amount in all-too-short a time; while I am quite certain I do not have the necessary constitution, I aspire to both his level of commitment and activity. Kōno Kensuke has been my teacher, my colleague, and my friend; his productivity, generosity, good humor, and open-mindedness continue to be an inspiration to me. Jay Rubin, has been there for me throughout this process and, with a few well-timed prods, got me to where I am today; he is now more family than advisor.

Above all, however, I would like to acknowledge the immeasurable contribution that my wife, Kasumi, has made to this work. She has made significant sacrifices to allow me to complete it, and it is to her that I dedicate this book.

Earlier versions of chapters 1 and 5 appeared as "Pure Art as Mass Culture: Industrialized Publishing and 'Modern Japanese Literature'" in *Books in Numbers*, ed. Wilt L. Idema (Cambridge: Harvard-Yenching Library, 2007), pp. 311–55, and "Accounting for Taste: The Creation of the Akutagawa and Naoki Prizes for Literature" in the *Harvard Journal of Asiatic Studies* 64:2 (December 2004), pp. 291–340.

● ● ●

Publishing and the Creation of

an Alternate Economy of Value

Demand . . . emerges as a function of a variety of social practices
and classifications, rather than a mysterious emanation of human
needs, a mechanical response to social manipulation . . . , or the
narrowing down of a universal and voracious desire for objects to
whatever happens to be available.

ARJUN APPADURAI, *THE SOCIAL LIFE OF THINGS*

In Mizumura Minae's semi-autobiographical novel *Shishōsetsu from Left
to Right* (The I-Novel from Left to Right, 1995) the narrator's mother
wheedles an old, vermillion-covered series of books out of a relative in
Yokohama before setting off for the United States. The one indication we
have in *Shishōsetsu from Left to Right* about the mother's motivations for
making a special trip to borrow a mountain of forty-year-old books comes
when we are told that she had obtained the series "for her daughter, whom
she would be raising in the United States."[1] This simple phrase captures the
mother's expectations of the series, which will become a singular resource
for her daughter, a literary youth who will have little access to other
sources of Japanese-language texts. As such, the series would partially
predetermine the act of reading both materially and conceptually. Materially it would limit what could be read by its contents; conceptually it
would influence how those contents could be interpreted through its or-
ganizational framework. That framework—modern Japanese literature—
implies that the texts not only have an organic relationship with one

another through the nation and through modernity, but also are somehow sufficient to represent the modern nation's literary production and perhaps the modern nation itself.[2] In reflecting on the series' impact later, when she herself has become a writer, Mizumura's narrator muses, "In the process of acquainting myself with the musty complete works of modern Japanese literature, at some point I fell in love not only with Japan, but with a Japan that existed before my birth."[3] It is, after all, not the literary quality—or value, in the sense of importance—of each individual work that draws the narrator's mother when she chooses the series, but an entire economy of such value, which in turn is legitimated through its association with modernity, its dissociation from a degraded form of fiction, and its interconnection with the nation itself.[4]

The series mentioned in the novel is the *Gendai Nihon bungaku zenshū* (Complete Works of Contemporary Japanese Literature), published by Kaizōsha between 1926 and 1931, which Mizumura's narrator rightly describes as being "the first complete works of modern Japanese literature."[5] The series marked a watershed in the production of literature, made possible by a concentration of print capital in Tokyo, the imperial seat.[6] This process of centralization had been under way through the second half of the Edo period (1600–1868) but accelerated rapidly right around the turn of the twentieth century.[7] The result was a small number of large publishers able to produce texts on an unprecedented scale and then sell those literary commodities to a market of unprecedented size.[8] The consolidation of cultural power—the ability to influence the dissemination, reception, and preservation of literary works—attending this concentration of economic capital provided for the creation of various instruments that allowed a small number of individuals to have a far-reaching influence not only on what people read, but also on how they read. The *Complete Works of Contemporary Japanese Literature* was only one of these instruments.

The influence of the series on Mizumura's narrator, while obviously exceptional, helps bring into relief the impact that extraliterary forces have on the understanding of literary value and literature itself. Many forces influence individual readers' conceptions of literary value, and often those forces are impossible to isolate. Some, however, are identifiable. This series, for example, did more than guarantee the material circulation of a specific set of texts under a rubric that positioned them as sufficient representatives of a national literary genius; it also conveyed an implied economy of literary value based on that rubric to a vast readership. This was an alternate economy to the extent that it claimed autonomy from the tyranny of the marketplace; it was new in the sense that it implied a different logic of value than that which underwrote earlier literature written in Japanese.[9] The finite cultural entity of modern Japanese literature, as instantiated in but not solely created by the series, relied on three powerful dichotomies: modern against premodern, the Japanese nation or linguistic community against non-Japanese communities, and literature against less worthy forms of writing. Standing between each of these dichotomies was a boundary, produced by and subsequently producing each side's mutual exclusivity. Inevitably these boundaries simplified complex realities in which dramatic difference was mixed with predictable similarity. When these three seemingly simple categories were evoked, however, the sequence of decisions behind the selection of the series' contents was obscured and the ambiguous boundary between the selected works and all others was reified. In this sense the *Complete Works of Contemporary Japanese Literature* helped manufacture the very entity it purported to reflect: modern Japanese literature.

The present study is meant to complement scholarship that questions these boundaries and considers the phenomenon of literature through categories other than the nation, modernity, or elite traditions.[10] My goal is to examine the way the existing, dominant boundaries were conceived and manifested, while remaining sensitive to the various interests of the parties involved and the tools used to realize those interests. I do this by focusing on immanent textual events: the physical objects—the old, vermillion-covered collection, for example—which readers held in their hands as they read, or at least placed on their bookshelves as a sign of personal cultivation. These are, after all, the only texts a reader can ever encounter: "particular, materially embodied, and historically mediated textual *instances* that inevitably bear traces of the complex economic, social, political, aesthetic, and bibliographical circumstances of their making."[11] It is these circumstances—the multiple value systems and the extraliterary forces behind the material reproduction of texts—that are the central object of this study.

The material reproduction of texts by the publishing industry enabled the alternate economy of value known as modern Japanese literature, which was originally produced discursively, to have the tremendous impact it did. Powerful instruments like the *Complete Works of Contemporary Japanese*

Literature (and later the Akutagawa Prize for literature) were made possible by specific developments in the publishing industry, particularly the expanding reach of that industry resulting from print capital's concentration in Tokyo. Today, when access to texts—whether educational, economic, or simply material access—is presumed (often mistakenly) to be reasonably unimpeded throughout the nation-state (if not the world), it is easy to project the present condition back in time, at least through the modern period. The reality of the matter, however, is that access to literature has not always been so ready; a history of the social existence of literature therefore must trace over time the reach of print both horizontally, to every corner of the nation-state, the empire, and the broader linguistic community, and vertically, through various economic and social strata.[12]

Literature's impact on the nation as a whole should not be presumed, even in the era of mass culture. This study traces the expansion of the Tokyo-based publishing industry into an industry that distributed an increasingly uniform supply of texts throughout a vast market. This examination of Tokyo's preeminence must not be taken as reifying the notion of a Tokyo-centered hegemony; it is precisely through historicization that this centrality can be recognized both for what it is and what it is not. Qualifiers such as "increasingly uniform" and "vast" (rather than the complete-sounding "national") signal the fact that even in this age of mass production any claim to a national (or supranational) market for print, implying complete access for all citizens, is hyperbolic. Needless to say, literary production was not homogeneous throughout the country, nor was consumption identical for each individual.[13] No single cultural product can link all members of a nation, nor can any center fully dominate the areas it considers peripheral. The centrality and importance of the Tokyo publishing world must be considered relatively and should not be interpreted as a complete or unchallenged hegemony even in the present day.

Although not hegemonic in its influence, the publishing industry expanded the audience for this new economy of value by an order (or two) of magnitude; even if modern Japanese literature's reach was not truly complete throughout the nation, it nonetheless derived authority from claiming a national audience. This transaction was almost certainly reciprocal: literature used the value attributed to the nation(-state) to contribute to its own prestige, and then the nation-state became able to use its possession of a modern national literary culture to reinforce that imagined community.

This is only one way the series functioned as an instrument of what has been called "capital intraconversion," through which the value, or symbolic capital, accumulated in the literary field could be exchanged for other forms of capital, whether economic, social, or political.[14] This capacity of intraconversion reveals the speciousness of literary value's claim to autonomy; this alternate economy of value was in fact intertwined with other forms of value, not the least of which was its exchange value as a commodity in the marketplace.

As value accumulated within the literary field and as its convertibility increased, the number of individuals who created and exercised various instruments to define literary value and thus exert power increased as well. This was likely the most lasting impact of mechanisms such as the *Complete Works of Contemporary Japanese Literature*: a reified alternate economy of value (which later would be associated with the concept of "pure literature") through differentiation (from, among other things, "popular literature" and thus a market-driven value system) and association (with modernity, the nation-state, and existing literary prestige).[15] In this sense the impact was less on specific works than on a conceptual space, the contents of which could shift over time.[16]

Of course print capitalism had as much to gain from the creation of this sphere as the nation(-state) did. As this study's focus on the publishing industry suggests, commercial interests had a great deal to gain from the establishment of this seemingly distinct value system. Print capital benefited greatly from the creation and valorization of a modern national literature because the concept itself interpellated and invested the largest number of potential readers, and thus consumers, in this literary economy and the works, the commodities, that value system elevated. It should also be noted that failure to be recognized within this new economy of value did not necessarily prevent works from being published; a vast array of works, much larger than the number linked to this new economy, were published because they shared sources of value directly recognized by the traditional economy, works often melded together under the rubric of "popular literature" and linked with the value of entertainment. The new alternate economy of value only *presented* itself as autonomous from the capitalist economy of value; as long as the works within that economy were published, however, they remained firmly embedded in the traditional economy as well.

The beneficial outcomes of this alternate economy should not be underestimated. It created a public space that allowed an unprecedented number and variety of individuals to be heard; the convertibility of the value produced within the field of modern Japanese literature enabled literary production that might not otherwise have been possible. Largely independent of political, religious, or governmental patronage, this value allowed a literary discourse that often stood in opposition to the cultural or political mainstream. Yet this enabling value came at a cost: an elevated sphere of modern Japanese literature necessitated that a large amount of literary production justify its very existence or be dismissed. The literary field presented as the product of a national aesthetic consensus was in fact a specific subset of literary production that had been culled from and elevated above a multitude of texts by a series of individuals, whose decisions were subjective and motivated. This should not be taken to mean that their assertions of literary value were unfounded, nor that the works lack identifiable value.[17] Rather the historical sources of these decisions were retroactively naturalized so as to appear to be resulting from a neat aesthetic consensus, which never existed.

Tracing the function of mechanisms such as the *Complete Works of Contemporary Japanese Literature* illuminates the role extraliterary forces play in the construction of the literary field; the absence of sources explicating the literary value systems informing the selections for that series, however, necessitates the examination of additional mechanisms. The contingency of literary value systems is readily apparent in the second instrument of cultural power that this book examines: the Akutagawa Prize for literature. Beginning in 1935 and continuing to this day, the Akutagawa Prize remains one of the most, if not *the* most, prestigious literary prizes in Japan. As with the *Complete Works of Contemporary Japanese Literature*, the Akutagawa Prize allowed actors not only to valorize specific works but also, in the process, to perpetuate a valorized literary field. Unlike the *Complete Works*, however, the Akutagawa Prize allows for these acts to be perpetual. Where the *Complete Works* created a singular opportunity to influence a body of works, the Akutagawa Prize allows actors to influence works to this day, creating a continuous flow of elevated literary commodities and reinforcing the economy of literary value at regular intervals. By referring to this distinction as "dynamic canonization" as opposed to the "static" mechanism of the anthology, we can highlight this advantage of the prize mechanism.[18]

I invoke the concept of a canon in only a limited sense, in an attempt to avoid a variety of implications sometimes associated with the term. Any suggestion of a state of being—something is either in the canon or out of the canon—obscures what is in fact a constantly shifting degree of authority. Similarly, despite the implication of universality, different individuals at different moments in time will have varying conceptions of the canon. And the stability of the canon should not be exaggerated: while reiterations of canonicity can stabilize a work's centrality, such status is never guaranteed. The connotations of stasis and universality inherent in the term can best be avoided if we remain focused on specific exercises of power, the mechanisms through which that power is exercised, the agenda informing those exercises, and the consequences of those exercises. The term also normally involves a religious, governmental, or educational authority that plays an active role in compelling adherence to the canon. My focus, however, is on the less directly suasive (though no less influential) role that publishing, and the material forms it produces, has on the dissemination, reception, and preservation of literary works. The Akutagawa Prize and Kaizōsha's *Complete Works of Contemporary Japanese Literature*, as two central instruments that played particularly important roles in the construction of a concept of modern Japanese literature, reflect the role that publishing plays in creating such an entity.[19]

The current study, rather than attempting to present a complete picture of all forces at work on literary production, might best be considered a series of essays on the topic. The essays link together into sections: the first is a macrohistory of literary publishing, which addresses the concentration of print capital in Tokyo, and the second is a microhistory of cultural authority, which describes two central mechanisms in the assertion of literary value that were made possible by that concentration. Between the discussions of the two mechanisms—the anthology and the award—I explore the discursive exercise of cultural authority that informed the material exercises. Together these chapters attempt to begin a historical reconstruction of the sociology of modern Japanese literature; needless to say, they amount to little more than a partial picture of a complex situation. Since this picture is partial, it is important to clarify what it will not be addressing. My focus is on the production rather than actual consumption of literature, though reception data are presented when available; often my conclusions regarding consumption are speculative, based on the potential for reception.[20] In addition, since the focus of this study is publishing as an industry and a system, my examination of the content of specific literary works is limited. Hopefully this will bring the materiality of literature into high relief without implying that the contents of texts are irrelevant. A study of literature that focuses on the materiality of texts rather than on their literary content is meant to complement rather than to replace studies of the texts themselves. Having said that, my goal is to show how dependent our experiences of literary content are on the material conditions of its production and consumption.

The first chapter addresses the history of book production and consumption in Japan, tracing the advancements in technology, the expansion of a market for literary commodities, and the development of an extensive reading community that resulted in Japan's modern publishing industry and the possibility of phenomena such as the *Complete Works of Contemporary Japanese Literature* and the Akutagawa Prize. At the same time I consider the notion of absolute rupture as it relates to a divide between a modern mode of literary production and the mode of production that preceded it, at least during the Edo period.[21] While granting the dramatic transformation that occurred at the end of the nineteenth century and the beginning of the twentieth, we can see the roots of a publishing industry concentrated in Tokyo (formerly Edo) in changes to the production and dissemination of texts starting no later than the seventeenth century.[22]

While it would be a mistake to imply a teleology to the events described, there was tremendous momentum toward capital accumulation in Tokyo. The second chapter explores the greatest challenge to that momentum, the near total destruction of the publishing industry in the Great Kantō Earthquake of 1923, and the ways Tokyo-based publishing was able not only to maintain its preeminence but also to reinforce it. Despite the extensive damage to publishing, printing, distribution, and retail businesses, and despite the existence of smaller-scale publishing operations elsewhere (particularly in the Kansai region—the Kyoto-Osaka area—to the west), within a matter of months Tokyo book and magazine publishing was quickly returning to its pre-earthquake levels. At the same time the groundwork had been laid for a national newspaper industry guided not by Osaka, the city with the largest newspapers prior to the earthquake, but to a certain extent by Tokyo. Finally, in destroying so many books the earthquake created not only a massive demand for new ones but also a concern over the preservation of older ones. An examination of the earthquake thus provides us with a detailed snapshot of both the industry and the marketplace on the eve of the events dealt with in the second part of the book.

The study then turns to two of the most influential mechanisms of cultural authority made possible by these developments in publishing. In chapter 3 I examine the *Complete Works of Contemporary Japanese Literature*, which gathered works written since the beginning of political modernity in Japan, the Meiji Restoration. Thanks to its reasonably low price—only one yen per volume, hence their name, "one-yen books" (*enpon*)—the series reached a wider audience than ever before. At its peak nearly 350,000 people were subscribing to the series; more readers gained access through means other than subscription: borrowing copies from friends, renting them from book lenders and reading groups, checking them out from libraries, or purchasing them at a discount when they later circulated in the used and remaindered book markets. For many reader-consumers the series was the first access they had to actual literary texts assembled systematically into a cultural entity known as modern Japanese literature. The series disseminated a set of texts throughout the empire (and beyond) in a physical format, the book, that continues to preserve them to this day.

The series succeeded beyond anyone's expectations; as the writer and publisher Kikuchi Kan noted, thanks to the series the "20–30,000 reader audience that literary books had enjoyed ha[d] suddenly swollen by ten to twenty times."[23] That is, there was more demand for the series than there had been for the works within the series; the whole was perceived as greater than the sum of its parts. Through its advertising campaign, one of the largest for any commodity up to that time, the series' impact on non-readers was similarly unprecedented. Even if one did not purchase the series, one could not help but be affected by this display. The result was a cultural prestige for modern Japanese literature recognized by a much larger population than ever before. Contemporary works in 1926 were likely perceived by many as discrete cultural products; while there was a concept of a canon of classical Japanese literature, the corresponding concept of a national cultural totality for recent literary production was only beginning to spread.[24] The *Complete Works of Contemporary Japanese Literature* dramatically accelerated this process, raising the cultural prestige of this subset of literary production. The intellectual historian Maruyama Masao described his personal experience of this expansion:

> If someone were to ask me why the explosive expansion in circulation [produced by Kaizōsha's series] led to the epoch-making change in the social status of writers and the novel, I would be at a loss. . . . I know there was a change, though, from concrete, personal experience. Whenever the latest volume of the series arrived, everyone was talking about it, even during recess at school. If you didn't know about that month's volume, you suddenly felt you were behind the times, intellectually. That might have been the case only because it was a middle school in a large city. Still, it was the case for everyone—not just students—that, whether you had read them or not, you had to at least know the names of famous Japanese and world authors and their works. After these one-yen book series appeared, this sort of information became "common knowledge."[25]

While an elevated sphere of literature, a modern national literature, was an established part of discourse among a small group of literary-minded elites in Tokyo, for many it was this series that realized the aspirations of that discourse.

At the time of its publication the series contributed to the solidification of a conceptual space in the minds of many citizens of the nation and the empire. The lasting contribution of the series was less on the specific body of works that it elevated than on the conceptual cultural entity that it consecrated: modern Japanese literature. This was the impact that Maruyama perceived as the social status of the art form rose. Thus even as the series had such concrete repercussions as leading the book-publishing industry into an age of dramatically increased production, clarifying copyright and royalty practices, illustrating the potential of advertising, turning writing from an insecure occupation into a potential source of wealth, and making select authors into celebrities, it also had a significant symbolic impact. As modern literature had not yet been widely incorporated into educational curricula, this series, rather than academia, conferred a nationally recognized cultural legitimacy on the new concept of modern literature itself even as it conferred similar legitimacy on the authors and works that it contained.[26]

There was a profound limitation to this mechanism's ability to confer legitimacy on specific literary works, however: its implicitly finite nature. It was this finite nature that allowed the publisher to offer subscribers an actual bookshelf at the completion of the subscription, built to specifications determined by the length of the series, leaving no room for additional texts. The anthology was by definition backward looking, claiming to present a full accounting of the important works. Although Kaizōsha struggled against this, expanding the series from its initial thirty-seven volumes to fifty and then sixty-three, the final result was the creation of a static canon of texts. Both cultural authority and print capitalism, however, needed a mechanism of dynamic canonization: new authors and works were needed to become new commodities; they also presented opportunities for cultural authority to be exercised and thus reproduced.

Before discussing the Akutagawa Prize for literature, which overcame this limitation, in chapter 4 I examine some of the most influential literary debates of the period in order to both illuminate the discursive field from which the anthology and the prize emerged and to explore the rhetorical mechanisms and concepts behind these material developments. I primarily focus on authors central to the Tokyo literary establishment to suggest the diversity of opinions about the proper form of literature. The debates are, at their core, about the ascription of literary value, particularly in the face of a marketplace that the critics see as attempting to assert a value system of its own. Throughout the debates critics resort to a conceptual division between desirable literature and literature marked by its *tsūzoku* (vulgar, mundane, or popular) nature.[27] The different ways this term is appropriated reveal not only the heterogeneity of literary agendas, but also the potency of the term as a tool for denigration and exclusion. In this chapter I also consider some of the critical writings on this subject by a central literary figure whose power and centrality in the literary field grew to the point that he became known as the doyen (*ōgosho*) of the literary establishment (*bundan*): Kikuchi Kan.[28] Kikuchi's early views on the topic of literary value are relevant for a variety of reasons: first, he frankly expressed many of the concerns that were arising about the need to clarify literary value; second, his position shows the influence of the most powerful alternate literary stream, proletarian literature, on this so-called bourgeois mainstream; and third, he reflects the attraction that nonelevated literature held for many writers, despite their protestations to the contrary. These essays in fact were written immediately prior to Kikuchi Kan's transition, in the eyes of much of the literary establishment, from an aspiring writer of "pure" literature to a compromised writer of "popular" literature, a distinction that was forming discursively in the course of these very debates.

In chapter 5 I return to material production, focusing on a mechanism that surmounted the limitations of the anthology: the Akutagawa Prize, which Kikuchi Kan founded along with the Naoki Prize. As had the *Complete Works of Contemporary Japanese Literature*, the Akutagawa Prize not only valorized specific works but also, in the process, perpetuated a valorized literary field: the modern literary economy that was a subset of the larger symbolic economy. This economy was made possible, as mentioned previously, by the assertion of various boundaries: modernity, the Japanese nation(-state), and an elevated subset of literary production. The Akutagawa Prize gives us the clearest insight into the function of that third boundary, a distinction it asserted using a discursive mechanism of power that was central to the formation and function of the prize: the concept of literary "purity." Such a notion implies that a work falls on one side or the other of such a boundary—Huyssen's "great divide"[29]—rather than recognizing the multiple spectra of quality that actually exist. Compromise in the face of economic pressures arising from modernization was for many an essential component of the distinction between "pure" and "popular." In 1933 Kikuchi defined the distinction this way: "Pure literature [*junbungei*] is that which the writer writes because he wants to; popular literature [*taishū bungei*] is that which is written to please people."[30]

The Akutagawa Prize, supported by this logic of differentiation, allowed Kikuchi and the other members of the selection committee to affect the dissemination, reception, and preservation of works they believed best adhered to their literary agendas in much the same way that the *Complete Works of Contemporary Japanese Literature* allowed its editors to do the same. What an examination of the workings of the Akutagawa Prize more clearly shows us, however, is that this agenda was not singular, nor was the literary value system informing its judges. The determination of the award recipients was contested even within the committee, often by parties with radically distinct value systems. Often in fact the award was given grudgingly, with the actors behind the instrument of power never fully satisfied with the way it functioned. We know this because we have unusual access to the instrument's inner workings: with each announcement of the award, *Bungei shunjū* magazine publishes the selection critiques of the committee members. In these critiques the committee members are often surprisingly frank about their appraisals of the winning works, the justifications for their positions, and their feelings about the effect of the award. What they reveal, in addition to the diversity of literary value systems, is the significant limitations individuals encounter in trying to utilize such an instrument to affect the course of literature. Even with these limitations, though, these instruments have had a significant impact on the dissemination, reception, and preservation of literary texts.

Despite the presence of economic pressures on premodern writers, critics invoking the distinction between pure and popular literature often pointed to the first decades of the twentieth century as being controlled by unprecedented economic forces; this was reinforced by the belief in a paradigmatic shift to a capitalist mode of production. The shift in the nature of the economy in general may have been more extreme than the impact it had specifically on writers. It is true that the scale of capital concentration increased dramatically in the Meiji and Taishō periods, and that this increase in scale had a profound impact. This is particularly true in questions of a national marketplace, as a marketplace of that magnitude required a dramatic concentration of print capital in Tokyo. The centralization of publishing (and cultural) capital in Tokyo was so dramatic that it was even able to surmount the city's near total destruction in the Great Kantō Earthquake of 1923. Yet the emphasis on rupture produced in the assertion of a binary—the creation of autonomous art versus the production of literary commodities for profit—suggests a prelapsarian state, implying acts of writing free of economic (or other nonliterary) pressures, rather than admitting the various compromises writers have historically been forced to make. It also ignores the ways commercial developments enabled many writers who, prior to this time, would never have had the ability to dedicate themselves to literature at all.

If its three justifying logics are destabilized, modern Japanese literature can be seen as the product of a series of exercises of power by individuals with particular aesthetic and nonaesthetic agendas who used various instruments—some discursive, some material—to elevate a specific subset of literary works. It is not that these works were undeserving of the attention they received; on the contrary, many of these works have repeatedly proved themselves worthy of the status they have enjoyed for most of the twentieth century. The treatment they received, however, was *not* solely the result of unique, intrinsic literary quality naturally revealed through the workings of time, but was also the result of a series of acts, some of them identifiable, that affected the treatment the works received and then naturalized the motivated acts themselves. The works normally thought of as comprising modern Japanese literature are ones that have suited certain individuals who had access to sufficient power, much of it made possible by print capital centralized in Tokyo, to actualize their vision of literature in a material form. As the extreme case of Mizumura's narrator illustrates, the material reproduction of fiction is the fundamental precondition for its social existence. When the contingency inherent in this material reproduction is exposed, the judgments they propagate cannot be seen as naturally revealed value.

This realization need not lead to simple cynicism or cultural relativism; instead it allows us to see the contingency of these acts that affected the dissemination, reception, and preservation of literary works.[31] The literary value systems informing these acts were multiple, not singular, and certainly not inevitable. By recognizing the contingency of the existing structures of valorization, we can recognize the flexibility of literary taste and the diversity of the literary arts. A historical study of literary production, assisted by a study of the publishing industry, allows us to recognize the constructed nature of modern Japanese literature, encouraging us to attend to alternate voices, genres, and media that have been pressed down by individuals so that other works might be lifted up.[32] Seeing literature as a contested field does more than help us to question ensconced conceptions of literary value, exposing what seems to be natural and inevitable as artificial and contingent; it helps us recognize the instruments that formed the field. This cannot be done in the hope that we will reach an objective standpoint in which exercises of power are eliminated. We cannot operate outside these mechanisms, but we can operate in fuller awareness of them. As we study the impact and relevance of texts in awareness of these mechanisms, we can also study the ways those texts and the concepts informing our thinking about those texts have been instrumentalized, either consciously or unconsciously, and the impact of that instrumentalization. In so doing, new groupings of literary works, new cultural entities, can be created in order to enlighten, to reveal, rather than to discipline or conceal. At the same time readers will be more prepared to resist transcendent claims to legitimacy made by these new configurations.

Modernity as Rupture

THE CONCENTRATION OF PRINT CAPITAL

> Nearly all theoretical discussions of art since the Industrial Revolu-
> tion have been crippled by the assumed opposition between art and
> the actual organization of society, which is important . . . but which
> can hardly be taken as an absolute.
>
> RAYMOND WILLIAMS, *CULTURE AND SOCIETY: 1780–1950*

Kaizōsha's *Complete Works of Contemporary Japanese Literature*, sold by subscription at the unprecedented low price of one yen per volume, eventually
attracted more than a third of a million subscribers and then drew even
more consumers when the books recirculated in the used and remaindered
book markets.[1] The success of this series led to an industrywide "one-yen
book boom." In fact the domestic market became so saturated with these
and other one-yen books that one entrepreneur traveled throughout the
Japanese colonies with a boxcar full of them, selling them at a fraction of
their original price.[2] With significantly lower barriers to their accessibility
the series permeated society to a deeper level than literary books had ever
done before.[3] This publishing project of unprecedented size placed a set of
fixed and durable texts in the hands of individuals throughout the nation,
the empire, and the global linguistic community. To this segment of society
the series made material a discursive abstraction that had been developing
over the previous four decades: a cultural entity now known as modern
Japanese literature, dominated by prose narrative produced almost exclusively in Tokyo and conceptually separate from the pre-Meiji national

literature being constructed almost simultaneously by *kokubungakusha* (national literature scholars).

In addition to such factors as political unification, compulsory education, and increased literacy rates, this development in literary publishing was made possible by a number of changes in the nature of the production and consumption of literature, which are traditionally associated with industrialization, modernization, and the capitalist mode of production: the mechanization of labor, the replacement of animate sources of energy by inanimate, a division of labor (usually allowing for the replacement of skilled labor by unskilled labor), the increased importance of capital (and a resulting concentration of capital), and a standardization of production that made possible the mass production of interchangeable commodities rather than unique artifacts. These developments allowed for the mass production of literary texts, a dramatic quantitative increase in capacity that enabled the texts to reach a market of unprecedented scope.

These changes in the publishing industry were part of what Harry Harootunian has called "the intensification of the process of capitalist modernization" and were analyzed within a "discourse [that] pointed to an emergent regime of 'modern life' and its production of an experience rooted in the mass consumption of commodity culture." Within this discourse these dramatic social and economic changes were often polarized: "modern life" came to be seen by many as "the moment Japan was overwhelmed by modernity."[4] Change was seen as rupture, largely associated with capitalism, "a totalizing process that affected every part of society."[5] Such a notion of rupture was clearly evident in the literary field. In terms of a general concern over the relationship between art and commerce it dates back at least into the Tokugawa period; in its specific concern over art in a capitalist system it dates back to at least the 1920s, when critics begin to distinguish the mass production of "popular literature" for profit from the production of "pure literature" unsullied by commodity culture. As publishers began to cater to the tastes of these readers, the argument goes, many writers were forced (or seduced) by the coercive power of the market to compromise their art. In this way the quantitative changes wrought by mass production were conflated with a qualitative effect, in which cultural artifacts were transformed into cultural commodities, producing a "mass" or "popular" literature.[6]

There is no doubt that the business of literary publishing, and therefore the economics of writing, changed profoundly in the decades leading up to the 1920s. Largely but not entirely enabled by technology imported from Europe and the United States, the dramatic increases in productive capacity in Japanese publishing resemble those seen in England during the nineteenth century. There, at the beginning of the nineteenth century, hand compositors could set around 350 words of movable type per hour, hand presses could print 200 to 250 sheets in the same amount of time, and paper was produced by the ream; by the close of the century a Linotype operator could set nearly four times as much type, a rotary newspaper press could print twenty-four thousand copies of a twelve-page newspaper in an hour, and paper was produced by the ton.[7] Similarly dramatic leaps in productive capacity were made in Japan. By 1929 the private printing company Shūeisha was operating an enormous German-made 128-page rotary press in order to print both the multivolume *Complete Works of Contemporary Japanese Literature* and *Kingu* (King) magazine, which in January 1927 became the first in Japan to reach a circulation of one million.[8]

The discourse of rupture, however, obscured significant continuities; it also obscured the advances made by commercialism in literary production over the preceding centuries. The developments of the late nineteenth century and early twentieth took place within a series of changes in print culture that go back at least to the beginning of the Tokugawa period.[9] Throughout most of the Tokugawa period print culture was a capital-driven industry producing texts in quantity by laborers with differentiated skills. Printed literary texts were commercial goods, and thus exposed to the pressures of the marketplace, before the mechanization of production. These cultural products gained ever broader geographical and social distribution among a readership expanding as a result of peace, improved economic circumstances, and increasing educational opportunities.

It is important therefore not to allow a discourse of rupture stemming from capitalist modernization to suggest a complete break with past modes of literary production.[10] In many cases the changes were ones of degree, as with the radical capital intensification and resulting centralization that allowed for the imagination of a marketplace coterminous with the nation-state (and later the empire.) This newfound access to this marketplace gave a specific body of literary works greater support for its claim to being a national literature, a claim made by Tsubouchi Shōyō and others when they tried to legitimize modern Japanese literature by linking it to the newly created Meiji nation-state and the discursive rupture of modernity. In this way technology, commerce, and community intertwined to help produce modern Japanese literature.

Changes in Technology: Producing Texts in Quantity

The technological revolution that occurred in print in Japan during the Meiji period (1868–1912) greatly transformed the industry: woodblocks were replaced by movable type, hand presses by engine-powered rotary presses, Japanese-style paper by Western-style paper, and Japanese-style binding methods by Western-style binding methods.[11] However, many of the factors that now seem to set the mass-produced literary commodities of the modern period apart from the cultural artifacts of preindustrial print were present in one form or another centuries earlier.

The first objects of print in Japan were the up to one million Buddhist invocations printed by order of Empress Shōtoku between 764 and 770.[12] From its inception print in Japan involved large-scale production. Needless to say these texts were not commodities in any straightforward sense; though they might have been created purely for their karmic exchange value they were not produced to function in a market. Once the sutras were printed they were inserted into small wooden pagodas; it is unlikely that they were ever meant to have a readership of any kind other than the divine. Nonetheless in many ways Shōtoku's sutra project was an instance of mass production; it is likely that the production involved the division of labor, with different individuals carving, inking, and printing the texts.

Despite the scale of this early printing project, until the end of the sixteenth century hand-copied texts remained far more common than printed ones. Large temples, which produced primarily religious and philosophical texts, dominated printing in the intervening years.[13] Although fiction was read throughout this period it was circulated primarily in manuscript form. Some literary printing did occur prior to the Tokugawa period; Buddhist monasteries, for example, published collections of Chinese poetry prior to 1590.[14] For the most part, however, printing was likely too expensive given the limited market, which had not yet benefited from the wide diffusion of education and literacy. When texts finally were printed for the marketplace they were not works of fiction; the *Setsuyō-shū* dictionary and encyclopedia, which was originally produced in the mid-fifteenth century, was one of the first nonreligious texts produced commercially. Thus certain elements of the mass production of print were in place prior to the 1590s in Japan. Texts were regularly produced in number, though most commonly these were religious texts produced by temples. These texts were produced using xylography, however, and not movable type, which is often considered central to the industrialization of print.

Movable type reached the Japanese islands from two sources at the close of the sixteenth century. The first type that reached Japan came with Jesuit missionaries in or before 1590 and was used until at least 1614, when the missionaries were officially expelled from Japan.[15] Although the primary products of the Jesuit press were religious, Jesuits produced other texts as well: a Japanese-Portuguese dictionary, a romanized version of the *Heike monogatari* (The Tale of the Heike), and a romanized translation of Aesop's fables.[16] They also produced texts written in Chinese characters (*kanji*) and the two Japanese syllabaries (*katakana* and *hiragana*), using lead type they had produced in Japan.[17] The press operated in areas in the southwest—Kazusa, Amakusa, and Nagasaki—far from the center of power in Edo, and is thus usually thought to have had limited impact on technological developments in print throughout the rest of the country.[18]

At almost the same time, around 1593, a set of Korean metal type was brought to Japan with Toyotomi Hideoyshi's army when it returned from its failed attempt to conquer the peninsula.[19] Unlike the Jesuit press, which seems to have had limited effect on domestic print technology, the technology brought from Korea was taken up by a wide variety of parties, including the government, temples, and private individuals.[20] The court used this type to print such works as the Chinese *Kobun kōkyō* (Classic of Filial Piety), which was produced by imperial order in 1593.[21] In 1597 a new set of movable type was produced, though in wood rather than metal.[22] This was likely due to two factors: insufficient technology to produce a cost-effective metal set and the greater desirability of wooden sets, which could be made with relative ease and were sufficiently durable for editions of limited size. This set of type was used to produce, again by imperial order, such secular works as an anthology of Sino-Japanese poetry (*kanshi*) by Moku'un (1597), the first two volumes of the *Nihon shoki* (The Chronicles of Japan, 1599), and the complete Confucian *Shisho* (Four Books, 1599).[23]

It is important to note that the technology for producing metal type did exist in Japan at this time; it was used by other operations around the country. Between 1606 and his death in 1616 Tokugawa Ieyasu had more than 110,000 pieces of movable wooden and bronze type made for a press in Fushimi.[24] The Fushimi press primarily produced political and historical works, some of substantial length, including the *Azuma kagami* (Mirror of Eastern Japan) in twenty-five volumes.[25] In 1616 the typeset was taken to the Kii domain. It is unclear what became of it after that; it seems to have been stored away, unused. The next known use of this typeset was in 1843, though two-thirds of the type was destroyed in 1846.[26]

The most relevant experiment in movable type during this early period, at least from the perspective of a literary historian, was that conducted by Suminokura Soan (1571–1632) and Hon'ami Kōetsu (1558–1637). Soan was a wealthy merchant and patron of the arts; Kōetsu was a talented artist in many media, including calligraphy and book design. These two men produced the *Sagabon*, illustrated movable-type editions of Japanese secular classics. Their operation, just outside of Kyoto, printed these texts between roughly 1608 and 1620.[27] Though they produced only thirteen works—including *Ise monogatari* (The Tales of Ise), *Hōjōki* (An Account of My Hut), *Tsurezuregusa* (Essays in Idleness), *Shin kokin wakashū* (New Collection of Poems Ancient and Modern), and *Hyakunin isshu* (A Hundred Poems by a Hundred Poets)—the volumes they created proved that the fundamental technological difficulties in reproducing illustrated, cursive literary texts had been surmounted in the first decades of the Tokugawa period.[28] The texts were not, however, widely circulated. It is believed that Soan and Kōetsu could produce runs of only roughly a hundred copies, each of which was extremely expensive; it is likely therefore that their readership was limited to individuals connected to the shogunate and those close to them.[29]

These early examples of movable type (*kokatsuji*) were eventually abandoned in favor of woodblock printing. In fact it seems that even the Saga press abandoned movable type for some of its later editions.[30] The preeminent scholar of the history of early type, Kawase Kazuma, estimated that while 80 percent of works known to have been printed between 1593 and 1625 were printed with movable type, that rate dropped to less than 20 percent between 1625 and 1650, and "virtually none" utilized movable type after 1650.[31]

A number of reasons have been put forward for this abandonment of movable type.[32] First, woodblock printing seems to have been better suited to the texts themselves, for both practical and aesthetic reasons. Although the *Sagabon* show that solutions had been discovered to produce the desired cursive script and to include the illustrations (though on facing pages) that were essential to many literary forms, blocks allowed extreme flexibility with no increased difficulty in production. Second, woodblocks were more economical for producing several hundred (or even several thousand) copies, a scale which became necessary for the bestselling books.[33] Third, woodblocks, once carved, could be stored away for use when sufficient demand arose, while economics demanded that type be reset for each subsequent use.[34] Fourth, woodblocks required less capital to produce.[35]

As the printing historian Nakane Katsu has observed, the technology of movable type, which is so commonly associated with a dramatic increase in production in Europe, was abandoned in Japan because it "could not respond to increasing demand." Movable type had been a reasonable approach to printing small quantities, such as the early print runs of a hundred or fewer copies. When texts increased in length, runs increased in size, and printings increased in frequency, however, woodblocks were the more economical means to print them.[36] As Peter Kornicki has noted, publishers "reverted to block printing to better respond to the demands of the market, and it is this familiar technology which governed the production of books for the remainder of the Tokugawa period." Block printing in fact remained the primary method for producing books until the 1880s.[37]

Paper, Presses, and Type: The Foundations of Modern Printing

Movable type appeared again in Japan in the mid-nineteenth century more as the result of the adoption of contemporary printing technology from the West than as a revival of these earlier movable type experiments in Japan.[38] Various modern letterpress technologies were imported into Japan over the next century, usually following advances in Europe and the United States, which were rapidly industrializing their print as well. The main technological advances behind letterpress industrialization were in three areas: paper, presses, and type. As a point of comparison, it is again worthwhile to trace developments that took place in England.[39]

In the production of paper there were two key advances. First, papermaking machines were mechanized through the use of the Fourdrinier machine, which was invented in 1798 but not put into widespread use until around 1830. Second, in order to provide the raw materials necessary for the productive capacity of these papermaking machines, processes were developed to use wood pulp rather than rags. This change occurred in the second half of the nineteenth century. The new machines were capable of producing continuous rolls of paper miles in length, essential for the high-speed presses that were produced around the same time.

Press technology underwent five important developments. First, iron presses were developed, beginning with the Stanhope press around 1800; while still manual, the Stanhope press allowed impressions to be made from a single pull. Second, the Koenig press, developed around 1812, introduced a steam-driven cylinder (pressing against a flat form) that powered the press. Third, papier-mâché stereotyping allowed molds made from flat forms to be curved; the Hoe rotary press, developed around 1860, replaced the flat form with a cylinder fitted with the curved plates produced by these molds. This paved the way for the fourth development, the introduction of a reel-fed paper supply, first introduced with the Walter press in 1869. As a result of these developments manual labor was largely eliminated from the printing process. The fifth development was the replacement of steam energy by electricity, which occurred at the end of the nineteenth century.

Much depended, however, on the mechanization of the casting and setting of type. The production of type rapidly shifted during the nineteenth century from Gutenberg-style hand-casting instruments to the Bruce pivotal caster, invented in 1838, which could produce six thousand pieces of type in an hour. This was replaced in 1881 by the Wicks rotary caster, which could produce sixty thousand pieces of type in an hour. The process of setting type needed to be accelerated as well, particularly to meet the needs of the newspaper and periodical presses. Various devices such as the Pianotyp (1840), Kastenbein (1866), and Paige (1894) mechanically set precast type. Perhaps a more important development occurred in 1872, when the first Linotype machine was invented. Made economically feasible by the Benton machine (1884), which punch-cut the necessary matrices, the Linotype machine cast its own type in slugs of complete lines, which were then assembled to produce the page. Linotype machines, which were developed commercially after 1886, rapidly became widely used. Monotype machines, developed in the last two decades of the nineteenth century, operated on a similar logic, though they produced type by the character rather than by the line, making corrections easier.

Many of these developments in printing technology from Europe and the United States were imported into Japan, where they were modified and improved to suit the language and the industry. In some cases, however, Japanese innovation in print technology happened in relative isolation from Western developments. Mid-nineteenth-century Japanese type experimenters seem to have been aware of the fundamental principles of Western movable type printing, though they lacked knowledge of some essential details. Although references to the Western printing press as early as 1763 have been found, it was not until the late 1850s that basic descriptions of the technology were published.[40] Nor were many of the earliest Japanese type experimenters aware at first of efforts by missionaries and scholars in China, who had been experimenting with Chinese printing since the early nineteenth century, and the solutions they had found to problems specific to printing larger character sets.[41]

Japanese experiments with metallic movable type began again around 1848. A number of different groups began working almost simultaneously (but not cooperatively) on creating metal Japanese type technology based on the Gutenberg model.[42] Three of these experiments deserve particular attention.[43] The first was led by Ichikawa Kanenori at the Institute for the Investigation of Western Books (Bansho Shirabesho) in Edo using a Stanhope press and a typeset the government had received as a present in 1850. The goal of the Institute's experiments was to print textbooks for the study of foreign languages. With much difficulty Ichikawa finally produced his first book in 1858 and continued to print textbooks until 1867, when the shogunate was on the verge of collapse.[44]

At nearly the same time, the Satsuma domain undertook the reprinting of Dutch books.[45] The domain hired Kimura Kahei III, a member of an Edo family of woodblock carvers, who used a Gutenberg technique with slight modifications adapted from woodblock printing. Although he began his work in 1854 he apparently was not able to print books until 1860. During his experiments he learned the new Western technology of electrotype. This led him to abandon his experiments and begin in 1864 to produce a typeset using the new technology. Although this was apparently a success, illness eventually forced him to abandon the project altogether.

The experimenter whose work succeeded on a large scale was Motoki Shōzō. Motoki was born into a Nagasaki family of interpreters of Dutch and, as a result, had extensive access to Western technology. Among other enterprises Motoki purchased a Dutch-made set of metal type and a manual press in 1848 and spent the following years attempting to reproduce the technology and create a syllabic typeface. Using this early type he was able to print a simple Dutch-Japanese dictionary in 1851–52.[46] In 1855 his operation was purchased and expanded by the Nagasaki city commissioner, who gave Motoki the resources to print books needed to confront the new threat of the United States.[47]

Still, until 1869 Motoki's operation did not greatly surpass the other Japanese experimenters, as he was still unable to produce a Japanese type in such a way as to make it commercially viable. This changed when Motoki sent an observer to the American Presbyterian Mission press in Shanghai. As a result he learned of the technological advances of William Gamble, who had adapted the new technology of electrotyping to Chinese characters and thus made it possible to produce thousands of matrices cheaply and quickly.[48] Having put this system into place at the Mission press, Gamble was hired in 1869 by Motoki to teach at his Movable Type Instruction Office (Kappan Denshūjo). Although his stay there was brief, it was long enough to convey the new technology. By 1870 Motoki's Nagasaki facility (Shinjuku Seizō Kappanjo) was producing type commercially.

Motoki's operation modernized even further when in 1871 he asked Hirano Tomiji to reorganize it. Albert Altman has described these changes: "[Hirano] discharged superfluous workers, cut the wages of those who did not produce, and adjusted wages to performance. He instituted a division of labour in the production process, appointed foremen and drew up a set of production standards for type. Finally, he inaugurated a system of fixed working hours and eliminated the customary after-lunch siesta."[49] The success of Motoki's operation allowed him to expand into Osaka, Yokohama, Kobe, Kyoto, and Tokyo. The Tokyo facility (Nagasaki Shinjuku Shutchō Kappan Seizōsho), run by Hirano, began by selling type made using the matrices and molds (three hand-casting instruments) he brought from Nagasaki. Later that year (1872) the facility began producing new matrices and molds and then began producing electrotype matrices and printing using electrotype plates.[50] In 1873 the company moved to a larger facility in Tsukiji (becoming the Tokyo Tsukiji Kappan Seizōsho in 1885), where it also produced and repaired manual presses.[51]

The development of the newspaper and periodical industry and the expansion of the new Meiji nation-state's need for official documents drove the industrialization of print centered on movable type. The government in fact became the primary competitor of the private Tsukiji foundry. The Printing Bureau (Insatsu-kyoku) was founded in 1875 as a result of centralizing various governmental printing facilities, which in turn had purchased much of their equipment from Motoki's Nagasaki foundry. At first the government focused on printing revenue stamps, paper currency, postage stamps, and postcards, but soon it was producing type for sale in order to profit from the heavy capital investment the foundry had required. In 1875 it began offering type for less than half the cost of the Tsukiji foundry. This led to a price war as more companies entered the industry; by the end of the 1880s the cost of movable type had fallen by 85 percent from its price in the early 1870s.[52]

The advances in movable type technology allowed newspapers, which had been printed by woodblock, to expand rapidly; this move to periodical publication marks one of the major developments in print in the modern period. Broadsheets (kawaraban) had been printed throughout much of the Tokugawa period, though they were produced only occasionally.[53] After Fukuzawa Yukichi traveled to the United States as part of a Japanese delegation in 1860 he began calling for the creation of modernized print, centered on the steam-powered cylinder press.[54] The first newspaper, the Nagasaki Shipping List and Advertiser, which as the name denotes was published in the southwestern city of Nagasaki, did not appear until 1861, and private daily newspapers began appearing after the Meiji Restoration in 1868.[55] The first daily newspaper printed in Japan, the Yokohama shinbun, was started by another disciple of Motoki, Yō Sonoji, in 1870; it started by using carved wooden type but also used cast metal type from the Tsukiji foundry beginning with the issue published on 26 September 1872.[56] By 14 June 1873 the newspaper (now the Yokohama mainichi shinbun) was printed entirely using metal movable type. The paper soon entrusted its printing to Shūeisha, founded in 1876, which developed into one of the largest private printing companies in Japan. The expansion of demand for newspapers seems to have been driven largely by war. The Satsuma Rebellion of 1877, for example, contributed to the first boom in demand for daily news.[57]

There were other important developments in the production of type. Type-casters were in use in Japan as early as 1876, when the Kappan Seizō Kōdōken, founded in 1874, purchased a manual Bruce-style pivotal typecaster, which pumped molten lead into a type mold using a spring-powered piston.[58] This remained the primary type-creating device in Japan until 1911, when the Cabinet Printing Bureau imported an automatic Thompson Typecaster. In terms of private companies purchasing the new type technology, in 1918 the Tsukiji foundry and the publishing company Hakubunkan's printing facility imported Thompson Typecasters, becoming the first private enterprises to put them to use. As mentioned earlier, however, the major innovation for mass-produced text was the creation of the Linotype machine. In 1903 the Cabinet Printing Bureau imported a Linotype machine from the United States. In 1912 the Printing Bureau also imported a Benson pantographic punch-cutting machine, which allowed a single master design to be used to produce various size matrices, thus making the Linotype machine more economical. The first private company to import a Linotype machine was Sanshūsha in 1928.[59]

Type was only one part of the puzzle; press technology, and the powering of those presses by engines, was also essential to the industrialization of print. In this area the government was often the driving force in importing and utilizing the latest technology. In 1883 the Printing Bureau of the Ministry of Finance was ordered by the Dajōkan to print the official gazette (*Kanpō*); the first was printed in July of that year. One million copies of the gazette were printed in the first year; before long it was printing nearly one million copies per month.[60] The government's increased printing demands forced the Bureau to adopt the latest technologies. In 1885 they installed two steam engines, one six horsepower and the other five, to run their stop-cylinder press and the lighting, respectively. Stop-cylinder presses dated back to at least 1877 in Japan, when the Tsukiji foundry imported a duodecimo sixteen-page stop-cylinder press; the flywheel of this press, however, was not driven by a steam engine, but by hand.[61] In the private sector Shūeisha imported a fifteen-horsepower engine in 1887 to drive its stop-cylinder presses.[62]

In 1889 a representative of the Cabinet Information Bureau was dispatched to the Paris Exhibition, where he learned of Hippolyte Marinoni's steam-powered rotary press, which allowed for automated double-sided printing and curved plates. By eliminating the flat form the press was capable of continuous printing. The rotary press required the creation of curved plates produced through stereotyping, which (as mentioned earlier) involves pouring hot metal into a papier-mâché mold made from a plate of type to produce a thin stereotype, which can be curved and fitted to the cylinder. The technology was first brought back to Japan from Australia in 1873 by Fujiyama Masahiko; it was first used in Japanese newspaper printing either in 1875 by the *Tokyo e-iri shinbun* or in 1876 by the *Yomiuri shinbun*. These curved plates allowed for the use of automated paper feeds and rolled paper; in conjunction with other existing machines that cut and folded the printed pages, unassisted printing became possible. In 1889 the Meiji government ordered three of the Marinoni rotary presses, one of which was to be used by the Tōkyō Asahi Shinbunsha.[63] In 1892 Ōsaka Asahi Shinbunsha imported a Marinoni press, followed by Ōsaka Mainichi Shinbunsha in 1893 and Hōchi Shinbunsha in 1896, the year Jiji Shinbunsha imported an R. Hoe rotary press from the United States.[64] In 1906 the Printing Bureau imported a new electrical generator and proceeded to switch all of their machines from steam to electricity.

These automated, continuous-feed presses required massive quantities of Western-style paper. After a failed enterprise undertaken by Hyakutake Yasubei in 1871, the first Western-style papermaking company was Yūkōsha, founded in 1872 in Tokyo when Asano Nagakoto imported a British papermaking machine and hired British engineers.[65] Perhaps the most significant papermaking company started around this time was Shōshi Kaisha, founded in 1873 by Shibusawa Eiichi and the three primary official money-changing houses: Mitsui, Ono, and Shimada.[66] The papermaking machinery was almost entirely imported from British and American companies. Despite the fact that the domestic companies had to compete with imported paper, the industry grew rapidly; Shōshi Kaisha, for example, grew into Ōji Seishi, which is now one of the largest companies in the industry. By 1890 the domestic industry was producing 6,757 tons of Western-style paper; that same year Japan imported an additional 5,000 tons.[67] It was not until 1892 that Ōji purchased a rewinder, allowing the company to produce the rolled paper necessary for the new Marinoni rotary presses. The next challenge was to shift from rags to wood pulp in order to meet the rapidly growing demand for paper; this transition occurred between 1890 and 1900. The demand for timber to produce this pulp became one of the pressures behind expansionist Japanese colonial policy over the subsequent decades.[68]

These developments in print technology may have been incorporated first into the production of newspapers, magazines, and government documents, but they gradually made their way into book production as well. The decision by the Ministry of Education in 1890 to print primary school textbooks with movable type rather than woodblock, in combination with the demand for war tales generated by the Sino-Japanese War of 1894–95, greatly stimulated the industrialization of the book publishing industry. One company that pioneered the use of these new technologies for book production was Shūeisha, the private printing company founded by Sakuma Teiichi in 1876. The company struggled at first because of the limited use of movable type for books, but finally stabilized when it won the right to reprint Nakamura Masanao's popular translation of Samuel Smiles's *Self-Help* (*Saigoku risshi-hen*, 1870–71).[69] One of Shūeisha's chief competitors, Hakushinsha, was the first to utilize rotary press technology for books and magazines. In response to the increased demand for print during the Russo-Japanese War in 1904–5, Hakushinsha, which was the printing house of the publishing company Hakubunkan, imported a web-fed Marinoni rotary press to produce its parent company's books and magazines.[70]

Bookbinding technologies also changed dramatically during this period. In 1873 the Printing Bureau hired an Englishman named W. F. Patterson to teach the basic techniques; one of the first books to employ these techniques was the Shūeisha-printed edition of Nakamura Masanao's *Saigoku risshi-hen*.[71] It took a number of years before the entire process—folding, gathering, sewing, cutting, backing, and casing—was automated. Most of these processes were mechanized over a span of some forty years: cutting around 1879, folding around 1889, magazine binding around 1904, and gathering around 1919. The transition from Japanese to Western binding methods was rapidly accelerated by their adoption for government-produced textbooks beginning in 1904.[72] As late as the beginning of the Shōwa period (1926–89), however, much of the sewing for bookbinding was still done by hand. Despite the relative delay in automating the binding process, the external form of print underwent changes at all levels. In 1885, for example, Tsubouchi Shōyō's *Shōsetsu shinzui* (The Essence of the Novel), the critical work thought by many to have launched modern Japanese literature, was bound in Japanese style. By 1900, however, as Peter Kornicki has written, "books, and the products of the newly emergent periodical press, were vastly different in technologies of production and in appearance from anything that had been available in 1800."[73]

FIGURE 1   Shūeisha's rotary press room, Ichigaya facility. From Dai-Nihon Insatsu Kabushiki Kaisha, ed., *Shichijūgonen no ayumi: Dai-Nihon Insatsu Kabushiki Kaisha-shi* (Tokyo: Dai-Nihon Insatsu Kabushiki Kaisha, 1952), xiii.

The 1920s also saw substantial advances in two other new technologies: offset printing and photocomposition. These technologies allowed for the reproduction of texts without the creation of metal relief stereotypes; they also allowed for the incorporation of high-quality images and multicolor printing.[74] Nonetheless letterpress printing still dominated the production of large-scale print, such as *King* magazine. Because of the scale and success of *King* in 1925 Shūeisha expanded its factories, made new type, and purchased a sixty-four-page rotary press in addition to its thirty-two-page rotary press (figure 1, above). This expansion gave the company the productive capacity necessary to undertake the production of the multivolume *Complete Works of Contemporary Japanese Literature* between 1926 and 1931. The success of that series and other one-yen collections led the company to add three more sixty-four-page rotary presses and the one hundred and twenty-eight-page rotary press previously mentioned, resulting in a printing capacity that dwarfed that of its early modern predecessors.[75]

Print and Commerce: The Edo Marketplace for Texts

There is no doubt that the technological improvements in printing produced greatly expanded capacity, but this striking expansion tends to obscure important continuities. The process of industrialization is often associated with a transformation of artifacts into commodities, with an implied transition from organic systems of authentic production to soulless systems of commercial production. Print technology was no different; yet, as Lucien Febvre and Henri-Jean Martin have written, "From its earliest days printing existed as an industry, governed by the same rules as any other industry; the book was a piece of merchandise which men produced before anything else to earn a living, even when they were . . . scholars and humanists at the same time."[76] Though noncommercial printing did precede commercial printing in Japan, implications of a prelapsarian print culture are counterproductive. While Febvre's and Martin's position may be extreme, it is important to recognize that the motivations driving the production of print have always been multiple, and thus any divide that suggests pure motivations preceding commercialization oversimplifies the present even as it romanticizes the past.

Of course print as a commercial enterprise predates the increases in productive capacity resulting from industrialization. One of the major features that set apart the preindustrial mode of production from the industrial was the size of the capital outlay necessary to undertake a printing. As mentioned previously, this was one of the reasons why Japanese printers likely stopped using early movable type and returned to woodblocks; whereas Gutenberg-style printing required a large initial investment to acquire type and a press, xylography required a smaller initial investment.[77] The capital outlay in xylographic printing was largely dedicated to the costs of wood, paper, skilled and semiskilled labor, and storage.

Though the initial capital investment was significantly smaller, the creation of books was still done on a proto-industrial model. Authors and artists, who usually could not mobilize this essential capital, were rarely the motive force behind the production of print. As the oft-cited illustration from 1818 (figure 2) shows, a bookseller (seated top center) would gather together (clockwise from upper right) a writer (*sakusha*), a copyist (*hikkō*), a printer (*hansuri*), a carver (*hangishi*), and an illustrator (*gakō*) to create and then print blocks. Sometimes, of course, a single individual performed more than one of these tasks; Saikaku, for example, illustrated a number of his own stories.[78] At the same time booksellers often employed well-known illustrators to increase the desirability of texts; Yoshida Hanbei, a famous illustrator from Kamigata (Kyoto and its surrounding cities),

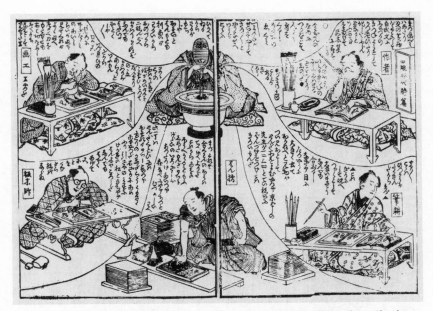

FIGURE 2 "Takarabune kogane no hobashira." Tōri Sanjin (writer) and Katsukawa Shunkō (illustrator). From Nagatomo Chiyoji, *Edo jidai no tosho ryūtsū* (Kyoto: Bukkyō Daigaku Tsūshin Kyōikubu, 2002), 8. Image held by Hōsa Bunko, City of Nagoya. Note that the name of the illustrator is given as Harukawa in Nagatomo; the name used here is the one given by Hōsa Bunko.

and Hishikawa Moronobu, a famous illustrator from Edo, also illustrated some of Saikaku's works.[79] The bookseller hired the writers, commissioned the carvers, printed the pages, bound the books, distributed them to other booksellers, and sold them himself. The bookseller provided the capital outlay and enjoyed the proceeds of that venture.

Control of the bookmaking process by a bookseller with sufficient capital was not the only continuity with the industrialized print culture that followed. Another was the assembly-line method of constructing books. Illustrations from 1802 (figure 3) show the process after the printer has completed his work (the final stage in the previous illustration). The printed pages are folded, put in order, cut into uniform size, covered, sewn, and sold.[80] While books were indeed being produced in much smaller quantities than in the industrialized period, they were nonetheless produced in assembly-line fashion, with a division of labor into tasks requiring little training. To this extent printed literary works were mass-produced

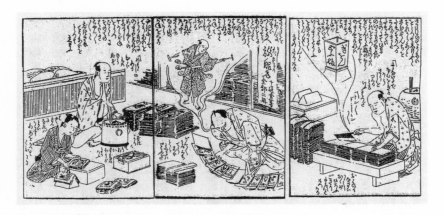

FIGURE 3 "Atariyashita jihon toiya." From the *kusazōshi* (picture books) by Jippensha Ikku. Various images from the 1802 *kusazōshi* in Nagatomo Chiyoji, *Edo jidai no tosho ryūtsū* (Kyoto: Bukkyō Daigaku Tsūshin Kyōikubu, 2002), 12.

commodities, assembled in a capitalistic mode of production utilizing a division of labor prior to the mechanization of literary production.

As with the technological developments described previously, there were also important discontinuities in the business of bookselling. The specialization of capital in the industry as a whole—dividing it into publishers, printers, distributors, retailers, and so on—did not occur until the close of the nineteenth century, and when it did it was largely due to the increased capital requirements of mechanization.[81] During the Tokugawa period most booksellers both produced and retailed their wares.[82] This is not the only discontinuity between preindustrial and industrial bookselling. There is also the matter of the significant difference in scope of the market for these texts. While the Edo market saw significant quantitative expansion, the industrialization of literary production—in conjunction with various other developments in the early decades of the new Meiji state—resulted in a quantitative expansion that came to be perceived as a qualitative change in the scope of the marketplace; books were now available to a national marketplace. To clarify this distinction it is worthwhile surveying developments in the marketplace for literary texts in Japan.

Commercial bookselling long preceded the Meiji period. Some booksellers likely existed during the Muromachi period (1392–1573), but clear evidence of commercial publishing appears soon after the restoration of peace by the Tokugawa regime and the developments in printing I described earlier.[83] As Peter Kornicki has written, "The means for commercial production and distribution may have existed [prior to 1600], but political disunity prevented the emergence of a national market for goods that could be readily exploited." Commercial booksellers have been identified in Kyoto as early as 1608.[84] The industry grew quickly. By 1702, according to the *Genroku taiheiki* (Genroku Chronicles), there were seventy-two booksellers in Kyoto alone. Osaka followed Kyoto; the first book produced there is thought to be the *Aseishū* (Frog in the Well Collection), published in 1671.[85] By 1696 there were thirty-four booksellers in that city. Edo booksellers date back to at least the Kan'ei period (1624–44), but as was the case in Osaka, the first books for sale came from Kyoto. By 1687 there were twenty-five booksellers operating in Edo.[86] Printing was by no means limited to these "three metropolises" (*santo*); provincial publishers often produced their own books or copied books produced elsewhere.[87]

These booksellers did not deal only in the books they printed; they formed guilds (*nakama*) that, in addition to protecting intellectual property and performing a censorship function for the government, also facilitated the exchange of members' books. This process of exchange was known as *hongae* (book exchange). Producers would sell their books to other booksellers in the guild at wholesale prices, usually 80 percent of the book's retail price. These wholesale transactions took place in two ways: through book exchanges recorded in ledgers (*nyūginchō* or *serichō*, depending on the location of the exchange) or through book markets (*seri shikai* or *hon no ichi*) at which only guild members or their agents (*seriko*) were allowed to buy books.[88]

There were other ways for individual booksellers to reach larger audiences, including copublishing (*aiaiban*) texts. In this system multiple booksellers would cofinance the production of a book and then share the rights to the finished product. This was usually done between booksellers in different cities, and thus different markets. Copublished texts allowed publishers not only to reach a larger number of consumers, but also to distribute the risks entailed in capitalizing a new publication. These networks soon linked the three metropolises of Kyoto, Osaka, and Edo, as well as some of the larger castle towns.[89] By the nineteenth century the networks extended to include many other major provincial towns. For most of the Tokugawa period, however, the majority of book transactions occurred within a given guild, limiting most large-scale movement of books to a single city. The transactions with booksellers outside the three metropolises and between the guilds of the three metropolises seem to have accounted for only a small portion of the total.[90]

The fall of the Tokugawa regime and the rise of the Meiji state only temporarily disrupted the growth of these retail networks. The guilds experienced a brief period of disarray during the political turmoil surrounding the Restoration, but were soon reinstated by the Meiji government, which recognized their usefulness.[91] The guilds continued until 1873, when the Meiji government dissolved them in the name of economic liberalization.[92] Modern associations of booksellers based on the guild system began to appear in 1887 with the creation of the Tokyo Shoseki Shuppan Eigyōsha Kumiai (Tokyo Book Publishing Businessmen's Association). While the new association no longer had the censorship function the guilds performed, it still ran an annual book market, produced a catalogue of books published by its members, and oversaw mechanisms of payment in member transactions.[93]

Bookselling in Meiji Japan:
Specialization, Consignment, and Fixed Prices

Three new developments in the marketing of print resulted from changes in the technologies of publishing and marked significant breaks with the past: specialization, consignment, and fixed prices. The new printing technologies allowed publishing in far larger quantities to meet the increasing demands of the Meiji state and of the growing population of readers emerging from the state's rapidly expanding educational system. At the same time the new technologies favored an increased concentration of capital that restructured the publishing industry. Few existing publishers were able to adjust to these new demands. In 1873 the membership roster of the Tokyo Shorin Kumiai (Tokyo Booksellers' Association) contained 145 publishers who had been in operation in the Tokugawa period; in 1887 the membership roster of the Tokyo Shoseki Shuppan Eigyōsha Kumiai (Tokyo Book Publishing Businessmen's Association) shows that only twenty survived the intervening years.[94] The industrialization of print culture in Japan saw the Tokugawa-period booksellers—the individuals and businesses that were often simultaneously printers, distributors, retailers, used bookstores, and even book lenders—disappear in the face of increased specialization that produced publishers, printers, distributors, and retailers.

A new system of retail sales involving ōurisabakijo (authorized retailer distributors) and urisabakijo (authorized retailers) emerged largely because of the system by which primary school texts were produced by the Ministry of Education and then reproduced and sold by private individuals.[95] Rather than being joint investors in a publishing project, these were exclusively retailers. The publishing company Hakubunkan created its own network of authorized retailer distributors (comprising 64 ōurisabakijo and 389 urisabakijo as early as September 1891).[96] In 1890 Hakubunkan created a separate company, Tōkyōdō, to handle the distribution throughout this network. It was around this time that companies specializing in distribution began to appear. By 1893 there were five main book distributors: Tōkyōdō, Hokuryūkan, Tōkaidō, Ryōmeidō, and Uedaya.[97]

These distributors took advantage of two contributions to the national infrastructure by the Meiji state that played particularly important roles in the expansion of retail networks for books: railroads and the postal system. Between 1872 and 1900 nearly four thousand miles of public and private railway lines were laid throughout Japan, allowing stock to be shipped more easily to different markets.[98] Meanwhile the new Meiji postal system began handling newspapers and books in 1871 and small parcels in 1892. Charges for freight shipped by train differed depending on the destination; by contrast, the postal system, which was used primarily for individual mail-order purchases, had a fixed rate based on weight that did not consider distance and in that sense unified the national marketplace.[99] These two methods of distribution increased the circulation of print, increasing even farther the reach of publishers.

The second major structural shift was from final sales to consignment sales, a move made possible by the new economic logic of scale. Because of the dropping cost to publishers of the single unit of production—whether newspaper, magazine, or book—any individual unit produced became dispensable. This led to a major shift in the way print was sold, to a system capable of bearing significant numbers of unsold units for the sake of exposure. Publishers began accepting returns in exchange for the ability to reach a far larger market, and bookstores were much more willing to accept stock from publishers that accepted returns because this allowed them to carry far more merchandise without bearing any risk themselves. The shift to consignment sales had another effect: because the large distributors regularly funded the publishing projects enabled by consignment sales, they were often given preferential deals on the books. As a result a clear divide was created between the major distributors, who collaborated for mutual protection, and the midsize and small distributors, who were often forced to get their books from the major distributors.[100] In 1914 central publishers agreed not to sell magazines to anyone other than the central six distributors, forcing smaller distributors and *sedoriya* (small-scale book resellers) to deal with the central distributors, thus creating a distribution hierarchy.

Some returns were allowed prior to the adoption of formal consignment systems in the first decades of the twentieth century.[101] However, the major transition to consignment sales began at the close of the Meiji period. In 1909 Jitsugyō no Nihonsha decided to accept returns of its popular women's magazine, *Fujin sekai* (Women's World), causing its circulation to surge.[102] Most other magazine publishers followed suit by 1915, with one exception: Hakubunkan insisted on a final sale system, which led to the downfall of the publishing house that had dominated the industry.[103] By the beginning of the Shōwa period it was supplanted by five major Tokyo publishers: Kōdansha, Shinchōsha, Kaizōsha, Heibonsha, and Chūō Kōronsha.[104] Beginning around this time, and particularly after the stunning success of *King* magazine in 1925, print capital and retailers focused almost exclusively on magazines because of their profitability.[105] The growth of the marketplace, however, only exacerbated an existing problem (for all but the consumer): price wars.

Individuals in publishing and distribution had long wanted to fix prices. It was only with the concentration of power in large companies and in increasingly powerful associations that this third major development became a reality. The fixing of retail prices for magazines began in 1914 and was largely achieved by 1919.[106] The relatively rapid establishment of fixed magazine prices occurred because most magazines were produced in Tokyo and distributed through the central distributors mentioned previously, who merely had to agree among themselves. The price of books, which were produced by a large number of publishers and distributed through a less regimented system, proved more difficult to control. In 1915 Iwanami Shoten instituted a fixed price system for its books, and in 1919 the Tokyo Shoseki-shō Kumiai (Tokyo Book Association) started their own system. When the Tokyo Association realized that it needed to control booksellers outside of its jurisdiction it pressed for regional associations to be formed. This led in 1920 to the new Zenkoku Shoseki-shō Kumiai Rengōkai (National League of Book Associations), which enforced a nationwide system of fixed prices. Once price wars had been eliminated by the establishment of fixed prices, the bookselling business stabilized and the number of bookstores increased dramatically, from three thousand in 1912 to six thousand in 1919 to more than ten thousand by 1927.[107] The combined effect of specialization (which allowed centralization), consignment, and fixed prices thus greatly expanded the marketplace for books.

The Magnitude of the Marketplace

Marketplace expansion had been an objective of booksellers in the Tokugawa period as well. One way to understand the magnitude of the marketplace during the Tokugawa period is to consider normal print runs and bestsellers. Within thirty years of the appearance of commercial publishers the market for books had grown significantly; one of the first bestsellers was the *Kiyomizu monogatari* (Tale of Kiyomizu, 1638), which is said to have sold two thousand to three thousand copies.[108] Demand was even greater in the second half of the Tokugawa period. It is said that two of the largest Edo publishers, Tsuruya Kiemon and Tsutaya Jūzaburō, would sell as many as thirteen thousand books each spring.[109] These were primarily the shorter *kusazōshi* (picture books), not the lengthier *yomihon* ("books for reading"). Evidence suggests that the demand for works of fiction as commodities to be owned, rather than merely borrowed temporarily, differed greatly depending on the genre. The bestselling authors may have sold more than ten thousand copies of less expensive works, such as *kusazōshi* and *kibyōshi* (satiric picture books).[110] *Yomihon*, the longer and less heavily illustrated prose genre, often sold in the hundreds, rarely more than twelve hundred copies, even for famous authors such as Kyokutei Bakin. The *yomihon* sales, however, occurred over a period of many years; in the case of *kusazōshi*, the shorter and more heavily illustrated prose genre, demand lasted only a matter of months, usually around the beginning of the year.[111]

When compared with the capacity for sales in the Meiji literary market, the difference made by these various developments is pronounced. Meiji literary bestsellers sold on a much larger scale. Two of the most popular were Ozaki Kōyō's *Konjiki yasha* (The Demon Gold, 1897–1903) and Tokutomi Roka's *Hototogisu* (The Cuckoo, 1898–99). Although *Hototogisu* sold only nine thousand copies in its first year, by the beginning of the Shōwa period it had sold as many as five hundred thousand copies.[112] By comparison, the average literary work was published in runs of fifteen hundred to two thousand throughout mid- and late Meiji. The Taishō period saw other bestselling literary works, such as Kurata Hyakuzō's *Shukke to sono deshi* (The Priest and His Disciples, 1917), which sold 140,000 copies, and the three-volume *Shisen o koete* (Before the Dawn, 1920), which sold around six hundred thousand volumes.[113] Even before the success of the *Complete Works of Contemporary Japanese Literature* the radically increased productive capacity of the publishing industry was readily apparent.

Community: The Question of a National Marketplace

In terms of production in large quantities, mass production occurred as early as the eighth century, and in the Tokugawa period xylographic production expanded to reach ever larger markets. In fact prior to the creation of broad distribution networks, it is possible that the demand for any given book rarely outstripped the productive capacity of woodblocks. However, for the concept of mass production (*tairyō seisan*) to be meaningful, to describe a scale of production fundamentally different from that which preceded it, it has to denote more than quantitatively increased capacity. It has to denote an increase so dramatic as to be perceived as resulting in a qualitative difference. The implied threshold is often the establishment of a national marketplace: an expansion of the market to include the masses (*taishū*), thus claiming a national audience and functioning as a shared culture, an element of a national self-imagination.

Scholars of the book in Japan have used the concept of a national marketplace for books—and the related concepts of a national readership and a national literature—to signify different things. One reason for this is the inherent impossibility of the idea: no work of literature is ever shared by every member of the national community. The problem also stems from the different perspectives of the scholars involved. Scholars of the book in the Tokugawa period are keen to show that books reached an unprecedented audience during that time, reaching the far corners of the country. This is undoubtedly true. From the perspective of a scholar of modern Japan who is used to broad, consistent penetration of the nation by media, however, this is not sufficient to constitute a national marketplace. It is unlikely that the majority of Japanese during the Tokugawa period—whether because of a low rate of literacy or lack of availability or affordability of books—had access to a common print literature. While print may have "become an accessible, familiar, and increasingly essential part of daily life" in Edo Japan,[114] it is unclear how uniformly available specific texts were throughout the country, a central precondition for any literature that might claim to be national.

Books produced in the city of Edo undoubtedly reached diverse parts of the country. The scholar Konta Yōzō, who has documented this broad reach, proposes that the Bunka-Bunsei periods (1804–30) marked the beginning of particularly extensive distribution. For example, he cites a prohibition by the Dewa-Tsuruoka domain in northeast Japan in 1812 against allowing children to read "new *kusazōshi* that have recently come down from Edo."[115] There is little doubt that books from Edo reached these domains at the far northern tip of Honshū even earlier than the Bunka-Bunsei periods; alternating attendance in the capital (*sankin kōtai*) would have made bringing books from the capital back to their domains relatively easy for elites beginning early in the Tokugawa period.

Konta describes the attention that particularly famous literary authors, such as Jippensha Ikku, Ryūtei Tanehiko, and Kyokutei Bakin, received from provincial readers and the speed with which their books circulated. As evidence he cites the case in which a book published on 1830.12.20 in Edo was on sale in the coastal city of Matsusaka (in what is now Mie prefecture, relatively near Osaka) by 1831.1.10.[116] Unfortunately this example (as with so many similar examples) tells us only about the heavily traveled corridor of the Tōkaidō highway between Edo and Osaka, an area that experienced something akin to cultural unification far earlier than any other in Japan. This does not necessarily mean, however, that a given work reached all or even most domains. The fact that a book rapidly reached a port city that was central to trade and was located between Edo and Osaka does not provide sufficient evidence that these books reached a national audience with anything resembling uniformity, let alone simultaneity. Of course the limited reader reception history available to us makes any specific case anecdotal and any final conclusion difficult. Future research into regional readerships may reveal a great deal of uniformity in booksellers' stocks, thus strengthening claims of a national audience in the Tokugawa period.

In the meantime, however, we should consider an anecdote that perhaps illustrates the limits of book distribution. The historian Nagatomo Chiyoji has recently written about one provincial bookseller in Matsumoto city (in what is now Nagano prefecture). The bookstore, Kenrindō Takamiya, which is still in operation, opened in 1797. At that time, according to the autobiography of the founder, most readers were forced to go to one of the three metropolises to buy books; on a special occasion they might have a messenger (hikyaku) buy books for them. Takamiya bought books during trips to Kyoto, Osaka, and Edo and from itinerant merchants. By 1850 Takamiya had become a regional retailer (and likely a local distributor) for the Izumiya bookstore in Edo.[117] It was thus the mid-nineteenth century before this rural domain relatively close to both Osaka and Tokyo had regular access to Edo books. In the most thorough study of this question to date, Nagamine Shigetoshi argues that print culture from Tokyo did not become regularly available in the provinces until as late as the Russo-Japanese War of 1904–5; it is his contention that this moment marks the creation of a national reading public, with significant homogeneity and simultaneity, that included a wide spectrum of society.[118]

Nagamine's contention alerts us to another problem involved in understanding the history of the distribution of texts: social penetration. It seems certain that provincial elites had access to books published in the three metropolises throughout the Tokugawa period.[119] Even if broad distribution to elites is granted, however, social penetration is a different issue. An important method of estimating the economic depth of the marketplace is to determine the financial accessibility of books by considering their prices during the Tokugawa period. On this point there is some disagreement as well. One scholar, stressing the accessibility of texts, writes, "The prices of books in the seventeenth century and most of the eighteenth century were high by comparison with the prices of other commodities, but at least by the late eighteenth century the lighter genres of fiction [kusazōshi] had become cheap and readily available, and were perceived to be so."[120] While perhaps true for some urban readers and the provincial elite, substantial economic barriers still remained.[121] This is particularly true of longer prose genres such as yomihon, kokkeibon (comic fiction), and ninjōbon (sentimental fiction). Bakin's yomihon, for example, cost as much as 26.7 monme, a price far too dear for the common reader.[122] The literary scholar Hamada Keisuke has adjusted the price of books to the price of rice: while a gōkan (bound picture book) in the first half of the nineteenth century cost about the same as two masu (approximately 1.5 kilograms) of rice, a five-volume yomihon would cost about a quarter of a koku (approximately 150 kilograms) of rice.[123]

Utano Hiroshi has attempted to adjust Edo book prices to contemporary levels, an exercise that is fraught with problems but which might provide a point of comparison. According to his calculations the cheapest books were kusazōshi, which cost anywhere from 175 to 3,850 yen (in November 1993, when the article was published, one dollar equaled 108.82 yen; thus $1.60 to $35.38), depending on the period, the length of the work, and the customer; some were more expensive. Saikaku's Kōshoku ichidai otoko (Life of a Sensuous Man) sold for the equivalent of 16,750 yen ($153.92) in the Genroku period (1688–1704) and 60,160 yen ($552.84) in the Tempō period (1830–44). A full set of Bakin's most famous work, Nansō Satomi no hakkenden (The Eight Dog Chronicles, henceforth Hakkenden), would have cost more than one million yen ($9,189.49).[124] While any such calculations are treacherous, it seems likely that kusazōshi would indeed have been within reach of many in or near cities, but perhaps fewer outside of them, and that only rare individuals could have afforded yomihon.

Despite these reservations about scope, there is little doubt that books were circulating in many parts of Japan in the Tokugawa period. We know that Bakin's works, for example, reached very remote parts of Japan; his *Hakkenden* was even read on the islands of Sado and Hokkaidō.[125] This is quite remarkable given that the book comprises 106 volumes, each usually selling fewer than 750 copies a year. The fact that *Hakkenden* in particular was read so broadly speaks to a problem with focusing on the industrialization of print culture and the mass production of the book as a product to be purchased and possessed. As mentioned previously, the notoriously long *yomihon* were produced in small quantities and sold at high prices. Nonetheless *Hakkenden* reached readers in locations as diverse as Sado and Hokkaidō. The explanation is simple: *Hakkenden* was not a commodity these readers purchased. *Kashihon'ya* (book lenders) greatly contributed to circulating books, particularly *yomihon*, which were purchased almost exclusively by book lenders. In 1808 there were 656 book lenders in Edo and around 300 in Osaka; by the 1830s the number in Edo had increased to 800.[126] Book lenders reached into the provinces as well; markings in some lending library books reveal that Osaka book lenders served clients on the main islands of Shikoku and Kyushu.[127] As Peter Kornicki writes, "By the early nineteenth century, it is clear that something akin to a nationwide network of booksellers and circulating libraries existed, which created a national readership for books."[128] Through this network books would pass from one lender to another after a given region's demand was tapped. In this way books moved from central lenders outward to provincial lenders, only to return to the center should they become old and rare.[129] Hamada, who has also asserted the existence of a national audience for literature during the Tokugawa period, has written, "By thinking about book lenders, one can think about the national readership that followed years or even decades behind the Edo readers' annual fads."[130]

One concrete example shows the limitations of the book lenders' reach. The publishing historian Asaoka Kunio has recently written about a bookseller and book lender, Koshikumo Minoji, who operated in Tochigi prefecture during the Meiji period.[131] When Koshikumo started his store in 1898 he carried books and local newspapers. In addition it is likely that his customers could have ordered any book or magazine published in Tokyo if—and these are significant caveats—they were aware of it and had the money. Once placed, these special orders took time to reach the customers; apparently it often took seven days to two weeks for books and magazines to arrive. A newspaper article from 1899 reports that it took seven days for a copy of the literary magazine *Shinshōsetsu* (New Fiction) to arrive. This special-order magazine was also more expensive for the rural reader: 23 sen, despite having a cover price of 15 or 16 sen. Though turn-of-the-century readers in rural Tochigi could purchase books from Tokyo many barriers remained.

Koshikumo began lending books in 1901; a record of his lending activities for the thirteen months from December 1901 through December 1902 remains. Most of the borrowers (80 percent) were from the former castle town of Karasuyama, where the bookstore was located. The town had a population of 3,915 at the time and was dependent on horse-drawn carriages, *jinrikisha*, and bicycles for transport and shipping until 1923, when a train line finally reached it. Literacy was probably not widespread; in 1907 only 12.58 percent of the population finished their four to six years of mandatory education. Books and magazines were lent for 2 to 15 sen, depending on the original price; most were lent for 3 sen. It is interesting to note that there were people in Karasuyama who were aware of and interested in Tokyo literary trends; Tsubouchi Shōyō's *Tōsei shosei katagi* (The Characters of Modern Students) was lent six times during those thirteen months, and the most commonly borrowed magazines were *Bungei kurabu* (Literary Club, lent twenty-two times) and *Shinshōsetsu* (lent ten times).[132] The vast majority of books borrowed, however, were not "pure" literature but *kōdan sokkibon* (transcriptions of storyteller performances) and detective novels. Perhaps most important, *Hakkenden* reached this audience in this popular *kōdan* form, a transcription of the story as told by Tanabe Nanrin.[133] This relatively late example shows that the contribution of these book lenders to the dissemination of print may be overstated. The author Tokuda Shūsei explained that it was not until the late 1880s that Tokyo-based publications—not only contemporary writing but also printed editions of classic authors such as Chikamatsu and Saikaku—became readily available in the lending libraries and bookstores of Kanazawa, a major city.[134]

There is no doubt that books were spreading throughout the islands of Japan during the Tokugawa period, reaching an ever increasing portion of the national audience. In fact focusing on books as commodities to be owned misses the true extent of this reach, as it fails to consider the reach of the book-lending trade, which greatly extended the dissemination of literature. Focusing on books, which few owned prior to the twentieth century, also overlooks the impact of the periodical industry. The first major forum for modern Japanese literary activity was the newspaper, which was superseded, at least in Tokyo, by the magazine.[135] In many cases these less expensive periodicals were also consumed without being purchased; newspaper reading rooms and magazine reading circles, the descendants of book lenders, appeared in short order to give broader access to these texts. Audiences were rapidly expanding throughout the Edo period, but claims for a national marketplace for literature during that period are accurate only in certain limited senses. As Jonathan Zwicker has recently written, the Edo marketplace was "marked not by simultaneity and uniformity," as we would expect from most contemporary conceptions of a national marketplace, "but by slowness and unevenness."[136]

One of the primary motivations behind discovering when the market for print became national is related to Benedict Anderson's concept of the "imagined community" that he argues plays such an important role in creating the political unit of the nation-state.[137] Peter Kornicki addresses the issue of Anderson's imagined community directly:

> As Edo came in the late eighteenth century to dominate commercial publishing and to disseminate its products by means of networks of book distributors and lending libraries that covered all urban communities of Japan, so the language of Edo was carried to readers who had never been there and became for them the language of access to mass-market popular literature and culture, a language that was uniformly transmitted throughout Japan.[138]

This observation focuses on one of the key unifying devices in Anderson's conception: a national language. To the end of creating a unified national language, it did not make a difference which books transmitted the language throughout Japan, as long as they came from a source that produced texts that were reasonably linguistically homogeneous. During the nineteenth century books produced in Edo undoubtedly reached almost every section of Japan; they were just not the same books. Many book lenders, for example, would not even order specific titles; they would simply order "this many revenge tales and that many warrior tales."[139] This speaks to another device that contributes to the creation of a national imagined community: a shared culture. The imagination of a shared print culture requires that the same books reach every part of Japan, preferably identified as essential representatives of Japanese culture.

Mary Elizabeth Berry has addressed at length the issue of cultural integration in early modern Japan. She persuasively argues that a "library of public information," made up of maps, personnel rosters, dictionaries, encyclopedias, and catalogues, existed during the Edo period. She concludes that such information was disseminated widely by commercial publishing and that it resulted in "an integral conception of territory, an assumption of political union under a paramount state, and a prevailing agreement about the cultural knowledge and social intercourse that bound 'our people.' "[140] Despite her frequent use of works by the author Saikaku to illustrate her points, however, she does not demonstrate the existence of a body of literary works that were widely distributed and thus shared by the population (nor need she to make her argument). Saikaku's works, for example, enjoyed an audience of unprecedented size, but regular access to the texts outside of urban centers for nonelites has yet to be established and should not be presumed. Of course there were tales—warrior tales, Buddhist tales, myths, folk tales, and so on—that circulated throughout much of the country in a variety of forms, and were thus held in common, since at least the twelfth century.[141] It seems likely that such tales produced the first shared sense of narrative culture on something approaching a national scale.

Another conception of a national literature involves a transition from the fluid texts produced during storytellers' countless retellings to the relatively fixed printed texts disseminated more or less simultaneously throughout the country. This difference is evident in a comparison between the kōdan sokkibon form of Hakkenden that reached Tochigi and the yomihon version of Bakin's text that would have been circulating through lending libraries. Rather than being a shared narrative culture, in which a common narrative core is expressed amid individual specific rhetorical flourishes, the presence of printed texts allowed a shared literary culture, in which a given work was common in all of its linguistic specificity.[142] Once circulated broadly, these relatively fixed literary works would presumably become part of the basis for claiming a shared national literary culture and would become the common bases against which future works were created. Literature would become common to a new community, one imagined to be coterminous with the nation-state and all of its citizens rather than only with a geographically concentrated elite.[143]

In attempting to discover when these uniform literary artifacts or commodities of print culture were disseminated widely enough to constitute a shared literary culture, the question changes from When did books reach every part of Japan? to When did the same literary texts reach every part of Japan? This was achieved in one sense much later, with the national school textbooks overseen by the Ministry of Education; an early example is the *Chūtō kokugo tokuhon* (Middle School National Language Reader, 1893).[144] This was part of a concerted effort to circulate portions of classical texts, intended as models for composition, throughout the nation. In a sense, then, the literature claiming a status independent of these classical models —modern Japanese literature—formed a culture of resistance, constructed as an alternative to this classical canon propagated by the state.[145] Having not yet been incorporated into the educational system, these works did not circulate widely, with the rare exceptions mentioned previously. As a result widely circulated texts such as the *Complete Works of Contemporary Japanese Literature* made more durable and accessible the concept of a modern national literature that had been forming over the past decades in newspapers and magazines, not only through the fiction they carried but also through their nonfiction articles and gossip columns about works and their authors. In this way such series, not to mention the periodical industry that laid the foundation for the series, were the result of a process perceptible prior to the industrialization of literary publishing but impossible without it; as with the process of industrialization itself, it marked both rupture and continuity.

Perhaps, however, the question of when texts reached a national audience is the wrong question to ask. Instead it might be better to pose the question this way: How did literary texts produced in Tokyo, primarily by a relatively small community of writers, reach an ever expanding audience of diverse readers—some within the nation-state, some within the empire's formal colonies, and others spread among a variety of communities throughout the world—marked as explicitly possessing a relation to Japan, be it nation-state, empire, or fictive ethnicity? Such a question would have to recognize the multiple positions of such readers relative to Japan, seemingly divisible between citizens who believe their membership in that collective to be unproblematic and subjects who have had membership in that collective forced upon them, but in practice often a much more complicated relationship that differs according to a variety of circumstances.[146] The answer to such a question would prevent us from seeing the nation-state frame as inevitable and would allow us to recognize both diachronic and synchronic differences among readers and their relationship to Japan. This allows us to problematize not only the claims of that Tokyo-based community on Japan, but also the nature of the entity they are claiming.

2

The Stability of the Center

TOKYO PUBLISHING AND THE GREAT KANTŌ EARTHQUAKE

Tokyo, the capital of the Empire, has been looked upon by the people as the centre of political and economic activities and the fountainhead of the cultural achievement of the nation. With the unforeseen visit of the catastrophe, the city has entirely lost its former prosperous contours but retains, nevertheless, its position as the national capital. . . . The general nation are ordered to assist in the realization of the government's undertakings and earnestly to fulfil their duty to the public, thereby strengthening the foundations of our Empire.

THE TAISHŌ EMPEROR AND THE PRINCE REGENT, IMPERIAL
EDICT ON RECONSTRUCTION

Kaizōsha's *Complete Works of Contemporary Japanese Literature* could be produced only by a highly centralized, capital-intensive publishing industry, such as the one in Tokyo. It was not, however, the first massive project that took advantage of the new possibilities created by this concentration and the networks that now gave Tokyo publishing access to such a vast market. One predecessor was the publishing house of Kōdansha's revolutionary *King* magazine, which it had begun planning at least as early as 1922.[1] Kōdansha's goal was to create the *Saturday Evening Post* of Japan, the first magazine that would capture a mass readership. These plans had to be delayed after a catastrophic earthquake struck the city of Tokyo, not only interrupting Kōdansha's plans, but also destroying much of the modern publishing infrastructure. Any examination of the centralization of print capital in Tokyo must explain how that preeminence was achieved despite this near total destruction of the industry in 1923.

On 1 September 1923 one of the greatest earthquakes in Japan's history struck Tokyo and the surrounding area, igniting fires that engulfed the eastern portion of the capital.[2] The Great Kantō Earthquake left the city half destroyed, temporarily depriving Japan of its political, economic, social, and cultural center. In the wake of the destruction speculation spread that the earthquake had ended Tokyo's predominance, that Japan's center would be relocated. The earthquake, however, had the opposite effect. Following the near total destruction of certain segments of Tokyo the government called upon the nation as a whole to rebuild the imperial capital. The enormous project not only displayed the national government's capacity to control the country's resources, but it also reaffirmed the city's status as the capital, a cultural, political, and economic entrepôt for the empire. Rather than proving that the center was still contested and therefore transferable, the earthquake reinforced Tokyo's centrality and preeminence.

The effects of the earthquake initially promised to be equally dramatic for Japan's print culture. As described in chapter 1, print culture had seen the largest publishing operations in the three metropolises of Kyoto, Osaka, and Edo (Tokyo). During the second half of the Tokugawa period the balance of power shifted east, from the Kamigata region to the seat of the Tokugawa shogunate in Edo.[3] The momentous changes in publishing during the Meiji period, which led to a concentration in the industry, rapidly accelerated this shift. Then the Great Kantō Earthquake decimated the industry's physical infrastructure in Tokyo. To make matters worse, a number of authors with sufficient means fled the city, primarily for the Kansai region. These events led some to believe that Kamigata publishing might regain its former stature. The publishing industry and the trajectory toward its centralization in Tokyo, however, proved far more resilient than anyone imagined.

Not only did the earthquake not derail this process of concentration, but it reinforced Tokyo's dominance in print culture in book and magazine form and led to changes in the newspaper industry that contributed to Tokyo's eventual rise in that medium, which Osaka had dominated since the inception of the industry in the 1870s. The earthquake precipitated structural changes within the Tokyo-based book and magazine industries as well. Because of special concessions made during the recovery period, avenues of book distribution were permanently broadened, enhancing Tokyo's access to a far-reaching market. The earthquake also highlighted some of the fundamental characteristics of the publishing industry, including flexibility and a relative lack of dependence on tangible assets. These characteristics allowed rapid recovery despite near total destruction of every segment of the industry and prevented the Kansai centers from mounting a significant challenge to Tokyo's dominance. Given the magnitude of the disaster Tokyo experienced, the recovery was truly startling.

Destruction: The Impact of the Earthquake on Tokyo

The violence of the initial shocks of the earthquake rendered many measuring devices inoperative, including those at the Central Weather Bureau. One of the surviving seismographs registered these shocks and indicated as many as fourteen hundred aftershocks over the next three months.[4] The earthquake, however, was dwarfed in its consequences by the fires that raged throughout the city over the next three days. By the time the conflagration had passed the disaster had destroyed a large portion of the metropolis, killed almost one hundred thousand people, and paralyzed the capital of the Japanese Empire.[5]

By the morning of 3 September roughly 44 percent of Tokyo had burned (figure 4).[6] According to the Land Survey Department, the destruction was concentrated in certain sections of the fifteen wards of Tokyo. Six wards in the eastern portion of the city suffered the greatest damage: Nihonbashi (100 percent destroyed), Asakusa (96 percent), Honjo, (95 percent), Kanda (94 percent), Kyōbashi (86 percent), and Fukagawa (85 percent). In the western portion of the city damage was limited. The five least affected wards were Akasaka (7 percent), Koishikawa (4 percent), Yotsuya (2 percent), Ushigome (933 *tsubo* [1 *tsubo* is approximately 3.3 square meters]), and Azabu (67 *tsubo*). The sources of the fires were diverse; there were up to 130 separate points of origin. The damage was not limited to the city of Tokyo. Relatively speaking, in fact, the disaster inflicted more damage on Yokohama, where fires destroyed 75 percent of residential properties.[7]

In most cases the fires did not spread quickly, but moved at speeds slower than one mile per hour, thus allowing many not only to flee, but also

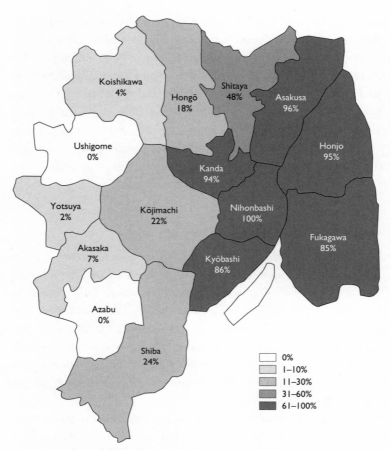

Koishikawa
4%

Hongō
18%

Shitaya
48%

Asakusa
96%

Ushigome
0%

Honjo
95%

Kanda
94%

Yotsuya
2%

Kōjimachi
22%

Nihonbashi
100%

Akasaka
7%

Fukagawa
85%

Azabu
0%

Kyōbashi
86%

Shiba
24%

□ 0%
□ 1–10%
□ 11–30%
□ 31–60%
■ 61–100%

MAP 1   Areas suffering fire damage after the Great Kantō Earthquake, by ward.

to take their valuables with them.[8] Nonetheless, though collapsing homes and workplaces produced some fatalities, the majority of deaths resulted from the fires. Although the exact number is still the object of some debate, the most recent research suggests that approximately one hundred thousand died as a result of the earthquake and the fires.[9] A large portion of the Tokyo fatalities occurred instantly, around four o'clock on the afternoon of 1 September. A firestorm that engulfed the park on the site of the former Honjo Clothing Depot (*hifukusho*) killed as many as thirty-eight thousand who had taken refuge at that evacuation center.[10] Had a similar calamity befallen Ueno Park, another of the designated refuge sites, fatalities would have been much higher.

FIGURE 4   An aerial view of post-earthquake Tokyo, 1923. Courtesy of the Yomiuri Photo Database.

The rest of Japan knew little of what was happening to Tokyo for many hours, as the earthquake had knocked out the thirty-nine telegraph lines connecting the city to the rest of the country. Seismic readings and the inability to contact Tokyo suggested that a major earthquake had struck.[11] The first specific information Osaka received about Tokyo was probably a telegraph sent by the Kanagawa police chief at 9:01 P.M. on the day of the earthquake and relayed by wireless from the steamship *Korea-maru*. It was concise: "At noon today a great earthquake struck, followed by great fires which have transformed almost all of the city into a sea of flames. Casualties are in the tens of thousands, transportation is still impossible, and there is no food or water."[12]

Damage to the infrastructure of Tokyo was profound. Rail lines suffered considerable damage and remained out of service for some time. Limited train service was restored on 6 September, but it was not until 31 October that roughly half was back in operation.[13] Postal service was temporarily halted within Tokyo and only gradually reinstated in the days and weeks that followed.[14] The earthquake also damaged the four major communications companies, including Teikoku Tsūshin (Teitsū) and Nihon Denpō

Tsūshin (Dentsū).[15] On 7 September the *Ōsaka asahi* newspaper reported that the Central Telegraph Office in front of Tokyo Station had begun accepting telegraphs, but only if they concerned disaster victims (*risai-min*).[16] Telephone use was similarly restricted.[17] Beginning on 4 September great efforts were made to establish a communication link between Tokyo and Osaka, which was completed around noon on 6 September. Newspapers particularly considered the link vital, enough so that, having realized its importance during the earthquake, *Asahi* opened a dedicated phone line connecting the two offices in June 1924, and in July 1924 *Mainichi* followed suit.[18]

The government moved rapidly to restore order. On 2 September an imperial edict placed Tokyo city and five surrounding metropolitan districts (*gun*)—Toyotama, Ebara, Kita-toshima, Minami-adachi, and Minami-katsushika—under martial law.[19] Later edicts on 3 and 4 September extended martial law to include all of Tokyo, Kanagawa, Saitama, and Chiba. Fifty thousand troops were mobilized under the direction of the commander of martial law in the Kanto districts (Kantō kaigen shirei-bu), which controlled regional administration and judiciary functions, banned assembly, censored newspapers and magazines, examined mail and telegrams, closed land and sea routes, and conducted house searches.[20] Martial law remained in effect for more than ten weeks, until lifted on 16 November.

The government realized that it also had to deal with potential economic disaster. Imperial Ordinance No. 404, issued on 7 September 1923, went under the heading "Ordinances Relating to Postponement of the Settlement of Liabilities and Other Financial Affairs."[21] This ordinance placed a moratorium on financial liabilities incurred prior to the earthquake in which settlement was due between 1 and 30 September, postponing the deadline for these debts for thirty days. This applied to debtors whose home or business was in Tokyo, Kanagawa, Shizuoka, Saitama, or Chiba prefectures or in areas designated by imperial ordinance as having been afflicted by the disaster. This moratorium did not apply to liabilities of public bodies, salaries and wages, bank deposits earmarked for the paying of salaries, and bank deposits of less than 100 yen. Imperial Ordinance No. 429, issued on 27 September, extended this period until 30 October. Imperial Ordinance No. 424, also issued on 27 September, arranged for the Japanese government to compensate the Bank of Japan for up to 100 million yen in losses incurred by discounting certain bills for persons and businesses in afflicted areas.

Almost immediately after the earthquake people began to search for information about the disaster. In 1923 residents of Tokyo and the rest of Japan received information about the world around them primarily through the medium of print. Radio was still a thing of the future for the general public.[22] Although the first permanent movie theater in Japan was opened in 1903, newsreels were not yet as common as they would later become.[23] After people recovered from the initial shock of the earthquake they wanted a broader understanding of what had happened; for this information they turned to books, magazines, and newspapers, the dominant forms of mass media at the time.

Contemporary Reactions: The Future of Tokyo's Cultural Centrality

Newspapers, which sent reporters into the city to collect information immediately after the earthquake, provided the first glimpses of the larger event. In addition to gathering factual information about the disaster, reporters also went to famous writers and intellectuals who lived in the city for their subjective impressions. Kikuchi Kan was one of a number of literati asked about the future of Tokyo. Shimanaka Yūsaku of the popular general interest magazine *Chūō kōron* (Central Review) visited his home on 3 September and asked for his impression of the earthquake's consequences. Kikuchi answered brusquely, "Listen, Tokyo culture is finished. From now on, cultural institutions are going to move to Osaka. I am thinking about moving there soon myself. That's my only impression."[24] The initial reports published in the Osaka papers projected catastrophic, long-term results from the disaster (figure 5).

Kikuchi was not alone in thinking that the earthquake was likely to reshape the cultural landscape. Many shared his ominous vision for both cultural production and one of its vital forums, the periodical press. An article in the *Ōsaka asahi shinbun* on 8 September spelled out the state of the magazine business in as much detail as was possible at the time and made certain predictions about the future of print culture in the wake of the earthquake.

FIGURE 5   Maruzen bookstore after the earthquake, 1923. Courtesy of the Mainichi Photobank.

MAGAZINES ANNIHILATED: FEW EXPECTED TO BE PUBLISHED
IN OCTOBER: A GREAT BLOW TO PRINT CULTURE

Most people probably think that print culture, with the exception of daily newspapers, was not greatly affected by the earthquake, because most magazines' September issues were shipped before the earthquake and have already been distributed to most regions of the country. In four or five days, however, when the twenty-four or -five magazines that are neatly lined up on shelves every month—the new children's magazines, women's magazines, and critical magazines—are supposed to arrive, people will probably find those shelves empty.

Even a quick glance at reports shows that, with *shitamachi* [the "low city" in the eastern portion of Tokyo: Kanda, Hongō, Nihonbashi, Kyō-bashi, and Shiba] completely destroyed, the majority of book and magazine publishers have burned, and up to eighty percent of book and magazine retailers have been wiped out. On top of this, because the bulk of essential printers were located in or around Shiba, Kyōbashi, Honjo, and Fukagawa, there is no way that the manuscripts of uncompleted books and magazines, as well as typefaces and printing machines, were not totally destroyed.

The printing facility for the publishing company Hakubunkan, which is located in Hisakata-chō in Koishikawa, had just finished installing five large printing machines it had ordered from abroad in April 1922. However, even these are said to have toppled and be inoperable. For the moment, magazine and book printing is stopped. Hakubunkan alone printed such titles as *Taiyō* [The Sun], *Bungei kurabu* [Literary Club], *Shukujo gahō* [Ladies' Illustrated], *Yakyū-kai* [World of Baseball], *Shinshumi* [New Tastes], and *Nōgyō sekai* [World of Farming] at the Hisakata plant. The majority of the plant's capacity, however, is dedicated to publications that claim far larger circulation, some reaching 200,000, such as Kōdansha's *Yūben* [Eloquence], *Kōdan kurabu* [Storytelling Club], and *Gendai* [The Present Day], as well as Daitōkaku's *Kaihō* [Emancipation] and Fujōkai-sha's *Fujokai* [Women's World]. As a result, the repercussions are severe. *Shinshōsetsu* [New Fiction, published by Shun'yōdō], *Fujin gahō* [Ladies' Illustrated, published by Tōkyōsha], *Jitsugyō no Nihon* [Commercial Japan, published by Jitsugyō no Nihon-sha], as well as other influential magazines are printed by Shūeisha, in Kyōbashi's Nishi Kon'ya-chō, which is also currently incapacitated. Genbunsha's *Shinkatei* [New Households] and *Shin'engei* [New Entertainment], printed by Toppan Insatsusha in Shitaya, are also incapacitated.

Given this information, it seems that it will be difficult for most magazines to go to print for some time. The examples presented here are taken from those companies located in destroyed districts or from verified accounts of destruction. When the damage caused to machines by tremors, the toppling of type cases, or machine stoppages, all of which occurred at the Shūeisha factory in the Ushigome area, are also taken into consideration, there can be no question that the printing capacity of Tokyo has been annihilated. Despite the fact that *Chūō kōron* and *Kaizō* [Reconstruction] are printed at factories in Ushigome, it is extremely doubtful production will resume with an October or November issue. Now is the time for the people of Kansai, who look to Kantō as the source of all culture, to devote all their energies to creating another great source of print culture here.[25]

The shift away from Tokyo was discussed as not only a cultural but also a political and economic shift. After the earthquake struck some suggested that the seat of government be moved out of the city; according to Edward

Seidensticker, certain elements in the military were even talking about the possibility of moving the government to the continent.[26] However unrealistic these suggestions may have been, they were sufficient in number to prompt the government to promulgate an imperial proclamation on 12 September reassuring everyone that Tokyo would continue to be the capital. The statement read as follows:

> Tokyo, the capital of the empire, has been looked upon by the people as the centre of political and economic activities and the fountainhead of the cultural achievement of the nation. With the unforeseen visit of the catastrophe, the city has entirely lost its former prosperous contours but retains, nevertheless, its position as the national capital. The remedial work, therefore, ought not to consist merely in the reparation of the quondam metropolis, but, in ample provisions for the future development of the city, completely to transform the avenues and streets.[27]

The future of Tokyo's academic activities was also questioned, this time by an influential Tokyo newspaper. "Academic Authority Shifts to Kyoto: Publishing World to Osaka" appeared on 8 September in the *Tōkyō nichinichi shinbun*. It quoted a Tokyo Imperial University professor by the name of Imai:

> There is nothing we can do but have students do independent research in Kyoto or Tōhoku until the [new Tokyo University] buildings are completed. It is suspected that, because libraries are the lifeblood of law and humanities departments, little authoritative scholarship will be produced [here] for the next several years and that, for this reason, scholastic authority may shift to Kyoto. It also seems that the general publishing world will, within a short time, move to Osaka. However, because the writing class, no matter how destroyed Tokyo may be, will not move to Osaka (many of their homes being in the suburbs and therefore having escaped damage), the center of publishing will probably return to Tokyo.[28]

Despite his extreme predictions, this Tokyo observer already perceived certain conditions that would limit a radical, permanent exodus from the city.

Realizing the Stability of Tokyo's Dominance

Comprehension of the effects of the earthquake deepened rapidly as the city got a clearer picture of what had happened. Only eight days after the publication of Imai's statement the same newspaper printed a recantation of his opinions. An article titled "Publishing World Centered in Tokyo as Always: Osaka Shift Theory Only Gossip" appeared in the *Tōkyō nichinichi shinbun* on 16 September:

> Although a rumor arose that Tokyo's publishing world would move to Osaka, the fact is that this has been disproved—particularly by the exceedingly energetic display of the magazine industry. It was decided by the Magazine Association that more than fifty different important magazines would release their October issues on October 1, continuing printing as always. Preparations are already underway.
>
> After surveying influential members of this industry, it seems that the capacity of printing facilities that escaped the fire alone exceeds the printing capacity of Osaka. Neither is the relationship between writers and publishers one that is easily broken. The only question is whether stereotype matrices have been destroyed or not. Given its current energy, the industry will recover within three months.
>
> Although roughly 300 different magazines appeared in stores prior to the earthquake, of these only around 50 are influential; although some will be weeded out, the majority will produce special earthquake editions.[29]

The rapid actions of the publishing industry to restabilize itself and the public announcements of its restabilization reassured industry watchers in the media, who in turn pacified the general public. By publishing their decisions in the newspapers, the Magazine Association (Tōkyō Zasshi Kyōkai) not only informed their dispersed membership of their decisions, but also presented the image of a unified front, calmly dealing with the situation they faced, able to resume business with only minor delays. In this way each of the forms of print media supported the others, creating the image of a stable industry.

By December observers had already gained enough distance from the events to recognize the improbability of a large-scale shift within the nation. Katagami Noboru, a professor of Russian literature at Waseda University, wrote in December that predictions of the future of writing were grim at the time of the earthquake:

> It is certainly a fact that for a moment—that moment when the convenience, tranquility, and pleasure provided us by a civilization centered in Tokyo was suddenly lost and when in order to obtain the minimum fundamental materials needed to survive, people had to exert all efforts and labors—the ruin of printing companies, booksellers, and the great city of Tokyo caused people to think that the publication and dissemination of the written word had lost its strength and that literature would thus wane.[30]

Given the large reading population in Tokyo it stands to reason that literature suffered when writers, readers, and publishers were forced to focus on sheer survival. The limited long-term effects on the trajectory of literature, however, were apparent to Katagami:

> This destruction, this obstacle, however, is more than anything else mechanical and external; along with the restoration of order to life in society, literature should be restored with relative ease. Today, for example, within two months of the earthquake and fires, a surprisingly large number of books and magazines are being published.[31]

In a matter of months speculation about the effects of the earthquake had deflated from Tokyo's complete eclipse to a slight production delay; the projections that the Kansai publishing industry might supersede Tokyo's faded quickly.

Although those projections proved to be wrong, they were not simply the result of regional boosterism. As we have seen, Tokyo had not always been the center of publishing; prior to the Tokugawa period Kyoto had dominated print culture. Even into the Tokugawa period, as influence shifted to the Kantō area, a tripolar constellation persisted: the merchant center of the country, Osaka, was "keeping pace with Kyoto and Edo as one of the centers of publishing culture."[32] Starting in the Meiji period and continuing until the earthquake, however, Kansai lost ground to Tokyo, whose dominance grew stronger by the year. Based on government statistics from 1922, Osaka and Kyoto published roughly one-third the number

TABLE 1   NUMBER OF PUBLICATIONS BY REGION, 1922

	Books	Magazines	Governmental	Total[a]	% of Total
Tokyo	8,856	9,084	2,069	20,009	41.3
Osaka and Kyoto	1,812	3,925	813	6,550	13.5

Source: Naimushō Daijin Kanbō Bunshoka, ed., *Dai-Nihon Teikoku Naimushō tōkei hōkoku* (Tokyo: Insatsu-kyoku, 1925), 413.

[a]Based on the total number of examination copies submitted to the government per the Publication Law of 1893.

of titles that Tokyo did, not including newspapers. While Tokyo dominated the publishing industry, Osaka and Kyoto nonetheless still possessed industries of some size. Neither did Tokyo control all organs of the print medium. Osaka had larger newspaper circulation in a market that was far from national, and Osaka's largest newspapers, the *Asahi* and the *Mainichi*, had already branched into the Tokyo market. Despite Tokyo's preeminence in publishing in terms of magnitude and reach Kansai remained a competitor that could not be ignored (table 1).

Despite this competition, however, the Tokyo publishing industry recovered rapidly. Although the vast majority of the industry was damaged or destroyed, a few key factories survived. Individual publishers, due to the inherent flexibility of the industry, operated even with their facilities destroyed, sometimes out of homes or hotel rooms. Within each segment of the industry cooperative organizations provided protection and balance amid the turmoil of the destruction and the resulting struggle for survival. Where this balance was not maintained, as in the newspaper industry, the restored market's composition was significantly altered. The individuals behind the industry were not purely rational economic actors; they had roots in and commitments to Tokyo they would not shift purely for temporary material advantage. Thanks to these factors, significant government intervention, and the extraordinary efforts of the individuals involved, Tokyo print culture recovered with such speed and vigor that Kansai could not overcome it.

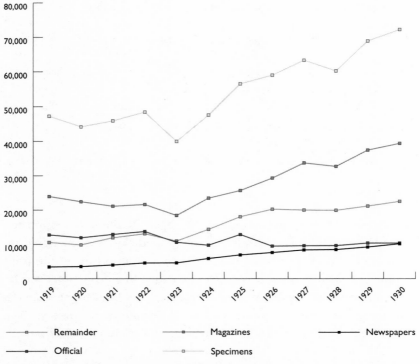

—□— Remainder	—□— Magazines	—■— Newspapers
—■— Official	—□— Specimens	

FIGURE 6   Number of titles published. Figures are from Yayoshi Mitsunaga, *Mikan shiryō ni yoru Nihon shuppan bunka: Kindai shuppan bunka*, Shoshi shomoku shiriizu 26, vol. 5 (Tokyo: Yumani Shobō, 1988), 293. See chapter 2, note 33 for further details.

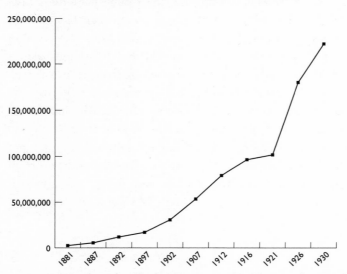

FIGURE 7   Estimates of total book and magazine sales. Figures are from Yayoshi Mitsunaga, *Mikan shiryō, ni yoru Nihon shuppan bunka: Kindai shuppan bunka*, Shoshi shomoku shiriizu 26, vol. 5 (Tokyo: Yumani Shobō, 1988), 289, 294. See chapter 2, note 34 for further details.

The Earthquake's Impact on Publishing

Certain government statistics provide us with a concrete image of the trajectories of the magazine, book, and newspaper industries, allowing us to see the repercussions of the earthquake in the years that followed. The total number of titles published each year can be approximated by examining the number of publications submitted to the Home Ministry for examination. As the decreases between 1919 and 1920 (-6.51 percent) and between 1927 and 1928 (-4.87 percent) reflect, growth in the number of titles produced per year was not steady. The years 1922–23, however, do reflect the greatest negative growth of the period, with 17.47 percent fewer titles printed in 1923. The response of the following two years (+18.97 percent and +18.89 percent, respectively) shows the rapid recovery of the industry as a whole. Not only was the disruption of the industry remarkably brief, but post-earthquake production showed a dramatic increase over pre-earthquake levels (figure 6, above).[33]

Total sales grew throughout the 1920s as well. Although only estimates, the graph in figure 7 (above) suggests the growing marketplace for printed matter in modern Japan.[34] Unfortunately we do not have estimates for the years 1922–25. The aggregate figures, though, point to a pronounced trajectory of growth. Based on these figures, overall sales recorded the smallest amount of growth between the years 1916 and 1921, at only 1.10 percent per year (on average). On the other hand, the period that includes the earthquake, 1921–26, reflects the largest growth since 1897–1902, and this average rate of growth per year (+15.36 percent) includes the drastic losses of 1923. The earthquake only momentarily hindered publishing's continuing growth.

Not only did the earthquake of 1923 *not* move the publishing (and cultural) center to Kansai, but it barely even disrupted the industry's growth. The two organs of the publishing industry dominated by Tokyo, books and magazines, emerged from the wreckage of the earthquake strong, though altered. The one organ dominated by Osaka, newspapers, emerged on a new trajectory, moving toward greater Tokyo centrality as well.

Recovery and Reorganization in the Magazine Industry

Collective effort and good timing helped the thriving magazine industry return rapidly to its pre-earthquake growth. A number of companies had

TABLE 2   EFFECT OF THE EARTHQUAKE ON LARGE PUBLISHERS

Company	Ward	Damage
Bungei Shunjūsha	Hongō	Damaged
Chūō Kōronsha	Kōjimachi	Little damage
Heibonsha	Kanda	Destroyed
Iwanami Shoten[a]	Kanda	Destroyed
Jitsugyō no Nihonsha	Kyōbashi	Destroyed
Kaizōsha	Shiba	Destroyed
Kōdansha	Hongō	Some damage
Sanseidō shuppan-bu	Kōjimachi	Destroyed
Shinchōsha	Ushigome	No damage
Shōgakukan	Kanda	Destroyed
Shufu no Tomosha	Kanda	Destroyed
Yūhikaku[b]	Kanda	Destroyed

Source: Makita Inagi, *Nihon shuppan taikan*, 2 vols. (Osaka: Shuppan Taimususha, 1928).

[a] Iwanami's wholesale division was the portion of the company destroyed.

[b] Yūhikaku's storehouse survived.

already distributed their September issues when the earthquake struck, and although the month of September was declared an official magazine hiatus many companies published special "earthquake editions" bearing an imprint date of 1 October and distributed soon thereafter. Many small magazines resumed publication within a matter of months, despite massive physical damage to publishers, most of whom were located in the worst hit areas of the city. In the long run, despite the severe financial losses caused by the earthquake, equalizing steps taken by the Magazine Association minimized permanent shifts in the industry's balance of power. This outcome must have seemed unlikely in the days following the disaster (table 2, above).

Noma Seiji, then president of the publishing company Kōdansha, played a central role in the magazine industry's recovery. At the time, Kōdansha put out some of the highest circulation magazines available, including *Yūben*, *Kōdan kurabu*, and *Gendai*. September issues of Kōdansha magazines were already on the market, and the October issues were either just completed or were at the printers. Although Kōdansha's warehouse was destroyed, no employees were injured.[35] Despite limited damage to the company's main offices in Dangozaka, it was impossible for the company to continue with business as usual. The earthquake had crippled the majority of printers, binders, distributors, and bookstores. According to Noma, soon after the earthquake he gathered members of the Magazine Association and representatives of the major distributors in order to plan a course of action.

The Tokyo Magazine Association (Tōkyō Zasshi Kumiai, renamed the Nihon Zasshi Kyōkai in 1924) was formed in February 1914 to encourage cooperation among magazine publishers.[36] From its inception, the Association was primarily designed to set fixed prices (*teika*), which members were obliged to enforce.[37] As a result of this coordination, magazine publishers had stabilized prices and protected their profits. This provided a substantial precedent for cooperative action to maintain profitability as well as a mechanism through which to realize such cooperation.

At Noma's urging, an extraordinary meeting of the Tokyo Magazine Association Secretariat (*rinji kanji-kai*) was held on 10 September, at which the attending representatives decided that none of the members would publish a magazine of any kind containing an article on the earthquake until 1 October. The following announcement was run in Tokyo newspapers at the time in order to reach members of the industry unreachable through normal channels:

URGENT NOTICE TO ALL MEMBERS OF
THE TOKYO MAGAZINE ASSOCIATION:

A special meeting of the secretariat of the Association was held on September 10 to discuss corrective measures in the wake of the unprecedented earthquake and fires. Given the incomplete recovery of delivery channels and the unavoidable circumstances attendant upon the reopening of businesses, with the major distributors in attendance the following resolutions were passed and shall be effected:

The resolutions that follow should have been decided by a plenary session, but given the current emergency situation, we recognized that calling such a meeting was impossible. We beg your understanding.

Be it resolved:

October issues of magazines shall be distributed as follows:

Children's magazines: October 1, 2
Entertainment magazines: October 3, 4
Young boy's, girl's, and youth magazines: October 5, 6
Women's magazines: October 7, 8
Others: From October 9 forward.

The preceding magazines must be published as October issues.

This advertisement has been used to notify members due to their dispersal.[38]

At the meeting they also decided how losses would be distributed. A return rate (*henpinritsu*) would be calculated based on May and June returns, and the distributors would be reimbursed for that amount for July, August, and September issue returns.[39] These were only a few of the flexible arrangements made for payments and other processes that required special considerations during the immediate aftermath of the earthquake and which allowed the industry to survive.

The Magazine Association was not the only collective organization that convened an emergency session in order to consider collaborative strategies of recovery. The Secondary School Textbook Association (Chūtō Kyō-kasho Kyōkai) held a meeting on 17 September to deliberate on corrective measures, the Tokyo Book Association (Tōkyō Shoseki-shō Kumiai) held an extraordinary deliberation meeting on 23 September, the Tokyo Magazine Marketing Cooperative (Tōkyō Zasshi Hanbai-gyō Kumiai) held an extraordinary executive meeting on 28 September, and the Tokyo Publishing Association (Tōkyō Shuppan Kyōkai) held an extraordinary executive meeting on 29 September.[40]

Despite these measures recovery was difficult for many magazines, and, particularly at first, many publishers despaired. At the time of the earthquake *Bungei shunjū* was only eight months old. Edited by Kikuchi Kan, at that time the magazine was printed and sold by the publisher Shun'yōdō. Circulation of the first issue had been three thousand, though it had climbed to eleven thousand by May and had remained at that level until the earthquake. The disaster destroyed Shun'yōdō's facilities and the September issue, which had just been completed but had yet to be distributed. The earthquake greatly distressed Kikuchi, even prompting him to write an essay in which he expressed an intention to give up publishing and become a farmer.[41] Still, as with other segments of the industry, *Bungei shunjū* recovered after all. Kikuchi made a public retraction of the statement shortly thereafter, and the magazine resumed printing two months later with its November issue.

The women's magazine *Shufu no tomo* (Housewife's Friend) was similarly disrupted but moved much more quickly to reestablish itself. Located in Kanda, Shufu no Tomosha's main offices were destroyed by the earthquake. Because the company that printed the magazine, Nisshin Insatsu, was not totally destroyed, Ishikawa Takemi, the founder of the magazine, was able to set up offices at the printer's facility.[42] Although the October issue was almost finished when the earthquake struck, it was abandoned, and work was begun on the *Tōkyō daishin daika gahō* (Great Tokyo Earthquake and Fire Illustrated), which was released in its place. By the morning of 4 September Shufu no Tomosha had erected a large hand-painted sign advertising the illustrated magazine at the site of the burned company offices and by 9 September had placed advertisements in newspapers throughout Japan. The company recovered rapidly after this, rebuilding on the site of the old offices.

Two of the most influential magazines of the day, *Kaizō* and *Chūō kōron*, recovered equally rapidly. Chūō Kōronsha, with offices in the famous Maru building and in Ushigome, suffered minor damage.[43] The offices in the Maru building were spared, though the company held most editorial meetings for the next two weeks at the home of the owner, Takita Choin, partly to be out of the disaster area and partly because of Takita's failing health. It was there that the October issue of *Chūō kōron*, titled *Daishinsai sōnan-ki* (Record of the Great Earthquake Disaster), was compiled. Kaizōsha, located in Shiba, was destroyed. Despite losing its central office, however, the company printed censor specimen copies of the October issue of *Kaizō* on 20 September and released the issue on 1 October. Shūeisha's Factory No. 1, spared due to its location in Ushigome-ku, Ichigaya Kagachō, printed the issue.

Many of the magazines that survived prided themselves on continuous publication despite the disaster's epic proportions. Most magazines with sufficient capitalization did survive and quickly resumed publication. Statistics suggest, however, that a large-scale winnowing of the industry occurred despite the rapid recovery of most of the larger magazines. The literary journal of the Shirakaba-ha (White Birch School), *Shirakaba* (White Birch), for example, ceased publication as a result of the earthquake. Prior to the earthquake there were some six hundred magazine titles; as of May 1924 there were only around three hundred.[44] Despite this winnowing, however, it is clear that the initial predictions of empty shelves throughout the country were wrong. The rapid recovery in fact must have given a quite different impression to readers, both in and outside of Tokyo: that the city's centrality could not be destabilized, even by a disaster of this size, and that its magazine culture, with new issues soon lined up on those shelves, could find a way to make even these events into profitable stories.

Tokyo's Gravitational Pull on Books

Unlike magazines, which tended to have a limited life span and thus were expected to be perpetually re-created, books were presumed to last, and therefore their loss was perhaps more keenly felt. The first concerns expressed over the loss of books focused on a potential scarcity of textbooks that might disrupt the academic cycle. The *Ōsaka asahi shinbun* reported on 7 September that schools were going to have problems getting their second-semester books because companies specializing in the printing of junior high school textbooks had been destroyed.[45] Depending on Tokyo's recovery, the article continued, the printing of next year's textbooks might also be in jeopardy. The public had legitimate reason for concern, as initial reports suggested that the earthquake had destroyed as much as 80 percent of the supply of textbooks for levels above middle school. Schools, the article reported, were to avoid price gouging by turning to used books, mimeographs, and lecture notes.

An article four days later in the *Ōsaka asahi shinbun* cited a telegram, received from Nihonbashi by the Osaka sales office for official national (*kokutei*) textbooks, saying that two large warehouses had been destroyed by fire and that as many as fifteen million books had been lost.[46] This was quickly dismissed as unlikely. Because books for the academic year's second semester were printed and bound in June and then sent to distributors around 20 August, the article concluded that many of the books (those in undamaged areas) must be safe. At the same time, the newspaper expressed concern that the likely loss of three or four million textbooks in the disaster areas would nonetheless disrupt many elementary school students' educations. If, however, factories or paper supplies were destroyed, they speculated, this would mean a delay not only in the replacement of textbooks for the second semester, but also in the printing of the next year's textbooks, which usually began in August. This fear, however, seems to have been unfounded. On 10 October the *Kokumin shinbun* reported that the textbooks needed in 1924 had already been printed.[47]

Despite the limited destruction of textbooks, the loss of other books was profound. According to Kobayashi Zenpachi, it was estimated in 1924 that the earthquake destroyed between six and eight million books from bookstore stock alone, not including those in publishers' and large distributors' warehouses.[48] More recently Okano Takeo estimated that between fifteen and sixteen million books were destroyed.[49] In Kanda alone 117 used bookstores were destroyed.[50] The destruction of so many books led to skyrocketing prices in the used book market, as "used books" became "rare books" overnight.[51] Some book prices quadrupled or even quintupled after the earthquake.[52] Tokyo's resulting demand for books was so extreme that it created a powerful gravitational force, pulling books to Tokyo from all over Japan. In an attempt to replenish stocks, used bookstores sent agents around the country and throughout the empire in order to buy books.[53] Two Osaka distributors, Sanbunsha and Seibun-kan, were cleared out by booksellers who hoped to buy up as many books as they could in the face of what appeared to them to be a book crisis.[54]

Not only did the earthquake rob Tokyo of its supply of books for sale, but it also deprived the city of important collections of books, some unique. Tokyo University's main library burned, destroying most of its collection of 760,000 books.[55] As with Tokyo itself, however, benefactors of the university did not allow it to simply fade away as a casualty of the calamity. In October 1924 *Gakushi-kai geppō* (Academia Monthly) reported that, through donations, the library had amassed over 270,000 replacement books. By the end of 1927 that number had increased to 550,000.[56] Tokyo University's was not the only collection destroyed. The Meiji University library lost 58,900 books, the private Ōhashi Library lost 88,304, and the Hitotsubashi Library lost 12,307. Twenty public libraries in the city of Tokyo lost a total of 103,505 books; eleven of those libraries lost more than 90 percent of their holdings.[57]

Many book publishing companies saw their facilities entirely destroyed by the earthquake. Iwanami Shoten was in its tenth year when the disaster struck. A twenty-year-old employee of the company in 1923, Kobayashi Isamu was in its Imagawakōji, Kanda, building when he felt the strong initial tremors.[58] Although the Iwanami building did not collapse, Kobayashi discovered that the buildings nearby had not been similarly spared. Not knowing what to do, he ran to the Iwanami store in Jinbō-chō. Iwanami Shigeo and his employees there were desperately trying to detach the sign over the storefront, which had been written by Natsume Sōseki. Unsuccessful in their attempt, Iwanami and his employees lost the irreplaceable sign to the fires. It was November when the company finally constructed a temporary building on the site of the Jinbō-chō store. Iwanami suffered roughly 800,000 yen in damages, losing two stores in Jinbō-chō, three storehouses in Imagawakōji, and a printing facility in Yūraku-chō.[59]

Some publishers lost unique master plates, thereby losing books that had yet to make it into print. At Heibonsha masters of the recently completed *Shingi jiten* (Dictionary of Shintō Deities) and *Kanwa jiten* (Chinese-Japanese Dictionary) were destroyed.[60] These were not the only new publications lost in the disaster; in fact the earthquake stymied book production in Tokyo, leaving it crippled for months. Prior to the earthquake the industry published an average of three hundred new hardcover books (*tankōbon*) per month. In September 1923 there were none; by April of the following year the total had risen to only 180.[61]

One very important title was published soon after the earthquake, Kōdansha's *Taishō daishinsai daikasai* (The Great Taishō Earthquake and Conflagration). This book not only revealed the extent of the disaster to readers starving to know what had happened to Tokyo, but it also helped the book industry as a whole recover and eventually even changed the way it operated. The story of its production demonstrates the difficulties faced in the days and weeks after the earthquake, the magnitude of the destruction to the publishing industry, and the energy with which some of these entrepreneurs approached these hurdles.

Noma Seiji wrote in his autobiography, *Watashi no hansei* (The First Half of My Life), that he had just sat down to lunch when the earthquake struck. Thinking to ride out what he expected to be a normal, mild earthquake, he remained seated. Soon, however, one of the roofs of the building across the lake on his property collapsed, raising a cloud of dust that made it look "as if a bomb had been dropped upon it."[62] The subsequent appearance of a number of his employees, who had come to verify his well-being, relieved him about the main office of Kōdansha in Dangozaka. That office emerged only slightly damaged. Employees had gathered important documents and stored them in protective cases during the initial shocks in order to protect them from subsequent fires. As described previously, Noma quickly called a meeting of the Magazine Association, which declared a one-month magazine hiatus.

Redefining the Book: Kōdansha's *Taishō daishinsai daikasai*

Kōdansha moved rapidly to make use of the hiatus, deciding to compile a book that would provide more information about the effects of the earthquake than the newspapers were able to provide. In planning for the book Noma met with representatives of the major distribution companies, including Tōkyōdō, Tōkaidō, Hokurikukan, and Seishundō. Noma, who realized the opportunity this presented, wanted to produce a run of 500,000 copies; the distributors hesitated committing to a run of larger than 150,000. They argued that with trains not running, with their trucks inoperative, and with more than 70 percent of their staff missing, they could not do it. They added that newspapers were not printing, that there would be no method of advertisement, and that if they printed in Tokyo they would have to find paper. By assuring them that arrangements had been made and that they could direct their advertisements at the bookstores rather than the customers directly, Noma convinced them to take on the project.[63]

The next problem was collecting orders. Kōdansha sent employees around the country to collect advance orders, which they relayed to Tokyo by telegram.[64] There were more problems, however. Unlike magazines, books could not be wrapped in newsprint and thrown onto a train. In theory, books had to be boxed, wrapped, labeled, weighed for postage, and addressed; it would have been impossible to handle all of this in the traditional manner. As a result one of the distributors' stipulations was that Kōdansha make arrangements to have the books shipped using magazine protocol. Through personal connections, Noma obtained permission for this convention-breaking step.

The Railroad Ministry granted special approval for Kōdansha to ship books by magazine protocol. Although Kōdansha paid the normal shipping rate for books, the Ministry granted the company permission to wrap them like magazines. In addition the books were distributed not only to stores specializing in books, but also to those specializing in magazines. At the time three types of stores existed; some exclusively sold books, some exclusively sold magazines, and some sold both. Getting access to all of these stores expanded publishers' retail network from three hundred to as many as ten thousand stores.[65] Although the distribution of books by magazine routes had been proposed before, various hurdles stood in the way: the distributors had relationships with regional associations that stood to lose with this new arrangement, administrative handling would be difficult, and it would have created problems for both the distributors and the bookstores if sales quantities were not on par with magazines. Despite these problems, Kōdansha went ahead with the project.

Noma still had to find paper. Having lost its stock to fire, one of the largest paper suppliers at the time, Chozō-shi, sent an employee to Osaka to buy paper. Noma considered entrusting the printing to Kansai printing companies—which he noted had developed greatly in recent years—but his relationship with Ōji Seishi held him back. When he contacted Ōji he discovered that fires had consumed the company's storehouse but spared their factory in Jūjō. As a result Ōji still had all of the paper that had recently been manufactured at the factory and gave Kōdansha its choice of the various remainders from existing orders. Unfortunately this did not suffice. Because the damage to a few of the paper machines was repairable, however, Ōji began fixing them and promised to produce sufficient quantities. The problem of art paper to print the first eighty pages of glossy photographs remained. The one supplier in the city, Nihon Kakō Seishi, had almost none left, and the job required some 1,050 reams.[66] Noma finally obtained imported art paper through a company that had just brought a shipment into the country. It was insufficient for Kōdansha's purposes— only the first sixteen of the eighty pages of photographs are on this paper— but it had to do.

Having secured paper supplies Kōdansha still had to find ways to advertise and print the book. Advertising for the new publication was an ordeal. Because it could not use newspaper advertisements, the company used other techniques, including hanging posters and sending postcards, six hundred thousand in all, announcing the book. Employees had to go to many different post offices both to get blank cards and to mail the finished

FIGURE 8   Hakubunkan after the earthquake. Courtesy of the Mainichi Photobank.

ones, but in the end Kōdansha succeeded in one of Japan's first mass mailings.[67] Printing facilities were secured after surveying surviving plants. The fires destroyed Hakubunkan Insatsu-jō's new printing facility, but its old facility, with only half the printing capacity, survived (figure 8). Kōdansha made arrangements with the company to print the book.

Because the government had placed a moratorium on banks, limiting daily withdrawals to 500 yen, cash remained scarce in the initial days and weeks after the earthquake.[68] Mitsubishi Bank put up the initial investment for the publication of *Taishō daishinsai daikasai* under a special dispensation, orchestrated through personal connections of Noma's. When the funding became available and all of the arrangements were made, the book was published and distributed to a readership eager to learn more about the events of the earthquake and to bookstores eager to have something to sell to that audience. Horie Tsunekichi, who was in charge of the book's production, said that a total of four hundred thousand copies were printed in three printings.[69] The sales from the *Taishō daishinsai daikaisai* brought much needed cash into bookstores, providing them with money to purchase more books.[70]

Fellow publishers censured Kōdansha for producing *Taishō daishinsai daikaisai* during the one-month magazine moratorium.[71] Many members of the Magazine Association were furious with Kōdansha for violating the spirit of the agreement, if not the word. Nagata Shin'nojō, acting on behalf of the president of Jitsugyō no Nihonsha, threatened to demand that certain bookstores not carry the book and that its advertisements be blocked.[72] These threats came to nothing, however, as stores, distributors, and readers eagerly bought up both *Taishō daishinsai daikaisai* and subsequent October magazine issues.

Taishō daishinsai daikaisai proved to the areas outside of Tokyo that the city had survived the earthquake and would recover; the stream of October magazine issues that flowed into their stores later that month reinforced this conclusion. Admittedly Kōdansha's success, in terms of speed of recovery, was an anomaly. Most book companies did not resume printing until 1924. Nonetheless the production of successful projects such as *Taishō daishinsai daikaisai* provided the producers of print culture with sufficient confidence to keep them in Tokyo, retaining access to copyrights and creative springs in the city. By using magazine distribution protocol to send the book to all stores selling print, Kōdansha set a precedent for the shipping of books that eventually became standard procedure, unifying the print retailers and increasing book sales.[73]

Challenging the Bipolar Structure of the Newspaper Market

Faster than the recovery of either the magazine or the book industry was that of the newspaper industry. At the time of the earthquake eighteen large daily newspapers were published in Tokyo.[74] Only three of these survived the fires; the *Tōkyō nichinichi shinbun*, the *Hōchi shinbun*, and the *Miyako shinbun* escaped serious damage because they were located in the Yamanote area of the city. Unlike the book and magazine industries, which experienced relatively uniform damage, this created an inequality of destruction within the industry, which contributed to lasting changes in the makeup of market distribution and company hierarchy.[75]

In 1923 newspaper companies were located for the most part in Nihonbashi, Kanda, Kōjimachi, Shiba, and especially Kyōbashi.[76] The three newspapers that survived were in Kōjimachi; the rest were destroyed. The damage to equipment seemed extensive and paralyzing at first. Ōta Masataka estimates that fires destroyed forty million pieces of movable type. Restoring toppled type cases into working order took more than ten days and nights. Because of power outages and other minor damage, even the

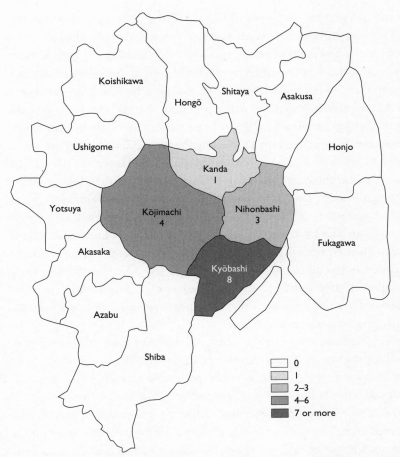

Koishikawa

Hongō

Shitaya

Asakusa

Ushigome

Honjo

Kanda
1

Yotsuya

Kōjimachi
4

Nihonbashi
3

Akasaka

Fukagawa

Kyōbashi
8

Azabu

Shiba

☐ 0
☐ 1
☐ 2–3
☐ 4–6
☐ 7 or more

MAP 2   Major newspaper company locations prior to the Great Kantō Earthquake. Primarily from Nagashiro Shizuo, ed., *Nihon shinbun shashi shūsei* (Tokyo: Shinbun Kenkyūjo, 1938).

surviving newspapers could not publish formal issues for a number of days after the earthquake. Instead they and other resourceful newspapers put out special hand-printed or mimeographed editions and commissioned printers and other newspaper companies in undamaged areas to print issues for them. The *Tōkyō nichinichi shinbun*, for example, was printed in Urawa; the *Hōchi shinbun* was printed in Maebashi and Mito.[77]

Hōchi shinbun's experience in the days following the earthquake illustrates the many challenges newspaper companies faced. According to Mitarai Tatsuo, the features head of the *Hōchi shinbun* at the time, his first

The Stability of the Center

77

concern was getting out a special edition of the newspaper. Because the company had experienced overturned type cases before, they had set aside enough in the basement to print a special edition in an emergency. Mitarai assembled such an edition using the limited type, but then realized that the rotary press would not run. Using a lithograph machine he printed masters by hand and mimeographed as many copies as he could. Around 1 P.M. on 1 September he gathered a number of employees, armed them with megaphones, and drove around the city selling these special editions.[78] By 4 P.M. *Hōchi* had released a special edition, produced in Maebashi, that it distributed to neighboring prefectures. The newspaper maintained emergency supplies of paper, which escaped the fire in the Sumitomo storehouse in Kyōbashi, and had a delivery en route that had not yet arrived when the earthquake struck. On 3 September it rushed a number of rolls of paper to Maebashi and produced more than ten thousand copies of another one-page special edition, which it sent back to Tokyo for distribution. On 4 September *Hōchi* printed fifty thousand copies of a special edition in Mito and sent it back into the city, while a half-page special edition was simultaneously printed at the main office.[79]

Power was restored on 5 September, and the three surviving newspapers resumed printing in Tokyo. *Nichinichi* began publishing on 6 September with a two-page edition, which experienced tremendous sales: pre-earthquake circulation figures of around 300,000 jumped to 610,050.[80] *Hōchi* published a two-page evening edition on 5 September, and *Miyako* published an eight-page evening edition on 8 September. The other newspapers took longer to recover. *Tōkyō asahi* resumed publishing with a four-page edition on 12 September, while *Yomiuri* published a four-page edition on 15 September. By 18 September *Tōkyō nichinichi* and *Hōchi* had returned to their pre-earthquake conditions; by 25 September so had *Tōkyō asahi* and *Jiji shinpō*. The damage, however, went beyond the production of the newspapers: "Their market of readers had been destroyed, their advertising revenue had been interrupted, and their regional distribution and sales systems were in chaos due to the suspension of publication."[81]

Two Tokyo newspapers, the *Tōkyō nichinichi* and *Tōkyō asahi*, were able to turn to parent companies in Osaka for assistance. The paper known today as the *Mainichi shinbun* began as the *Nihon rikken seitō shinbun* in Osaka in 1882. The name changed to the *Ōsaka mainichi shinbun* in 1888, when it shifted from strictly political content to general news. In 1906 the company purchased the *Denpō shinbun* in Tokyo and renamed it the *Mainichi denpō*. This merged with the *Tōkyō nichinichi shinbun* in 1911, retaining the name *Tōkyō nichinichi* until 1943. Management located in Osaka ran both the Tokyo and Osaka papers.[82] *Tōkyō nichinichi*, having survived the fires, put out special editions and recovered rapidly.

Tōkyō asahi shinbun, which was destroyed by fire, recovered quickly with the assistance of its parent company, the Ōsaka Asahi Shinbunsha, which was established in 1879 and expanded into the Tokyo market in 1888.[83] Two rotary presses that Osaka had already sent prior to the disaster were destroyed at the Shiodome train station in the earthquake. On 3 September a warship arrived in Shibaura from Osaka loaded with copies of the *Ōsaka asahi shinbun*. The next day a dispatch from Osaka arrived at the Imperial Hotel by car, with five thousand copies of the Osaka paper and 10,000 yen in cash. As bank withdrawals were limited, the newspaper valued this cash highly; it allowed Asahi to bargain with companies such as Nisshin Insatsu and Hakubunkan for the use of machines in their factories. By 12 September Asahi had received type and factory workers from Osaka. According to the *Tōkyō asahi* business report for the second half of the year (May–October), Ōsaka Asahi Shinbunsha provided a total of 100,000 yen in assistance.[84] Thanks to Osaka's help, *Tōkyō asahi* began publishing both morning (eight-page) and evening (four-page) editions beginning on 1 December 1923. *Tōkyō asahi* did not surpass *Nichinichi*, which had moved in front of *Tōkyō asahi* prior to the earthquake and whose lead the earthquake strengthened, but both overcame the earthquake in better condition than other papers.[85]

Figures from 1919 to 1932 reflect an increasing concentration of market share among the major Tokyo newspapers, with marked growth by the two Osaka subsidiaries.[86] Starting with shares of 7.3 percent and 4.8 percent, respectively, *Tōkyō nichinichi* and *Tōkyō asahi* climbed to 14.7 percent and 13.1 percent in 1925 and to 20.6 percent and 19.8 percent in 1930. The other major Tokyo papers were unable to match this growth. A general concentration of market share followed the earthquake as well; the six papers charted in figure 9 (*Tōkyō nichinichi*, *Tōkyō asahi*, *Hōchi*, *Yomiuri*, *Jiji*, and *Kokumin*) possessed a total market share (of this narrowly defined market) of 35.8 percent in 1919, which exploded to 83.2 percent in 1930.[87] Prior to the earthquake newspapers originating in Tokyo dominated the Tokyo market; after the earthquake newspapers with Osaka lineages, such

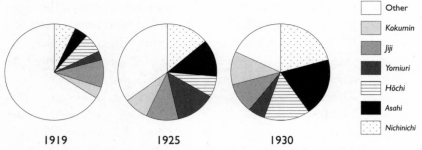

FIGURE 9 Tokyo newspaper market shares. From Yamamoto, *Kindai Nihon no shinbun dokushasō*, 245.

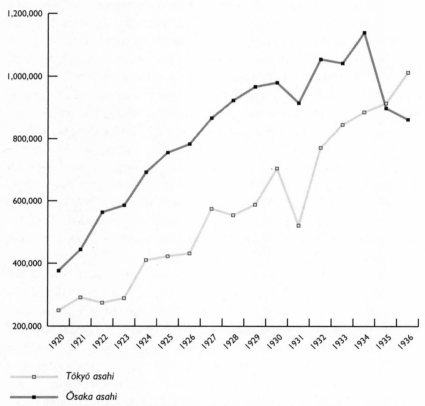

FIGURE 10 Growth in *Ōsaka asahi* and *Tōkyō asahi* circulation. From Yamamoto Taketoshi, *Kindai Nihon no shinbun dokushasō*, Sōsho gendai no shakai kagaku (Tokyo: Hōsei Daigaku Shuppankyoku, 1981), 410.

as *Tōkyō nichinichi* and *Tōkyō asahi*, started to replace them. Such competition between Osaka-based newspapers and Tokyo-based newspapers was soon replaced by a much more complex model, which included the Tokyo subsidiaries' growing influence on their Osaka progenitors.

The graph in figure 10 tracks the growth of *Tōkyō asahi*'s circulation in relation to the main Osaka office. The Tokyo edition of the newspaper experienced a dip in circulation in 1921–22. The following year (that of the earthquake) growth was relatively small, but it was nonetheless greater than the preceding year. The year following the earthquake, 1923–24, *Tōkyō asahi* showed an unprecedented growth in circulation of 41.72 percent. In the years that followed, the Tokyo branch of the paper continued to experience greater growth than Osaka, eventually overtaking it in 1935.[88]

On 1 September 1940, exactly seventeen years after the earthquake, the New *Asahi shinbun* Order (*Asahi shinbun no shintaisei*) went into effect, and the papers stopped denoting "Tokyo" and "Osaka" in their titles. This was part of a larger program to unify the regional, semiautonomous Asahi papers into one centralized paper. Appointed as part of the system, the new editor in chief, Osaka head editor, Tokyo head editor, and Nagoya head editor were all former *Tōkyō asahi* editors.[89] These appointments reflected a power shift fueled by the growing newspaper market in Tokyo and the resulting growth of the Tokyo subsidiaries. Due to actions of the Osaka-based papers during the earthquake, *Asahi* and *Mainichi* had come to dominate the Tokyo market; in the end, however, those very actions may have helped Tokyo gain greater influence over the only portion of Japanese print culture that it had not already come to dominate.

Supporting Industries: Printing, Distribution, and Paper

For any of these segments of the publishing industry to recover, certain supporting industries, which had also sustained serious damage, had to be rebuilt; the earthquake struck the printing, distributing, and paper industries as hard as it struck the publishing industry. Many printing companies, for example, were based in the center of the city. It is very important to note that three of the largest printing companies—Hakubunkan, Shūeisha, and Nisshin—were damaged but not destroyed. Nonetheless the damage to the industry as a whole was profound. Although the data in table 3 are limited to some of the larger printing houses, overall statistics are also

TABLE 3   EFFECT OF THE EARTHQUAKE ON PRINTING COMPANIES

Company[a]	Facility	Ward	Damage
Chūgai Insatsu		Kanda	Destroyed
Fuji Insatsu		Koishikawa	Slightly damaged
Hakubunkan	Hisakata-chō facility	Koishikawa	Partially collapsed
Isshiki Kappan		Kōjimachi	Destroyed
Insatsu-kyoku		Kōjimachi	Destroyed
Nakaya Insatsu		Kyōbashi	Destroyed
Nisshin Insatsu		Ushigome	Damaged
Nomura Insatsu-jo		Kōjimachi	Burned
Ōe Insatsu		Azabu	Partially damaged
Ōkura Insatsu		Kyōbashi	Destroyed
Risōsha		Ushigome	Survived
Sankyō Insatsu		Kyōbashi	Destroyed
Sanshūsha		Kanda	Destroyed
Shūeisha	Main offices	Kyōbashi	Destroyed
	Print sales office	Nihonbashi	Destroyed
	Factory No. 1	Ushigome	Partially collapsed[b]
Tōa Insatsu		Kyōbashi	Destroyed
Tōkyō Insatsu		Kyōbashi	Destroyed
Toppan Insatsu	Main office	Shitaya	Heavily damaged
	Main factory	Mukōjima	Destroyed
	Branch factory	Honjo	Destroyed
Tōyō Insatsu		Shiba	Destroyed
Tsukiji Kappan Seizō-jo		Kyōbashi	Destroyed

Sources: Tōkyō Insatsu Dōgyō Kumiai, *Nihon insatsu taikan, sōgyō nijūgo-shū-nen kinen* (Tokyo: Tōkyō Insatsu Dōgyō Kumiai, 1938), 312–20; Kawada Hisanaga, *Kappan insatsushi: Nihon kappan insatsushi no kenkyū* (Tokyo: Tōkyō Insatsu Gakkai Shuppanbu, 1949).

[a] Of damaged factories of pre-earthquake size of more than one hundred workers and of companies mentioned elsewhere in this chapter.

[b] The machines in Shūeisha's Factory No. 1 were repairable.

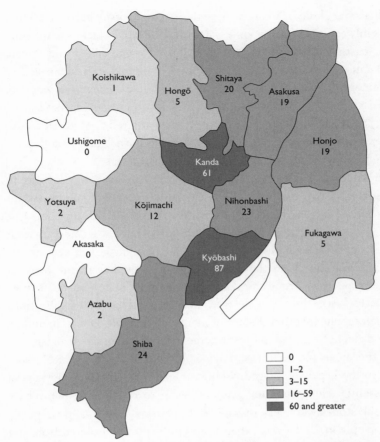

	0
	1–2
	3–15
	16–59
	60 and greater

Map shows Tokyo wards with factory destruction figures:
Koishikawa 1, Hongō 5, Shitaya 20, Asakusa 19, Ushigome 0, Honjo 19, Kanda 61, Yotsuya 2, Kōjimachi 12, Nihonbashi 23, Akasaka 0, Fukagawa 5, Kyōbashi 87, Azabu 2, Shiba 24.

MAP 3   Factories destroyed in the Great Kantō Earthquake, by ward. From Kaizōsha, ed., *Taishō daishinkasai shi* (Tokyo: Kaizōsha, 1924), 76–77. Shading represents degree of fire damage suffered by ward.

available, as seen in map 3. Damage to the printing industry, as these figures show, was substantial: 94 percent (296) of the total number of factories sustained at least some damage.[90]

While losses of material assets to the industry were extensive, deaths were limited. Of the 212 member companies of the Tokyo Publishing Association (Tōkyō Shuppan Kyōkai) in 1923, 167 suffered material losses due to the earthquake, but only 4 individuals were killed. Of the more than 1,800 members of the Tokyo Book Association (Tōkyō Shoseki-shō Kumiai), 956 members suffered material losses due to the earthquake, but only 17 individuals were killed. Fires destroyed the Tsukiji Kappan Seizō-jo, the first print facility equipped with a point system and the largest facility at the time for type-casting. Of 689 workers there, only one was killed and 3 were injured. This was the product of good fortune. Many factories had fixed days off, commonly the first and the fifteenth; as a result many factories were not heavily occupied.[91] Of the 9,070 factory workers prior to earthquake, 73 (0.8 percent) were killed and 38 (0.4 percent) were injured.[92] Material losses, however, were substantial: 280 printing factories burned and 16 collapsed. Damage to the industry was estimated at 16,828,780 yen.[93]

Yano Michiya, a doctor of engineering who surveyed the damage to printing factories in the wake of the earthquake, made many important observations about the effect of the earthquake on the printing industry. His survey, which also included small printing houses located in "rear tenements and back alleys," helps explain the earthquake's impact on the industry.[94] In addition to the damage to type, whether in the form of destroyed type or upturned cases, a number of other factors made printers particularly susceptible and delayed their reconstruction. Publications with photographs required the use of many combustible agents, including ether and alcohol; this led to fires in some printing factories. Also, because most of the largest pharmacies supplying photo-developing chemicals were located in the heavily damaged Nihonbashi area, there was a shortage of these essential elements after printers began to reestablish themselves. Lithograph stones were very susceptible to damage as well, and when the limited supply in Osaka was exhausted more had to be ordered from the only area that produced them, a region in Germany.

All of this damage to printing companies, however, actually allowed companies to convert to newer technology. Printing technology had been developing quickly in the decade or so prior to the earthquake, with such advances as offset printing (introduced as a concept in Japan in 1911 but not incorporated into the printing industry until later in the Taishō period); Thompson Typecasters (*Tomuson jidō katsuji chūzōki*, introduced in the private sector in Japan in 1918); rotary photogravure (*rōtarii fotogurabia*, first used in the private sector in Japan in 1920); and Huebner's photocomposition (HB *purosesu*, first used in the private sector in Japan in 1920). Shūeisha, for example, imported German-made automatic paper-feeding photogravure presses in August 1925 to replace equipment lost in the fires.[95]

TABLE 4   EFFECT OF THE EARTHQUAKE ON DISTRIBUTORS

Company	Ward	Damage
Hokuryū-kan	Nihonbashi	Destroyed
Tōkaidō	Kyōbashi	Destroyed
Tōkyōdō	Kanda	Destroyed
Ueda-ya	Kanda	Destroyed
Shiseidō	Nihonbashi	Destroyed

Source: The "Damage" column's data come from Kaizōsha, ed., *Taishō daishinkasai shi* (Tokyo: Kaizōsha, 1924), 84.

Distribution was another subsidiary industry to publishing that was severely affected by the disaster. Until 1919 eight companies had dominated magazine distribution: Tōkyōdō, Tōkaidō, Hokuryūkan, Ryōmeidō, Seishundō, Uedaya, Bunrindō, and Shiseidō. In the years immediately preceding the earthquake Ryōmeidō went out of business and Bunrindō fell into decline.[96] The remaining five largest companies (Seishundō distributed to only one part of Tokyo) were located in the areas most damaged by the fires.[97] The damage was tantamount to nearly complete destruction of the physical assets of the industry. (See table 4, above.)

Practically the only physical assets that survived of Tōkyōdō, the largest distributor, were its seven safes. The company's main building, in Jinbō-chō, survived the earthquake but burned to the ground roughly three hours later, as did Tōkyōdō's returns warehouse in Nishiki-chō. It was not until 8 September that the safes had cooled sufficiently for them to be opened.[98] Having experienced a fire at the company before, many of the employees knew what to save first, such as financial records. Because the records survived the company first settled its books for August and then sent invoices to various shops around the country. As a result it had collected 500,000 yen by the end of September. The appearance of Kōdansha's *Taishō daishinsai daikasai* created a deadline for the reconstruction of Tōkyōdō and the other large distributors.[99] Tōkyōdō built a temporary barracks in Nishiki-chō, Omote Jinbō-chō, and was back in business by 1 October.

Hokuryū-kan, another of the largest distributors, lost its offices and

TABLE 5   EFFECT OF THE EARTHQUAKE ON MAJOR PAPER PRODUCERS

Company[a]	Facility	Area	Damage
Ōji Seishi	Main office	Shiba	Destroyed
	Factory	Jūjō	Damaged
	Factory	Kita-toshima-gun	Destroyed
Fuji Seishi	Main office	Kyōbashi	Destroyed
	Factory	Adachi-gun	Damaged
	Factory	Edogawa	Damaged
Mitsubishi Seishi	Factory	Fukagawa	Damaged
Kyūshū Seishi		Marunouchi	No damage
Chūō Seishi		Marunouchi	No damage
Kokura Seishi	Branch office	Kyōbashi	Damaged
Hokuetsu Seishi	Branch office	Nihonbashi	Destroyed
	Factory	Ichikawa	Damaged

Source: Togai Yoshio and Nihon Keieishi Kenkyūjo, Seishigyō no hyakunen: Kami no bunka to sangyō (Tokyo: Ōji Seishi, 1973), 133–40.

[a] Companies are listed in descending order of size, based on production in 1921.

all of its merchandise to fire.[100] Fortunately it, like Tōkyōdō, secured important documents and cash in fireproof safes, which survived the blaze. As a result of the Magazine Association's decision to begin publishing magazines on 1 September, Hokuryū-kan began building temporary barracks for its offices on 12 September. In the weeks following the disaster the company distributed magazines and the Taishō daishinsai daikasai from these barracks. In order to obtain cash it sent out employees to collect debts. Despite the debts being extended by imperial edict, Hokuryū-kan was able to collect a great deal of money between 14 and 25 September, providing liquid assets that allowed the devastated company to remobilize rapidly.

Losses were so drastic that Shiseidō and Ueda-ya were eventually forced to merge with Seishundō into a single company, Daitōkan.[101] In this way the earthquake accelerated a process of consolidation and centralization that played such a key role in the modernization of the publishing industry, as seen in the previous chapter. Daitōkan, Tōkyōdō, Tōkaidō, and Hokuryūkan became the four major distributors that dominated the business until the Second World War.

The paper industry suffered damage similar to that of the other industries, having been located in many of the same areas. Five of the seven largest paper producers suffered damage (see table 5 on p. 86). Of the 160 paper-producing members of the Tokyo Paper Trade Association (Tōkyō Shishō Dōgyō Kumiai), 146 lost offices or storehouses to the fires.[102] Damage for some of the larger companies was substantial: Ōji suffered 4,830,000 yen in damages; Fuji, 3,350,000; Mitsubishi, 680,000; Dai-Nihon, 680,000; Kokura, 79,000. Fifty-five million pounds of paper—roughly one month's worth of production—were lost.[103] Immediate measures to fill the demand for paper led to shifts in sources. Despite roughly equal circulation before and after the earthquake, daily demand in Tokyo for paper produced in the city dropped from 550 rolls (enough to make 2,700,000 eight-page newspapers) to 300 rolls, with imported paper and paper produced outside of the Tokyo area making up the difference.[104] Fifteen factories were located in areas surrounding Tokyo, and for most of them damage was relatively light. Many began operation again within the month. In addition the moratorium, the guarantee of promissory notes, and a loan from the Bank of Japan greatly facilitated the rapid recovery of the paper industry.

The Impact of the Earthquake on Publishing

In addition to the extraordinary resolve of individuals, three factors accelerated the recovery of the publishing industry immediately after the earthquake. The first was the survival of essential factories: four major printing factories, located in the only slightly damaged Koishikawa and Ushigome wards, survived the disaster and thus allowed printing to resume quickly. As the managing director of the distributor Hokuryū-kan wrote, "Because of the lucky coincidence that the four major printing factories were only slightly damaged, the publishing world and our business [distribution] stabilized rapidly and were never in jeopardy."[105] The second was cash (and financial records), which in many cases survived the disaster thanks to fireproof safes.[106] Cash was essential to the perpetuation of many companies. In the weeks after the earthquake the possession of currency was indispensable for negotiating the arrangements necessary for companies totally deprived of facilities of their own. Because of the dispensability of most physical assets to publishing and distribution companies—Suzuki Toshio has said that publishers really require only a desk and a telephone—the preservation of key records and the possession of cash allowed the companies to relocate and begin business.[107] The third was collective action by industry associations. In the same way that they had determined the makeup of the modern publishing industry, these groups maintained sufficient industry stability and provided essential assistance that allowed their members to recover more quickly than they would have otherwise.

The nature of the destruction also contributed to the survival of Tokyo publishing. As many of the larger companies were in buildings capable of riding out the earthquake itself, employees survived the tremors and fled the oncoming flames. This resulted in relatively few deaths in the industry, allowing most workforces to assemble the next day at whatever spot had been designated as the temporary offices of their company. Few of the companies opted to abandon the city, and many chose to rebuild on the site of their destroyed offices. For these reasons workers and their employers found themselves willing and able to remain in Tokyo and thus set about the natural next step of reconstructing their lives.

What was initially perceived as the destruction of Tokyo proved to be only a temporary setback—and to some an opportunity for greater development and modernization. The publishing companies that produced the three most prevalent forms of print culture—books, magazines, and newspapers—were not nearly as affected by the earthquake as one might have expected. They were not, however, unaffected. The destruction of massive quantities of books led to an increased demand for those published by the recovering companies; book publishers took advantage of the extraordinary circumstances to expand into distribution and sales networks that had traditionally been limited to magazines. At the same time, the earthquake awoke in people a realization of the frailty of print. Many came to recognize the continued vulnerability of texts, even in an age of mass production, and the need to consider ways to preserve them. The magazine industry, which suffered drastically as well, was able to create a brief recovery period through collective action and then harness various alternative subsidiary industries to continue publishing with hardly a pause. The newspaper industry, which the earthquake initially reduced to a state of technological infancy, seized on people's desire to know more about what they had experienced. Though Kansai-based firms initially profited from the disaster, even this development eventually contributed to greater Tokyo centrality. As the Tokyo market expanded, the Tokyo branches' authority grew, leading eventually to their central role in this vast market.

Geographical specificity ravaged certain areas of the print culture industry and spared others. The lines of destruction had been drawn, more or less by chance, in a way that left just enough infrastructure for the industries to rebuild rapidly. The desire to rebuild fueled the creativity necessary to overcome the greatest material deprivations. In the end Tokyo gained enough momentum to carry it over this tremendous, unforeseen, tragic hurdle. Had Tokyo occupied a less stable position of cultural centrality, perhaps Kansai could have indeed, in the absence of a center, taken the lead in the production of print. Instead Tokyo stood poised to seize control of new possibilities presented by the Great Kantō Earthquake of 1923— including more flexible shipping arrangements and the increased printing capacity of factories rebuilt using improved printing technology—to dominate a broader market than ever before. It was this centralized industry that allowed a small group of writers and critics, primarily located in Tokyo, to present a vast audience with literary works it valorized as part of an alternate economy, modern Japanese literature.

3

The Static Canon

KAIZŌSHA'S COMPLETE WORKS OF
CONTEMPORARY JAPANESE LITERATURE

Those who are in a position to edit anthologies . . . are obviously
those who occupy positions of some cultural power; and their acts
of evaluation—represented in what they exclude as well as in what
they include—constitute not merely recommendations of value,
but . . . also determinants of value. Moreover, since they will usually
exclude not only what they take to be inferior literature but also
what they take to be nonliterary, subliterary, or paraliterary, their
selections not only imply certain "criteria" of literary value, which
may in fact be made explicit, but, more significantly, they produce
and maintain certain definitions of "literature" and, thereby, certain assumptions about the desired and expected functions of the
texts so classified and about the interests of their appropriate audiences, all of which are usually not explicit and, for that reason, less
likely to be questioned, challenged, or even noticed.

BARBARA HERRNSTEIN SMITH, *CONTINGENCIES OF VALUE:*
ALTERNATIVE PERSPECTIVES FOR CRITICAL THEORY

On the eve of the transition to the Shōwa period, which began on 25 December 1926, Tokyo enjoyed a concentration of print capital and a magnitude of readership that was unprecedented and that allowed a small minority to exercise a dramatic degree of control over the literary culture of the
nation. This process of concentration had seemed to come to an abrupt end

on 1 September 1923, when the Great Kantō Earthquake nearly annihilated the Tokyo publishing industry. The centralization of print culture in the imperial capital persisted, however, and even, in some ways, accelerated as a result of the disaster. In the years immediately following the earthquake the publishing industry rebuilt itself by not only continuing to feed the demand for print created by a growing literate and economically stable reading audience, but by replacing many of the books that had been lost in the catastrophe.

Thanks to this new demand publishing was, for a time, able to limit the impact of a domestic economy that was generally struggling. Despite an economic upturn soon after the end of the First World War the Japanese economy entered into a recession following the stock market crash of 15 March 1920. This crash led to the collapse of a number of small banks and businesses and further strengthened the zaibatsu (large holding companies). Fortunately certain factors, such as spending on public works, rising real incomes, and expanding domestic demand for heavy chemicals and electricity, tempered the downturn. The recession deepened in 1923 because of the damage caused by and the huge costs of reconstruction following the Great Earthquake.[1] Much of the reconstruction was financed by the government's decision to rediscount bonds and loans, only half of which had been paid off by 1926, leaving roughly 200 million yen in bad loans outstanding.

Despite the general economic malaise in much of the publishing industry in 1925, one company, Kōdansha, remained strong thanks to such successes as Taishō daishinsai daikasai.[2] Encouraged by that success, Kōdansha decided to push through with a project it had considered before the earthquake: King magazine.[3] Large-scale advertising began in September 1924, and the first issue, published in December of that year, sold its complete run of 740,000 copies after three printings.[4] The reach of King continued to grow, selling 1.3 million copies in November 1927, 1.4 million in January 1928, and 1.5 million in November 1928.[5] The general interest magazine Bungei shunjū, by comparison, sold 183,000 copies of its 1927 New Year's issue, a circulation that its more prestigious rival Chūō kōron could only dream of achieving.[6]

Kōdansha's growth impacted other sectors of the publishing industry as well. One of the companies that enjoyed the most direct benefit was Shūeisha, the company that printed King. The publishing phenomenon of King allowed Shūeisha to make substantial improvements to its physical plant. To handle the massive printing demands, the company installed a domestically produced thirty-two-page rotary letterpress in May 1925 and a German Albert sixty-four-page high-speed rotary letterpress in November 1925. It also completed the expansion of its Ichigaya factory, which it had begun in October 1920.[7] Shūeisha approached the close of 1926 with a printing capacity that was unprecedented for a private Japanese firm.[8]

While *King*'s impact on the reading practices of the nation (and empire and diasporic communities) was significant,[9] it was Kaizōsha's *Complete Works of Contemporary Japanese Literature* that built upon *King*'s success and took advantage of this expanded printing capacity and had the more profound effect on modern Japanese literature. Not only did this series make a single image of contemporary literature available to a much larger audience than ever before—including consumers throughout the country and Japanese speakers living abroad—but it also invested that literature with a prestige it had not previously enjoyed. The series assured consumers that Japan, like other advanced nations, had a contemporary literature; it also made that literature affordable.[10] As a result it simultaneously sacralized and commodified an array of authors, many of whom were still alive to reap the benefits of those processes. The most lasting effect of the series, however, was not the material impact it had on specific works and authors but its reification of a conceptual space, in which distinct works were linked in a constellation of literary value and national importance. It was an effect its compilers would likely have rejected. What Kaizōsha reified through the *Complete Works of Contemporary Japanese Literature* was a conception of an entity—modern Japanese literature—that persists to this day, and which helped transform the production of a small-scale Tokyo-centered literary scene into not only a national but also an imperial culture.[11]

The Origins of a Revolutionary Idea and Its Predecessors

The initial decision to produce the series stemmed not from a grand plan to manufacture a national or imperial culture, but from a pressing and practical concern: Kaizōsha's need to escape from imminent bankruptcy in 1926. Yamamoto Sanehiko founded the publishing company in 1919 and it had gained significant status through its flagship magazine, *Kaizō*.[12] Thanks in part to a variety of inventive schemes, including reportage from China, sponsorship of visits by Chinese scholars, and even bringing Albert Einstein to Japan, *Kaizō* had come to rival the older and more established *Chūō kōron*. The company also enjoyed success in publishing books, particularly the Christian reformer Kagawa Toyohiko's novel *Shisen o koete* (*Before the Dawn*), which became one of the bestselling novels of the Taishō period. The company's success continued until 1923, when the earthquake devastated Kaizōsha along with the rest of the industry. The company's main offices were burned to the ground and its printing facilities were destroyed; Kaizōsha's losses amounted to 1.2 million yen and some eight hundred thousand books lost.[13] In the aftermath of the earthquake *Kaizō*'s circulation dropped to twenty thousand to thirty thousand issues per month.[14] This decrease was compounded by the government's censorship of *Kaizō*'s issue of July 1926, which was prohibited from sale because of the inclusion of Fujimori Seikichi's play *Gisei* (Sacrifice) and Kurata Hyakuzō's novel *Akai reikon* (Red Soul). These factors (among others) left Kaizōsha in severe economic distress, running 120,000 yen in the red in 1926.[15] Yamamoto had mortgaged his house and, according to his daughter Sayoko, had even contemplated suicide.[16] The *Complete Works of Contemporary Japanese Literature* was an all-or-nothing gamble to save the company.

Yamamoto did not even have sufficient capital to launch the series, so he had to convince many individuals to work with him on credit. He consulted with the president of Denpō Tsūshinsha, Mitsunaga Hoshio, who agreed to do the initial advertising on credit despite the fact that Yamamoto was already deeply in debt to his company.[17] Similar arrangements were struck with the printing company Shūeisha and Kaizōsha's paper supplier.[18] He asked even more of the distributor Tōkyōdō. The company had just begun selling its own *Meiji bungaku meicho zenshū* (Complete Collection of Famous Meiji Literary Works) earlier that year; this series of Meiji-period novels sold for roughly 2.50 yen per volume and was published at the rate of about one volume per month.[19] According to Ōno Magohei, who negotiated with Yamamoto, Tōkyōdō suspended publication of the series in order to help Kaizōsha. Yamamoto then asked for a significant loan to help him start the project, which Ōno supplied.[20] This was not an unusual event; the largest distributors often acted as financiers for publishing ventures.[21] With this support in place, Kaizōsha was able to begin planning its groundbreaking series.

There were a number of precedents for a multivolume series that gathered various authors under a single imprint. Examples from the Meiji period onward include Yoshioka Shoseki-ten's eighteen-volume *Shincho hyakushu* (New Authors Anthology, 1889–91), each volume containing one or more novellas by a single author; Hakubunkan's twenty-four-volume *Nihon bungaku zensho* (Complete Library of Japanese Literature, 1890–92), of what would now be considered premodern or early modern works, and eighteen-volume *Meiji bunko* (Meiji Library, 1893–94), which contained multiple stories by one or more authors; and Min'yūsha's eight-volume *Kokumin shōsetsu* series (People's Fiction, 1890–96), each volume of which contained a selection of works by various authors. The famous literary publisher Shun'yōdō's fifteen-volume *Shōsetsu hyakka-sen* (Selected Fiction by Various Authors, 1894–95) contained works by various authors in each volume; each of the ten volumes of *Shun'yō bunko* (Shun'yō Library, 1897–98) was a single novel; and each of the forty-five volumes of *Gendai bungei sōsho* (Contemporary Literature Library, 1911–14) included multiple works by single authors.[22] Akagi Seizō's *Akagi sosho* (Akagi Library, 1914), also known as the "10-sen Library," which primarily contained translations, contained more than one hundred volumes. Uemura Shoin's twelve-volume *Gendai daihyō-saku sōsho* (Library of Representative Contemporary Works, 1914–15) contained various works by single authors. Although these series resembled the Kaizōsha series in many ways, none explicitly bracketed off a modern national literature, and only the *Nihon bungaku zensho* made an equally ambitious claim to completeness.

A few predecessors in the years immediately preceding the *Complete Works of Contemporary Japanese Literature* bore an even greater resemblance. Some of these resemblances were trivial: the publishing company Yūhōdō offered the people who bought its whole set of classics a free bookcase, as Kaizōsha would eventually do;[23] others, such as Nantendō Shobō's *Kindai meicho bunko* series (Library of Famous Modern Works, ca. 1922–24), were based on a conception of modern literature. Most volumes of this series, which expanded to at least twenty-five volumes, contained a single work by a single author and only cost 50 sen per volume. This series was not based on a conception of a national literature, however, and included not only novels by Tokuda Shūsei, Tayama Katai, and Masamune Hakuchō, but also novels by Tolstoy and Mérimée.[24] The greatest resemblance may have been borne by a classical literature series that immediately preceded the *Complete Works of Contemporary Japanese Literature*. In 1925 Yosano Akiko, Yosano Hiroshi, and Masamune Atsuo (the younger brother of Masamune Hakuchō) announced their *Koten bungaku zenshū* (Complete Works of Classic Literature) in the September issue of *Myōjō* (Morning Star). The editors originally hoped it would contain a thousand volumes, published at a rate of fifty per year. Some 266 volumes were eventually released between the start of the project and 1944. The initial announcement promised that the series would "bring the classics to the citizenry [*koten no kokuminka*]," including works from Japan (*wagakuni*) from the beginning of writing to the end of the Tokugawa period and spanning a wide variety of topics, including ethics, literature, economics, law, and agriculture.[25] The *Koten bungaku zenshū*, while perhaps implicitly recognizing a distinct modern period through omission, was still explicitly based on a transhistorical model.

Only the *Complete Works of Contemporary Japanese Literature* connected the nation with a specifically modern literary entity in the form of a large, finite series of inexpensive volumes. The specific source of this particular configuration is a matter of some debate. One story speaks to an idealistic impulse behind the series: the author and political activist Fujimori Sei-kichi and his wife, after working for a year in a factory, suggested to Yamamoto that he should publish inexpensive books, perhaps at 50 sen per volume, because the masses wanted to read but could not afford books.[26] Believing it impossible to profit on 50-sen books, the story concludes, Yamamoto did not act on that suggestion directly. Another story speaks to the commercial potential of inexpensive books: Yamamoto apparently received a similar suggestion after the Great Earthquake from Tanizaki Jun'ichirō, who suggested that Kaizōsha try selling a few of his books at one yen each.[27] A final theory presents the most prosaic, and perhaps therefore most likely source, describing the idea for the series as coming from Yama-moto's chief editor, Fujikawa Yasuo.[28] Whatever the source of the idea, in 1926 Yamamoto Sanehiko had made up his mind to commit the fate of his company to the *Complete Works of Contemporary Japanese Literature*, an ambitious collection of authors and works.

Selecting the Contents: Kimura Ki and the Meiji Bunka Kenkyūkai

Once the fundamental plan was decided, the specific details of the se-ries had to be determined. Yamamoto asked the literary critic Kimura Ki (1894–1979) to select the series' contents along with Takasu Yoshijirō, who had been in charge of *Kaizō's* literature column at the magazine's inception.[29] Kimura had long wanted to produce a Japanese version of the *Harvard Classics*, which he had purchased in 1920 and which had been so influential in his education.[30] He suggested to Yamamoto that, rather than a series of popular authors' most famous works, the series should try to be more comprehensive, addressing culture since the Meiji period as a whole; the title he initially proposed was the *Meiji bungaku zenshū* (Complete Works of Meiji Literature).[31] In undertaking this large-scale project, Kimura consulted with his friend and colleague Yanagida Izumi (1894–1969) on the arrangement, contents, construction, and chronological history volume (*nenpyō*) of the series.[32] The contents they gathered were extremely wide-ranging, including nearly six hundred authors and two thousand works.[33]

The personal reading histories of Kimura and Yanagida illustrate the limited access individuals had to texts even in the first decades of the twentieth century. Kimura, the son of the village mayor, grew up in the small mountain community of Katsumada-mura in Okayama; Yanagida, the son of the village head (*kochō*), grew up in Toyota-mura in Aomori. As their fathers' offices suggest, the two possessed advantages, both educational and economic, that other members of their communities would not have enjoyed. Kimura was exposed to literature almost exclusively through his textbooks and magazines, particularly *Bunshō sekai* (World of Writing), which he read from its first issue in 1906. It was to the issue published in April 1907, which contained brief biographies of 230 authors in its special supplements, that Kimura attributed his decision to become a researcher of Meiji literature. Despite his family's status, he did not have enough money to buy many magazines, so he briefly joined a subscription club with fellow students in order to gain access to a wider variety of titles. It was not until he went to live with his older brother in Osaka that Kimura gained access to many of the books he had read about.[34] Yanagida similarly had limited access to texts. His view of modern Japanese literature was formed, as Kimura's had been, by special issues of magazines that appeared in 1904, 1908, and 1912. Like Kimura's, Yanagida's family was not in a position to buy a great many books. Fortunately for him, however, he had an older brother who had attended school in Tokyo and a mother who was a voracious reader. As a result he read whatever he could find. Unlike Kimura, Yanagida also had access to a library that subscribed to a number of magazines. Once he went to Hirosaki to attend higher elementary school he was able to borrow books from a tea distributor that lent books on the side and purchase used books and back issues of magazines.[35] Both Kimura and Yanagida thus had personal experience with the difficulties of obtaining texts in rural Japan.

Kimura and Yanagida became members of a group called the Society for the Study of Meiji Culture (Meiji Bunka Kenkyūkai), a group for which the preservation of texts was a crucial undertaking. The Society was formed in November 1924 partially in response to a perceived crisis: members feared that the print culture of the Meiji period was not being preserved and that there existed the real possibility that much of it would be lost. At the end of the Taishō period many shared the fear that large swaths of Meiji culture could simply disappear. Not only were texts not being reproduced, but the earthquake had recently destroyed the Tokyo Imperial University main library, nearly all of the Tokyo-based publishing industry, and much of the supply of new and used books in the city. The creation of the anthology in 1926 provided Kimura and Yanagida with the opportunity to reproduce vital Meiji texts.

The scholar Sekii Mitsu has written on the connection between the Society's goals and the creation of the *Complete Works of Contemporary Japanese Literature*.[36] Challenging those who argued that an essentially Japanese aesthetic unified all of Japanese literature, the Society applied a rigorously historicist approach to the study of the Meiji period. For them the Meiji differed fundamentally from the periods that preceded it; the only way to come to terms with this alternative zeitgeist was to examine as broad a range of cultural products as possible. For Kimura and Yanagida this meant preserving as wide an array of Meiji-period writings as possible.[37] It was this desire to reconstruct an overarching picture of a culture that prompted Kimura to suggest that they "should construct [the series] in such a way that it comprehensively examines all types of literature from the Meiji period. . . . In so doing, one would glean an understanding of culture as a whole."[38] As Sekii puts it, the Society was interested in the "noise" (*zawameki*) of the period, not just a narrow band of highly polished production.[39] Paradoxically Kimura's and Yanagida's goal in editing the series, inclusion, ran contrary to an effect often attributed to anthologies, exclusion.[40] The resulting series achieved this goal to a surprisingly great extent, given its essentially commercial nature, even as it reinforced the centrality of that more narrow definition of literature. Little is known about the specific criteria considered in the selection of the works, so the resulting structure will be the primary source of the following analysis.

Arishima Takeo, Arishima Ikuma

Shimamura Hōgetsu, Ikeda Chōkō, Nakazawa Rinsen, Katagami Noburu, Yoshie Kogan

Satomi Ton

Satō Haruo

Akutagawa Ryūnosuke

Kikuchi Kan

Chikamatsu Shūkō

Kume Masao

Shōnen bungaku (Juvenile Literature)

Rekishi shōsetsu (Historical Fiction) and *Katei shōsetsu* (Domestic Fiction)

Gendai gikyoku meisaku (Famous Works of Contemporary Theater)

Kikō zuihitsu (Travel Essays)

Gendai Nihon shi, Gendai Nihon kanshi (Contemporary Japanese Poems and *Kanshi*)

THE COMPLETE WORKS OF CONTEMPORARY JAPANESE LITERATURE (ADDED VOLUMES)

Volume Contents (Authors or Themes)

Gendai tanka, Gendai haiku (Contemporary Tanka and Haiku)

Shakai bungaku (Social Literature)

Itō Sachio, Nagatsuka Takashi, Takahama Kyoshi

Hasegawa Nyozekan, Uchida Roan, Takebayashi Musōan

Suzuki Miekichi, Morita Sōhei

Okamoto Kidō, Nagata Mikihiko

Kubota Mantarō, Nagayo Yoshirō, Murō Saisei

Ishikawa Takuboku

Yamamoto Yūzō, Kurata Hyakuzō

Yoshida Genjirō, Fujimori Seikichi

Hirotsu Kazuo, Kasai Zenzō, Uno Kōji

Sensō bungaku (War Literature)

Shinkō bungaku (New Literature)

Shinbun bungaku (Newspaper Literature)

Shūkyō bungaku (Religious Literature)

Kosugi Tengai, Yamada Bimyō

Iwaya Sazanami, Emi Suiin, Ishibashi Shian, Kikuchi Yūhō

Oguri Fūyō, Yanagawa Shun'yō, Satō Kōroku

Tamura Toshiko, Nogami Yaeko, Chūjō (Miyamoto) Yuriko

Koizumi Yakumo, Raphael Koeber, Noguchi Yonejirō

Shinmura Izuru, Yanagita Kunio, Yoshimura Fuyuhiko, Saitō Mokichi

Kagawa Toyohiko

Osaragi Jirō

Shinkō geijutsu-ha bungaku (New Art Literature)

Puroretaria bungaku (Proletarian Literature)

Gendai Nihon bungaku dai nenpyō (Timeline of Contemporary Literature)

The impact of an orthodox narrative regarding Japanese literary modernity, which had been developing over the previous decades, can be seen in the *Complete Works of Contemporary Japanese Literature*. The first single-author volume, for example, is dedicated to Tsubouchi Shōyō, the author of *Shōsetsu shinzui* (The Essence of the Novel). The series, however, diverges from this narrative in important ways. For example, it should be noted that the famous treatise—which is often credited with having launched Japan's literary modernity—does not appear in his volume.[41]

An examination of the first volume tells us a great deal about the logic of the series as a whole. That volume marks the debt the collection owes to a concept of political modernity; *Meiji kaika-ki bungaku-shū* (Literature from the Meiji Civilization and Enlightenment Period) links works to their coincidence with the "civilization and enlightenment" movement of the early Meiji period. To an extent the series adheres to the broad meaning of the term *bungaku* (in this case "letters" rather than "literature") that dominated into the early twentieth century.[42] An example is Katō Hiroyuki's treatise of 1870, *Shinsei taii* (Outline of True Government). Most of the works in the first volume, however, adhere to the narrow definition of *bungaku* as imaginative fiction. It includes Kanagaki Robun's *Aguranabe* (Sitting around the Stew Pan), Fukuzawa Yukichi's *Katawa musume* (The Deformed Girl), Kawashima Chūnosuke's adaptation of Jules Verne's *Around the World in Eighty Days* (*Le tour du monde en quatre-vingts jours*, 1872), Tōkai Sanshi's *Kajin no kigū* (Chance Meetings with Beautiful Women), Suehiro Kenchō's *Setchūbai* (Plum Blossoms in the Snow), Sudō Nansui's *Ryokusadan* (The Local Self-Government), and works by Aeba Kōson, Katō Hiroyuki, Baba

Tatsui, Nakamura Masanao, Narushima Ryūhoku, and Hattori Bushō. Most of the works originally appeared before the conventional beginning of literary modernity in 1885, with the publication of *Shōsetsu shinzui*.[43]

This introductory volume, which was not shipped until January 1931, is a model of accessibility. The script of *Aguranabe*, which is cursive in its original, woodblock-printed form, is presented in clear type with a syllabic gloss and includes reproductions of sample illustrations from the original printing. As a result this version became far more legible than even the popular original, published in 1871. This accessibility is perhaps the most notable aspect of the volume, which contains texts in a variety of original "languages." The dialect-filled Japanese of *Aguranabe* is followed by the mixed contemporary and classical grammar of *Katawa musume*, followed by the *kanbun kundoku* (a Japanese rendering of literary Chinese) version of the adaptation of the originally French *Around the World in Eighty Days*. Most, but not all, literary Chinese in the volume is rendered in *kanbun kundoku-tai*; small portions of text, such as long quotes in *Kajin no kigū*, are left in their original format, though with tools to assist in comprehension, such as *kunten* (reading marks) and *furigana* (pronunciation guides). For example, the adaptation of *Around the World in Eighty Days*, which contained few glossed words in its original version, glosses nearly every word. As a result this volume not only preserved texts that Kimura deemed deserving, but also lowered the barrier to accessibility to the texts for a greatly expanded audience.

One way to gain access to the value system informing the creation of the series is through the limited paratext that is present in each book.[44] In the explanatory notes that conclude the introductory volume Kimura explains the period covered as that in which Japan began to experience Westernization, the process through which Japan took in the system and culture of capitalism. He then goes on to describe the effort he has made to represent not only the key voices behind these sociopolitical developments, such as Fukuzawa's, but also voices of holdouts from the Edo period, including Robun's. Kimura's introduction also makes clear that he does not see a complete rupture, with one tradition ending and another beginning; instead he sees writers such as Aeba Kōson continuing the older tradition in the present. It is evident, however, that Kimura recognizes that some of his selections will be questioned. He ends the introduction with an apology of sorts for the texts therein contained: "Anyone who considers these works of the civilization and enlightenment period—or the works of people like Osaragi Jirō or Kikuchi Kan—to be totally uninteresting is mistaken in doing so. The interest, the significance of those works can only be appreciated by those willing to consider the intervening passage of time and the difference in the period."[45] Kimura is not attempting to construct a timeless canon with his series. In fact he is specifically selecting texts in order to represent the changing notions of value that history has shown.

The resilience of a broad definition of *bungaku* is apparent in a number of the theme-based volumes of the series. The *Shinbun bungakushū* (Newspaper Literature) volume (number 51) underscores Kimura's attempt to cling to the broad definition of literature, even as he recognizes the growing dominance of the narrow definition. The works he collected in the volume are not serialized newspaper novels, but critical nonfiction essays on topics as diverse as Lenin and the establishment of the Diet. He writes, "The tendency to see journalism as opposed to pure literature [*junsei bungaku*] and to exclude it from the sphere of *bungaku* is a misunderstanding of both newspapers and *bungaku*."[46] He argues that this is particularly true in terms of styles of writing, given the immense impact newspapers had during a period of great linguistic confusion (*bunshō konran-ki*), when Western languages, *kanbun*, and Japanese (*wabun*) were thrown together, side by side. The *Shakai bungakushū* (Social Literature) volume (number 39), published in September 1930, similarly depends on the broad definition of literature. This volume is made up of critical essays by such socialist thinkers as Nakae Chōmin, Kōtoku Shūsui, Sakai Toshihiko, and Ōsugi Sakae. The timing of this volume and the breadth of its distribution say something about how dangerous the government did (or more importantly did not) consider this thought in 1930. The *Shūkyō bungakushū* (Religious Literature) volume (number 52) is a collection of critical essays on religion rather than a collection of religion-themed fiction.

The series also contains volumes dedicated to schools that were being removed from the dominant definitions of pure literature. Again, however, the prefatory material presents a historicized view of this shift in literary status. In the introduction to the *Rekishi/katei shōsetsu-shū* (Historical and Domestic Fiction) volume, *katei shōsetsu* (domestic fiction) authors (such as Tokutomi Roka, Kusamura Hokusei, and Kikuchi Yūhō) are described as having been central to the literary establishment in the early Meiji 30s (1897–1902). The editor, presumably Kimura, refers to the genres of *katei shōsetsu* and *rekishi shōsetsu* (historical fiction) as the genres in which authors "construct the most interesting pages."[47]

Another school was that of proletarian literature, which was at its peak of influence when its volume (number 62) was released in February 1931. Some of the texts are censored; the penultimate page of *Kani kōsen* (The Cannery Boat), containing a scene critical of the emperor, was removed entirely by (or at least for) the censors, but given that the author of the novel, Kobayashi Takiji, would die in police custody in 1933, the fact that so much of it was included is notable.[48] Despite the politically progressive nature of the anthology's publisher, the guest editors of this volume still found their inclusion to be perverse. Eguchi Kan and Kishi Yamaji, who wrote the introduction to the volume, were fully aware of the irony of including proletarian works in this most capitalist of enterprises, even if it did come from the politically progressive Kaizōsha. They write:

> In 1930, a number of our comrades in the Nihon Puroretaria Sakka Dōmei (Japan Proletarian Writers' League) were stolen away by the hand of the ruling class. To date, we have offered up any number of martyrs from our literary movement. The more we proceed along the one true path, in fact, the more sacrifices will likely follow. The many troubles that will accrue to our movement are foreseeable because only ours is the true movement to construct a proletarian literature, possessing a power to permeate the laboring and farming classes and move the masses in the direction they must go.
>
> This volume was not compiled and published, however, to aid in this struggle. It resulted from a recommendation by Kaizōsha for the expanded *Complete Works of Contemporary Japanese Literature*. We have gathered together the most "famous" works (thus far) of nine members of the Nihon Puroretaria Sakka Dōmei in order to show you, the beloved readers of this complete works, this literature, which has developed at such a startling pace and now promises to succeed Naturalism as Japan's primary literary school.
>
> Of these nine authors, no fewer than four are martyrs. Put another way, those four are comrades who did the greatest work and fought the fiercest fight for Japan's proletarian literature. We must do everything

we can to save those four comrades and their families. Fortunately, because this publication performs that function, it is for us first and foremost a project done to relieve their suffering.

You readers have thus far, through your reading of the "literature" of all sorts of "famous literati," made those bourgeois literati rich. Many of them have used their earnings to buy land, build homes, purchase stocks, and debauch themselves.

We comrades, through our "literature," strive not for various luxuries such as homes and land, but for xx.[49]

Why are our situations so different? Needless to say, it is because our literature is class literature. Therefore we write only for the final class, the proletariat, which will destroy this class society; we write only for the new, correct society. It should come as no surprise that the present ruling class is not pleased with our work.

xx guarantees us a stoning in place of gold, and guarantees them (all bourgeois writers) gold instead of a stoning. However, even as our literature has stones of xx shower down upon it, step by step—or perhaps leap by leap—it spreads, growing closer to the proletariat and to readers of good conscience.

At this point, you, by taking this volume in hand, rather than making us rich, have aided our beleaguered literary movement and supported those comrades who went before us and were stolen away. For this we will repay you by telling you the absolute truth of this world through our literature.

Whether or not the editors of the volume did successfully manipulate the series for their political ends, the volume itself shows both the catholic vision of Kimura and the dominance of the "bourgeois" literary lineage in the series.

The vast majority of the remaining volumes are dedicated to individual authors whose inclusion comes as little surprise. The volumes include prose fiction, verse (in multiple distinct styles), essays on a variety of subjects, translations (including *Hamlet*), diaries, and a number of other forms. Despite this variety, however, the series gave prose fiction a centrality that has persisted; the literary critic Miura Masashi has even suggested that the series established fiction's dominance of the literary field.[50] Only twenty-five of the eventual sixty-three volumes were dedicated to a single author;

the rest were dedicated to multiple authors, schools, or genres. The series even possessed a slight amount of ethnic diversity, the most obvious examples being the translated works of Lafcadio Hearn (included under his Japanese name, Koizumi Yakumo) and Raphael von Koeber.

The gender biases of the editors, and of the modern literary establishment itself, are abundantly clear in the anthology.[51] While female authors are included in genre-determined volumes, such as the *Gendai tankashū/gendai haiku-shū* (Contemporary Tanka and Haiku, volume 38), only two volumes name female authors on their spines. Of the initial volumes, volume 9 is dedicated to the female author Higuchi Ichiyō and the male author Kitamura Tōkoku. When the series was expanded, the editors once again seem to have felt compelled to dedicate one of the volumes to women; volume 56 is dedicated to Tamura Toshiko, Nogami Yaeko, and Chūjō (Miyamoto) Yuriko. The promise of gender-blind treatment suggested by Ichiyō's grouping with Tōkoku was betrayed by the grouping of the three female authors in the second volume, which segregated them within the series and suggested that their greatest common element was their biological sex.

Compositions in languages other than Japanese were considered appropriate for the series; lengthy, untranslated passages in the original English, French, and Italian are also included. This goes along with the linguistic diversity within the Japanese language that implicitly functions as one of the unifying characteristics of the series itself. In addition to vernacular Japanese one finds representative pieces of other forms of written Japanese: *kanbun* (literary Chinese), *kanbun kundoku*, and *kobun* (classical Japanese). Though the emergence and growing sophistication of the vernacular can be seen as the works move forward chronologically, the linguistic diversity of the first decades of the modern period are preserved in the series, despite its construction for a large readership without the highest level of literacy. Kimura's and Yanagida's conception of contemporary Japanese literature was—consonant with their vision of the project—exceptionally broad.

Negotiating Rights: Material Limitations to the Series

Kaizōsha had to overcome a number of obstacles in assembling the series; the first of these was to secure the legal rights to reprint the works. In theory this would have involved gaining the *shuppan-ken* (publication rights, which are granted for specific projects or lengths of time) from the individual who held the *chosaku-ken* (authorial rights, which were valid for the life of the author and thirty years after his or her death, but which were transferable), usually the author. But during the Meiji period, despite the efforts of early crusaders such as Fukuzawa Yukichi and a number of major legal developments, in practice writers' rights remained somewhat vague.[52] Asaoka Kunio has shown that the standard practice during much of the Meiji period was for writers to transfer (*jōto*) their *chosaku-ken* to publishers for a one-time payment.[53] As a result publishing companies, such as Shun'yōdō and Hakubunkan, controlled the rights to many Meiji writers' works and thus held a lot of power in determining the nature of literary collections. As a relatively young publishing company, Kaizōsha held the rights to few works, forcing them to negotiate with multiple publishers.

When Kaizōsha began assembling the Nagai Kafū volume of the series, for example, it was forced to negotiate with Hakubunkan for the right to include *Amerika monogatari* (Tales of America).[54] Kafū had sold the rights for the stories to Hakubunkan in 1907 for 50 yen, and the rival publisher initially moved to block the inclusion of the story in the Kaizōsha series. In the end Kaizōsha convinced Hakubunkan to sell the rights for 5,000 yen, one hundred times what they had paid Kafū for them. Kaizōsha presumably found the investment reasonable because by the time it was negotiating for the contents of Kafū's volume the company already had a large number of subscribers and was thus guaranteed sufficient income to make it worthwhile. Hakubunkan, which was not planning a competing series, must have seen the 5,000 yen as being more than the volume alone could have hoped to return in future printings. This is a pivotal point: the story was more commercially valuable as part of the series than it was on its own. In this concrete economic sense the framework of the anthology added value to the literary work. When another publishing company, Shun'yōdō, decided in May 1927 to create its own one-yen book series, the *Meiji Taishō bungaku zenshū* (Complete Works of Meiji and Taishō Literature), it assembled a very different Kafū volume.[55] Shun'yōdō, which previously had published a six-volume Nagai Kafū collection, already possessed rights to a number of works, which it was not willing to relinquish to Kaizōsha. Perhaps Shun'yōdō felt its anthology's framework added similar value, or perhaps their decision was not entirely based on economic rationality.

Shun'yōdō, which had long been the central publishing house for literature, took umbrage at the audacity of Kaizōsha to produce such a series, and the two companies clearly functioned with competitive mindsets about the selection of works for the collections.[56] For example, Kaizōsha tried very hard to get Shun'yōdō to sell them the right to publish Ozaki Kōyō's *Konjiki yasha* (The Gold Demon). Shun'yōdō had the rights to many of Ozaki's most famous works, including *Konjiki yasha*, *Kyara makura* (Aloeswood Pillow), and *Kokoro no yami* (Darkness in the Heart). Although Yamamoto went to great lengths to convince Wada Toshihiko, the president of Shun'yōdō, to allow him to publish them, Wada refused. The only major work Yamamoto was able to get, again for 5,000 yen, was *Tajō takon* (Passions and Griefs).[57] Yamamoto even thanked Wada in the pages of *Kaizō*.[58] As a result Kaizōsha's collection of Ozaki's work is almost completely different from Shun'yōdō's collection.[59] The fact that Kaizōsha was willing to spend large sums of money for the right to include specific works reveals the works' symbolic importance. In both cases Kaizōsha felt compelled to include a minimum number of key works in order to legitimize the volume as a whole.

Just as specific works were necessary to legitimize a single volume, specific authors were necessary to legitimize the series as a whole. In some cases authors contributed more to the authority of the series as presences, or brands, than through any of the specific works contained in their volumes. Shimazaki Tōson's volume, for example, contains only essays and none of his fictional works because Shinchōsha owned the complete rights to the novels and was unwilling to negotiate for their use.[60] In the preface to his *Complete Works of Contemporary Japanese Literature* volume, Tōson conceded that the series was the result of his having given away all of his novels and poems to other collections, and he tried to stem perceptions of the collection as a "meaningless exercise."[61] In the *Kaizō* issue of June 1927, Kaizōsha announced that Shinchōsha had given its permission for them to publish *Haru* (Spring), saying that it would get the story to subscribers somehow. The Tōson volume had already been sent out at that time, so Kaizōsha included *Haru* (and his story *Arashi* [Storm]) in volume 36, the travel essay (*Kikō zuihitsu*) volume, which was published in August 1929. The fact that Kaizōsha thought it needed to do this, even after the volume had been released, suggests that there was some dissatisfaction with the Tōson volume's contents. Tōson had to be represented, however, despite the limited literary value that his included works might have had, in order to legitimize the collection itself.

Natsume Sōseki's volume similarly contains complete versions of only three of his most celebrated works (*Botchan*, *Kusamakura* [Pillow of Grass], and *Michikusa* [Grass on the Wayside]), omitting other famous works, such as *Mon* (The Gate), *Sorekara* (And Then), *Sanshirō*, *Meian* (Light and Darkness), and *Kokoro*. Kaizōsha bargained with the Sōseki Zenshū Kankō-kai, a cartel of three publishers that had formed to produce a complete Sōseki collection, to get eight lesser known works in addition to the three mentioned above. The publishers of Sōseki's complete works, unwilling to undercut the demand for their own collection, were naturally reluctant to allow the inclusion of the more popular works. Since some important works would have been essential to maintain the legitimacy of the volume and omission of Sōseki from the Kaizōsha collection would have severely damaged the authority of the *Complete Works of Contemporary Japanese Literature*, Kaizō was willing to go to great lengths to get the works it did.

Editorial Intervention

That is not to say, however, that Kaizōsha accorded any great reverence to the autonomy of individual works within a given volume. In many cases only selections (*shō*) of works were included (though to Kaizōsha's credit they were marked as such). Some selections show more editorial intervention than others. For example, only parts of Sōseki's work *Garasudo no uchi* (Inside My Glass Doors)—fifteen of the original thirty-nine installments—were used in his volume. The edition contains a commentary (*kaisetsu*) written by the scholar and Sōseki disciple Komiya Toyotaka. After stating that he thinks that Sōseki's writing was at its most beautiful and most pure during his illness, he writes:

> The segments I excerpted from *Garasudo no naka* . . . share a unified air—a kind of melancholy richness [*shimeyaka na uruoi*]—[so] for convenience's sake I have set them up as an independent work. The selected segments share this special richness because they are Sōseki's nostalgic recollections of his distant past. Certain readers might be interested to compare these short pieces with the recollections of his distant past interspersed throughout *Michikusa*.[62]

Komiya selected segments that in his opinion created a more coherent work from a less coherent one. As a result he changed *Garasudo no uchi* from a highly variable collection of short pieces to a unified narrative, dismissing the structure (or lack thereof) that the author had chosen for the work. In this case even Sōseki's considerable authority was not sufficient to protect his work from editorial intervention.

Atsuko Sakaki has discussed the impact that editorial intervention had on Tōkai Sanshi's *Kajin no kigū*. According to Sakaki, this impact was substantial. The edition of the story that appeared in the series "gives the nostalgic impression that it attempts to reproduce the original" by including reproductions of original illustrations, prefaces, and postfaces. Sakaki argues, however, that these gestures actually reinforced "the irrevocable gap between the original and the duplicate" by shrinking these reproductions to a scale that makes them difficult to decipher. At the same time commentaries that had been present in the original were omitted, thus erasing the involvement of individuals other than Sanshi in the production of the text. As a result the "dialogic or multivalent quality [of the text] was significantly neutralized in the 1931 edition. . . . The text was reduced to the linear flow of the story, and the initial readers' claims to participation in its making . . . were submerged in a demonstration of singular narrative authority established by the exclusion of exterior voices."[63] It is Sakaki's contention that this intervention resulted in the erasure of marks of the text's "premodern literariness," obscuring the text's simultaneous participation in both "modernity" and "premodernity." Such a claim does not require that the editors had such ends in mind; it is sufficient that the editorial interventions would have had that effect on readers.

Despite the many compromises that were made in the assembly of the collection, some individuals involved in the project invested significant time and effort in the series and took the project as a whole very seriously. Certain authors also got involved with the contents of their volume, recognizing not only the commercial potential of the series but the impact it would have their literary legacies. Izumi Kyōka constructed his volume with an eye toward literary history, carefully including representative works from various genres and periods in his career.[64] The series was also driven by an editorial staff—in addition to Kimura Ki and Yanagida Izumi—that worked extremely hard on the accuracy of the series, despite remaining anonymous.[65]

The role of the anonymous editors in fact became an immediate subject of debate. Satō Haruo raised two specific complaints about the compilation of the series in his essay "Ichienpon no ryūkō" (The One-Yen Book Fad), published in April 1927.[66] On the one hand, Satō took issue over the use of the word zenshū (complete works), when the one-yen books were in fact actually senshū (selected works).[67] He was right to make this criticism. Though no one would have thought that every work of contemporary Japanese literature appeared in the series, the title nonetheless implied a kind of completeness and, in so doing, carried a particular rhetorical force. Satō also criticized Kaizōsha for keeping the editors anonymous, despite the fact that the company must have consulted people when collecting the works. Satō felt that naming the individuals would raise their sense of responsibility for the project, and implored publishers to remember that theirs was an industry that could not be driven solely by economic necessity, but must consider the merit of the works as well.

By allowing the editors to remain unnamed at the time of the series' publication Kaizōsha was able to preserve an illusion of objectivity for a process that was in fact a clear exercise of cultural power. In so doing the decisions of the editorial team were naturalized, creating the impression that they were the result of an inevitable order. As Kōno Kensuke has written:

> The limited form of the zenshū forces the editors to decide who should be given their own volume and who should be put together to share a volume. Moreover, because the editors were not named, it gave the impression that a consensus based on a literary common knowledge was achieved at some point. Literary selection and exclusion, ranking and stratification were done, quite before everyone's eyes, in the creation of anthologies.[68]

The act of creating such a zenshū demanded a ranking of writers, even when the head editors were consciously trying to create as inclusive a collection as possible. The literary historian Tanizawa Eiichi has gone so far as to say, "The person who determined the ranking of Meiji and Taishō writers was none other than Kimura Ki." In so doing, Tanizawa continues, Kimura "became the arbiter elegantiarum of the Meiji-Taishō literary establishment."[69]

Kimura Ki did not work alone, however, nor did he create a hierarchy that was entirely capricious or idiosyncratic. Kimura functioned within a small literary establishment that possessed a rapidly solidifying conception of modern Japanese literature, divided from the literature of the past, with certain writers and works that had been elevated from the rest. This discourse had already found material form in such works as the *Bungei hyakka zensho* (Encyclopedia of the Literary Arts, 1909) and other histories of the literary arts in modern Japan.[70] Nonetheless the specific aesthetic sense informing the series, though limited by material constraints and existing conceptions, belonged to Kimura, and the benefits produced by the series were bestowed on the works he chose according to the hierarchical structure he determined. The more lasting effect of the series, however, was its reification of a conception. More than any specific author or work, the series consolidated the cultural prestige of a space that later figures filled differently, often informed by a definition of literature far narrower than Kimura's.

Selling the Series: Rhetoric and Revelry

The impact of this conception was determined by the size of its audience. Once Kaizōsha had laid out its plan for this massive gamble, the next step was to sell it. Again *King* magazine proved to be an invaluable precedent; many of Kaizōsha's advertising techniques, as well as its attempt to reach a national marketplace (and beyond), were modeled directly on the magazine.[71] Advertising, every possible manifestation of which Kaizōsha employed to publicize the series, was central to the company's strategy. Flags, banners, and signs were erected near as many bookstores as possible. Throughout the country boys wearing *hanten* coats with the insignia of the collection were sent into the streets, which were littered with handbills and posters. Fliers were dropped from towers and planes. *Chindon-ya* troupes (brightly dressed street performers) were employed to herald the new release. Politicians, scholars, entrepreneurs, teachers, artists, and all manner of literary figures lent their names to the advertising.[72] A fleet of taxis was hired to take Kaizō employees to bookstores to distribute sample books, arches were constructed in front of larger bookstores, and salesmen were dispatched as far as Taiwan and Hawaii.[73] According to Yamamoto himself, advertising cost well over 100,000 yen (figure 11).[74]

In addition Kaizōsha utilized its magazine *Kaizō* to stir up interest in the series. In the special issue of *Kaizō* in December 1926, titled *Meiji bungaku no omoide* (Memories of Meiji Literature), the plan of the *Complete Works*

FIGURE 11 Cars advertising the series *Complete Works of Contemporary Japanese Literature*. From Matsubara Kazue, *Kaizōsha to Yamamoto Sanehiko: Yamamoto Sanehiko's Kaizosya* (Kagoshima-shi: Nanpō Shinsha, 2000), 150.

was linked to a reevaluation of Meiji literature, creating a type of scholarly atmosphere around the series. In this issue eleven essays of either recollections or debate were collected, marking the beginning of the scholarly reevaluation.[75] Contributors to this reevaluation may not have realized that they were prepping the market for a forthcoming product.

At least some of the writers involved in a nationwide lecture series on the literary arts (*bungei kōen-kai*) sponsored by Kaizōsha were fully aware of their function; Akutagawa Ryūnosuke was quoted as complaining that he "had been made to stand [before the audiences] in place of a billboard."[76] Throughout 1927 the company held lectures in Tokyo, Hokkaidō, Shin'etsu (Nagano, Niigata), Kansai, and Kyūshū. Between twenty thousand and thirty thousand people attended the Tokyo lecture, held at the Ryōgoku Kokugikan.[77] Takei Shizuo and Shōji Tatsuya have both written in great detail about the grueling tour of Hokkaidō and Tōhoku by Akutagawa in May 1927, which may very well have hastened his mental and emotional collapse and subsequent suicide.[78] These lecture tours brought famous writers face to face with the general public in open meeting places, while simultaneously disseminating a specific view of literary value in line with the logic of the collection itself. As part of this series a film was shot which depicted the daily lives of many famous literary figures of the time (including Kume Masao, Akutagawa Ryūnosuke, and Tokuda Shūsei, to name a few) and was shown during the lecture series.[79] Following a trend to include images of authors in their books, this film took the next step in the creation of a celebrity culture for writers.[80]

Both the intensity of the blitz and the nature of Kaizōsha's advertising strategies can be most readily seen today in the newspaper advertising campaign the publishing house undertook to publicize the series.[81] The hyperbole of the rhetoric appears in the earliest advertisements:

> With the slogan of "letting you read good books cheaply," our company is carrying out a great revolution in the publishing world, releasing the art of the privileged class before all the nation [zenminshū]. One for each household! Life without art is truly like the wilderness. Why, though we Japanese [waga kokujin] possess a great Meiji literature worthy of the attention of all the world, is it not made the possession of the nation [zenminshū-ka] as England's Shakespeare is? This is why our company has undertaken this grand project, unprecedented in our country, of producing one million sets—we are counting on them to become the beloved reading of every household in the country. Japan's greatest source of pride! This collection of each and every representative work of the great authors of Meiji and Taishō is the greatest miracle of the contemporary period. The fact that more than 1,200 pages of famous works can be read for a mere one yen is the greatest miracle of contemporary Japan.[82]

This first advertisement cites democratization, Shakespeare, revolution, and national pride on the international stage to help elevate the series through, for want of a better term, legitimacy by association. The symbols and discourses Kaizōsha appropriated to elevate the importance of its product created rhetorical linkages between this modern literary canon and the nation, the emperor, and Japanese ethnic identity itself.

The first linkage meant to produce value in the series is that between literature and the nation. The rhetoric leaves no doubt about the series being an important national event:

> Literature is the "wellspring of life" that symbolizes the highest culture of mankind, enriches each of our lives, and cultivates a beautiful vitality in us. The Japanese literature of the Meiji and Taishō periods, in particu-

lar, having deftly absorbed the quintessence of European literature and making it its own, has become the equal of the most recent European literature. No—it has even surpassed it. That is the proof of the great advances made by Japanese culture.[83]

Even as the advertisement launches with a transnational humanism, it quickly morphs into a nationalistic call, stressing international competition:

Art is eternal! Meiji literature, which strives to be seen as a peer of the world's literatures, is the sole essence of Oriental culture! The fact that we possess this Meiji literature, which contains a notable revolutionary passion, is the pride of all Japanese citizens! The immortal *Complete Works of Contemporary Japanese Literature*, filled with everlasting masterpieces, is approaching![84]

Linkages to individuals work in a similar fashion. In one, the famous economist Fukuda Tokuzō is quoted as commenting, "[This series] will give Japan one more thing to be proud of before the international community" (figure 12).[85] More than the call to national pride, the importance here is the linking of the series—and of modern literature—to alternative forms of authority, this time through association with Fukuda and the pro-democracy activist Yoshino Sakuzō. The most extreme example of linkages to powerful individuals occurred in an advertisement that appeared in November 1926, when it connected the series to the emperor himself. After announcing that "Irie [Tamemori], the Grand Chamberlain, has given us permission to include (and will be copying for us) poems by the Meiji Emperor and Empress, each a world-class poet, in the *Complete Works of Contemporary Japanese Literature*," the advertisement discusses "the Meiji emperor as a poet" (figure 13).[86] The series not only purported to represent the national genius, but also contained the literary production of the embodiment of the Japanese people, the emperor.

The positive rhetoric of the advertisements also contained implied challenges to the readers:

Look at this! This reaction! Door-to-door visits! We are truly in the thick of it! One per household! With this call in mind, bookstores in big cities such as Tokyo and Osaka and small cities in every prefecture have even begun selling the series door to door—it is an unprecedented success.[87]

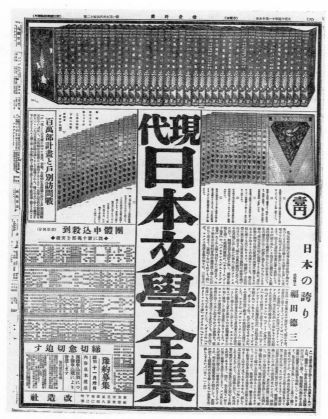

FIGURE 12   Fukuda Tokuzō and the *Complete Works of Contemporary Japanese Literature*. *Yomiuri shinbun*, 18 November 1926, morning edition, 6.

By stressing a national reach and broad national participation, the advertisement preys on people's fears of being left out of a new national event, a new national culture. No excuse is sufficient to avoid participation in this event, not even economic constraints:

> Look at the tearful faces of the poor people who so readily commit their one yen, which they earned through blood and sweat. Look at the austere housewives happily throwing in their one yen, even if it means cutting back on their daily goods.[88]

To miss this opportunity is, finally, to betray Japan and thus one's identity. A large note in the corner clarifies this: "To lack this collection is a disgrace

FIGURE 13 "The Meiji Emperor as a Poet." *Yomiuri shinbun*, 30 November 1926.

upon a household." The advertisement then leverages Natsume Sōseki's fame to continue emotionally blackmailing potential consumers:

> The great Sōseki, who possessed noble blood and pure tears, also possessed a modern sensibility truly unparalleled in the Meiji or Taishō periods. As for his purity of character, like artesian water each and every drop was the essence and the flower of the Yamato race. . . . These significant works of art should be read by every man and woman in our country. . . . Can one who has not read this Sōseki collection, one who cannot appreciate this collection, truly be called a Japanese gentleman or lady?[89]

The Static Canon

A fear of failing Japan is not the only anxiety utilized in the advertising rhetoric; Kaizōsha uses the very fears of commodification that its own series inspired, absolving itself by accusing its competitors of contributing to the downfall of the nation (and, by extension, the empire) as a whole:

As one compares the many collections that are thought up in a moment, planned with only commerce in mind, and comprised of works chosen solely for their entertainment value, to one that was assembled in good conscience, through a revolutionary struggle, and comprised systematically, with literary history in mind, as the years pass surely their relative value will become apparent. Randomly chosen stories thrown together can only lead to confusion in the minds of readers. We must caution everyone that struggle, passion, and purity have been lost from nearly all enterprises in this world, and that if we do not fundamentally reform the attitude, common throughout contemporary Japan, of casually *imitating* without recognizing *vices* of any type, the new Japan will inevitably experience the path of ruin in the end.[90]

By linking itself to sources of authority outside of the literary field—democratization, ethnic pride, the nation-state (and thus the imperial state), a humanist view of art, civilization, the academy, ethnic identity, and the emperor himself—the series attempted to establish its own authority. The series then interpellated consumers, demanding that they prove their commitment to the national project through purchase of the series.

The Impact of Subscription Sales

Purchasing the series was in theory an all-or-nothing proposition; individual volumes were not, at least in principle, for sale. Kaizōsha made the decision to sell the series by subscription, following the subscription publishing law (Yoyaku Shuppan-hō) instituted in 1910.[91] Subscriptions could be taken by mail in response to advertising in magazines or newspapers, or they could be taken in person at bookstores or at the Kaizōsha company headquarters. Although consumers initially had the option of paying for the series in one (discounted) lump sum, few seem to have taken this option. Instead most sent a one-yen down payment to the company and then made monthly payments of one yen until the completion of the series. The down payment was to be used to cover the cost of the final volume.[92] Subscribers who canceled midway lost their deposit. Although distributors initially argued that they should hold the deposit, Kaizōsha ignored their request.[93] By collecting deposits Kaizōsha was effectively given an interest-free loan that enabled it to rebuild itself and finance the publication of the series.

Although some consumers applied directly to Kaizōsha, retail stores and regional book merchants handled most of the subscriptions.[94] Advertising for the series in the *Tōkyō asahi shinbun* on 3 November 1926 claims that bookstores in Tokyo, Osaka, and every prefecture in the country had begun door-to-door visits to hawk the series.[95] Many retailers enthusiastically distributed the series because it provided them with business each month with little risk.[96] Retail booksellers' sales increased 20 to 30 percent as a result of the *Complete Works of Contemporary Japanese Literature* and the many other one-yen book series that followed it. As had been the case with the *Taishō daishinsai daikasai*, some stores that had carried only magazines began to sell one-yen books. In fact some bookstores subscribed to the series themselves, presumably to offer them for retail sale to shoppers who had missed the application deadline or wanted only specific volumes.[97] Demand for the series in Kyūshū was so intense that it produced significant stresses for Kaizōsha. The company had initially linked up with the Kinbunkai network of retailers, which had stores in most major Kyūshū cities, using the chain to facilitate Kaizōsha's lecture series.[98] When the Kagoshima store Kinkaidō put up a sign claiming to be a special agent of Kaizōsha, the Kagoshima Booksellers Association (Shoten Kumiai) called for a boycott of Kaizōsha among its members. Yamamoto Sanehiko contacted the Association personally and assured them the sign would be removed. The incident illustrates the importance of the series to regional retail stores, as well as the importance of those stores to Kaizōsha.[99]

Most consumers did not have access to the stores that subscribed in order to sell the books individually and so were not able to buy individual volumes. By purchasing the series by subscription consumers broke with the traditional logic of book sales through retailers. Whether a consumer took a book off a shelf at Maruzen and examined it or a bookseller familiar with the consumer's tastes examined it for him or her, the consumer would make a decision based on a variety of factors, including content, author, and publisher. In the countryside consumers would make selections in consultation with a retailer with whom they often had a long-term relationship.

The *Complete Works of Contemporary Japanese Literature*, which was purchased in much the same way as magazines, changed this. Although the contents of the series were described in some detail (and with reasonable, though not total accuracy) in the very earliest advertisements, later advertisements were much more ambiguous about what the series would contain.[100] Subscribers made their commitment, finally, to a concept: modern Japanese literature.

Unimaginable Success: Speculations on Reception

The series was a tremendous success. Although sales statistics are debated, most agree that the collection attracted roughly 230,000 subscribers by the close of its first subscription deadline of 30 November 1926.[101] Kaizōsha responded to subsequent demands to join the series—as well as to the competition of Shun'yōdō's series—by opening a second enrollment period that lasted from roughly 23 April until 31 July 1927 (figure 14).[102] By the end of that period the total number of subscribers had climbed to at least 340,000. This should have marked the peak of circulation for the collection because subscribers could quit after this time but in principle they could not join.[103] The estimate of at least 340,000 is supported by Nagai Kafū, who years later noted in his journal that a total of 339,350 copies of his volume (released in September 1927) had sold.[104] The figure of 340,000 subscriptions represents only a momentary peak and does not apply to complete sets of the series because subscribers did quit and volumes were printed only in the quantity necessary. An estimate of how much attrition occurred is possible. In order to entice subscribers to continue until the end, Kaizōsha offered a bookcase to everyone who did so (figure 15). Loss through canceled subscriptions must have been a problem from early on in the process because these bookcases were offered as early as 3 May 1927.[105] By January 1931 the number of subscribers, based on the number of bookcases that the company estimated it would have needed at that point, had dropped to roughly 50,000.[106]

Despite this drop the series must be seen as radically increasing the size of literature's readership, as most literary volumes up to this time had enjoyed a much more limited circulation. Although some authors, such as Shimada Seijirō, reached audiences that extended beyond the small, mostly Tokyo-based literary readership, even big names like Mori Ōgai and

FIGURE 14　Deadline announcement for second enrollment in
the subscription series *Complete Works of Contemporary Japanese
Literature. Yomiuri shinbun*, 31 May 1927, morning edition, 6.

Nagai Kafū had first runs of only a thousand copies in the early Taishō
period.[107] In most cases a book that achieved sales of ten thousand copies
would have been considered a bestseller.[108] The dramatic difference between the sales figures of the *Complete Works of Contemporary Japanese
Literature* and those of most literary works suggests that people desired the
entity modern Japanese literature more than they wanted specific works of
modern Japanese literature. At the same time the low price of the series
likely tapped a demand for the texts that had previously been untapped.
This second interpretation has been the standard one for these statistics;
they marked a turning point in the history of literary dissemination in

The Static Canon

FIGURE 15   Bookcase offer advertised as an incentive to subscribe to the
Complete Works of Contemporary Japanese Literature. Yomiuri shinbun,
3 May 1927, morning edition, 5.

Japan, with the series permeating every stratum of Japanese society. There
is no doubt that the level of production was unprecedented, but the limited
reception data that we have indicate that subscribers to the series were not
from as broad a cross-section of society as is often supposed.

Although the *Complete Works of Contemporary Japanese Literature* enjoyed a readership far larger than that of most literary works, in terms of social penetration it was not as deep as the sales statistics might suggest. After
examining the small number of extant surveys and taking into consideration various other forms of data available, Nagamine Shigetoshi concludes
that one-yen book purchases were most common among urban intellec-

tuals, female students, salaried workers, and rural landowners. Due primarily to financial constraints, purchases were not common among large segments of the population, including non-landowning farmers, youth group members, and urban factory workers.[109] During its subscription period the *Complete Works* likely saturated certain segments of society—members of the urban, salaried classes and rural, landowning classes—and left others less affected.

In the absence of large surveys and thorough statistics on readership, scholars such as Nagamine have turned to estimates of household expenditures during the period to help them understand the marketplace for literature. Maeda Ai was one of the first scholars to perform such a reconstruction. In his discussion of expanding readership for women's magazines in the decade preceding the *Complete Works*, Maeda gives concrete examples of expenditures in middle-class homes for reading material. Using Minami Hiroshi's definitions of "middle class"—an annual income between 500 and 5,000 yen per year—Maeda concluded that 2.38 percent of households were middle class in 1903, 5 percent in 1917, and fully 11.5 percent met an adjusted standard (800–5,000 yen) in 1925.[110] By that definition nearly 1.4 million households were middle class by 1925. The growth of this middle class resulted in an increased demand for print culture, to which the publishing industry immediately responded. The magnitude of demand is apparent in contemporary household budgets, calculated by the Tokyo metropolitan government, differentiated by occupation; the expense category relevant to reading was "self-cultivation expenses" (*shūyōhi*). In 1922 the average monthly self-cultivation budgets for some representative middle-class occupations (60–80 yen per month) were 2.2 yen for public servants, 2.37 yen for elementary school teachers, 2.55 yen for police officers, 2.1 yen for transportation workers, and 1.47 yen for bank employees. That same year police officers and transportation workers earning less than 60 yen per month spent an average of 46 sen and 56 sen, respectively.[111] As disposable income decreased, so did self-cultivation expenses.

Ariyama Teruo has explored surveys to give an even clearer picture of monthly self-cultivation expenses in the years leading up to the *Complete Works of Contemporary Japanese Literature*. In 1926 the family of a salaried worker with a monthly income of 150 yen or higher spent an average of 2.47 yen on cultivation expenses, suggesting that this stratum had sufficient means to subscribe to such a series. Households with an income between 100 and 120 yen, however, spent only 1.65 yen per month on such purchases and thus might not have been inclined to buy even this low-cost series. Wage laborers, whose income averaged 120 yen per month, spent only 1.11 yen on cultivation expenses. Newspaper subscription (which at roughly one yen per month would have consumed most of this budget) was common among working households, but full-price magazine (at 50–70 sen) and book (at 1.50–2 yen) purchases remained out of reach.[112] These figures, however, are from a survey of Tokyo households and thus reflect higher wages than existed in other cities; the national average salary in 1926 was only 102.07 yen per month.[113] All of these data reinforce the notion that social permeation of the series, when sold at full price, was likely limited.

Beyond a National Marketplace

There was another market for the series that should not be overlooked: the colonies.[114] The *Complete Works of Contemporary Japanese Literature* and other one-yen book series sold well in the colonies from the start. Uchiyama Shoten, a Japanese bookstore in Shanghai that opened in 1920, was a popular spot not only for Japanese expatriates but also for Chinese intellectuals and professionals associated with Japanese enterprises in China. The poet Kaneko Mitsuharu wrote that Uchiyama Shoten was the "teat from which Chinese received their intellectual nourishment," and the famous author Lu Xun was a customer. According to Uchiyama Kanzō, the founder, his store distributed a thousand sets of the *Complete Works* in China.[115] Uchiyama Shoten was not an exception in this regard. Matsumoto Shōhei, who was in charge of distribution to Korea and Manchuria for Tōkyōdō at the time, recalled that one-yen books continued to sell well in the colonies even into the war years, long after demand had died off in Japan. The one-yen books, which were originally priced 20 percent higher in the colonies, sold so well that overseas bookstores were happy to carry them despite having to bear added shipping costs and complete additional paperwork.[116] Most important, overseas bookstores were plentiful. In 1928 Taiwan's Booksellers Association (Shoseki-shō Kumiai) had 66 members, growing to 106 by 1938; the Karafuto Book and Magazine Sellers' Association (Shoseki Zasshi-shō) had 88 members; the Manshū Book and

Magazine Sellers' Association (Shoseki Zasshi-shō) had 110 members; and the Chōsen Book and Magazine Sellers' Association (Shoseki Zasshi-shō) had 323 members.[117] Though small in comparison to the combined memberships of the Tokyo and Osaka associations (4,400 members), these colonial bookstores still represented a significant market and suggest considerable consumption of the series throughout the empire.

Both inside and outside Japan there were also ways that individuals gained access to the series without subscribing. Subscriptions to the *Complete Works* were not limited to individuals; Kimura Ki mentions that schools and libraries also subscribed to the series.[118] These volumes circulated to a far wider readership. The Sōseki volume, for example, was borrowed twenty-two times from the Nagoya Public Library in November 1927 alone.[119] Kaizōsha's advertisements enumerated organizations that were subscribing to the series, claiming that schools, youth groups, banks, companies, newspapers, hospitals, factories, and government agencies were ordering dozens, or even hundreds of subscriptions as groups. One advertisement lists nearly 150 such groups.[120] This is just one of many ways that readers might have gained access to the series without subscribing individually; there were also book lenders, reading rooms (*jūran-jo*), factory reading rooms (*kōjō tosho-shitsu*), and both commercial and informal reading circles (*kaidoku-kai*). Magazine reading circles also circulated one-yen books.[121]

Soon after their retail release the volumes began to circulate on the used and remaindered book market as well, often at a significant discount from their original low price. This brought the series to more strata of society than the original subscription period had. One of the key players behind the sales of one-yen books through these sales networks was Bandō Kyōgo. Bandō's company, the Teikoku Tosho Fukyūkai (Imperial Book Dissemination Society), sold these books throughout Japan and the Japanese colonies.[122] Bandō's commercial expedition to the colonies was not the only one. It is well known that after the one-yen book boom came to a close, Kawano Shoten purchased 300,000 volumes of the *Complete Works* for 12 sen per volume.[123] Less well known is that Kawano Shoten often sold such remaindered books in the colonies.[124] According to Matsumoto Shōhei, even after retailers in Japan began to refuse to handle one-yen books, groups such as the Taira Shōkai in Changchun (Shinkyō) and Lushun (Ryojun) took on as many one-yen books as they could get.[125] It was during this round of circulation that the *Complete Works* went on sale in São Paulo. Copies of the Satō Haruo, Okamoto Kidō, and Kikuchi Kan volumes were offered beginning as early as 1933.

Reactions within the Publishing Industry: The One-Yen Book Wars and Their Impact

The success of Kaizōsha's gamble led many of its competitors to imitate it. Following Kaizōsha's lead, Shinchōsha presented its *Sekai bungaku zenshū* (Complete Works of World Literature) in January 1927.[126] This series was even more successful than Kaizōsha's, attracting as many as 580,000 subscribers.[127] For many this series provided access to world literature that had previously been blocked not only by an economic barrier, but also by a linguistic one. With the entrance into one-yen book publishing of Shinchōsha, a large and respected firm at the time, many other firms soon followed, and the one-yen book wars began. Over the next five years more than two hundred one-yen book *zenshū* were published, covering a broad spectrum of subject matter.[128] Publishers competed furiously, increasing pages and decreasing prices, thus cutting profit margins until they were untenable.[129] By 1931 virtually every publisher had joined in on this price slashing and mass production of books.

Perhaps the most relevant of these other one-yen book series to modern Japanese literature was Shun'yōdō's fifty-volume *Meiji Taishō bungaku zenshū*, which began in May 1927.[130] Unlike Kaizōsha, Shun'yōdō had a long history of publishing literary works, possessing both cultural prestige and legal control over many texts. Kaizōsha was clearly intimidated by Shun'yōdō's entry into the one-yen book wars; it responded to the announcement with its second call for subscribers. The competition between these two collections, which the *Complete Works of Contemporary Japanese Literature* ultimately won, has been thoroughly analyzed by Takashima Ken'ichirō, who identifies three important reasons why Kaizōsha's series succeeded in the end.[131] First was the syllabic gloss, which Shun'yōdō's series lacked, thus limiting its potential market.[132] Second was Kaizōsha's broad scope, which it was forced to adopt because of its inability to get many major works; the *Complete Works* includes 586 authors and 1,960 prose works and plays (poems not included in the total), while Shun'yōdō's series includes only 268 authors and 923 prose works and plays. Furthermore many one-yen book consumers did not possess the cultural literacy required to distinguish major works. Third was Kaizōsha's six-month lead, which forced Shun'yōdō to try to seduce customers away from a subscription to which they had already made a financial commitment. Takashima also discusses the long-term impact of the series on the two companies. Future sales of works contained in the series, at least in the immediate future, suffered as a result of inclusion. This had little effect on Kaizōsha, which had owned few of the rights to works in the first place. In Shun'yōdō's case, however, the company cannibalized the long-term profitability of its catalogue for the sake of its series.

Despite the scale of the one-yen book boom, ever shrinking margins made the series profitable for only a limited number of publishers. In fact in some cases the success of a one-yen book collection ultimately hurt the company. As just described, Shun'yōdō failed despite, or rather because of the success it experienced with its *Meiji Taishō bungaku zenshū*.[133] As the one-yen book wars heated up, profit margins were cut further and further in a constant competition over page totals, paper quality, and binding quality.[134] Often the subscriptions did not meet expectations, and the collection, which publishers were forced to see through to the end because of the subscription publishing law, became a burden rather than a boon. Prices of all types of books, not just one-yen books, were forced down.[135]

The series temporarily expanded retailers' profitability, but not all the gains were lasting. In the long run many retailers found themselves overstaffed in subsequent years and some were forced out of business, having expanded their workforces by 20 to 30 percent to handle the boom.[136] One of the lasting changes for retailers concerned their expectations. The one-yen book boom put bookstores in the habit of returning books rather than trying to exhaust every possible means of selling them first. Although the *Complete Works of Contemporary Japanese Literature* most likely did not accept returns, later series did. In Matsumoto Shōhei's experience during his years at the distributor Tōkyōdō, this marked a shift in retailers' thinking from an active "Let's try to sell whatever we have" to a passive "We will only carry what sells."[137]

The boom changed demands made on distributors, particularly on the simultaneous delivery of products throughout the country, or at least by region. Because of the increased traffic through both distributors and retailers, detailed delivery schedules were calculated to ensure relatively uniform timing in distribution and to minimize shipping costs.[138] Distributors (at the insistence of publishers and retailers) tried hard to get deliveries to bookstores in a given region to arrive at the same time, but it was too complicated; on 1 June 1927 the publishers and major distributors sent a joint statement to bookstores around the country apologizing that simultaneous delivery would be impossible.[139] In many cases both bookmaking and distribution companies were overwhelmed by the load. Books were often sent out before their bindings were dry and distributors were often forced to find alternative shipping methods. This sort of pressure was in some ways new to the industry; prior to this time retailers rarely demanded uniform delivery.[140]

Regardless of the huge success that the series marked for authors and publishers, a number of other problems produced by the series have been identified. In 1928 the notoriously (and hilariously) cantankerous historian, social critic, and satirist Miyatake Gaikotsu self-published a pamphlet titled *Ichien ryūkō no gaidoku to sono rimendan* (The Evils of the One-Yen Fad and Its Inside Story) in which he enumerated—only half ironically— sixteen negative repercussions of the one-yen books.[141]

> Recklessness of one-yen book publishing houses.
> Dilution of respect for books.
> Corruption of one-yen book authors and translators.
> Loss of faith in the subscription publishing system.
> Evil influence on the rest of the publishing world.
> Creating problems for financiers.
> Weakening the masses with a literary poison.
> Decadence of those newly rich through royalties.
> Setting a precedent of untrustworthy advertising.
> Extravagant waste of domestic paper.
> Furthering the evil practice of unfair criticism.
> Debasement of book-making techniques.
> Obstruction of the means of communications on a grand scale.
> Exacerbation of general economic recession.
> Hindrance to shipping on a grand scale.
> Breeding of discontent among scholars.

Although Miyatake's concerns are hyperbolic, there are a number of concrete negative repercussions discernable from available statistics and subsequent trends. The most dramatic was the damage the boom in one-yen book sales did to other books during the period 1927–31. As might be expected, sales of older, more expensive books dropped sharply.[142] Reduced profit margins made the publication of books expected to sell only five hundred to a thousand copies all but impossible; even as the threshold for bestseller status itself was increased by an order of magnitude during this period, so too were publishers' expectations for sales. Increased concentration of publishing and sales capital also created problems for small publishing ventures.[143]

On the other hand, there were of course positive repercussions for the industry. Distributors profited from the increased volume of books passing through bookstores. Fukuda Ryōtarō of the distribution company Hokuryū-kan claimed that as a result of this volume, stores received on-the-spot clerical training and became more business-like, finally keeping track of their inventories and account books.[144] Perhaps the longest-term impact on the industry was the creation of the Iwanami Bunko (Iwanami Library) series, Iwanami Shoten's low-cost alternative to the collections that were swamping the market at the time.[145] The success of this series created a format, the inexpensive *bunkobon* (small, soft-covered books), that is now central to the publishing world and performs the invaluable function of keeping many books in print.[146] While the effect of the one-yen book boom on the publishing industry may have been dramatic in the short term, its long-term effects were more limited.

The effects of the one-yen book boom, specifically of the *Complete Works of Contemporary Japanese Literature*, on writers were equally significant in the short term. Many "poor literati" (*binbō bunshi*) of the Meiji and Taishō periods became "one-yen book *nouveaux riches*" (*enpon narikin*) overnight.[147] Tokyo's *Kokumin shinbun*, using tax office and other statistics, calculated in 1927 that the ten main collections available at that point had attracted 1,415,000 subscriptions for a total projected income of 58,885,000 yen.[148] The article noted that Kikuchi Kan would receive the greatest amount in royalties, 250,000 yen. The following year the magazine *Fujin kōron* looked at these one-yen book nouveaux riches and what they were doing with their newfound wealth. According to the article, Tanizaki Jun'ichirō, Kōda Rohan, Satō Haruo, Yoshida Genjirō, and Satomi Ton had all built homes using their royalties; others built additions, restored old homes, purchased land, took trips abroad, invested in companies, or wasted it through "profligate spending" (rōhi).[149]

The dramatic profits from these series forced publishing companies and authors to be more attentive to copyrights. Although some authors, such as Mori Ōgai and Natsume Sōseki, had taken a keen interest in the specifics of their contracts and the control of their rights—Sōseki going as far as to help finance the creation of Iwanami Shoten in order to have more direct control over his publications—many writers had sold the complete rights to their works to publishers. While an author's right to his or her writings— his or her intellectual property—had been protected by law since at least 1875, a manuscript sale system (genkō kaitori seido) continued in practice for most authors. With most literary books selling in very small runs, in many cases it was more profitable for authors to sell their manuscripts outright.[150] During the Taishō period, however, more authors began to insist on a royalty system (inzei seido). Kaizōsha seems to have paid at least some of the authors included in its Complete Works a royalty of roughly 12 percent.[151] Although this led to a general move toward the royalty system, Satō Haruo complained that the resulting standard royalty percentages— usually 10 to 12 percent, sometimes as low as 6 or 8 percent—marked a setback. According to Satō, established writers who had been in a position to demand royalties prior to the series had grown accustomed to rates of 15 or 20 percent.[152] As the stakes increased dramatically for all concerned parties, the contracts of the Meiji period were replaced by clearer delineations of rights and obligations.

Writers were not the only people to benefit from the increased income from royalties. According to one source, Shinchōsha paid 30,000 to 40,000 yen to each of the translators of the Sekai bungaku zenshū; it is believed that Toyoshima Yoshio, the translator of the first work of the series, Les Miserables, earned at least 100,000 yen for the three-volume translation. At the time the going rate for many famous writers who also did translations—such as Tanizaki Jun'ichirō, Satō Haruo, and Masamune Hakuchō—was 10 yen per page.[153] As with original works, the one-yen book collections resulted in a standard royalty rate; for translators this was 6 percent.[154] The series also raised questions about responsibilities to original authors; Havelock Ellis was infuriated to discover that Studies in the

Psychology of Sex had been translated (as *Sei no shinri*) without his permission.[155] The series also affected the qualifications sought in translators. In response to tight deadlines, translators were now often chosen based on their ability to translate rapidly, while slower translators were avoided.[156]

The one-yen books did not benefit all writers. A clear divide was created between authors who appeared in these series and thus found themselves with new economic freedom and those who had not been included. For aspiring authors the one-yen book years and the years immediately following the boom, roughly 1927–34, were extremely difficult. In his essay "Kanbatsu-toki no jumoku" (Trees in a Time of Drought) Kanō Sakujirō likened young writers at this time to trees suffering through a drought and placed specific blame on the economic downturn and the one-yen book boom.[157] This economic hardship was particularly noticeable because it followed on the heels of a relatively prosperous period for authors, what Yamamoto Yoshiaki, following Kanō, calls "the golden age of the *bundan* [literary establishment]," the period of high demand for fiction by periodicals that occurred between 1919 and 1925. This drought continued even after the end of the *Complete Works of Contemporary Japanese Literature* and many other one-yen book series in 1931. The appearance of new literary journals, such as *Bungakukai* (October 1933) and *Bungei* (November 1933), marked a resurgence of demand for new literary works and led to the literary revival (*bungei fukkō*) of the mid-1930s.[158]

The Impact of the *Complete Works* on Readers and Literature

The *Complete Works of Contemporary Japanese Literature* is often dismissed as having had little impact on its consumers, who are described as having purchased little more than a piece of furniture. It is very likely that many subscribers were attracted to the series as a symbol of education and social status; Shiobara Aki, for example, has described the central role that book-lined studies had in the "cultured home" (*bunka jūtaku*) movement.[159] In 1929 the cultural critic Ōya Sōichi wrote that sitting rooms were often furnished with "three-legged chairs and two or three one-yen anthologies."[160] The fact that Kaizōsha hired the famous designer Sugiura Hisui to design the cover—and gave him specific instructions to think of the books as interior decorations—shows that the company was well aware of this facet of their commodity.[161] The statistics presented previously suggest the magnitude of the series' market, though not necessarily its reading audience.

Thanks to the work of Ueda Yasuo and others we have anecdotal (or testimonial) evidence about the readership of the series, which shows us how much the collection affected certain individual readers who went on to be writers and critics. Ueda breaks down the readers into three types: those who bought the series themselves, those whose family members bought it, and those who borrowed it from friends. Authors such as Setouchi Harumi, Kuroi Senji, Hoshi Shin'ichi, Yoshioka Minoru, and Tamiya Torahiko and critics such as Matsuura Sōzō, Aeba Takao, and Tanemura Suehiro have all written about the central role the collection played in their early literary educations. Many of the readers who bought it (as a whole or as individual volumes) did so years later. One was the author Minakami Tsutomu, who bought the volumes "in bundles" in 1940, when they were available for 5 sen each. Many others, such as the literary scholar Kamei Hideo, discovered them decades later in relatives' collections. The Akutagawa Prize–winning author Furuyama Komao, who was born in the Korean city of Sinuiju, began to read the series in 1935 as a middle school student; his father, a physician from Japan, had bought them for his son.[162] This was a pattern repeated decades later, in the 1960s, when the protagonist of Mizumura Minae's *Shishōsetsu from Left to Right* moves to the United States. These are just a few of the writers who were profoundly affected by this and later anthologies. One publishing historian wrote, "Literary anthologies were the fundamental materials through which world and national literatures—centered on the novel—were systematically absorbed in [Japan]."[163]

Many of the series' consequences were more far-reaching and abstract than those just listed. Such anthologies played a central role in the understanding of the works as national literature. In many ways the series created and defined the very entity it purported to describe. As previously mentioned, the fact that it described a totality—a canon, with fixed boundaries—is conveyed in the use of the term *zenshū*, or "complete works." An advertisement in *Yomiuri shinbun* on 11 November 1926 declared, "A complete [kanzen na] library of contemporary literature for so little money!" As a result of its own self-inflating advertising rhetoric, the series presented itself to consumers as whole unto itself, as sufficient. By creating a "complete works"—and then providing subscribers with a bookcase built to fit the series and only the series—Kaizōsha implied to readers that what they were purchasing was not only part of a tradition, it was the tradition in its entirety.

Despite rhetorical linkages to the literary tradition that preceded it in Japan—and that borrowed that tradition's authority for itself—this new entity was more than a mere subset of that tradition; to some extent it came to be perceived as an independent system. The series was committed to the historical rupture attributed to the Meiji Restoration, as illustrated by the first volume of the series, a collection of *Meiji kaika-ki bungaku*. Concretely speaking, the *gendai* in the *Complete Works of Contemporary Japanese Literature* referred to the period since 1868. That Kaizōsha chose to title the series *gendai* (contemporary) rather than *kindai* (modern) is simply the result of shifting terminology; there is no doubt that the editors thought of the series as the product of a new Japan, a Japan that had gone through the epoch-making changes often referred to as modernization.[164] Though the term was not yet *kindai*, the concept was: a period considered so radically distinct from that which preceded it as to warrant thinking of it as fundamentally other and thus distancing its literature from the literary tradition. This series justified its existence by highlighting that rupture while simultaneously reifying it.

Linked as it was to the nation, as a national literature, the series simultaneously claimed to be the representative product of the people and their shared culture. This must have been a particularly powerful connection in 1926. The passage of the Universal Manhood Suffrage Law in 1925, the result of a nearly three-decade movement to expand suffrage by eliminating economic barriers to enfranchisement for men, had more than quadrupled the enfranchised population, from three million to thirteen million.[165] The *Complete Works* likely benefited from the new investment these ten million newly enfranchised citizens had in the nation-state (and empire) of Japan. Komori Yōichi has written that subscription to *King* magazine represented "proof of citizenship," in that it allowed consumers to participate in the first explicitly national periodical.[166] Subscription to the *Complete Works* would have represented similar participation in a representative culture of the nation. The scholar Tanizawa Eiichi has written, "Given its scale, it inevitably became a national [*kokumin-teki*] event. The important decisions made in the collection's editing naturally produced a 'common sense'—a commonly accepted standard—among the citizens of the nation [*kokumin no jōshiki*]."¹⁶⁷ The series and the cultural entity that it represented reinforced that very community.

Geographically and politically, however, "Japan" did not merely denote the nation-state in 1926. At that time Korea, Taiwan, and the southern half of Sakhalin were part of the Japanese Empire and were therefore part of Japan. As mentioned earlier, Kaizōsha sent sales agents overseas to sell the series from the beginning. Later, after the subscription period was over, the Teikoku Tosho Fukyū-kai successfully sold the remaining books at a radical discount in Seoul, Manchuria, and Taiwan. In addition mass emigration to other regions, particularly North and South America, had created large informal colonies abroad. When the *Complete Works of Contemporary Japanese Literature* was still being published the empire expanded to include much of Manchuria, over which Japan held de facto control following the Manchurian Incident of 18 September 1931. Throughout these years policies of integration were being instituted in an attempt to solidify the connection; one of the main tools of integration was language. Substantial research into reception within the colonies is necessary to determine the actual function these texts had in the imperial project.¹⁶⁸ It is conceivable, however, that the decision to include a full syllabic gloss, thus making the works comprehensible for readers with a lower level of literacy, made the collection accessible not only to a larger body of native speakers, but also to new non-native-speaking imperial subjects. To the extent that the texts and the essays by editorial staff that accompanied the texts reflected Tokyo dialect, the series may have contributed to linguistic assimilation and hierarchization within the nation as well, by reinforcing Tokyo dialect as the standard.

Finally, and perhaps most important from the perspective of literature, the series contributed to the creation and elevation of the concept of modern literature itself. Even those who chose not to purchase the series were presented with a cultural entity linked with the nation, the emperor, and ethnic pride. There is no doubt that literature gained in broad cultural prestige as a result of the series, even as Tokyo intellectuals were decrying the series for its commodification of the literary arts. According to Maruyama Masao, whose perception of this change has already been mentioned, the average parent and teacher at the end of the Taishō period thought that "a middle school student who spent all his time reading novels was doing one of two things: avoiding his studies or corrupting his morals."¹⁶⁹ After the *Complete Works of Contemporary Japanese Literature* was published, reading literature became a more respectable cultural pursuit; hence the nonreading use of the series, commonly claimed by critics, as a piece of furniture that consumers bought only as a signifier of cultivation.

Even as the general concept of literature received a boost in prestige from the series, so too did a specific way of conceiving of a modern Japanese literary tradition. A specific literary lineage, focused on Tokyo-based literary production and ignoring various alternative voices, gained a tremendous purchase in readers' minds. This lineage was then structured into primary and secondary authors, schools, and genres. The author Furui Yoshikichi has written that he read through the series well aware of the structure within which the series presented each work, and has commented on how that structure affected the way he perceived those works.[170] Despite Kimura Ki's and Yanagida Izumi's intentions to produce as broad a survey of writing as possible, the series nonetheless largely adhered to an already conventional image of modern literary development, with narrative-dominated prose literature, stemming from Tsubouchi Shōyō's *Shōsetsu shinzui*, passing through an initial moment of linguistic heterogeneity to arrive at *genbun itchi* (unification of speech and writing), and marginalizing genres that did not suit the Tokyo literary establishment of the day.

The Tokyo publishing industry was central in the dissemination of the Tokyo literary establishment's vision of modern Japanese literature. In most studies of canon formation in other national literatures the focus has been on the educational establishment as the primary mechanism. While there is no doubt that academia played an important role in canonization in Japan, anecdotes such as Maruyama's suggest that contemporary literature did not yet have a significant place in general education,[171] even though universities and higher schools—particularly Tokyo Imperial University, Waseda University, and the First Higher School—were centers of literary activity. Thus contemporary Japanese literature did not yet have a place in the consciousness of a broad segment of the population. Having been so widely distributed, the series acted to legitimate the works it contained. That is not to say there was spontaneous creation of legitimacy for previously unrecognized works; not only was Kimura Ki affected by existing discourses of literary value, but Kaizōsha legitimated the series as a whole through the invocation of various other sites of power. Yet it was Kimura who was central to the decision about what works would or would not be included; his individual aesthetic, though constrained, guided the series. Without the publishing industry to actualize those decisions, however, they would have had no impact. Although educational institutions may indeed wield a great deal of power in the definition and perpetuation of a relatively stable literary canon, the publishing industry also wields power; the agenda it constructs is informed by mandarins, but it is often realized by merchants.[172]

The Limitations of an Anthology

The one-yen books are rightfully seen as the harbingers of inexpensive book publishing through mass production, as contributors to the expansion of the reading market, and as catalysts to the modernization of the publishing industry.[173] It could also be said that the publication of the *Complete Works of Contemporary Japanese Literature* contributed to the reevaluation of contemporary culture since the Meiji period, and that it helped revive the book market after the mass destruction of the Great Kantō Earthquake. The repercussions the series had on related industries, including paper, printing, and bookmaking, are far-reaching and complex.[174] The boom initiated by the series pulled the book-publishing industry into the age of mass production, clarified laws, illustrated advertising potential, turned writing into a well-paid occupation, and made certain authors into stars. Most important, however, the boom defined and disseminated a contemporary Japanese literary canon to the nation and beyond.

No canon remains entirely stable over time; instead there is a series of individual historical moments in which cultural authority of one form or another is exercised in order to affect the dissemination, reception, and preservation of specific literary works. The effects of any such exercise are finite; many of the works contained in the *Complete Works* no longer enjoy a dominant position in literary discourse. Nonetheless the specific impact of this series was far-reaching. The works contained in the series were, through the act of its publication, invested with a specific cultural value and made available to a broad segment of the citizenry. The series determined what works many people would read and how they would read them. In so doing it influenced the direction in which literature would proceed, as those readers sometimes developed into the next generation of writers. Kaizōsha's and Kimura Ki's selections, as constrained as they were, possessed a form of power that molded opinions for decades. The example of Mizumura Minae's narrator exemplifies this reach. At the same time, though, her narrator shows the limitations of this power. As the narrator recognized, her image of Japan in the late 1960s and early 1970s was of "a Japan that existed before [her] birth." The conception of modern Japanese literature reified in the *Complete Works of Contemporary Japanese Literature* terminated in December 1931, when the series was completed and the bookcase was full. The canon it produced was static, and, from the perspective of Mizumura's narrator, literature was frozen in time. Works, including Mizumura's own, continued to be written, however, and this series was of no use to anyone who might wish to influence the reception of these subsequent works.

The *Complete Works of Contemporary Japanese Literature* produced a *static* canon. Once the Kaizōsha series had completely shipped (and was neatly stored in its finite bookcase), it no longer had the capacity to canonize future authors and profit from that transfer of cultural authority. This dilemma was partially solved by Iwanami Shoten, which created the inexpensive *bunkobon* in reaction to the one-yen book boom. By creating an open-ended series, Iwanami set in motion a mechanism for a kind of canonization that continues to operate to this day. What Iwanami Shoten did not sufficiently consider was the preservation of its own cultural capital. By producing so many titles the authority the series initially possessed was diluted over time, to the point that today *bunkobon* have limited authority. Nor did the series adorn its contents with any specific aura. The Kaizōsha series labeled its contents "Contemporary Japanese Literature," thus associating the individual works with an imaginary entity that benefited from consumers' desire to be modern, their identification with the nation, and their aspirations for elevated cultural status. One mechanism of cultural authority that was dynamic but that also bestowed an aura appeared in 1935, when Kikuchi Kan created the Akutagawa Prize.

Both mechanisms allowed the Tokyo literary establishment, acting in concert with the Tokyo-based publishing industry, to have a significant impact on the nature and direction of this new cultural totality, modern Japanese literature. This should not be interpreted, however, as suggesting that the Tokyo literary establishment was monolithic and that its members possessed a homogeneous view of literary value. Quite to the contrary, even among the writers and critics now seen as making up the core of that establishment there existed a wide diversity of opinions about literary value. The discursive field of Kimura Ki and Yanagida Izumi was one of contention, not consensus. While chapter 5, dealing with the Akutagawa Prize, will show how this heterogeneity of opinions affected the function of material mechanisms of cultural authority, we must first turn to the discursive field of the Tokyo literary establishment and to the various conceptions of value that dominated it.

4

Defining and Defending Literary Value

DEBATES, 1919–1935

In general, a number of historic debates . . . would find themselves
clarified, or more simply annulled, if one could bring to light, in
each case, the complete world of distinct and often contrasting sig-
nifications which all the relevant concepts . . . are given in social
struggles within the entire field (where they function, originally, as
terms of denunciation or insults . . .) or within a subfield of those
who claim them as emblems. . . . Nor should we forget that the
meanings of these words, eternalized in theoretical discussions by
dehistoricizing them . . . constantly change in the course of time.

PIERRE BOURDIEU, *THE RULES OF ART: GENESIS AND STRUCTURE*
OF THE LITERARY FIELD

The success of the *Complete Works of Contemporary Japanese Literature*
meant that works of fiction that many Tokyo-based authors and critics had
long imagined as forming a national literature now were shared, to an
unprecedented degree, by a significant portion of the nation and the empire; this was largely thanks to the developments in the industry described
earlier. The market's embrace of this commodified concept of modern
Japanese literature created a paradox: the works were now *popular* in a
quantitatively undeniable way. For many of these central authors and critics, this was yet another incursion of commercialism into their cultural
production, an incursion that threatened to replace artistic demands with
the demands of the market. Precisely because the market had found a space

for modern literary production, authors and critics found it essential to assert the existence of an alternate economy of value, one that could not be conflated with a text's commercial viability.

As mentioned previously, although the *Complete Works of Contemporary Japanese Literature* represented one of the first material manifestations of the cultural totality known as modern Japanese literature, it did not create this totality out of nothing. For established writers and critics in Tokyo the concepts of modern Japanese literature and an alternate economy of value that informed it likely preceded the *Complete Works* by at least three decades. Kimura Ki and Yanagida Izumi made their decisions about which authors and works would be included as participants in this existing discourse, which was not conducted solely within the academy. One of its primary sites was the literary magazine, most of which were based in Tokyo; in the pages of those magazines the discourse often took the form of debates (*ronsō*).

In order to understand how publishing worked as a mechanism of cultural authority it is essential to understand this discursive sphere, from which many of the conceptions of literary value emerged. Though the debates within the pages of these literary magazines reached only a small group of people, primarily literati in the Tokyo area, those individuals possessed a disproportionate amount of influence on the course of literary production. The opinions formed in these contentious dialogues had a far greater indirect than direct effect on the perception of literature by helping to mold the thinking of the writers, critics, and publishers who produced literary works. It should not be presumed, however, that this literary establishment enjoyed a clear consensus about the nature of literary value. The debates examined in this chapter, despite representing only a small fraction of that discursive field, clearly reveal this. Differences of opinion about the nature of literary value existed even among the most central writers and critics. These differences were often aired in print, as individuals not only defended their own positions but also worked to influence the positions of their peers.

Certain mechanisms of cultural authority were exercised within these literary debates. Though these mechanisms were discursive rather than material they share an important connection with the mechanisms that are the primary object of this study: they were sites of contestation themselves, in which individuals struggled to define the nature of literary value and, in so doing, influence future literary production. This chapter examines a variety of debates, some preceding the *Complete Works*, some contemporaneous with that series, and some in the years following the series and coinciding with the creation of the Akutagawa Prize for literature. The first group of critical writings, focusing on the early musings of Kikuchi Kan, not only illuminates the thinking of this pivotal figure, but also reveals that concerns over literary value preceded Kaizōsha's series. The second group of critical writings comprise what is now known as the "I-novel debate." These essays show us that figures at the center of literary production had significant misgivings about the value of the putative genre, which is often described as being more or less interchangeable with the category of "pure literature" during the modern period in Japan. The third group of critical writings come from two debates: one over a proposed new genre, "pure fiction," that reveals the ambiguity many felt about a solidifying divide between "pure" and "popular" literature, and another that attempts to reinforce the distinction by divorcing it from the qualities of the literary work altogether.[1] Taken together the debates reveal questions about the nature of literary value, the elusive factor that determined whether fiction was art or entertainment, which plagued Tokyo literati during the interwar period.[2]

Through these debates one gains a sense not only of the absence of consensus even at the center about the nature of literary value, but also of the rhetorical mechanisms that individuals employed to strengthen their claims and disparage those of their adversaries. The key rhetorical mechanism of this sort was the term *tsūzoku* (vulgar, mundane), which was always situated in an implied binarism made up of things that were pure, artistic, and worthy and those that were compromised, interested, and not worthy.[3] This binarism is clearly linked to the classical binary of *ga* (elegant) and *zoku* (inelegant).[4] Even in the last decades of the nineteenth century one sees the *ga-zoku* binarism used in this formulation; Shōyō's *Shōsetsu shinzui* is one example. Both the *jun-tsūzoku* binary and the *ga-zoku* binary, in their inherent ambiguity, possess tremendous flexibility. Komori Yōichi has discussed how Shōyō utilized the *ga-zoku* binary to represent various other binaries: the present versus the past, contemporary novels versus historical tales, the language of Kamigata versus the language of Edo, *waka* versus prose, and the upper classes versus the lower, to name a few.[5] In all cases Shōyō uses the seemingly spontaneous hierarchy of *ga* over *zoku* to impute a natural order and therefore obviate the need for argument, let alone a questioning of the binary structure itself. The same is true of the term *tsūzoku*, which appears again and again in the debates. As Suzuki Sadami has written:

> From the early Meiji 20s [1885–90], when "political novels" were criticized in accordance with Tsubouchi Shōyō's theories, groups of writers and critics have disparaged other groups of writers using the word *tsūzoku-teki*. At the height of Naturalism's power, the Ken'yūsha's art-for-art's sake philosophy was dismissed as *tsūzoku-teki*. Even as the meaning of *tsūzoku* changed over time, the custom of contempt toward it persisted.[6]

It is unlikely that the historicization of the term *tsūzoku* will annul the debates that took place, as Bourdieu suggests in the epigraph to this chapter; the clarification of its history, however, does illuminate its function as part of a struggle within the field.

It was the fear of the marketplace that allowed for these rhetorical tools, such as the term *tsūzoku*, which could be used to valorize certain characteristics while demonizing others. As it appears in the following debates, the division the term *tsūzoku* pointed to is often one between literary value that stems directly from commercial value and literary value that claims autonomy from the market. Because the works celebrated as the highest literary achievements were becoming (profitable) commodities as a result of a vastly expanded publishing industry and marketplace for texts, many felt that the market itself threatened to become the final arbiter of literary value.[7] This resulted in a fear of aesthetic debasement, the symptom of which was persistent questioning of the foundation of literary value, if not the market. The question that comes up again and again, however, is this: What should the basis of that value be, if not the market (which is often presumed to be a crystallization of base human desire)? Different individuals propose different answers, but little consensus is ever achieved about the basis of the distinction. Rather than doubting the usefulness of the binary in a capitalist economy, however, the distinction is rarely doubted and is regularly invoked, always to support the agenda of the invoker.

Authority, Objectivity, and Art: Kikuchi Kan's Early Criticism

Early writings by Kikuchi Kan, the publisher and writer who went on to a central role of power in the literary establishment, reveal his ambivalence toward the role of critics as arbiters of value and suggest a widely held desire to identify an objective standard that would justify their authority. Less than a year after his story "Mumei sakka no nikki" (Diary of an Unknown Author) attracted the attention of the literary establishment, Kikuchi had already begun to express his frustration with the activities of literary critics.[8] Such frustrations are evident in an article he published titled "Hihyō-ka no kengen" (The Authority of Critics).[9] He begins with a series of questions:

> What exactly *does* a critic do? Is it simply judge works without trepidation, as many are wont to do today? Is it to pass value judgments fearlessly on all works, assuming the pose of one with the judgment of a god? Where do critics get this sort of authority from? What is the yardstick [*monosashi*] by which they arrogantly judge all these works? Do they simply trust in the universality and absolute accuracy of their personal yardstick?[10]

He then raises a number of problems with the state of contemporary Japanese criticism. First, in the absence of an objective standard, critics are forced to rely on three areas of ability: their cultural education (*kyōyō*), their life experience, and their ability to appreciate (*mikairyoku*) art; yet it is the rare case when a critic has all three abilities in sufficient quantity. Second, the critic becomes the judge, jury, and executioner for works that are often produced by an artist more complex than the critic—and thus beyond his proper comprehension—and leaves the author without any right of appeal. Third, critics possess disproportionate influence over readers and are too eager to pass judgment on an author on the basis of a single work. For Kikuchi these weaknesses undermine the authority of literary critics to make simple judgments of value. That does not mean that Kikuchi does not see legitimate activities for the critic. Critics can use works to talk about issues in society; they can explain the author's craftsmanship; they can even catalogue an author's artistic tendencies. In the end, however, they avoid the question of what the basis for objective evaluation might be.

Gentlemanly criticism, Kikuchi concludes, is that which finds the beauty in a work of art rather than claiming to measure a work's beauty objectively.

In *Shinchō* in July 1919 Kikuchi continued venting his frustration by attacking what he called "impressionistic criticism" (*inshō hihyō*).[11] His essay "Inshō hihyō no hei" (The Vices of Impressionist Criticism) begins with a question: "Recent criticism—particularly literary criticism—has no authority [*ken'i*] and has become simply reading material [*yomimono*] for literary magazines and newspaper literature columns, rewarded with sneers from authors and having nothing to teach the *bundan* in general. Why is that?" Impressionist critics, by Kikuchi's definition, were those who justified their subjective evaluations through recourse to Saintsbury's dictum "The primary requirements of a critic are that he has the capacity to appreciate a work and that he can express that appreciation."[12] This, in Kikuchi's opinion, causes the critic to indulge himself in a shallow egocentrism, in which he tries to find himself in an author's work.[13] Have critics, Kikuchi asks, reflected on the nature of this "self" that is the basis of their criticism? While it is acceptable for someone as great as Saintsbury to engage in such egocentric criticism, Kikuchi declares, it is unacceptable for "uncultured rabble [*uzōmuzō*], lacking any appreciation for art, to say 'Using this work as a pretext, I shall speak about myself.'"[14] Though subjective criticism could be a valuable tool in the right hands, in the wrong hands it is disastrous.

For Kikuchi the solution is a more objective criticism, which can resort to reason as its standard, though he recognizes that such a standard might not actually be out there to be found.

> If critics are to contribute to literature and to life—as Matthew Arnold would have them do—then lukewarm appreciation and unidealistic, standard-less impressionist criticism must be abandoned. A new standard must be sought for literary criticism, new value and significance must be discovered from contemporary literature, and development in that direction must be spurred. In the March issue of *Shinchō* I described the vice of critics arbitrarily judging the work of others without possessing a fair and accurate yardstick. What I want now is the creation of a new measure with which everyone can agree. As an author, it is unacceptable to me to have the value of a work vacillate due to groundless, rambling impressions. Those who are satisfied with impressionist criticism are dilettantes, with no demands or ideals for literature or their own lives.[15]

Here, in this early essay, is the intellectual background for the material steps Kikuchi later took when he established the Akutagawa Prize for literature. Criticism had a valuable role to play in the social functioning and development of literature—in the definition and defense of literary value—but it needed an objective standard that would not be subject to the vicissitudes of subjectivity. In his call that such a standard must be "created" rather than merely "recognized" Kikuchi seems unsure that such a standard exists; such a standard, he implies, would earn its legitimacy through calls to reason and general consensus.

In contrast to Kikuchi's apparent elitism regarding critical activity, his attitude toward creative activity was much more populist. The following year he wrote "Geijutsu to tenbun—Sakka bon'yō-shugi" (Art and Natural Ability: Theory of Ordinary Authors), which appeared in *Bunshō sekai* in March 1920 and which raised issues that would reappear throughout *bundan* debates of the period.[16] In his typical rhetorical style he begins the essay by posing a question: "It is often said that to be involved with art—in this case, literature—you must possess a certain special gift [*tenbun*]. Without such a gift—disposition, sensibility, sentiment—one cannot be involved with art. . . . But is that so? Is literature a vocation best left to the select few?" Are only the select few allowed the joy of creating art (*sōsaku*)? Needless to say, Kikuchi believes that the answer is no, that the pleasure of writing should be available to everyone. Nor should critics block access to works that are the products of common minds:

> The time of lionizing the works of witty and brilliant geniuses as if they were rare gems has passed. The literary aristocracy of a minority of geniuses dominating the rights of creation is a thing of the past. This is an age in which the free expression of geniuses' imaginations share the floor with the expressions of average people's imaginations—imaginations they share with the vast majority.

In Kikuchi's opinion, "The period when strange sensibilities, offbeat emotions, and varied lifestyles are prized as the subject matter of works has passed."[17]

Despite this apparent democratization of literary value, a clear binary between men of common capacity and men of genius forms the basis of the argument. Kikuchi always had doubts about whether or not he possessed innate ability and thus into which category he fell. This was a concern that many of his contemporaries shared. Kawabata Yasunari, for example, wrote in his diaries on more than one occasion between 1915 and 1917 about his concern that he was not a genius. As Yamamoto Yoshiaki has shown, these concerns were reactions to reading *The Man of Genius* (*Tensai-ron*, trans. 1914) by Cesare Lombroso (1835–1909). This book was influential for many writers in the literary establishment, including Akutagawa Ryūnosuke, Arishima Takeo, and Satomi Ton.[18] It proved a pseudo-scientific explanation for a belief in the divide between writers who possess genius and those who do not, and by extension a divide between an elevated literary sphere and mere fiction. Kikuchi's essay also shows one of the strategies that developed in response to that binary structure: inversion. By describing their sensibilities as merely unusual, Kikuchi tries—counterintuitively—to valorize the works of common men. While clearly an attempt to resist the hierarchy imposed by the binarism, he remains unable to break free of the fundamental concept of a clearly demarcated polarity.

At one level these three essays suggest the insecurity of a young author who is reckoning with powerful forces as he attempts to establish himself. It clearly depicts the power of critics, at whose influence Kikuchi bridles and under whose scrutiny he labors. At another level these essays, written in the years preceding Kaizōsha's *Complete Works*, reveal both a concern with the nature of literary value and a certain way of thinking about that value. The simultaneous desire for an objective standard and the conviction that one has not yet been found intermingle with a firm belief that literary talent is something either possessed or not possessed. The romantic notion of the genius both solidified and mystified the nature of literary value, obscuring specific characteristics that might comprise it behind an ambiguous belief in an unbreachable divide.

Social Relevance and Literary Value: The Debate over Form and Content

Two years later Kikuchi entered into a famous debate about the nature of literary value. In July 1922 he published an essay in *Shinchō* titled "Bungei sakuhin no naiyō-teki kachi" (The Content Value of Literary Works).[19] The essay was written partially in response to Satomi Ton's essay "Bungei kanken" (Literary Blinders) and was partially a continuation of his own "Sakka bon'yō-shugi." In "Bungei sakuhin no naiyō-teki kachi" Kikuchi asks why he is sometimes moved by work that he considers artistically inferior and sometimes not moved by work that he considers artistically superior: "Sometimes I read a work I think is very skillfully written [umai], but am not touched by it. Other times I read a work I think is very poorly written [mazui], but am touched by it. . . . How can this be explained?"[20] He poses two possible answers to this question: either the work has a "precious sense of reality [tattoi jikkan ga kaite aru]" or it describes an experience not easily had. Whatever the reason, he writes, the latter work possesses some value that the former work does not.

Kikuchi concedes that any question of value in works of art leads to the question of the nature of art itself. He believes in the position put forward by Benedetto Croce and J. E. Spingarn, that art is expression (geijutsu wa hyōgen nari).[21] But he argues that content has an ability to touch people that is divorced from the artistic quality of its form. He cites the material for Akutagawa's "Mikan" (The Tangerines), which touched him even before it had taken its final artistic form, when the author told him about it.[22] He also cites the example of his own Onshū no kanata ni (The Realm Beyond), the material for which touched him when he originally read it in an artistically void travel pamphlet. Kikuchi explains this fact by writing, "Of the various materials used in literary works, many were brilliantly sparkling gems of humanity before the author touched them with the magic wand of their artistic form."[23] Artistic form in fact does not increase this value, which he calls content value. However, he cautions, the term "content value" is chosen simply out of expedience and could be called real-life value; it could also be further subdivided into moral and intellectual values. Most important, this value is essential in literary works.

Just asking art to provide deep impressions (kanmei) is not enough. He asks, "Is art, simply for the sake of art, really that important in a person's life?"[24] Pure art forms, such as sculpture, have limited ways in which they can connect with life. Literature, however, since it can deal directly with life, has an infinite capacity to connect with it. Artistic expressions make life better, but only slightly; they are the smell of food to the starving man. It is the content (or real-life) value that is truly important to human life. Kikuchi concludes with the statement for which he is best known: "Life first, art second."[25]

Satomi Ton responded to these assertions in his essay "Kikuchi Kan-shi no 'Bungei sakuhin no naiyō-teki kachi' o bakusu" (Refuting Kikuchi Kan's "Content Value of Literary Works"), published in Kaizō in August 1922.[26]

His primary concern in the essay is what he sees as an artificial dualism of form and content in the discussion of literary works. For Satomi the two are indivisible. Regarding the two examples that Kikuchi offered, he writes:

> What if the material for the stories "Mikan" and *Onshū no kanata ni* were entirely the fictional creation of the authors? What would Kikuchi then have the authors "touch" with "the magic wand of their artistic form"? Imagine the riot as the number of authors soared, with everyone running around picking up these "gems of humanity" until they were exhausted.[27]

Satomi argues that Kikuchi has underestimated the contribution of the writer in the creation of the content and the value Kikuchi perceives in that content.

In his essay Kikuchi had written, "I believe there exists in the work value other than artistic value." This additional value, the measure of a work's power to move the reader, he provisionally named "content value." Satomi rephrases Kikuchi's assertion thus: "I believe there exists in the work a value of materials and models apart from [the author's] literary labor."[28] If this is the case, Satomi suggests, that value should be called "extrinsic value" rather than "content value." In rephrasing Kikuchi's primary statement in this way, however, Satomi exposes the complex discourse from which Kikuchi had seized the terms "value" and "labor." Whether consciously or not, Kikuchi had linked his ruminations on literary value to contemporary debates over the value of labor and the exploitation of that labor to create surplus value. Satomi's rephrasing of Kikuchi's comment more clearly situates the novel as a commodity produced by the labor of the author. As such, the price of the commodity is determined by the value of the raw materials combined with the value of the labor invested in that commodity's creation. Even as he attempts to dismantle Kikuchi's distinction between form and content, Satomi exposes the influence on Kikuchi's argument of a larger discourse on how one should properly value (and compensate) labor.

Kikuchi, on the other hand, was not concerned as much with a distinction between content and form as with affect, particularly an emotional reaction of concern over social injustice. Reading *Shisen o koete* by Kagawa Toyohiko, Kikuchi had been moved. It was clear from sales figures—the book was a groundbreaking bestseller—that others had found something moving in it as well. Yet Kikuchi felt that the work did not possess a level of artistry worthy of his reaction. It is this conundrum that led him to write the original essay and pose the original question: What affected him about the work? For Kikuchi the story marked a new type of representation. In it a Christian intellectual youth goes into the slums of Kobe and tries to improve the lives of the people he finds there. What was new about the story was that the novel was written after the author had actually entered the slum, lived among the destitute, and had direct interaction with the members of that underclass. Kikuchi was not alone in being moved by the work; in addition to general readers, the novel captured the attention of Christian and Marxist reformers who wanted to improve working people's living conditions. What Kikuchi perceived in the response to this work was that readers had been moved by a valuable emotion: rather than nostalgia or sentimentalism, they were moved by what Kikuchi believed to be a legitimate idealism and compassion.[29]

Satomi, however, does not accept (what he believes to be) Kikuchi's basic assertion, that the value art has in relation to life stems from its portrayal of magnificent thoughts, feelings, or acts. Satomi believes that Kikuchi credits form when in fact he should credit subject matter. The problem with this position, according to Satomi, is that Kikuchi cannot get beyond seeing art as an elegant pastime (*fūryū inji*).[30] This suggests that Satomi adheres to a broader definition of art that presumably contains a role for art in society or life, though he is not specific (at least here) about what that definition might be. He believes that when Kikuchi claims "Literature is important to the administration of the state,"[31] his description of its value suggests that it has nothing to offer that scholars, religious figures, politicians, entrepreneurs, and workers are not already providing. Satomi defends the value of deep artistic impressions (*kanmei*), saying that such impressions are what an encounter with literature should result in, rather than evaluation (*hyōka*). For him there is no division between form and content, and thus one cannot be touched by a work that is not good. He concludes by asserting that a true appreciation of art recognizes the contributions of the artist as essential to the impact of the work.

What kept Kikuchi from holding a similar position from the beginning, presumably, was the fact that he knew he would face disparagement from the literary establishment if he simply claimed that *Shisen o koete* was great art. He was trying to explain the fact that he was moved by a work that was not recognized as art by powerful literary authorities. He was advocating to that literary establishment an expansion of its criteria (which he likely imagined were held in consensus)—or perhaps a complete reconsideration of them—to include the idealism and compassion elicited by a work's subject matter and its treatment. His exploration into possible alternative sources of value in literary production was perceived by Satomi to be a devaluation of artistic expression and a belittling of the existing role of art in society.

When Kikuchi responded to Satomi with his essay "Sairon 'Bungei sakuhin no naiyō-teki kachi'" ("'The Content Value of Literary Works' Revised") in *Shinchō* in September 1922, however, he backed away from a vision that incorporated this "extrinsic value" into the criteria for the evaluation of a work of art. He begins by stating that he was not arguing a theory of "form and content" and that perhaps he should have used the term "practical value" (*kōri-teki kachi*) or Satomi's "extrinsic value." What he was referring to had no relation at all to the content or form of literature. He stresses that works need not have content value or moral value to be magnificent art. Art is form: if the form is excellent, then the art is excellent. For Kikuchi, however, it is not enough for a work to simply be magnificent art. He concedes that art does serve humanity through its ability to lift one's heart (Aristotle's catharsis) and improve one's life, providing a "rapturous intoxication [*kōkotsu-taru tōsui*]." Many, however, live full lives without music, for example. Wouldn't it be an overstatement to claim that mankind is better or our hearts are purer because of that intoxication?

Kikuchi wants art to deal with the material that has the most meaning for people's lives. He cannot be satisfied with Strindberg, no matter how perfectly he expresses what he sees when he looks at a spider web, how it makes him feel, and how it moves him. But when Strindberg writes about his daughter's character or circumstances, it has more value for readers. Writing about spiders and about daughters can be of equal artistic value (in fact, writing about spiders can be of greater artistic value), but the former will have little content or real-life value. He then extends this criticism to the classics, such as the works of Chikamatsu and Shakespeare, which he feels have become too detached from our contemporary experience.[32] Satomi was right, Kikuchi says, to call this extrinsic value. It is not a measure of artistic value, but a measure of the value of art to society and mankind.

More important than Kikuchi's and Satomi's contorted debate over the divisibility of form and content is Kikuchi's attempt to include social relevance among the criteria used to judge literary value. Though Kikuchi was not a member of the proletarian literature movement (which was posing the largest threat to the centrality of the existing literary establishment) and in fact was often singled out by that movement as an example of the result of a corrupting bourgeois influence on literature, he nonetheless had what the proletarians would often dismiss as "liberal" tendencies: a growing (though politically amorphous) concern for social inequalities. While he may not have been as politically committed as the proletarian movement would have wished him to be, he was nonetheless influenced by the broad reevaluation of social injustice that fueled both the proletarian movement and the Taishō democracy movement. This debate, as well as his earlier essays, show how questions over literary value plagued this young author in the years preceding the *Complete Works of Contemporary Japanese Literature*.

Solidifying Binarisms: The I-Novel Debate

Kikuchi Kan was not alone is his desire to identify the basis of literary value; the same theme can be recognized in many debates, including one of the most important of the time, what later came to be called the "I-novel debate," which coincided with the launching of the *Complete Works of Contemporary Japanese Literature*. At its most basic, the debate centered on the relative merits of novels that portray a broad tableau, exploring multiple characters' ideas and emotions, and those that keep a tighter focus, fixing on a single interiority, usually more or less related to that of the historical author. The latter works were grouped together using a term that emerged in the course of this very debate: the I-novel (*shishōsetsu*). At another level, however, the debate was over the nature of literary value, over what literary works should be. The different opinions expressed by authors and critics expose the significant contestation occurring at the heart of literary production in Tokyo.

Nakamura Murao's essay "Honkaku shōsetsu to shinkyō shōsetsu to" (The Authentic Novel and the Mental State Novel), often examined for its contribution to the formation of the I-novel genre, appeared in January 1924 in *Shinshōsetsu* and launched the debate.[33] Ironically this essay did not support the genre; instead its main focus was the current state of the Japanese literary world, which Nakamura saw as dominated by the mental state novel (*shinkyō shōsetsu*; here not used to differentiate from the term *shishōsetsu*, which did not yet exist) at the expense of alternative literary forms.[34] Nakamura expresses his concern over the fact that the mental state novel is becoming such a powerful force in the literary world. Influential authors such as Satō Haruo, Kasai Zenzō, and Nagai Kafū were all producing works in this vein.[35] Nakamura feared that mental state novels had replaced the previous dominant form, naturalism.

> In each period, there will invariably be various changes both in how authors see and feel things, and in how they express those thoughts and feelings. As long as it is impossible to establish a fixed standard of value, one cannot say which method is good, which is bad, or to which one should adhere. Think of trends in summer hats: last year, when wide brims were in fashion, wide brims were considered good. This summer, with narrow brims having come into fashion, now narrow brims are considered good. Perhaps it is like that. Watching people's and trends' ups and downs in the literary establishment, I feel that something is wrong. In summer hat fashions, wide brims are good until narrow ones are. The same is true in the literary establishment, where the change is always dizzying; when trends pass, they usually do so without leaving much of a trace.[36]

Rather than presuming the objective value of forms currently being celebrated by the literary establishment, Nakamura echoes Kikuchi's concerns over how to address the apparent absence of a fixed standard of value.

For Nakamura, rather than representing consensus, broad support within the literary establishment for one conception of literature represents a mere trend or fad (*hayari*). These trends do not result from the recognition of objective value, but instead are propelled by herd psychology (*gunshū shinri*).[37] With parasol fashions, for example, one scorns a person breaking with the current trend or following a now past trend even when one is unable to defend logically that scorn. What those breaking with trends are doing just feels wrong intuitively. Nakamura accepts that there is no philosophical basis or aesthetic standard for trends in parasols and hats. Could the same be true, he wonders, for literary trends?

Can it be all right to follow blindly, simply controlled by herd psychology? Reflecting on the remnants of the various trends and -isms that have risen and fallen in the Japanese literary world recently, could anyone not be as uneasy as I am? When the epicureans [kyōraku-ha] are in ascendance, everyone shouts, "Long live epicureanism!" When humanism is in ascendance, everyone shouts out for humanism. It is the same for kobanashi bungaku [short anecdotes; reference unclear] and mental state novels. Accurate criticism must be lacking. The fact that a certain belief or tendency is popular is necessarily significant. It is the spirit of the times. What is warping the development of literature, however, is the idea that, as with trends in summer hats and parasols, authority simply reflects transient fads and that this makes it impossible to put a work in its proper place through proper criticism.[38]

For Nakamura, despite the fact that much current criticism is simply the result of herd mentalities supporting baseless fads, behind the trends remains an unwavering absolute yardstick against which proper criticism (seitō na hihan) can accurately measure works. With this objective measurement made, upstart works can be put in their proper place. Without it, the proper development of literature will be warped.

Nakamura disagrees with what he calls "so-called progressive thinkers" who believe that the nature of the novel cannot be clearly defined. In order to bring a novel into existence the writer must make certain promises and accept a certain form. If he or she does that, then proper criticism can place the work in a certain category, saying, "This is a true novel," "This has the characteristics of a novel," or "This is not a novel." Since that form is discernible, proper criticism can also determine the quality of a given manifestation of that form. Proper form can determine superior types of novels from inferior types. Ironically, for those who see this debate as pivotal in the establishment of the I-novel as the central genre in modern Japanese literature, Nakamura argues that the mental state novel is a fad whose day will pass. He contends that what he refers to as the "authentic novel" (honkaku shōsetsu) is, objectively, the superior form. There are reasons, he explains, why people do not realize this and continue to invest their creativity in lesser forms of the novel: people want the wrong things from literature and lack proper criticism to make them aware of this fact. Not only is this the case for the general reader, but it is also true of the critics in the literary establishment. Impressionist critics are rampant, and there are no critics who will set aside their own likes and dislikes and judge works (*kanshō hihan*) "from the true path of literature"—that of the authentic novel.[39] At present, as authentic novels are scorned as *tsūzoku* novels, works are not in their correct position in an aesthetic hierarchy.[40] Nakamura fears that no one judges works objectively; everyone simply follows the trend and shouts, "Long live the mental state novel!"

For Nakamura there is an objectively superior form for the novel, which is apparent to any trained critic who can set aside his or her own subjectivity long enough to see it. In fact he argues that some of the novels considered *tsūzoku* novels are such objectively superior types. There is also a social role for critics who can suspend their subjectivity in this way: they can illuminate readers, who otherwise would simply be carried along on the tide of trends. Nakamura concedes that works produced by these trends do have some value to literature: they make literature more complex and add to its development. The danger in these trends is that critics who should know better get so caught up in the trends themselves that they cannot judge accurately. Literature is developing, he asserts, and there is a proper way for it to develop. Without a recognized objective scale, inferior works might be valued more highly than superior works, leading to the production of more works of an inferior type. This would cause literature's development to warp away from its proper course. It is the proper critic's responsibility to act objectively and prevent this from happening. The creation of a novel is a contractual agreement that requires the work to take a certain form. Proper (objective and insightful) criticism can (and must) discern the degree to which that contract is fulfilled.

Nakamura calls for a group of objective critics to disregard their subjective reactions to literature (which cannot be trusted) and recognize the fixed standard of value that is there for them to find. Once this is done, the development of the novel can be readjusted so that it returns to the most direct path to perfection. In many ways Nakamura's concerns fall in line with those expressed by Kikuchi in his early writings, particularly the concern that subjective criticism was causing long-term harm to the development of Japanese literature. The solution he proposes is similar as well. In order to condemn subjective criticism, one must believe that nonsubjective criticism is possible; for such objective criticism to be possible, an objective standard must exist. When critics can step out of their subjectivity and discern this objective standard, proper criticism can take place that will valorize works with transcendental value rather than simply reinforcing temporary trends.

Ikuta Chōkō's "Nichijō seikatsu o henchō suru akukeikō" (The Negative Tendency to Prioritize Daily Life) continued the attack on mental state novels six months later, in July 1924, in *Shinchō*.[41] His primary concern with the form is that it willfully ignores true greatness in its obsession with the common. Great men, Ikuta writes, have banal sides to their personalities. Uncommon inventors are common men when they are not inventing; uncommon soldiers are common men when they are not fighting. That simply makes them human; it does not detract from their greatness. Writers in the literary establishment today, he laments, are unsatisfied with just humanizing these uncommon men and insist on making them utterly banal. They do this by describing the inventor when he is not inventing, the soldier when he is not fighting. They express only the common sides of these people by focusing on their everyday lives. This is particularly true when the subject becomes the writers themselves. As Ikuta put it sharply, "I need not point out how common uncommon writers can be when they are not writing."[42]

Ikuta saw this process as part of a global social phenomenon: democratization. He believed that democratization was an often misguided attempt to raise a large social group that had been kept down. Rather than raising them to the heights achieved by the minority, it would obliterate whatever gains the minority had achieved and eliminate that group's ability to help the majority, which cannot help itself.

> Today, when the remnants of the nobility that attempted to pull everyone up to the heights it occupied are gone, and the democracy that attempts to pull everyone down to the same base level is reaching every corner of the world, the fact that the great majority of the literary establishment is contending for foolish honors and merits, as if they were smashing idols, does not seem that strange after all.[43]

The elitism here is similar in some ways to that expressed by Nakamura in discussing the critic-reader relationship. Frustrated over their low circumstances and running amok in their newfound power, the majority (including members of the literary establishment) smash the delicate achievements of their predecessors and betters without realizing that those accomplishments are beyond their ability. A clear line is drawn between the tastes of the masses, which are seen as necessarily inferior, and the political empowerment of the masses through democratization.

If a man is a great writer, according to Ikuta, it will naturally be in his writing that his greatness will be most clearly evident. If his true nature is shown more clearly outside his work, then perhaps he is more a great man than a great writer. While an author may become a bit different, a bit more polished, and a bit more affected in his work than he is in real life, he more than makes up for that by approaching an ideal humanity in his nobility, profundity, subtlety, and purity. Nietzsche, Ikuta suggests, is a good example: from his letters it is clear that he was an average man in his daily life; it is in *Thus Spake Zarathustra* that he becomes most himself. In a sense Nietzsche begins to live Zarathustra's life, to become the great Zarathustra himself:

> If normal, common, banal people gather fragmentary writings of geniuses like Goethe and Nietzsche that solely express their daily lives, discover some similarity to their lives in the lives of these men who are so utterly dissimilar to them, and as a result feel a so-called "intimacy" with that genius, they are free to do so. If they then, however, imagine that that similarity is the essence of the genius's daily life or, even worse, that that aspect of their lives defines the absolute truth about that genius, they are completely mistaken and are forgetting their place. It is a debasement of those geniuses.[44]

It is perfectly acceptable for the average man to find commonalities with an uncommon man, but he would be profoundly mistaken to then conclude from those commonalities that they were equals.

How does one judge such a great man, according to Ikuta? There are those geniuses, like Byron, whose genius is obvious to all; but there are also those geniuses, like Emerson and Shakespeare, who appear no different from an ordinary man and whose uncommonness is apparent only to another uncommon man's eye. Ikuta explains that Shakespeare's true worth is made known through his works, not through his sketchy biography.[45] The sharper the insight brought to Shakespeare's works—the more uncommon the appraising eye—the more sharply Shakespeare, and his value, will be perceived. That is to say, if you don't recognize the genius, it is simply because you yourself do not possess genius. Ikuta does not comment on the logical implication of this claim, that the perceptible magnitude of this sort of genius (and thus the value of the artist and his or her works) would then be limited to the genius of the greatest observer. It is also unclear whether or not that observer would be able to communicate that genius to anyone else. Thus such a writer could possess only as much (or as little) communicable or effective genius as any given observer. Ikuta does not dismiss this group of geniuses—those whose genius is not immediately apparent to all observers—so it is safe to presume that he does believe that there exist critics (such as himself) who can fully discern that genius and convey it to others. His argument, which distinguishes between genius and mediocrity, seems to demand that criticism—the disciplining of reading practices—be ceded to a ruling critical class, despite the implications contained in his logic of evaluation.

At the same time as he makes this argument about great men, Ikuta also criticizes mental state novels at a simpler level, suggesting that the form itself functions as a shield for creative deficiency. Authors, he argues, think of mental state novels, which are actually not so easy to write, as something they can write with little difficulty; they also know that it is a relatively well-compensated form in the literary establishment. By contrast authentic novels are more challenging, providing none of the excuses to authors that the mental state novel provides. For example, authors of mental state novels can respond to criticism by saying, "That's how it happened, so there's nothing I can do." Authors of authentic novels have no such recourse and thus can be criticized in a variety of ways, including on the grounds of artificiality. This is why it doesn't pay to write authentic novels in the literary establishment: mental state novels are easy, readily defendable, and lucrative. In this way Ikuta explicitly recognizes the role of extraliterary concerns, particularly the marketplace, in the creation of art and inverts a hierarchy that typically elevates the I-novel, as the representative form of pure literature, through contrast to the *tsūzoku*.

Following in early 1925 was Kume Masao's famous essay "Shishōsetsu to shinkyō shōsetsu" (The I-Novel and the Mental State Novel), which appeared in two parts in the Bungei Shunjūsha publication, *Bungei kōza*.[46] Kume begins by defining the mental state novel: "A mental state novel is a novel in which the author, in describing an object, tries to express his 'feelings' [*kokoromochi*]—more complexly put, his impressions reflecting his view of life [*jinseikan-teki kansō*]—from a given time, rather than trying to reproduce a reality (though it is fine if he does this as well)."[47] He then moves on to a discussion of the I-novel, a form he believes is related (but not identical) to the mental state novel, which he argues is the foundation (*konpon*), the true path (*hondō*), and the essence (*shinzui*) of the art of prose. He bases this conclusion on his experience as an author, explaining that writing I-novels provides him with the most spiritual peace (*anshin ritsumei*), and as a reader, pointing out that he believes he can trust and read I-novels more directly—once he has ascertained that they are true— than other works.

For such a novel to be art and not autobiography or confession, its form (*hyōgen*) must be artistic. Kume gives concrete examples of works that are and are not I-novels: Tolstoy's *A Confession* has its artistic elements, but it is not an I-novel; Rousseau's *Confessions* has various novelistic aspects, but it is not an I-novel either. Strindberg's *Confession of a Fool*, on the other hand, is an I-novel. As for Japanese examples, Kume is willing to concede the status of Natsume Sōseki's *Wagahai wa neko de aru* (I Am a Cat) as "a marvelous classic [*koten*] of modern [*kinsei*] Japanese novels," but he believes that it is really only a display of Sōseki's technical finesse, increasing a kind of *tsūzoku* interest.[48] While the work seems artistic, it only has an artistic skin or frame. On the other hand, Kume expresses his admiration for Sōseki's *Garasudo no uchi*, though he omits it from discussion because he believes that it is not a novel. For a representative Japanese I-novel, Kume gives the example of Kikuchi Kan's series of short stories that were known as his "Keikichi" works, though he expresses some misgivings about them as well.

For Kume an I-novel may have either a first- or a third-person narrator, but that narrator must not be a character created by the author; it must be the author himself. Perhaps, he concedes, a few of the greatest authors (Tolstoy, Dostoyevsky, Flaubert) were able to put themselves into their characters. Still, the moment such transference to a character takes place, a sense of distance, or fictionality (*kyokōkan*), creeps in as well, and though it might still be excellent reading it ceases to be trustworthy. This is why Kume says he has in the past referred to *War and Peace*, *Crime and Punishment*, and *Madame Bovary* as no more than grand *tsūzoku* novels. They are just artifice, just things to read. With these comments Kume enters into one of the fundamental issues in the debate that will be defined as "pure literature" versus "popular literature": entertainment. For Kume the label *tsūzoku* novel is roughly equivalent to that of popular literature: fiction not worthy of serious consideration, fiction that is not art and thus serves no higher purpose than entertainment and is no more than "something to read."

Kume ended the first half of his essay with a reiteration of his position on the nature of art:

> The foundation of all art is the self. For this reason, the direct expression of the self without the pretext of the other—in prose literature, the "I-novel"—clearly must be the true path, the foundation, and the essence of literature. Enlisting the other is no more than a method of making art *tsūzoku*. . . . Therefore, everything other than the I-novel is a *tsūzoku* novel.[49]

He concludes the first part of the essay with an analogy, writing that the most beautiful artificial flower does not equal even a stem of a wildflower.

By the time he writes the second part of his essay a month later, Kume seems to have received some feedback from his peers that prompts him to clarify what he is and is not trying to do. He writes, "Through this discussion, I mean neither to advocate nor to publicize the 'I-novel.' I am not trying to define the criteria for what a novel is, and I am definitely not trying to construct the category of novel."[50] He then enters into a discussion of the role of aesthetics. Aesthetics, he says, should be descriptive, not prescriptive. It is only when one is going to discuss the social or ethical problems raised by a work's moral elements that one can say "It should be this way" or "It shouldn't be that way." He assures us that he wants to limit himself to a description of how things are or were and limit himself to his own experience. Despite those self-proclaimed limitations, he nonetheless goes on to reiterate his belief that the I-novel is the fundamental form of literature and thus is the most frank, direct, and trustworthy. For that reason, why would one feel the need to look for other forms?

If there is a problem with the I-novel, Kume suggests, it is not with the form but with the self that is being observed. He refers to Kikuchi Kan's essay "Sakka bon'yō-shugi." Kume agrees with Kikuchi's proposition that if even an average person's existence is described realistically, that description has value as literature. Only those who truly recognize their "self" and are able to realistically express that self in their writing can be considered artists and can produce I-novels worthy of preservation. The question lies in the condition that it be realistically expressed. Realistic expression, Kume cautions, is not realism—that is, the description of the thing as it is. To express a self realistically a "condenser of the self" is necessary: a mental state that accurately "fuses, filters, concentrates, agitates, and then harmoniously reproduces the self." If an I-novel possesses such a mental state, then it becomes something worthy of "receiving literature's garland [ka-kan]."[51] He stresses that the sort of I-novel or mental state novel he is referring to is not a passing fancy or simply a temporary trend in the literary establishment. It is the source of the novel, to which literature must eventually return.

Despite his claims to the contrary, Kume is presenting a normative vision for literature; in fact, as Seiji Lippit has pointed out, it is a vision for a "specifically Japanese literature."[52] By describing a border between the *tsūzoku* novel and its opposite, which includes but may not be limited to the mental state novel, and a border between that which is art and that which is not art, he is simultaneously prescribing such a border. Those who "truly recognize" their "self" and who have the ability to express that self after a process of condensation have the ability to produce an I-novel worthy of preservation. Part of their greatness comes from what the works can do: they can provide the author with the most (on a continuum) spiritual peace and readers with material they can trust. Without that trust, even the most excellent work becomes *tsūzoku*. Perhaps this is because the reader remains defensive toward the work, allowing it to arouse only a base *tsūzoku* interest. Such a work is "only" something that is entertaining to read; it is not art, which has a higher purpose. Despite Kume's claim that he is not actively advocating the I-novel, the statement that it is objectively the foundation of the novel and the source of the novel's art is decidedly normative.

The next foray into the defense of the I-novel came from Uno Kōji, with his essay "'Shishōsetsu' shiken" (My Views on the "I-Novel"), published in October 1925 in *Shinchō*.[53] Like Kume, Uno sees the mental state novel as a superior subset of the I-novel. He writes that one of the reasons the literature presently being produced by the literary establishment is often inferior is that writers are not sufficiently describing their mental states but are focusing on the minutiae of their daily lives. The other current trend is for writers to assume that readers realize that a given work is a continued discussion of the writer's own life. As such, they omit details that were

spelled out in previous works. This threatens the autonomy of the works—
for Uno, a precondition of a proper work of art. An autonomous work of art
such as a novel must have equal value no matter who reads it and no matter
what information the reader brings to the reading.

Unlike Kume, Uno feels that the authentic (objective) novel described
by Nakamura does dig down into the author's self, but that I-novels simply
do it more directly. Uno also warns that Japan should not expect to produce
a writer who can write a superior authentic novel, such as Balzac. It is here
that Uno enters into ethnic essentialism, claiming that the Japanese instead possess a character appropriate to the writing of mental state novels.
Just as Japan cannot expect a Balzac, neither can the West expect a Kasai
Zenzō. Uno focuses on Kasai, who he feels is the greatest example of a
Japanese I-novelist. For Kasai "art" was "living," rendering irrelevant a
ranking such as Kikuchi's "Life first, art second." The novelist capable of
this is rare. This sort of novelist, Uno states, does not have the leisure
(yoyū) to write about someone's daughter (mi mo shiranu naninani reijō),
workers (kōfu), geisha, old tales, or vendettas.[54] First he must write about
himself. Not that the I-novel is the only way to unify life and art. Uno
believes that for Japanese, however, the most natural way to write about
one's deepest self is in the form of an I-novel. Having established the
special connection between the Japanese and the I-novel, and having declared Kasai Zenzō to be the greatest practitioner of that form, Uno asks the
following question: From the heights that Kasai's works (particularly Kohan
shuki [Notes from the Lakeside] and Haoto [The Sound of Wings]) have attained, don't many works seem tsūzoku? This division between that which
is vulgar and that which is not is emblematic of Uno's approach, which,
while strong at times, remains more flexible and relative than other critics.
In the logic of his question tsūzoku becomes a label of a novel of lesser
quality rather than of a novel that is categorically different.

In May 1926 Satō Haruo joined this discussion in a radio lecture titled
"Ihi roman no koto" (The Ich-roman).[55] He started his presentation by
mentioning a letter that he had recently received from a bookseller, who
said that the literary establishment had been extremely boring of late and
that he wanted to publish a new author who was not following the current
boring trends. Whether or not there actually was such a letter, it does seem
that so-called I-novels were glutting the literary market and that dissatisfaction with the form was developing. In his lecture Satō argues that the

I-novel is more significant than the market suggests and that authors have a responsibility to write them.

> This is because an author does not live for worldly fame or profit. Because he lives solely to describe the true shape of things, he does not think about what the world might consider ugly or awkward, nor whether something might hurt his reputation, but only labors to describe the true shape of things in detail. . . . More than anything else, speaking frankly is the social responsibility of the literary writer . . . in contrast to average people [*sezoku no hito*], who only think about such things as appearances, fame, and profit.[56]

This is writing as a sacrifice for the good of mankind, by a writer who dismisses everything a broad readership might offer, particularly fame and wealth. The success or failure of the I-novel depends on the ability of the authors to carry out this important task. If the I-novels that are being produced today are boring, that is not because the form itself is boring, but because the enthusiasm of the authors is lacking. The writing of true I-novels is an act of great significance. "For me," Satō writes, "the value of the *ich-roman* is born of the fact that it is written with this sort of commitment [*kesshin*]."[57] He calls for writers who care nothing for such mundane desires as fame and wealth, thus implicitly condemning those who are concerned with the market value of their works.

Responsibility for the success or failure of an I-novel does not lie entirely with the writers, however. Readers who consider the work to be something that might appear on the society or gossip pages of the newspaper, Satō adds, make the already difficult process of self-exposure even more uncomfortable for writers. The readers must take a crucial step deeper into the work. If one does not take that step, there is no value in reading the work. For the interaction to have value, the reader must approach the work with sincerity and seriousness that approaches that of the writer himself. Authors of I-novels should not avoid pain or be defensive, but should labor with sincerity for the good of society. Readers should recognize the author's struggle with his fate and should try to empathize with that struggle. If readers can read deeply in this way, then they can discover things about themselves as well. Writers write I-novels for the good of truth and mankind; profit and fame have no place in determining its value. For readers, it is the source of truth and a monument to the sacrifices the writer has made on their behalf.

Almost a year later, in March 1927, Satō wrote another piece on the I-novel issue, "'Shinkyō shōsetsu' to 'honkaku shōsetsu'" (The "Mental State Novel" and the "Authentic Novel"), which appeared in *Chūō kōron*. This is a much less fervent essay, focusing primarily on determining why the mental state novel has so much purchase in Japan. First, however, he deals with prescriptive attempts to direct the course of literature and make value judgments between the mental state novel and the authentic novel, categories whose objective existence he does not question. Whether writers decide to make literature spiritual training or a way to re-create a world is up to them, Satō writes; it is a decision based in their characters. Authors' views on life make them choose one or the other; thus trying to determine which is better is like debating whether an orchid is better than a cherry blossom. We are free to declare that we like one flower more than the other. We cannot, however, tell a cherry to flower like an orchid. Satō asks a different question: Why do so many orchids flower in Japan's soil?

Part of the reason lies in the national character (*kokuminsei*) and part in the age (*jidai*). Satō sees the I-novel as being the natural product of literary youth, who are prone to self-examination and possess limited life experience. The reason Japanese literature's most perfect product is the psychological novel is because its writers are young. Now that many of these writers, like Satō, have been writing for more than ten years, that youth has come to an end. The writers are not only coming of age; they are coming of age into a literary marketplace that differs significantly from the one they entered. The youthful phase of many Japanese writers coincided with a decade, he laments, that was not a lucrative one for writers. He does concede that the material rewards of a writing career have improved in recent years, though he adds, "While I am not sure how it would compare to that of a capitalist, the material compensation we receive from society is greater than that given to the average person of comparable labor and talent."[58] The problem is that writers are recognized only as entertainers and not as public figures.

Amid these changed circumstances, Satō suggests, the writers find themselves facing a new series of challenges, some of which are produced by the very market that has ameliorated their material struggles. These now mature writers realize that their passion has faded, their imagination has decreased, their self-examination is numbed, their experiences outside themselves are few, and their observations are impoverished. Nonetheless they are carried along on the wave of thriving journalism and are not allowed silent reflection. They are forced by the market to produce, despite the fact that they have lost the traits necessary to produce quality products. For Satō the circumstances that produce these semidesiccated writers distort the I-novel into the mental state novel. Thus the I-novel and the mental state novel are each products of their age—the I-novel emerging from a literary world dominated by young authors and the mental state novel emerging from one dominated by old authors—and of writers who, for different reasons, can write nothing else. The market then becomes either an artificial sustenance to a literary movement whose time has passed or an economic barrier to natural authorial development.

Hirabayashi Hatsunosuke's "Sokkyō-teki shōsetsu o haisu" (Abandoning the Improvised Novel) was published in *Shinchō* in November 1927.[59] He begins by addressing the difference between artistic works and *tsūzoku* works. For him the essential, primary concern of art is that the artist is creating (*sōzō*) something, or at least laboring (*doryoku*) with the desire to create something. Mundane works lack this creativity. On the other hand, truly excellent works of art will also possess the universality that draws a mass readership. Unfortunately, Hirabayashi writes, most works today lack that desire to be creative and are instead improvised (*sokkyō-teki*). This improvisation means there is no polishing of plots, no careful selection of material, no reflection on the thoughts and actions of the characters, and no necessity. Such works are only a snapshot of one's daily traffic. For a work to be a true novel it must include, for example, some very unusual incident or something that strongly moved the author. In many works today, he complains, there is no anguish, no remorse, no joy; the protagonist experiences neither cheerfulness nor skepticism.

Recently everyone, he writes, from middling writers to new writers in literary coterie magazines to the proletarian writers, is jotting down fragments of their banal, content-less lives and calling it a novel. They are too busy fooling around to be selective of their material, to create a plan, or to refine their prose. Such habits, Hirabayashi warns, inevitably lead to the attenuation of creative powers. The current decay is the fault of what he sees as an inability of the Japanese since the Meiji period to be constructive. In the case of prose, it is the fault of realism. Realism effectively destroyed falsehood and ornamentation in literature, but it did not construct anything in their place. At first, he admits, when some authors sought the "truth" of life with a pious and solemn attitude, noteworthy works were created. This is no longer the case.

Nor does Hirabayashi let nonrealist or non-I-novel literary forms off the hook. Popular literature, he writes, focuses on things of secondary importance, such as the structure of the story's plot, the succession of external incidents, and cheap tricks. Popular authors, by investing work in researching material and constructing plots, have had some success attracting readers and deserve some recognition. Popular literature, however, is not the way to save the novel. To do that, the primary element must be recovered: namely, the desire to create. Writers must apply themselves diligently and with devotion (*shōjin kokku*). It is virtually impossible to succeed without effort, even for a genius.

Hirabayashi sees the current crop of novels as lacking not only the basic building blocks that popular literature has maintained—plot, prose, structure—but also that element which popular literature by (his) definition lacks: creativity. Writers must not only have a drive to create that they invest in their work; they must also labor diligently, if not monastically. Religious metaphors appear throughout his essay, such as in his description of the solemn and pious attitude of the early realists and the monastic devotion that he calls upon writers to apply. His contribution to the debate shifts the discussion away from advocacy for either the I-novel or the authentic novel to a search for first principles that draws from both sides of this (imagined) generic divide.

The I-novel debate begins with Nakamura and Ikuta contrasting the mental state novel (at that point referring to what comes to be known as the I-novel) with the authentic novel, but they are not valorizing the former at the expense of the latter. Rather both men see the recent trend of the mental state novel as an aberration into a lesser form. It is the creation of this schema—in which there are two types of literature, easily distinguished, one legitimate and one illegitimate—that is most germane to this study. Though Uno Kōji makes gestures toward breaking from this binarism, the essential dynamic of the debate is simply to reverse the order of the binarism to favor one's view. Thus Kume inverts the dichotomy of the mental state novel and the authentic novel set up by Nakamura and

Ikuta, claiming that the mental state novel is the highest achievement. Kume, however, discovers a more powerful discursive tool in the term *tsūzoku*, a term which (as Uno alone seems to recognize) seems to be descriptive but in fact is simply dismissive. The flexibility of the term is evident throughout the debate. By labeling the inferior pole of the binarism *tsūzoku*, one taints that pole and thus hampers the hierarchy's reinversion. This binarism between *tsūzoku* and *jun*, between the trivial (or even vulgar) and the pure, becomes the basic logical structure for the debates that follow.

Flexing the Inflexible: The Pure Fiction Debate

Eight years after Hirabayashi's essay and four years after Kaizōsha completed the publication of the *Complete Works of Contemporary Japanese Literature*, a similar question about the proper nature of literature drew statements by a number of writers and critics, many of whom had come to positions of prominence in the literary establishment during the period under discussion. Two of these were Yokomitsu Riichi and Kawabata Yasunari, who were perhaps the most famous writers of "pure literature" at the time.[60] Both of these writers had benefited greatly from the patronage of Kikuchi Kan, who made them members of the selection committee for the Akutagawa Prize, which was formed the same year this debate began. The resulting essays, known today as the "pure fiction" debate, show the way conceptual structures that appeared in various nascent forms in the I-novel debate had reified, shifting from contingent heuristic devices to inevitable ontological realities.

In April 1935 Yokomitsu Riichi wrote "Junsui shōsetsu-ron" (Theory of the Pure Novel) for *Kaizō*, in which he speculated on the future of literary purity in the face of commercial publishing.[61] The impetus for the essay was the so-called *bungei fukkō*: the widespread belief that modern Japanese literature was undergoing a literary revival at the time. In his essay Yokomitsu agrees that such a revival is taking place, but disagrees about its location. He argues that the only place a revival can occur is among "*tsūzoku* novels that [are] pure literature [*junbungaku ni shite tsūzoku shōsetsu*]*.*" To support his claim and to launch his argument, Yokomitsu quotes some recent observations by other literary critics that he considers to be particularly insightful. Although removed from their original contexts, they nonetheless illustrate some of the positions held by literary figures at the time that might seem unusual today. For example, Kawakami Tetsutarō comments that, if a pure novel could be produced in today's literary establishment, it would appear only among *tsūzoku* novels; Kōda Rohan states that the division between pure literature and *tsūzoku* novels should never have been made; and Kobayashi Hideo declares that were he "pressed by a foreigner to name a single representative Japanese author" he would offer Kikuchi Kan's name, a claim that would have been seen by most as provocative, as Kikuchi was by this time known as a popular novelist.[62]

In the essay it quickly becomes clear that Yokomitsu has a complex view of generic divisions within literature. Despite declaring admiration for Kōda's dismissal of the division between pure and *tsūzoku* literature, he nonetheless divides contemporary literature into five types: *junbungaku* (pure literature), *geijutsu bungaku* (artistic literature), *junsui shōsetsu* (the pure novel), *taishū bungaku* (popular or mass literature), and *tsūzoku shōsetsu* (*tsūzoku* fiction). The highest of these, according to Yokomitsu, is pure fiction (*junsui shōsetsu*; a distinction from pure literature, *junbungaku*); unfortunately few if any works of pure fiction have actually ever been produced in the Japanese literary establishment.[63] Contemporary readers of Yokomitsu's essay must have been baffled by these distinctions.[64] Though Marxist theorists (and some others) tried to distinguish mass literature from *tsūzoku* novels, the two designations were likely interchangeable for many readers. As for the first three designations, it is doubtful anyone would have perceived a difference among them.

In clarifying these divisions, Yokomitsu first turns to the most discussed (and relevant) divide: the one that exists between pure literature and *tsūzoku* novels. He cites two factors that are frequently raised in distinguishing one from the other: chance (*gūzen*) and sentimentality (*kanshōsei*). Pure literature, the argument goes, is that which lacks these two devices, while *tsūzoku* novels are those that utilize them. Unfortunately, Yokomitsu retorts, no one has clearly defined these two terms. Some critics suggest that the only way to recognize these characteristics is to possess sufficient taste to *intuit* them; others argue that any person of reasonable intellect can distinguish them, as they will inevitably stand out as abnormal or unrealistic.

Yokomitsu deals first with chance. He criticizes pure literature for eliminating chance entirely, considering it to be vulgar and unrealistic, and instead focusing solely on the mundane aspects of life. This ignores the fact that moments of chance do occur in daily life, and that these moments are often the most moving events one experiences. Because these events are so moving, chance is therefore directly related to sentimentalism, because the use of extraordinary events to affect readers is a form of sentimentalism. He is quick to caution, however, that this is not actually a criticism. He would rather see authors show creativity by using such sentimental mechanisms, which by their nature focus on the more moving moments in life, than show no creativity by focusing solely on the picayune.

He then lists two criteria to which chance will conform in a pure novel as he wishes to define it: first, it will occur in moments that naturally (though not necessarily) arise from the majority of the structure of the novel, which is dominated by noncoincidental events; second, the presence of coincidental events will actually heighten the realism of the novel as a whole by recognizing the role chance plays in real life. Yokomitsu cautions, however, that in properly utilizing chance and sentimentality in a pure novel, the portion of the work devoted to the mundane must sufficiently outweigh the portion devoted to the unusual in order to assure the realistic framing of those exceptional events. For this reason the pure novel cannot be a novella; in order to "flesh out the ideas" of a pure novel, "one or two hundred pages are simply not enough."[65]

Yokomitsu then moves to a more concrete description of how a pure novel is written. After defining the pure novels that have appeared thus far in Japan as those in which "the author lives believing that he is the only one that thinks about things," he points out the "simple" fact that, in real life, each individual has his own private thoughts. He then asks, "If the author has realized that characters appearing in his work are not beings who think the same way he himself does, then what sort of realism should the author —of whom there is only one—employ?"[66] That is to say, how do you depict others' interiorities without simply replicating your own? He wants to move beyond the I-novel, which is premised upon the belief that the author can understand (and thus represent) only his or her own interiority. This leads to Yokomitsu's introduction of his conception of the "fourth person," a focal point that would allow each character to possess an autonomous interiority, independent of the interiority of the author.

The desire to bring in realistically portrayed interiorities that are not simply replicas (or facets) of the author's interiority (and thus, in the case of an I-novel, the narrator's) harkens back to Nakamura Murao's praise of what he calls the "authentic novel." Key to the discussion of literary value, however, is Yokomitsu's deconstruction of the use of chance (its presence or absence) to define an objective boundary between pure literature and *tsūzoku* literature. According to Yokomitsu, modern man is himself constructed by chance; to display coincidence in a work is to display the reality of modern life and therefore to be pure. Realism, not the absence of chance, is essential to true purity. To eliminate chance, by extension, is to become *tsūzoku*. That which is pure grasps the chance inherent in modern existence; that which is not eliminates it. The realism that is held up by most pure literature is a superficial realism, which ignores a deeper reality.

In closing his treatise Yokomitsu describes other examples of the vicissitudes inherent in literary judgment:

> The English novel *Tom Jones* went through the 18th century considered a *tsūzoku* novel; recently, however, the English literary establishment revived it as a pure novel. If we went carefully through the *tsūzoku* novels of Japan, perhaps we would find pure novels there as well. I recently received a copy of Stendhal's *The Charterhouse of Parma*. This is a model pure novel. . . . If it were to have appeared in the Japanese literary establishment, however, it would have been dismissed as a *tsūzoku* novel.[67]

This echoes the judgments with which he started the essay, in which he declares that, according to their criticisms of chance, the contemporary Japanese literary establishment would consider Dostoyevsky, Tolstoy, Balzac, and Stendhal to be *tsūzoku* novelists.[68] It is important to note that, as with Kume Masao years earlier, the seemingly inarguable greatness of these authors despite contemporary definitions of what made literature great created a palpable sense of contradiction.

Nakamura Mitsuo responded to Yokomitsu's essay in the May issue of *Bungakukai*.[69] Nakamura begins his essay by stressing the importance of literary debates (and the theories they produce) to the development of literature: "Despite the obvious fact that literary history is made up of a series of creative works written by authors, at least in Japan the normal course of events since 'The Essence of the Novel' and Futabata Shimei's *Ukigumo* (Floating Clouds) has been for new theories to blaze new trails for new literature."[70] According to Nakamura, in Japan, at least during the modern period, theory precedes (and therefore perhaps determines) production.[71] That is not to say that he considers this an ideal state of affairs; in fact he believes the confusion of the pure novel debate is the direct result of confusion among practicing authors who have "faithfully adhered to the insanity of contemporary literature."[72]

As for the categories of pure and *tsūzoku*, Nakamura is a pragmatist. He writes, "Whether they are mistaken or correct, these two categories definitely exist in our country's literary establishment today." He argues that Yokomitsu's criteria for the distinction—sentimentality and chance—are insufficiently clear. But then he adds, "That is not his fault, though. Nearly all of the conceptual terms in use by the literary establishment reveal this sort of ambiguous character if examined closely." To consider what makes a novel *tsūzoku*, Nakamura examines *Crime and Punishment*, which Yokomitsu labeled a *tsūzoku* novel because of its regular use of coincidence and sentimentality. Nakamura argues that the mechanism of chance in *Crime and Punishment* does not debase the work, as it might in a novel of less psychological profundity, but rather makes possible a greater realism that is achieved by the work as a whole: "The only thing that is necessary [rather than coincidental] is Raskolnikov's thought, which completely brings to life his character as it is given flesh through countless chance events."[73]

While this might seem to be in agreement with Yokomitsu, it is not meant to be. Nakamura denies that a reality constructed from a mass of chance events is *tsūzoku*: "Coincidences 'that move people in daily life' are the true basis of daily life. If one faithfully depicts a reality containing contingencies that move people, one is not writing a *tsūzoku* novel. It is a pure novel. If you move away from that reality, it will cease to be moving. The invention of coincidences detached from reality is not creation, it is fabrication."[74] Nakamura's distinction, of course, is arbitrary. He claims that *Crime and Punishment* is a pure novel because it does not veer from reality, yet he is subjectively determining whether its frequent use of coincidence has or has not veered from reality. This, however, seems to show his unease with accepting Yokomitsu's terms, but not his concepts. Yokomitsu also believes that chance has the capacity to be, but is not necessarily, realistic; his proposed "pure novels," in contrast to the *tsūzoku* novels from which they are born, will be those that attain that reality.

Nakamura then takes his discussion in another direction, as he interprets Yokomitsu's treatise as a reaction against the triviality (or normalcy) of the I-novel. Nakamura reads the desire to break with normalcy that Yokomitsu associates with the *tsūzoku* novel as the creation of an alternate morality within the text that opposes conventional morality.[75] Following this logic, Nakamura is critical of Shiga Naoya and his novel, *An'ya kōro* (A Dark Night's Passing): "Despite his fiercely individual style, he never transcended his age's morality." Instead Nakamura praises authors who broke with the I-novel tradition and, by extension, with the age's morality, such as Izumi Kyōka. Meiji-period authors, while frantically introducing Western literary innovations, in this regard never veered from Edo literary tradition in their actual writing: "Just as the writers of the Edo period had, they never wrote works that broke with the common sense [*ryōshiki*] of society. The peculiar half-breed offspring of this feudal literary tradition and the techniques of Western literature is the I-novel, our country's unique literary form."[76] For Nakamura it is this ability to break with conventional morality that sets one group of works apart from another. While he has dispensed with Yokomitsu's criteria—chance and sentimentality—he preserves the binary structure.

As for Yokomitsu's proposed narrative perspective, the fourth person, Nakamura disagrees with his assertion that a viewpoint can be achieved that transcends a given self-consciousness. Any such perspective would be a delusion: "If there is self-consciousness that is separate from an individual's thought, it is no more than an abstraction created for one's amusement." This is not, however, a limitation; in fact it is the premise of all self-understanding achievable through art. Characters other than the dominant consciousness cannot have independent consciousnesses, nor should they: "A man's image is only made clear in the mirror of another. . . . To live in this world is to discover new images of oneself in the depths of other people."[77]

Moriyama Kei also published a response to Yokomitsu in May 1935, though his appeared in the pages of *Bungei*.[78] Moriyama grants that Yokomitsu's definition of the distinction between *tsūzoku* and pure—the presence or absence of chance and sentimentalism—is the most commonly held one, and even elaborates on it, saying, "It is a fact that the primary characteristic of *tsūzoku* literature is that it appeals to readers' interest through many nonsensical chance incidents and developments, and that moreover it appeals to the naïve tears and common ideas of readers under the dominant ideology of the day."[79] Moriyama, however, does not believe that this is a sufficient definition of the divide between *tsūzoku* and pure.

Moriyama first dispenses with a distinction between *tsūzoku* literature and *taishū* (mass) literature that would suggest that *taishū* literature is produced in order to be read by the masses and to result in their being uplifted. Instead he says that the term *tsūzoku*, when referring to *tsūzoku* fiction and *taishū* literature, is strictly speaking vulgarity (*hizoku-sei*). This is not as clear a conclusion as one might think, however, because he then gives "vulgarity" a new definition. It is not, he states explicitly, vulgarity from the perspective of moral teaching; it is the failure to "peel off the mask" of "truths prescribed by the dominant ideology" and reveal their essential falsehood. "Therefore," he writes, "the sentimentality and chance in vulgar [*hizoku na*] novels reflect the author's fundamental complacency toward reality."[80]

When the mask is peeled away by an author who is not complacent toward reality, Moriyama contends, not only will the flaws of the dominant ideology be revealed, but the historical necessity of specific incidents that seem coincidental will also come to light. The mistake of pure literature is that, while it does portray some coincidence, it is only the coincidence experienced by individuals who are not representative of their age, who "bear no essential significance in the general progression of history," thus rendering pure literature "ineffectual." Proletarian literature makes the similar mistake of focusing on boring individuals, when "the social reality in Japan—in economic, political, and daily life—possesses far more radical incidents, paradoxes, and superficially coincidental individuals than the social reality portrayed in proletarian literature." By discovering the function or significance of phenomena that might appear to be meaningless, the author can "illuminate a 'Japanese reality' that would at first glance seem coincidental and confused."[81] Moriyama is careful to clarify that he does not believe in a simple mechanistic view of the world, in which all events are necessary. In discussing the difference between *tsūzoku* and pure literature, however, the use of chance as a defining difference misses a deeper level of interconnectedness or relevance that literature has the power to illuminate and which the dominant ideological structure may be invested in concealing.

Kawabata Yasunari responded to Yokomitsu's essay in " 'Junsui shōsetsu-ron' no hankyō" (Responses to "Theory of the Pure Novel"), published in *Shinchō* in July 1935.[82] He begins by asking why Yokomitsu's description of his personal difficulties in creating a pure novel has been taken so seriously by the literary establishment and, by extension, what this tells us about Yokomitsu's position within that establishment. Yokomitsu's April essay elicited, by Kawabata's count, more than nineteen essays and one symposium (*zadankai*), which was published in *Sakuhin* in May.

Kawabata discusses Yokomitsu's theory of the split between pure and *tsūzoku*. He disagrees with Yokomitsu's definition of sentimentalism as that which would not stand up to the critique of a reasonable intellect. He points out that the line between sentimentality (*kanshō*), an illegitimate emotional reaction, and being moved (*kandō*), a legitimate emotional reaction, is hard to determine. In fact Kawabata has a problem with the distinction between pure and *tsūzoku* literature itself:

> It is of course also the case that the term "*tsūzoku* novel" is no more than a term used within the literary establishment for the sake of convenience. Needless to say, the border between *tsūzoku* novels and pure literary novels is not clear. In comparison to the pure literary novel, which is normally determined by literary establishment criticism, the *tsūzoku* novel is generally entrusted to the likes and dislikes of the masses of readers, does not have a uniform standard of criticism, and includes a greatly uneven body of very different works. For that reason it is hard for us to fix our sights upon.

What Kawabata does not address, however, is the process by which a given work comes under the scrutiny of literary establishment criticism. Were he to do so, he would be forced into the difficult position of naming the criteria that determine literary purity. He explicitly refuses to claim any logical defensibility for the divide. Ever the pragmatist, however, he writes, "In our literary establishment, the two [types of literature] exist in fact" and therefore must be dealt with despite their logical ambiguity.[83]

Kawabata then recounts some of the statements made by these other critics and authors on the distinction. Most of these follow lines of argument we have seen before; two, however, raise new and provocative arguments for the divide. Kawabata quotes Kataoka Teppei, who writes, "Probably what makes *tsūzoku* novels *tsūzoku* is that they provide people with easy consolation. Artistic novels are artistic novels because they are based in beauty that does not provide easy consolation."[84] This argument foreshadows critical views of literature as consolation, and thus as a mechanism for perpetuating existing social relations. Ikumi Kiyoharu, on the other hand, writes that the difference between the two is originality and the creative drive behind that originality: "Pure literature is that which is filled with new life (or new thought), and *tsūzoku* novels are those which simply attempt to reproduce the forms pure literature provides."[85] For Ikumi, Kawabata concludes, "*tsūzoku* literature is merely a mechanical activity: the monthly, repeated manufacturing of works."[86] This argument conjures up images of Grub Street and the hack writer, who produces fictional commodities utterly devoid of insight or invention as a laborer in capitalism's culture industry.

Kawabata ends by writing:

> For some time I have wondered whether the contemporary novel was not actually more *tsūzoku* than not. In addition, there is reason to believe that the distinction between *tsūzoku* and non-*tsūzoku* may, relatively quickly, become indiscernible and that in the future there may come a time when *tsūzoku* novels come to be seen as having been more accurate representations of reality. As the various writers have suggested, that is due to the flagging creation of pure literature today.[87]

Kawabata was right: postwar critics have argued that the literature dismissed as popular (and celebrated by the Naoki Prize) is more truly literary than those works admired as pure (and celebrated by the Akutagawa Prize). Despite his questioning of the internal logic of the divide, however, Kawabata nonetheless believes that it does exist and, in his final analysis, reveals his acceptance of that flawed logic.

Throughout the debate, despite the fact that attempts to clarify the factors that would objectively determine the qualitative difference between a *tsūzoku* novel and a pure novel are repeatedly foiled in their specifics, the critics cling to a schema that keeps the two separate. The attempt to come to terms with the diversity of quality and kind they see in the works around them forces critics like Yokomitsu to subdivide the categories and to call for works that blur the categories, without ever taking the next step to move beyond those very categories. At the same time certain themes resonate throughout the debate, as they have throughout the previous debates; the primary example is a fear of the masses and the marketplace.

Illegitimate Motivations: The Pure Literature and Amateurism Debate

Given the fact that a fear of the marketplace so clearly provided the foundation for the debates, it seems to have been only a matter of time before the distinction between the pure and the *tsūzoku* would be located in the nature of that literature's production, rather than in the works themselves. This is the gist of Kume Masao's "Junbungaku yogi-setsu" (A Theory of Pure Literature and Amateurism), which he published in April 1935 as part of a series in *Bungei shunjū*. Kume introduces himself as a man who writes *tsūzoku* novels as an occupation (*shokugyō*) and plays golf as a hobby (*dōraku*). What he wants to talk about this time, he asserts, is pure literature as a pastime (*yogi*).

> First of all, what gives people the wrong idea about pure literature's external social existence—in other words, its market price [*shika*]—is the belief that pure literature must be professionalized [*shokugyō-ka*]. Precisely because people think of pure literature as an occupation, they must view popular [*taishū*] literature as an enemy and an obstacle. If they were to view pure literature as a pastime, they would realize that its market price and everything else about it is simply in a different category.[88]

Kume defines a pastime as an activity that is not professional, that is done apart from one's livelihood, as a "relief from the true hardships of life [*shinken na seikatsu no kyūbatsu*]."[89] The cries of self-appointed pure literature writers who are supported by journalism are laughable, he writes. Since pure literature was originally a pastime—and thus, in a good sense, spontaneous and naturally occurring—pure literature that is pressed to meet *Chūō kōron's* or *Kaizō's* deadlines or that is written on an order from or at a length set by *Shinchō* or *Bungei shunjū* is strange. He mocks Hirotsu Kazuo, who called on pure writers to "regain the newspaper novel columns." Newspapers no longer require literature, pure or impure, for anything more than decoration. Popular literature, the literature produced as a result of external pressures, should not be attacked for the commercial value that is the basis of its existence (*sonzai-teki shōgyō kachi*), but rather for its market price, which exceeds its worth, or for its overproduction. According to Kume's logic, the determining factor of whether literature is pure or popular is the impetus under which it was created, and is thus external to the content of the work itself. Pieces produced as the result of an overwhelming desire to write are pure; pieces produced for any other reason are not.

Hirotsu Kazuo, whose call to "regain newspaper novel columns" Kume had attacked, responded in "'Junbungaku yogi-setsu' ni kotau" (A Response to "A Theory of Pure Literature and Amateurism"), published in *Junbungaku no tame ni* (On Behalf of Pure Literature, May 1935). Hirotsu writes that what Kume is arguing as a principle is the theory of literature as sacred vocation (*bungaku shinsei-ron*). Most people, according to Hirotsu, agree with the principle. Kume does not want sacred literature to be inspired by professionalism (*shokugyō ishiki*) or subsistence need (*jissei-katsu*), but instead by a desire to write. In reality, however, it is laughable to think that you could get paid for so-called pure literature and even more laughable to think that it is unfair that you cannot. Hirotsu believes Kume is reacting to a fear of the influence of commercial writing on literature. He finds this concern bitterly ironic, as it was this influence that he has been warning the literary establishment of since newspapers recovered from the Great Earthquake. At that time he wrote:

> The leftist theory of a sense of purpose should not be feared, but recognized for the ally it is. Instead, it is another sense of purpose [that should be feared]: the sense of purpose held by [manifestations of] journalism [*jaanarizumu*] like *Kingu* magazine, which is changing literature gradually and destroying literature's liberalism [*jiyū-shugi*]. We must defend ourselves against that now.[90]

Now the developments that Hirotsu warned the literary establishment of have come to pass:

> Many members of the literary establishment were drunk with the one-yen book boom that followed, and believed that literature's liberalism would thrive forever. Meanwhile, [manifestations of] journalism like *Kingu* magazine had gradually begun destroying so-called pure literature's citadel. Any number of times I begged the members of the literary establishment not to sit idly by dependent on others for their livelihood, but to join forces to acquire a right to life. I needled them by raising the example of how sumo wrestlers had made an association among themselves, saying that it was not too late but that if they let this opportunity pass it would be the end. Despite my harsh wording and even the

proposition of a plan to acquire that right to life, no one in the literary establishment paid me any heed. . . . Now the time has passed and the situation for pure literature has developed into what Kume described as "the cries [of a pure literature] controlled by journalism."[91]

Still, Hirotsu wishes to present a possible strategy for literature. When he argued that pure literary writers should advance into the field of newspaper novels, he did not mean with literary establishment novels (so-called to avoid confusion with pure literature) as they were. Perhaps Kume would consider what he proposes to be popular literature, but even Kume does not think that all popular literature is equal. Hirotsu believes that it is still possible to pioneer new areas in the field of popular literature. If literature produced under the influence of commercial publishing is by definition popular, then perhaps it is possible to produce superior works within that sphere.

In so claiming, Hirotsu recognizes the capacity to produce art within a fully capitalist economy, even as he implicitly clings to an ideal realm outside of print capitalism, in which authors write without having to negotiate the forces of the market. Even as Hirotsu identifies the porousness of the binary—that is, the ability to produce works of literary value even while functioning within the market—he remains unable to slough off the binary itself, revealing how firmly it had established itself in the minds of the literary establishment in Tokyo.

The Gradual Reification of a Discursive Schema

Debates such as these made up the discursive space that produced not only Kimura Ki and Yanagida Izumi, the creators of the *Complete Works of Contemporary Japanese Literature*, but also Kikuchi Kan and the writers of the Tokyo literary establishment. The I-novel debate and the pure novel debate, the two major debates that involved members of the *bundan*, frame the development of a certain logic over the course of the interwar period. Though the essay by Nakamura Murao that started the I-novel debate in early 1924 argued the relative merits of two fairly distinct views of literature, one committed to the representation of multiple interiorities and the other convinced of the ultimate unknowability of other interiorities, what emerged from the debate was a schema in which only the binary structure remained. When Kume Masao shifted the diction of the binary from authentic novel (with multiple interiorities) and mental state novel (with a single interiority) to I-novel and *tsūzoku* novel, he laid the groundwork for a powerful mechanism of discursive cultural authority. By labeling the alternative to his own literary preference with the derogatory (and ambiguous) term *tsūzoku*, Kume created a term that had the ability to elevate certain works at the expense of others, without being forced to clarify the elements that determine that value.

By the end of the pure novel debate of 1935 this binary schema had been fully absorbed into the discourse on literary value. The debate began with Yokomitsu attempting to find gradations in the black-and-white schema, yet feeling compelled to define those gradations using contorted combinations of two basic terms: pure (the type of literature that is art) and *tsūzoku* (the type of fiction that is not). Despite his desire to reflect continuity of value, he was so locked into a rhetoric of discontinuity that he felt compelled to limit himself to this emaciated vocabulary (and in so doing reproduced the binary schema). As the debate developed various theorists tried to pinpoint the elements that determined the location of the divide between that which was pure and that which was not. After a series of failures Kawabata Yasunari stepped forward to declare a seemingly obvious fact: that such a clear divide could not be determined logically. Kawabata's conclusion, however, was not so obvious. Rather than dismiss the arbitrary binarism, he embraced it in all its ambiguity, accepting it as a fait accompli.

When the attempt to discover intrinsic elements that could determine purity failed, the focus shifted to extrinsic factors, as seen in the pure literature and amateurism debate. Though this extrinsic element was present from the creation of the schema—in the form of a fear of the marketplace—this was the first time that a critic attempted to make those external factors the sole determination of whether or not a work was pure. The problems with this approach are multiple and obvious, including the fact that such a determination demands historical knowledge of the work's production, which is not always available. Nonetheless in the frantic (and almost invariably vague) defense of a clear line between art and nonart, a focus on the conditions (and motivations) of production is common.

Despite the ambiguity (and logical indefensibility) of the line believed to separate pure and nonpure fiction, Kawabata was right to claim (in July 1935) that the distinction existed in fact. Such a clear divide did exist within the literary establishment in Tokyo at that time. Though the schema had originated in this discursive sphere, however, the material presence of the divide alluded to by Kawabata was not directly created by this discourse. The publishing industry was directly responsible for the reification of that divide. The divide between pure and nonpure literature in interwar Japan was definitively established the very year that Kawabata made his assertion, when Kikuchi Kan created the Akutagawa Prize for pure literature and the Naoki Prize for mass literature.

The Dynamic Canon

THE AKUTAGAWA AND NAOKI PRIZES FOR LITERATURE

It would be romanticizing to assume that formerly art was entirely
pure, that the creative artist thought only in terms of the inner consistency of the artifact and not also of its effect upon the spectators.
. . . Conversely, vestiges of the aesthetic claim to be something autonomous, a world unto itself, remain even within the most trivial
product of mass culture. In fact, the present rigid division of art into
the autonomous and commercial aspects is itself largely a function
of commercialization.

THEODOR ADORNO, "HOW TO LOOK AT TELEVISION" (1954), THE
CULTURE INDUSTRY: SELECTED ESSAYS ON MASS CULTURE

A variety of mechanisms, in addition to the *Complete Works of Contempo-*
rary Japanese Literature, contributed to the dissemination, reception, and
preservation of literary works. As mentioned previously, these included
literary histories and lectures, newspaper columns, textbooks, and works of
literary criticism. Needless to say, literary awards played an important
function in this process as authoritative celebrations of works, authors, and
literature itself.[1] Of these, the award that is considered the first major prize
for modern Japanese literature and which continues to be the highest profile award is the Akutagawa Prize. While it is often argued that the Akutagawa Prize has never been awarded to a central canonical work and that
many famous authors never received the award, there is little doubt that it
has affected not only its recipients, but also the conception of an elevated

literary field. Receipt of the prize does not, as history has shown, guarantee perpetual canonical centrality. Nonetheless Akutagawa Prize–winning works enjoy greater dissemination, partially predetermined reception (as a work worthy of consideration), and extended preservation (through reproduction, if nowhere other than in the *Complete Collection of Akutagawa Prize–Winning Works* [*Akutagawa-shō zenshū*]).[2] In addition by reminding the public every six months that such a field still exists and that the field warrants both attention and celebration, the Akutagawa Prize perpetuates the conception of modern Japanese literature itself.[3]

These benefits are not the result of a consensus on literary value among experts, despite the appearance that this is precisely what they result from. Instead, as with the *Complete Works of Contemporary Japanese Literature*, a variety of both literary and extraliterary factors are at play in the process of deciding which works will enjoy consecration and which will not. While the *Complete Works of Contemporary Japanese Literature* revealed many of the commercial forces that affected inclusion in the series, the literary value system of the series' editors could only be inferred from the contents. The Akutagawa Prize, however, provides direct insight into the multiple literary value systems behind the celebration and reveals the absence of consensus and the contingency not only of the extraliterary factors behind such acts of cultural authority, but also of the literary factors themselves.

Naturalizing Contested Values

In January 2000 a crowd of reporters gathered in a large banquet room at Shinkiraku, an exclusive restaurant across from the Tsukiji market in Tokyo, waiting for the novelist Miyamoto Teru to appear. Miyamoto was the representative of the Akutagawa Prize selection committee, which had just completed its deliberations for that season's recipient of the prestigious literary award. The committee, composed of established writers who were (with one exception) former recipients of the prize themselves, had made their selection from a short list of seven works.[4] After entering, Miyamoto sat at the front of the room, announced the recipients—two authors were awarded the prize—and then accepted questions from the audience. Reporters immediately asked, not unexpectedly, how the committee had arrived at its choices. Miyamoto dismissively responded, "It's obvious if you take even a cursory glance at the stories."[5] His suggestion that the literary value of the winning works was self-evident obscured the fact that the works received support from only the slimmest majority of committee members.[6]

Miyamoto's dismissive response perpetuated a misrecognition of the nature of the prize—misrepresenting the subjective practice of bestowing it as objective and disinterested—and in so doing naturalized its consequences and concealed its essential interestedness.[7] Rather than being an objective identification of literary value, the awarding of this prize was an exercise of power that had direct consequences for the works that received the prize, the authors of those works, the authors who made up the selection committee, the publishing industry, the concept of literature, and perhaps even a Japanese identity. It was an exercise of power in which all parties had vested interests. In being honored for the "objective value" of their writing, the two awardees received not only the award and the prize money, but also a form of symbolic capital. This symbolic capital resembles other forms of capital, for which it can often be exchanged, and takes the form of benefits usually grouped under the rubric of canonization: legitimacy, as the works and authors are recognized as appropriate objects of serious academic attention; publication (and attendant income), as publishers flock to the recipients with requests for manuscripts; a place in cultural memory, as the writers are added to dictionaries and anthologies of modern Japanese literature; and a vastly expanded readership, as the publishing industry makes authors and their works into objects of national attention. The awarding of the prize produces a moment of celebrity as well. From the announcement of the award in 1934 the media has followed the Akutagawa Prize with great interest; today it is a national event.[8] As a result the Akutagawa Prize overcomes the limitations faced by the finite *Complete Works of Contemporary Japanese Literature*; its biannual exercise creates a dynamic canon, producing a continuous stream of elevated works.

Miyamoto's posture of disinterest was particularly noteworthy because it ignored the fact that symbolic capital was both produced and reproduced through the award. The honor of acting as a committee member, even if often dismissed by the members themselves as burdensome, reproduces the power of the committee and reminds readers of its members' importance and centrality in the literary field—the constellation of competitive relationships among literary producers and consumers who struggle for various forms of capital. In the act of defining literary "purity," the members establish a boundary that allows them to determine legitimate literary art. The Naoki Prize, which was bestowed later that night upon a writer of "popular" literature, is then defined as the antithesis of this legitimate art and dismissed by all those who are invested in the existence of a clearly bounded elevated literary field, which in the late 1920s began to be referred to as "pure" literature.[9] According to this logic of literary purity, the Naoki Prize merely celebrates well-written *fiction*, while the Akutagawa Prize celebrates *literary art*. Thus the Akutagawa Prize, a biannual celebration of pure literature (*junbungaku*), elevates specific works of fiction above other works of fiction into a realm that is perceived to be qualitatively different. In the process it reifies that realm, reproducing its legitimacy and perpetuating all of the industries that depend on pure literature, from literary publishing to academia.[10]

The boundary between pure literature and popular literature has been examined before; some scholars have claimed a single meaning for the term "pure," while others have traced the history of the term's referents.[11] As chapter 4 revealed, this might be the wrong question to ask of the term. Rather than focusing on what the term "pure" *meant*—what literary qualities it indicated at different points in history—it is much more important to focus on how the term *functioned*. An examination of its function, as a term that produces the very difference it appears to describe, reveals the power inherent in the invocation of that distinction.[12] The ability to elevate works into the category of pure literature is a form of power. Miyamoto's comment, however, epitomizes the internalization of this power that makes its prescriptive subjectivity appear to be descriptive objectivity. Instead of being revealed as a motivated selection made by a small number of individuals with both vested interests in the process and plural (sometimes conflicting) systems of literary value, the award presents itself as a process through which objective literary value is revealed. Miyamoto's response conceals the contingency of the value systems informing the decision, creating the illusion of a uniform system of purity.

A study of the early history of the Akutagawa Prize performs multiple functions. First, it reasserts the subjective nature of the award by dissecting its construction and first years of function.[13] Second, it reveals the contingency of literary values by showing how many of the early selections deviate from certain broadly accepted beliefs about literary value in modern Japan and thus about the nature of modern Japanese literature itself.

This is especially telling given that authors central to this conception of the literary field made those selections for the purpose of defining the future of modern Japanese literature. Third, it raises the question of how the functioning of power in the Japanese literary field has determined both the contours of that field and the epistemological structures with which it is studied.

The History of Literary Distinctions

The history of literary prizes in modern Japan predates the establishment of the Akutagawa and Naoki Prizes by more than half a century.[14] When considering literary awards as acts of awarding distinction, the history is even longer. In a sense all publishing that involves the selection of works involves the awarding of distinction. Although the comparison can be taken too far, it is worthwhile to recognize certain similarities. When magazine editors select a work for publication, for example, the author receives recognition and prestige and sometimes a material reward in the form of payment. This transaction is not unilateral. In selecting a work for a prize or simply for publication, a publisher wagers that the work will bring him both economic and symbolic returns. That is, he hopes that the work will not only increase sales, but also enhance his magazine's reputation. In the case of a magazine, selecting multiple works distributes both the risk and the potential reward. The more works a publisher selects for his magazine, the less the magazine's success depends on any given work.

Contribution (*tōsho*) magazines and contributors' columns (*tōkōran*), in which works that were submitted by readers were selected and published without the intervention of a patron, may be the earliest modern vehicles for granting distinction to unknown writers; as such they functioned as a path into the outer fringes of the Tokyo-based literary world. The contribution magazine *Eisai shinshi* (Genius Magazine), which began in 1877, was one of the first of these for-profit magazines. Newspapers and larger magazines, in contrast, would usually purchase or commission works from established authors and from new writers recommended by established authors.

When literary coterie magazines (*dōjin zasshi*) began to appear in large numbers in the early Taishō period (1912–26), contribution magazines like *Eisai shinshi* began to decline.[15] Coterie magazines differed from contribution magazines in one important way: they were normally funded, written, produced, and read primarily by coterie members. They also performed a function in the system of literary recognition: coterie magazines were often sent, gratis, to established editors, critics, and writers in order to gain attention for their contributors. This gateway was open, however, only to those who had access to sufficient resources to produce such a magazine. For those individuals both contribution magazines and literary coterie magazines resembled literary awards in that they distinguished certain works and rewarded them with publication. In granting distinction, however, the magazines differed from literary prizes in two respects: the prestige they bestowed was implicit, and the publisher's risk was spread among multiple works.

Kenshō shōsetsu (prize-winning novels) were works of fiction that had been selected for publication by newspapers from submissions and then printed in their pages; as a result they received explicit prestige. In principle at least, the material benefits of the award became secondary to the prestige itself.[16] *Yomiuri shinbun* created the first *kenshō shōsetsu* in 1894, after Nakai Kinjō, a newspaper reporter and essayist, proposed an award for historical novels and scripts. Selected by the authors Tsubouchi Shōyō and Ozaki Kōyō, the first recipient of these awards was the critic Takayama Chogyū; his work was serialized in the paper and he received a watch.[17] In contrast to the contribution magazines, *Yomiuri shinbun* and its judges wagered their symbolic capital on a single recipient at a time, a strategy that increased the recipient's prestige.[18] Other newspapers, the *Ōsaka mainichi shinbun* in 1901 and the *Ōsaka asahi shinbun* in 1904, subsequently created similar awards for longer fiction (*chōhen*). All of these newspapers bestowed their awards on an irregular basis, often as part of another celebration, such as the thirtieth anniversary of the newspaper's founding. As a result the award celebrated not only the work, but also the newspaper. The newspapers saw literature as possessing a certain value, whether cultural cachet or entertainment value, that could benefit the newspaper. Though literature profited from this transaction, the primary purpose of the award was not the amplification of literature.

Not all early literary awards were bestowed on specific works. From 1908 until 1912 the magazine *Waseda bungaku* (Waseda Literature) bestowed its "Words of Praise" (*Suisan no kotoba*) on an author for his (all recipients were men) general contribution over the course of a year. The authors

Tayama Katai, Shimazaki Tōson, Masamune Hakuchō, Nagai Kafū, Tokuda Shūsei, Tanizaki Jun'ichirō, Ogawa Mimei, and Osanai Kaoru all received the award. Unlike earlier awards, this honor bestowed by the magazine was entirely symbolic; there was no trophy, no prize money, no ceremony, and no publication. Because *Waseda bungaku* was seen as the central coterie magazine, the prestige of being selected was considered reward enough.[19]

All these awards were privately sponsored. There were also forms of distinction bestowed by the government. Though not awards, they nonetheless consecrated authors and works.[20] Two years after the High Treason Incident in 1910, for example, the Ministry of Education formed a committee for the "protection and cultivation of literature," fearing that Western influence was corrupting it.[21] One of its first (and last) acts was to award Tsubouchi Shōyō a medal and 3,000 yen in prize money for his contributions to literature. Again the benefits of the transaction were reciprocal. Not only did the authors selected to serve on the committee gain in prestige through this governmental recognition, but the government benefited from association with the cultural capital possessed by those authors. The intimate connection with the government, and the tacit support for the government that such a connection would convey, led some literati to refuse the honor.[22]

Kenshō shōsetsu provided a way for authors to win recognition from the literary world without relying on patronage. The goal was to advance through the ranks of publications until one reached the Dragon Gates (*tōryūmon*) to the literary establishment: the large general interest magazines *Kaizō* and *Chūō kōron*.[23] Having one's works published in these journals represented a significant achievement: that one had, to some extent, made it. Though not the highest paying publications, they were the most prestigious.[24] When these journals began to solicit works for their own prize competitions, new authors had the chance to bypass publications lower on the hierarchy. The *Kaizō kenshō sōsaku* prize was started in 1928 to celebrate the tenth anniversary of the magazine's founding.[25] Not to be outdone by its rival, in 1930 *Chūō kōron* founded the *Bundan andepandan* (literally, "independent of the literary establishment") *Chūō kōron kenshō*.[26] These soon became the most prestigious literary awards.[27] After the creation of the Akutagawa and Naoki Prizes, *kenshō shōsetsu*, *Kaizō*'s and *Chūō kōron*'s included, precipitously declined in importance.[28]

The Illusion of Parity: The Decision to Establish the Awards

Planning for the Akutagawa and Naoki Prizes began soon after the death of the author Naoki Sanjūgo on 24 February 1934. Kikuchi Kan, who was a close friend of Naoki's, dedicated the April 1934 issue of his literary magazine *Bungei shunjū* to his memory.[29] This was only the second issue dedicated to a deceased author; the first had been for Akutagawa Ryūnosuke, another old friend of Kikuchi's. It seems that Kikuchi did not consider these memorials sufficient. In his monthly column in April 1934 he revealed his intention to create two literary awards: "Iketani Shinzaburō, Sasaki Mitsuzō, Naoki—one by one my closest friends have died. I am plagued by increasingly desolate thoughts. I am considering creating something here at the company called the Naoki Prize as a memorial, to be awarded to a rising author of popular literary art [*taishū bungei*]. I am also considering creating an Akutagawa Prize, to be awarded to a rising author of pure literature [*junbungaku*]."[30]

Having decided to create the awards, Kikuchi then had to decide how they would function. Originally he envisioned a *kenshō shōsetsu* type of award, in which a committee would judge and make a selection from new manuscripts submitted directly to *Bungei shunjū*. Eventually he was persuaded to introduce a new award format; rather than choosing from unpublished manuscripts, the award would be given to works that had already been published, not only in commercial magazines and newspapers, but also in coterie magazines.[31] During the prewar period literary coterie magazines supplied most Akutagawa Prize–winning works.[32] For this reason coterie magazines experienced an increase in status even as they assumed a position of subordination to *Bungei shunjū*, which appointed itself the ultimate arbiter over the value of their publishing decisions.

The "Announcement of the Akutagawa and Naoki Prizes" was published in *Bungei shunjū* in January 1935; the regulations for the Akutagawa Prize read as follows:

> The Akutagawa Prize shall be awarded to an individual for the best work produced by an unknown or rising author and appearing in any newspaper or magazine (literary coterie magazines included).
>
> The Akutagawa Prize shall consist of a prize (a watch) as well as a cash award of five hundred yen.

The members of the Akutagawa Prize Committee shall select the recipient of the Akutagawa Prize. The committee shall be made up of the following people, all of whom are old friends of the deceased with long ties to Bungei Shunjūsha: Kikuchi Kan, Kume Masao, Yamamoto Yūzō, Satō Haruo, Tanizaki Jun'ichirō, Murō Saisei, Kojima Masajirō, Sasaki Mosaku, Takii Kōsaku, Yokomitsu Riichi, and Kawabata Yasunari. (Not in any particular order.)

The Akutagawa Prize shall be awarded every six months. When there is no appropriate recipient, the award shall not be presented.

The Akutagawa Prize recipient's work shall be published in the pages of *Bungei shunjū*.[33]

The regulations for the Naoki Prize were nearly identical, probably because Kikuchi wanted to establish parity between the awards. The few differences are thus all the more significant. To begin with, the Akutagawa Prize celebrated the best original work (*sōsaku*) by a rising author, while the Naoki Prize rewarded the best popular literature (*taishū bungei*) written by a rising author. In addition, though Kikuchi, Kume, Kojima, and Sasaki served on both committees, the Naoki committee was stocked with established authors categorized as writers of popular fiction, including Yoshikawa Eiji, Osaragi Jirō, and Shirai Kyōji. Finally, winners of the Akutagawa Prize were published in *Bungei shunjū*, while Naoki award winners were published in the less prestigious *Ōru yomimono* (All Fiction). In each respect the Naoki Prize adhered to the institutional boundaries that were forming according to the discursive divide between pure and popular literature. The creation of the two separate awards helped to solidify this division, which was at the time still logically ambiguous and strongly contested.

Just as Kikuchi chose writers marked as popular for the Naoki Prize committee, he selected writers he deemed pure for the Akutagawa committee. Not surprisingly the primary qualification for membership on the Akutagawa committee seems to have been affiliation with *Bungei shunjū*. As early as 19 December 1934 criticisms were being leveled against the award for this bias.[34] Indeed the committee members were for the most part a closely interrelated group whose elite educational backgrounds were similar, if not identical, and whose careers had long been linked.[35] In addition they were all authors who had known each other for many years and had been established for more than a decade when Kikuchi brought them together in 1935.[36]

The two committees handled their responsibilities differently. According to Osaragi Jirō, the Akutagawa committee was made up of strong-willed and opinionated people, none of whom would compromise on his position. Their debates would go on for hours. The Naoki committee, on the contrary, often made their decisions easily, perhaps because they took the award less seriously.[37] Osaragi, for example, once suggested facetiously that they leave the selection to Kawabata so as to avoid the work of selection.[38] In addition, because the Naoki Prize tended to reward consistent production, the committee members often had recipients in mind in advance. In contrast to the light-hearted approach of the Naoki committee, the Akutagawa committee acted as if it were making decisions that would affect the future direction of the literary tradition.

Another difference between the two awards deepened the divide between pure and popular literature. Although initially the recipients of both prizes were announced in the pages of *Bungei shunjū*, only the Akutagawa Prize–winning work was to be published there, while the Naoki Prize–winning work was to be published in *Ōru yomimono*, the company's less prestigious popular magazine.[39] This arrangement gave *Bungei shunjū* control of both awards, allowing it to claim the authority to announce the best work of popular literature without contaminating its pages with the work itself.

The Selection Mechanism: Choosing the First Recipients

The selection process required substantial time and effort before a list of manageable size could be drawn up for the committees to consider. In theory any work published in the six months preceding the selection process was eligible to win the prizes. Two winnowing stages were introduced into the selection process to handle the large number of eligible pieces. In March, over seven months before the final selection, one hundred requests for recommendations were sent by mail to members of the literary establishment.[40] Within days the receipt (or lack thereof) of these cards requesting recommendation unintentionally created what one newspaper article named a "card class" within that community.[41] For some authors, the article reported, failure to receive a card could be interpreted as a blessing;

for example, the author Ōtani Fujiko's failure to receive a card gave rise to gossip that she might win the award.[42] In response to its request, the publishing house Bungei Shunjūsha received recommendations from a diverse body of contemporary writers, including Ibuse Masuji, Niwa Fumio, Funahashi Seiichi, Ozaki Kazuo, Tokunaga Sunao, Itō Sei, Hirabayashi Taiko, Takeda Rintarō, Hayama Yoshiki, and Hayashi Fumiko.

Using these recommendations the Bungei Shunjūsha staff compiled a preliminary list, which was then given to Takii Kōsaku and Kawabata Yasunari, who were charged with producing a short list.[43] For the first award Takii and Kawabata presented the Akutagawa committee with a list that had been narrowed down to five works. The two committees met four times between 14 June and 10 August, when, with all eleven members of both committees present, the final decision was made and the results were announced to the press.[44]

The first Akutagawa Prize was given in September 1935 to Ishikawa Tatsuzō for his novel, Sōbō (The Emigrants).[45] As Kawamura Minato has pointed out, in selecting this work the committee ignored the most prominent literary forms of the time: the conversion (tenkō) works renouncing affinity for the proletarian movement, the various works in the I-novel tradition, and the modernist stories of the New Sensationists (Shinkankaku-ha).[46] Instead Sōbō tells the story of a group of semiliterate Japanese peasants and their experiences of being processed at the Emigration Office in Kobe prior to their departure for Brazil. The narrative primarily focuses on a young woman, Onatsu, and her younger brother, Magoichi. Because individuals had to emigrate as families to receive government subsidies, Onatsu has abandoned the man she loves to travel to Brazil with her brother, who dreams of success there. The story focuses on Onatsu's and Magoichi's experiences, but not exclusively. Touching on large contemporary events of 1930, such as the London Naval Conference and bribery scandals involving high-ranking government officials, Sōbō also explores many other characters' experiences, effectively capturing the mass of people and their diverse situations.

The first Naoki Prize went to Kawaguchi Matsutarō for his novella Tsuruhachi Tsurujirō (Tsuruhachi and Tsurujirō) and other recent works.[47] Tsuruhachi Tsurujirō is the story of a pair of shinnai (a type of chanting [jōruri]) performers, Tsuruga Tsurujirō and Tsuruga Tsuruhachi. After one of their frequent quarrels Tsuruhachi decides to quit and marry the son of a

Ueno restaurant owner. Her married life proceeds smoothly, but Tsurujirō's fame and talent wane over time and he starts to drink heavily. Three years later the two hold a reunion performance. Realizing how much she misses performing, Tsuruhachi decides to leave her husband to return to her art. Despite his desire to reunite with Tsuruhachi, Tsurujirō, who realizes how much she stands to lose, turns her away for her own benefit.[48]

In contrast to the literary prizes that preceded them, the Akutagawa and Naoki Prizes exposed their inner workings. *Bungei shunjū* made public the composition of the selection committees, then on 10 August 1935 the magazine made the reasons for the selections public as well. Along with the announcement of the winning works, readers were presented with the selection critiques (*senpyō*) of each committee member. The selection critiques for the first Akutagawa and Naoki awards speak directly to the differences between the two, the imperfections of the selection process, and the nature of the values informing the decisions.[49]

While the Akutagawa committee members expressed different opinions concerning the criteria that should be used to determine the recipient, few expressed confusion about the selection process. The Naoki committee members, in contrast, declared their uncertainty from the start. Osaragi Jirō began his critique, "The difficulty stems from the fact that it is not clear what popular literature is." As Osaragi's perplexity reflects, the Japanese terms for "popular" contain the same ambiguity as the English term. Could something be popular prior to its consumption? That is to say, were writers popular because they wrote the sort of *tsūzoku* things the people like, or were writers popular because the people liked what they wrote? Could something be accurately judged popular before the people had spoken through the marketplace? Kojima Masajirō's comment, which seems to be addressing this question, suggests not: "I was against the selection of an author as famous as Kawaguchi. But, having heard the argument that an unknown author could not be considered a popular [*taishū*] author, I finally conceded to giving the award to a famous author."[50] If established fame was the criterion for selection, however, there would be no need for the selection committee, for the highest sales would reveal who had the greatest popularity. The fundamental logic of the award demanded that popularity be a quality inherent in a work.

In the end Osaragi decided to award the prize to Kawaguchi for being so prolific and for having drawn attention to the early Meiji period in his writing. Initially, however, he had thought to give it to Hamamoto Hiroshi, "one of the few who have put in real literary effort in the field of popular literature, where few ever work hard."[51] Osaragi suggests that in valuing "literary effort" the Naoki Prize is on the same spectrum as the Akutagawa Prize, rather than being an award for an alternate genre. Both committees sought to reward literary achievement without implying that there may be multiple ways to define that achievement. More important, Osaragi's comments suggest a class basis to success in the respective fields: while the Akutagawa Prize's pure literature relied upon genius, the Naoki Prize's popular literature depended on literary labor.

Reaffirming this link between labor and the Naoki Prize, Yoshikawa Eiji contradicted Osaragi, writing, "[Kawaguchi] does not have enough experience with literary hardship." According to Yoshikawa, an author should not be rewarded for a single good work: "Though I have no objection to this decision [the selection of Kawaguchi], from my experience as an author, in the field of popular literature, the skillful production of one or two works is not the sort of thing to deserve showers of cheap praise. One should praise an author only when his consistent production, lifestyle, and spirit have captured the public."[52] In Yoshikawa's view, popular literature was more a craft than an art. While an artist could, theoretically, create great art accidentally, an artisan could be considered great only for continued high-quality production. To make matters more complicated, from Yoshikawa's perspective it was not even sufficient for the author to have produced consistently strong work. The quality of the work could be judged only if one knew something about the craftsman himself; the craftsman had to have a certain excellence of character and commitment to be worthy of praise.

The matter of artist versus artisan was clearly put by Sasaki when he wrote, "In my personal opinion, popular literature requires a kind of artisan-like [aachizan-teki] quality that is refined over time, as in the saying 'practice makes perfect.'" As for considering the character rather than simply the work of an author, Sasaki wrote, "The only regrettable thing for Kawaguchi is that, while no one on the Akutagawa committee knew Ishikawa and the decision was made solely on the basis of his works, even [Kawaguchi's] attitude toward life . . . was brought into the discussion.

While there are many drawbacks to being unknown, there are also many drawbacks to being known."[53] The Naoki Prize was awarded not for a literary work of particular excellence, but on the basis of an evaluation of an artisan's lifestyle and character.

The selection committee realized that they were not entirely free to define popular literature and the criteria for the prize. Kikuchi Kan, despite presenting the two awards as being homologous, had a different agenda for the Naoki Prize than he did for the Akutagawa. Osaragi described Kikuchi's conception of the prize as follows: "Simply put, the policy was this: the Akutagawa Prize was for a [specific] work; the Naoki Prize was for [overall] ability." From the beginning it was an unwritten rule that a Naoki Prize–winning writer had to show the potential to have a long and prolific career. Kume and Osaragi argued that this placed too great a demand on the selection committee, but Kikuchi stood fast; he needed new writers who could produce material for his magazines.[54]

Though Kikuchi did not demand the same from Akutagawa Prize authors, the future potential of authors was clearly on the minds of Akutagawa selection committee members.[55] Takii Kōsaku—who went on to be the longest-serving committee member in Akutagawa Prize history to date, participating in eighty-six selections over forty-six years—wrote the following in his selection critique: "If I found an author's works generally to be inferior and I was unsure about his ability, I could not recommend him to the reading world even if I were to find a single work by that author that I found to be excellent. Therefore I looked for authors about whose skill I had no doubts, and in whose capacity I could place my confidence." Kume Masao evinced this concern for the future when he wrote, "[Sōbō]'s solid style gives me great confidence that we can expect a lot from [Ishikawa] in the future."[56] This distinguished the Akutagawa and Naoki Prizes from most other awards, particularly kenshō shōsetsu, which celebrated a given work with no explicit regard for the author's future career.

There were other similarities between the awards. Kume, who acted on both committees, wrote, "[Ishikawa Tatsuzō] understands tsūzoku-teki writing methods, and I mean that in a good way. There are not many 140- or 150-page works these days that you read right through in a sitting." At the same time he ended his brief critique of Kawaguchi by stating, "If he should now become more diligent as a pure [junsui na] writer, then the granting of this award will have even more meaning."[57] Pure works improved with the incorporation of popular techniques, while popular works benefited from the writer's diligence and purity. The two categories blurred even here, where they had been reified to appear as ontological realities.

The purity the selection committee found in *Sōbō* was not that of the so-called I-novel.[58] Although the definitions for what makes up this genre vary, they have in common the presence of what Irmela Hijiya-Kirschnereit has called a "focus figure," often identifiable as the author, whose life becomes the central preoccupation of the text.[59] Kume Masao is frequently quoted as having given the most succinct description of the genre's centrality to the modern Japanese literary tradition. In 1925, ten years before the first Akutagawa Prize was given (and as part of the I-novel debate discussed in chapter 4), he wrote, "In the final analysis, the basis of all art lies in the self. It follows that the form that expresses the 'self' directly and frankly, without pretense and disguise, that is to say, the I-novel, should become the main path, the basis, and the essence of the art of prose."[60] Yet *Sōbō* has no single focus figure, nor are the characters to be identified with the author.[61] Kikuchi wrote, "Most new authors recently tend to write on the monotonous subject of themselves; in contrast, Ishikawa depicts a group of illiterate emigrants . . . in a skillful way that results in a powerful work."[62] In contrast to his earlier celebration of the I-novel form, Kume praised *Sōbō* for its unique subject matter: "One feels compelled to read the story because the experiences are interesting and the material is unusual" (ASZ 1: 335). Rather than demanding that Ishikawa plumb the depths of his own consciousness and experience to reveal a (universal) truth of existence, Kume seems to be calling for writers to look outside themselves at disparate others.

This attention to others, particularly those of lower social classes, was common to proletarian literature, the genre most literary histories depict as distinct from bourgeois pure literature. Yet in commenting on the works short-listed for this prize for pure literature, certain committee members explicitly and positively referred to proletarian literature and criticized pure authors. Kawabata Yasunari, for example, states, "Among those [in my proposed short list], Watanabe Kan and Asai Hanako recently emerged from the working class. I was quite moved by the proletarian subject matter and the authors' lives. One doesn't often see this kind of author among the new members of the enervated art-for-art's sake school [geijutsu-ha]."[63] Kawabata's public statement suggests that some writers of pure literature felt sympathy for (and to some extent solidarity with) the proletarian literature movement. By printing his alternate list, Kawabata also displayed his resistance to the direction the selection process took.

Rather than seeking a fixed set of literary qualities that might be implied in a singular definition of purity, the committee preferred stylistic freshness. Kume expressed concern in fact that Sōbō was insufficiently innovative in its style; Nagai Tatsuo recalls one committee member's comparison (he thinks it was Kume Masao) of the two prizes: "Roughly speaking, the Akutagawa Prize is a proper young lady. What we buy first and foremost is freshness and youth. Even if two or three years pass and she comes to be slightly tainted by the world, the judges are not to be blamed. What we bought was the freshness of the works. In contrast, the Naoki Prize is an apprentice geisha. What we are after is not just the winning work, but a person who is going to continue to produce."[64] While the Akutagawa Prize was nominally for pure literature, the selection committee had no clear definition of literary purity.

Whatever the committee was seeking, one thing soon became obvious to them about this mechanism of cultural authority they had created: they did not have complete control over it. This lack of control is apparent in the prewar selection critiques of the Akutagawa Prize, which often expressed a general dissatisfaction about the selection or about the public reception to their selections. Dissatisfaction arose because decisions were rarely unanimous and the power held by committee members greatly varied.[65] For the first competition the individual with the most power, Takii Kōsaku, determined the final short list. Satō Haruo explicitly recognized Takii's power: "I am a supporter of Dazai's work, but I was put in a bind when 'Gyakkō' [Against the Current] was short-listed instead of 'Dōke no hana' [The Flowers of Buffoonery]. . . . Of course, I suppose that 'Dōke no hana' didn't fit Takii's demands for realism and that is why he short-listed 'Gyakkō' instead."[66] Takii had included only one of Dazai Osamu's works on the short list, thereby eliminating the other from consideration; in that way his demands for realism overruled Satō's appreciation of the imaginative.

Kikuchi Kan had created a powerful mechanism for the consecration of young authors, but its actual functioning disappointed him. His comments concerning the first awards touch on a number of points:

For the purposes of selecting the Akutagawa Prize I read works by new authors for the first time in a long while. I was disappointed. I found their freshness false, nothing more than trivial detail. In fact, it struck me that literature hadn't progressed at all in the last ten years. I particularly felt that the writing style, decked out with all sorts of novelties, had made the works increasingly inaccessible to all but a select few, to the point that I felt they were alienating themselves from a general readership. Being read by the masses is a necessity for popular literature. For pure literature as well, the more it is read by the masses, the better.[67]

Things were not turning out as Kikuchi had hoped. If he believed that his award would discover and celebrate the new hopes of modern Japanese literature, he was disillusioned by what he found. In closing he isolated what he believed was one of the key problems in the pure literature of his time: that authors had no eye toward readers outside of the literary establishment. In effect Kikuchi was agreeing with Kume, saying that pure literature required a certain popular quality, or at least that it needed to keep a broad body of readers in mind.

The official comments by the prize recipients illustrate both the prestige brought to the awards by their namesakes and the different perceptions of the two prizes. As was fitting for the recipient of the Akutagawa Prize, Ishikawa wrote in extremely polite language about how flattered he was to be honored in the name of a genius like Akutagawa, how uncertain he was that he could produce good work in the future given his limited talent, and how he would nonetheless work hard to do so. In contrast to Ishikawa's flowery and humble words, the winner of the first Naoki Prize, Kawaguchi, wrote with blunt frankness: "During his lifetime Naoki scorned my work and barely read any of it. Of the one work he did read, *Dassōpei* [The Deserter], he warned me, 'Too much explanation. Use more description.' Despite our long friendship, this was the first and last literary advice I received from him. I bet that old baldy, hearing that I had received the Naoki Prize, is down in his grave grinning at the irony."[68] Though presented as equals, the Akutagawa and Naoki Prizes never were treated as such, even by the recipients.

As Satō Haruo's comments suggest, Dazai Osamu and his works were on the minds of a number of committee members. Undoubtedly the award and the distinction it could convey were on Dazai's mind as well. From the time he read the announcement of the award's establishment, Dazai had lobbied to be selected as the first recipient. The award would have meant a lot to his career as a writer, which had only recently begun in earnest. He had entered Tokyo Imperial University in 1930 but did not graduate. He had been publishing in Aomori coterie magazines for many years and had begun establishing himself in Tokyo. In his personal life he suffered a series of problems, including a nearly fatal case of appendicitis, and made multiple suicide attempts. By the time the first Akutagawa selection committee met, Dazai was deeply addicted to Pavinal, a form of morphine, which he had begun taking as a painkiller after the surgery for his appendicitis. His addiction had become so profound that abstention left him mentally unstable. Perhaps he felt that the award would justify his life choices to his parents, from whom he had become estranged. His drug habit, his need for social approbation, and his profound ambition made him desperate for the money and the legitimacy that the prize would bring.

What stood between Dazai and the award was not lack of literary talent. Kawabata Yasunari, like Satō, expressed an appreciation for Dazai's writing; his recommended short list included both "Gyakkō" and "Dōke no hana." He had reservations, however, about Dazai's physical and mental condition: "I regretted that dark clouds in his personal life at the moment seem to be keeping him from expressing his talent more clearly."[69] These comments about his personal life led Dazai to write a harsh letter to another Bungei Shunjūsha magazine, *Bungei tsūshin* (Literary Communications). In it he makes reference to a recent story of Kawabata's, asking, "Does keeping small birds and watching dancers perform constitute such an admirable life?" He continues, "I felt, deep in my vitals, the perverse, hot, strong, Nelly-esque affection you must have for me." He then intimates that not only was Kawabata not solely responsible for his decision, but that he was likely coerced into making it, and that someone else must have written his selection critique. "In those words of yours I sensed 'worldly pressures' [*seken*] and the suffocating odor of 'financial relationships.'"[70] Kawabata responded in the following month's issue of *Bungei tsūshin*: "Mr. Dazai does not understand how the committee functions. It would be best for him not to indulge in wild speculation or groundless suspicion."[71] Dazai's more inflammatory accusations aside, Kawabata's comments reveal how extraliterary factors, such as an author's personal conduct, affected the decision-making process.

The passage of time has shown that the Akutagawa Prize was not essential to Dazai's achieving the approbation he so strongly desired. The likelihood that he would eventually win recognition was obvious to at least one member of the committee as well. Shortly after the heated exchange of letters, Dazai was introduced to Satō Haruo and began lobbying him for the second Akutagawa Prize. Satō, who thought highly of his ability, feared for Dazai's well-being and, in cooperation with Dazai's mentor, Ibuse Masuji, had him hospitalized.[72] At the same time he tried to reassure Dazai that his failure to receive the award was not catastrophic. Satō later recalled how he had gone about consoling Dazai:

> It was really tough when Dazai was begging me for the award. We weren't going to select Dazai, nor Dan [Kazuo]. "Even if you two don't get the award, you are going to gain more fame than the award can provide, so don't brood over it. Look, I didn't win the Akutagawa Prize either." That was how I consoled them. I even joked with them, saying, "Let's form an obscure writers' society. Let's force them to recognize how great we obscure writers are."[73]

The Dazai incident reminds us that the Akutagawa Prize never became the sole bearer of cultural authority, but it also shows how quickly its power grew and how quickly writers recognized that power. At the time the incident played yet another function. Dazai's and Kawabata's exchange was public, appearing in the pages of *Bungei tsūshin*; Satō's response to Dazai's letters and visits appeared in *Kaizō* (November 1936).[74] While Kawabata's and Satō's actions suggest that they respected Dazai's ability and cared for him as a person, they nonetheless showed little hesitation in exposing his desperation to readers. This public display elevated Kawabata's and Satō's reputations as literary kingmakers and helped fix the Akutagawa Prize in the general imagination as a Dragon Gate for emerging talents.[75]

Kikuchi originally said that he wanted the award ceremony to be a grand event, in the hopes that it would play a major role in the literary world. In the end, though, little ceremony accompanied the first presentation. In December 1935 he explained, "I had wanted to hold a *bundan* celebration, but I was extremely busy traveling and in the end lost the opportunity altogether."[76] The response of some newspapers, which he thought took the award to be nothing more that a publisher's gimmick, dissatisfied him.[77] He criticized the press coverage in his October "Rubbish Bin" column:

I resented the fact that, even though we cordially invited each of the newspapers to the Akutagawa and Naoki Prize announcements, some newspapers did not write a single line about it—especially when the announcement of something like the Nikakai [Nika Association] Exhibit selection is made before a whole array of photographers. Which has more value as a news item—more social value even: one of the countless selectees of the innumerable exhibitions or the sole recipients of the Akutagawa or Naoki Prizes? They're idiots. They even announce the Literary Chat Society [Bungei Kon'wa-kai] award.[78]

The press coverage would eventually satisfy Kikuchi's expectations. In October 1936 he praised the media's response to the awards:

For the winner as well as for the selection committee members, the extremely positive reception of the Akutagawa Prize was the realization of a dream. Thanks to that reception, the September issue of *Bungei shunjū* sold very well—yet another reason for celebration. I would be ecstatic if the authority of the Akutagawa Prize grew like this with each new prize. As for the Naoki Prize, though it wasn't especially well received, it wasn't badly received either. It seems everyone understood our reasons for giving the award.[79]

The Naoki Prize was not enjoying the same degree of attention, but this did not overly concern Kikuchi, because the Akutagawa Prize was rapidly becoming the powerful mechanism that he wanted it to be. Aside from providing publicity for Bungei Shunjūsha, the award had already begun to produce concrete benefits for its recipients. For Ishikawa one result of winning the award was that the commercial magazines on which his livelihood depended treated him more generously. Ishikawa later recounted that prior to winning the award, he would take his work to *Chūō kōron* and *Kaizō* only to be rebuffed; after the award they came to him, not only for his writing, but also for his photograph.[80]

By design Bungei Shunjūsha did not simply bestow the award and then turn its back on the winning authors. As had been stated explicitly in the announcement of the award, the company assumed some responsibility for cultivating the authors it had chosen. Generally it followed through on this promise. A case in point concerns Ishikawa's first work after winning the prize, *Shinkaigyo* (Deepsea Fish), which was treated roughly by the critics.

Sasaki urged a head editor at Bungei Shunjūsha to encourage Ishikawa to keep writing, reminding the editor of their commitment to cultivating the author after the award.[81] At first the publishing house extended such support even to its short-listed authors, publishing their stories in *Bungei shunjū* as well.[82] Consequently the magazine was dedicating so many of its pages to these writers that by December 1936 Kikuchi was compelled to comment, "Every month since September we have been running the works that were short-listed for the Akutagawa Prize; January's issue will carry Tsuruta's and Oda's works. The result is that the Akutagawa Prize dominates *Bungei shunjū*'s 'new works' section. It would be a bore if this section were effectively to lock out established authors of the *bundan*; therefore starting next time the short-listed works will be published separately in book form."[83] Roughly two years after its inception Kikuchi's Akutagawa Prize threatened to dominate the entire magazine. Despite Kikuchi's dissatisfaction with the prize's initial reception, it quickly became powerful. Contributing to its growing authority were several factors: the Dazai incident, the prestige of the committee members, the association of the award with a well-respected writer, and the concrete career benefits winning authors received. Even as it gave young writers the imprimatur of its distinguished committee members, the Akutagawa Prize reproduced and amplified the committee members' authority and allowed them to affect directly the development of modern Japanese literature. By wielding the ambiguously defined but decidedly effective designation of purity, the committee elevated fiction that best adhered to their literary ideals and allowed them to affect the course of literary development.

The Early Years of the Prizes, 1935–1941

The Akutagawa and Naoki Prizes continued to be awarded twice a year through the end of 1944, after which they took a four-year hiatus as a result of the Second World War. Over the course of those first twenty competitions (1935–44) twenty-one Akutagawa Prizes and fifteen Naoki Prizes were awarded. During that time the official composition of the selection committees remained largely consistent. Until 1943 the only changes were as follows: the writer Uno Kōji joined the Akutagawa committee in the sixth competition (fall 1937) and the Naoki committee in the eleventh competition (spring 1940), and the writer Kataoka Teppei joined the Naoki committee in the thirteenth competition (spring 1941).[84] Despite this consistency each selection process was unique, as the committees confronted different issues each time they convened. Every six months the committees considered a new group of works and interpreted their responsibilities in light of the contemporary cultural and political situation.[85] The vicissitudes in the selection process reveal the strengths and weaknesses of the awards, the forces at play on their selection, and the various desires of the individuals involved.

The episodes that follow have been reconstructed using both the selection critiques and subsequently published reminiscences of committee members, and are thus inevitably highly subjective. They are intended to illustrate the value systems each committee member brought with him to the table when selecting the awards.

CRITICISM, COLONIALISM, AND THE I-NOVEL: THE THIRD AKUTAGAWA PRIZE

Some of the award competitions and selection critiques help us to extrapolate the guiding principles of the committee members. The two works awarded the Akutagawa Prize for the first half of 1936, Oda Takeo's "Jōgai" (Outside the Castle) and Tsuruta Tomoya's "Koshamain-ki" (The Chronicle of Koshamain), are particularly useful in this regard. The committee members' deliberations illuminate not only these principles, but larger issues as well: the capacity of works to contain criticism of the government during the war years, the centrality of the I-novel form to modern Japanese literary production, and the complex relationship between the colonies and the home islands during the period of the Greater Japanese Empire.

"Koshamain-ki" purports to be the record of a third-generation Ainu chieftain.[86] Set in the early Tokugawa period, the story follows Koshamain as he flees his home village of Setana (on Hokkaidō) after deceitful and conniving Japanese who have begun to colonize the island kill his father, just as earlier they had killed his grandfather. Narrowly escaping Japanese forces that have been sent to kill him, Koshamain survives thanks to sacrifices made by village chieftains who have yet to succumb to the invaders. More of an epic than a novella, the narrative depicts Koshamain becoming an adult and learning various skills as it builds readers' expectations for a denouement in which Koshamain repels the Japanese menace and saves his culture from destruction. In the final scene, however, the story abruptly deviates from readers' expectations. Koshamain meets a Japanese lumber-jack who invites him to share a drink with a group of fellow lumberjacks remaining on the island for the winter. Koshamain, who has been careful to avoid the saké he knows the Japanese have used to corrupt his people, finally accepts a drink to show his willingness to make peace. When he turns to leave, the formerly friendly Japanese lumberjacks grab him, stab him in the back (literally), and then race one another across the river to rape and murder his wife and mother. The story closes with Koshamain's body floating downstream to a formerly sacred spot, where rats and crows peck at the corpse.

"Koshamain-ki," which uses the long-established tradition of veiling political criticism in historical events, can be read as a surprisingly overt attack on Japan's imperial ambitions and the means the Japanese used to achieve those ambitions. In an afterword included in a postwar reprint of the story, Tsuruta makes this explicit: "My point was that reflection about the Japanese attitude toward other ethnicities was essential, particularly given the invasion of Manchuria underway at the time."[87] The government did not suppress the story despite its harsh portrayal of Japanese. The unfettered publication of this story, not to mention the attention it subse-quently enjoyed as a prize recipient, belies the common image of the literary world during the rise of the militarist government as barren and incapable of producing anything critical of the militarist regime.[88] Per-haps the story escaped censorship because the timing of its publication in *Bungei shunjū* was fortuitous, before the Cabinet Information Committee (established in July 1936) was fully functioning and before the crackdown on left-wing writers the following year.[89] It is also possible that many contemporary readers did not view the story as criticism. The selection critiques betray no awareness that it could be read as controversial; they make no excuses for its inflammatory content. The critique closest to recognizing the critical aspect of the story came from Murō Saisei, who states (rather ambiguously), "In its depiction of resistance to a terrible, irresistible force, the tale contains extremely harsh criticism of 'civilization' and 'barbarism.' "[90]

Nonetheless the relevance of the story to contemporary imperial expan-sion was noted by some commentators at the time. In an article in the *Asahi shinbun* on 9 September Yamakawa Kikue suggested that the piece brought to mind the European conquest of indigenous Americans, the East India

Company's domination of India, and even the recent fall of the Ethiopians to the Italians, all examples of "the fate of an undeveloped [*mikai*] people that come in contact with a civilized people possessed of more advanced weapons and organization." In an article in the *Yomiuri shinbun* on 25 August Katsumoto Seiichirō put a Marxist spin on the same reading, applauding the work as one "that accurately depicts the toppling of northern undeveloped [*mikai*] people by the expansion of capitalism, and is thus a work of the new generation in the most precise sense, a new generation informed by a materialist view of history." It is unclear whether these comments are critical of the processes they describe, however. While they could be read as implicitly criticizing imperialism (including Japanese imperialism), they could just as easily be read as noting a process of social evolution (as described by Herbert Spencer) or historical materialism (as explicated by Marx). In the end the work was not suppressed, although censors did keep a close eye on Tsuruta's works and did not allow the story to be turned into a film.[91]

Reactions to the two works chosen to receive the third Akutagawa Prize reveal unexpected praise for the epic and scorn for the I-novel. In the afterword to the postwar reprint of "Koshamain-ki," Tsuruta explained that he had chosen the epic form in order to break away from the "extremely tedious naturalism that dominates Japanese literature." Apparently the selection committee approved of this move, giving the work nearly unanimous support. While the antinaturalist "Koshamain-ki" was, as an article in the *Yomiuri shinbun* of 9 September put it, "universally praised," the other Akutagawa Prize–winning work, "Jōgai," which Itō Sei labeled an I-novel, was not.[92] Katsumoto Seiichirō, who had raved about "Koshamain-ki," put it bluntly when he declared that the selection of "Jōgai" to share the prize was "clearly a failure for the Akutagawa Prize selection committee."[93]

In addition to being an I-novel, "Jōgai" is one of many Akutagawa Prize–winning works of the prewar period that take a pronounced interest in people and places outside Japan. Of the twenty-one prewar and wartime Akutagawa Prize works, fourteen either take place abroad or focus on non-Japanese characters.[94] "Jōgai" tells the story of Shigetō Yōichi, a young man who goes to the Japanese Consulate in Hangzhou to work as a clerk (*shokisei*) in the Foreign Ministry. Kawamura Minato has examined the marked tendency of both the winning and short-listed works to focus on the "outer territories" (*gaichi*; Japan's settlements, colonies, or occupied territories) and other areas of Asia.[95] He notes twelve such works between 1935 and 1944 and asserts that the prewar prize "even played the role of stimulating the appearance of a literature that collaborated with foreign expansion strategies. It would not be an overstatement to say those literary works were running a three-legged race with the period's social trends and the ideology of national policy."[96] As we have seen in "Koshamain-ki," however, it would be incorrect to say that all the works displayed expansion in a positive light. Nonetheless it is clear that the Akutagawa selection committee was fascinated with works that placed Japan in an international context, both multiethnic and multilingual, and favored works that took up this topic. The committee rewarded looking out as much as (or more than) it did introspection.

The outer territories were, the literary critic Hashizume Ken argues, more than just a source of material for modern Japanese literature. According to Hashizume, from 1935 to 1945 the Japanese home islands were a sterile environment for literature, with leftist, nihilistic, and liberal writing largely suppressed. Police and the military constantly watched *tenkō* writers, and even authors not specifically under observation felt some pressure. Consequently many writers fled to the *gaichi*, and their experiences there were reflected in the prewar Akutagawa Prizes.[97] Hashizume's account does not explain why works written in Japan were chosen during the repression and then celebrated despite it. Any work produced abroad that received the Akutagawa Prize, no matter how free the writers may have been abroad, was scrutinized as closely as one produced in Tokyo. While many authors may have composed subversive material abroad, the prize-winning works published and celebrated in Tokyo enjoyed no special freedom.

From the beginning Sasaki Mosaku was calling on the committee to use the Akutagawa Prize to "let some fresh air 'inside the walls'" of existing pure literature. This "fresh air" included voices from the Japanese colonies, which the committee was keen to encourage. Take the tenth award, for example. In his selection critique Takii Kōsaku comments on the ethnic Korean author Kim Saryang, whose "Hikari no naka ni" (Into the Light) was short-listed, as follows: "I was happy to see that such a talented writer had been produced in Korea." Takii points out that the committee had considered pieces from a collection of stories by writers living in the Japanese puppet state of Manchukuo, and he congratulates the writer Kitamura Kenjirō for having created a literary magazine there and for publishing "pioneering [*kaitaku shite iru*] Manshū literature."[98] A year later a story by Ushijima Haruko from a similar collection was short-listed for the twelfth award.

An interest in the outer territories was again expressed on the occasion of the thirteenth award, which went to "Chōkō Deruta." Of the author, Tada Yūkei, and his circumstances Takii Kōsaku stated, "Not only does he reside in Shanghai; his work also appeared in a Shanghai-based magazine. Needless to say, at a time like this, it seems a good idea for us to bring attention to these facts through the Akutagawa Prize." As this quote suggests, however, colonial literature was usually a product of place, not identity or ethnicity; nearly all of these authors of "local literature" (*genchi bungaku*; that is, literature that is not produced in Japan, and more specifically, Tokyo) were ethnic Japanese. Despite the attempt to include colonial production in a new conception of contemporary Japanese literature, ethnic differences (and stereotypical understandings of those differences) had not been erased under the assimilation policies of the new imperial regime. During the twelfth selection process, for example, Kawabata Yasunari praised the short-listed story by Ushijima Haruko: "She described the baffling character of the Manshū people as it is, baffling." Difference and the exoticism that accompanied it were highly desirable to most, though not all, committee members. As early as the fourth award Satō Haruo declared, "Thus far too many novels about foreign countries [*gaikoku shōsetsu*] have received the award."[99]

The committee's uniform praise for "Koshamain-ki," a work that was neither realistic, contemporary, nor introspective, shows yet again that the criteria for literary value held by the committee members—writers central to the modern literary tradition—were not monolithic. It also shows that in 1936 works critical of the military government's policy could still be celebrated, even if that criticism could not be explicitly recognized. The selection of "Jōgai" follows a trend established by *Sōbō* and carried on throughout the early years of the prize whereby the committee carefully attended to the world outside of the main islands, particularly in the new colonies of the Greater Japanese Empire.

The selection process for the sixth competition resulted in the Akutagawa and Naoki Prizes being awarded to two authors who went on to play important roles in the history of modern Japanese literature: Hino Ashihei, whose *Mugi to heitai* (Wheat and Soldiers, 1938) set off a pro-war literary boom, and Ibuse Masuji, now seen as a central writer in the modern literary canon. The events surrounding the selection of these two writers reveal numerous contingencies inherent in the awards. The process by which Hino's "Fun'nyō-tan" (A Tale of Excrement) was selected to receive the Akutagawa Prize illustrates not only the inequality of opportunity for writers from different geographical regions in Japan, but also the caprice of the selection process and the importance of extraliterary factors in the decision making. The process by which Ibuse's "Jon Manjirō hyōryū-ki" (John Manjiro, a Castaway's Chronicle) was selected to receive the Naoki Prize reveals once again the lack of parity between the two awards, despite Kikuchi's intentions.

A string of coincidences allowed Hino Ashihei, a nearly unknown author, to receive the Akutagawa Prize.[100] His "Fun'nyō-tan" came to the attention of the committee as a result of the survey of literary figures that Bungei Shunjūsha had conducted before creating a short list. In that survey the works that received the most recommendations were Wada Den's "Yokudo" (Fertile Land) and Mamiya Mosuke's "Aragane" (Ore).[101] Hino's story came to light only because it had been recommended by Tsuruta Tomoya, whose "Koshamain-ki" had won the Akutagawa Prize for the first half of 1936. A native of Fukuoka, Tsuruta had come across another story of Hino's in the Kyūshū literary coterie magazine *Toranshitto* (Transit). This led him to "Fun'nyō-tan," which appeared in another Kyūshū literary coterie magazine, *Bungaku kaigi* (Literature Meeting). As Hashizume Ken points out, it is remarkable that the work made the short list on the basis of a solitary recommendation from an author who had himself been short-listed on the basis of a single recommendation.[102] Although this incident reveals the committee's willingness to consider stories produced outside of Tokyo—some would argue that the committee preferred such works, particularly when they were from the colonies—it also illuminates the practical difficulties such works had in attracting the attention of the committee. Had it not been for Tsuruta's link to these provincial coterie magazines, the committee would not have discovered Hino's story. These mundane logistical problems produced a geographical bias in the nominally national literary award.

These coincidences merely got Hino's story short-listed; another series of contingencies, which Uno Kōji described in 1952, resulted in its selection.[103] Despite Tsuruta's strong support for the work, "Fun'nyō-tan" survived the process of elimination precisely *because* Hino was unknown. As Kume Masao put it in his selection critique, the other candidates were all writers who "were already 'registered'; who had already 'mounted the stage.' That is to say, they had already appeared in magazines like *Ch'uō kōron* and *Kaizō*."[104] Wada's story, considered excellent by much of the committee, was too long. The story was also rumored to have been selected to receive the Shinchō Prize, so the committee did not consider it seriously.[105] According to Uno, the committee felt that Mamiya's story was also a little long, had a weak ending, and had a somewhat *tsūzoku* feel; Uno quotes Kume Masao's description of the story as "a failed proletarian work [*puroretaria-kuzure*]."[106] The selection committee was on the verge of not awarding a prize when Uno suggested awarding it to Hino. Both Satō and Kume had found Hino's work interesting, if in bad taste. Murō Saisei expressed his aversion to such writing—as the title indicates, it was a tale of night soil—until Uno pointed out that Saisei's own writings were similarly sordid.[107] The story's selection depended less on its literary merits than on contingency and a process of elimination.

"Fun'nyō-tan" depicts a man struggling to restore his family's wealth by entering into the night soil business. Unable to turn a profit, the protagonist, Hikotarō, falls on hard times and is forced to leave his wife and family and live alone in a small shack next to his warehouse. Though he is able to secure a contract through the town boss to become its designated night soil collector, that contract turns out to be less profitable than he had imagined and results in further economic distress. It is only through the auspices of the town boss's son-in-law that Hikotarō is able to renegotiate his contract with the town and turn the business around. Just when the business is becoming profitable, however, it is nationalized, with only a quarter of the proceeds going to Hikotarō. He continues working with the company and, in the process of its operations, regularly comes into conflict with local toughs. In the final scene he snaps. In a rage he begins heaving the contents of the night soil buckets at his tormentors, screaming at them as he too becomes covered with excrement.

The selection committee convened for five days, during which time Kikuchi read Hino's story (he had not originally read it), and the other members read other stories by Hino, which they requested from *Bungaku kaigi*. None of the committee members wanted to commit himself to an unknown author without some further evidence that he would continue to produce fiction. The notes from the meeting, which were also published, state that two or three committee members thought highly of Hino's other works, including "Fugu" (Blowfish) and "Yamaimo" (Yam). Each member, the notes assured readers, prudently reflected on his decision. This comment was likely meant to stem criticism that the work had received the award simply as the result of a process of elimination. Indeed from the committee's perspective, the story had merits that went beyond its literary value: it was topical and it made for good advertising.[108]

At the time the prize was awarded Hino was on active duty on the front lines in China, and the committee took advantage of the situation, asking the critic Kobayashi Hideo, who was in China, to deliver the news.[109] Kobayashi was initially apprehensive about how the military would react to his request to hold a small ceremony. When he first approached Hino's commanding officer, the officer replied that he had never heard of the Akutagawa Prize. When Kobayashi likened it to the Order of the Golden Kite (*kinshi kunshō*) military award, however, the officer was delighted and immediately ordered that a ceremony be held (figure 16). In his report from the front Kobayashi described the scene:

> With commanding officer S, commanding officer M, and lieutenant S from the press corps in attendance, the whole unit lined up in the courtyard of the headquarters. My heart pounded when I heard the orders "Attention! Listen up!" but I forced myself to speak the ceremonial phrases as if delivering orders myself. After words from corporal Hino and commanding officer S, the ceremony ended. It was the kind of simple, serious ceremony one would expect at the front. I was a little overwhelmed by it all, but I was very happy. Hino was also overjoyed.[110]

Not only was the military happy to perform the ceremony; it even began treating this new celebrity in its midst with favor. Soon after the ceremony

FIGURE 16   Kobayashi Hideo and Hino Ashihei. Courtesy of Mainichi Photobank.

Hino was transferred to a relatively safe post in the Central China Contingent Information Division. In this case the benefits of winning the award were more profound than having one's picture taken—for the award may have saved Hino's life.

Despite its investment in a concept of literary purity, the Akutagawa Prize remained anything but pure. At the same time much authority was to be gained by an association with literary purity. The point is perhaps best seen in terms of the growing gap between the Akutagawa Prize and the Naoki Prize, a gap made extremely clear in the selection of Ibuse Masuji as recipient for the Naoki Prize.[111] Given literary tastes today, it is deeply ironic that Hino received the Akutagawa Prize while Ibuse received the Naoki Prize; at the very least it suggests the contingency of literary tastes and the heterogeneity of an author's output over the course of his or her career. The question of whether the Naoki Prize was appropriate for Ibuse was asked by contemporaries as well.[112] A few selection committee members were hesitant to offer Ibuse the award out of concern that he might be insulted and not accept it.[113] Trying to finesse the decision, Kikuchi Kan explained, "A new path was opened for the Naoki Prize when it was given to Ibuse. By awarding him the prize, we are not saying that his writing is popular [*taishū*] literature; we are saying that in his literature we discovered a popular quality [*taishū-sei*] that we liked."[114] Fortunately for them, Ibuse took no umbrage. In recalling the event he recounted that, just before he received the award, a special-delivery letter arrived from Sasaki Mosaku asking him to come to the offices of Bungei Shunjūsha immediately.[115] When he went there, Sasaki said to him, "Between us, it has been decided that your "Jon Manjirō hyōryū-ki" will be given the Naoki Prize. . . . Would you accept it even though it is the Naoki Prize and not the Akutagawa Prize?" Ibuse responded to the seriousness of their concern with humor, asking, "Will I get a watch too?" Assured that he would, Ibuse told Sasaki he would happily accept the prize. Ibuse's response is perhaps less telling than the committee members' concern, which reminds us that the parity of the two awards was understood to be fictional even at the time.

For literati invested in the concept of pure literature, the Naoki Prize possessed far less prestige than the Akutagawa Prize; for both the general public and many authors its prestige was nonetheless significant, as the incidents surrounding Ibuse's receipt of the award make clear. Despite his humor and the selection committee members' concern, Ibuse took the Naoki Prize seriously. When he went to Bungei Shunjūsha to receive it he dressed in formal Japanese attire (*hakama*). In contrast to Ibuse's seriousness, Kikuchi's actions perhaps reflect his true feelings about the award, the importance of which he defended again and again in print. Kikuchi, an avid Japanese chess (*shōgi*) player, merely glanced over his shoulder at Ibuse for a moment, quickly turning back to the board. An assistant brought the award and the certificate to Kikuchi, who merely passed them to Ibuse without looking up. At first, Ibuse says, he thought that Kikuchi wanted him to learn some moral from this; later he realized it was just that Kikuchi found him less interesting than the *shōgi* game. Still, Ibuse was not the only person who took the honor seriously. On his way home from the Bungei Shunjūsha offices he stopped by a restaurant he frequented in Ginza in order to pay off his debt there. The woman who ran the restaurant had learned of the award from the paper and quickly realized that he was paying his bill with that money. She then said to him, "Because this is auspicious money, I am going to use it for my daughter's [university] entrance exam." Despite the indifference to the Naoki Prize shown by such individuals as Kikuchi, who were attached to the concept of an elevated literary sphere, many persons, like Ibuse and the restaurant proprietor, did value the award.

THE ACT OF REFUSAL: THE ELEVENTH AKUTAGAWA PRIZE

A testament to the power of the Akutagawa Prize is that it has been re-fused only once, when Takagi Taku declined the eleventh award in spring 1940.[116] A graduate of the First Higher School and Tokyo Imperial Univer-sity, Takagi was an instructor of German at the First Higher School and at the Mito Higher School and the nephew of Kōda Rohan. Given his back-ground and position, perhaps he felt no need for the recognition the award had to offer. There are other theories about why Takagi refused the award. He initially told reporters that he preferred another work he had written, which had been passed over for an earlier Akutagawa Prize, and that he did not want to accept the prize for what he considered to be a lesser story. Later he attributed his decision to skepticism about literary prizes. How-ever, according to the author Sakurada Tsunehisa, a close friend of Takagi, Takagi refused it because he thought that it would then be given to Saku-rada for his story "Kairo no shō" (Dew on the Shallots), which had also been considered.[117]

Whether he was conscious of this motivation or not, Kikuchi was furi-ous about Takagi's refusal:

> The accuracy and propriety of the selection are the responsibility of the selection committee and not of the recipient. Once an author puts a work into print, he should leave praise and criticism to others; if praise is going to bother him, he should not publish in the first place. Par-ticularly in the case of the Akutagawa Prize, once the unofficial decision has been made, the honor has already been conveyed; after that it is just a matter of the money. Though he flaunted his modesty by refusing the award, he had actually already received its benefits. It is the same as Sōseki's refusing the doctorate of letters; the act gave him even more prestige because he did it publicly. When one doesn't graciously accept recognition such as this it creates problems for the selection committee. Such a refusal calls into question the ability of the committee members, and that is unacceptable.[118]

Kikuchi's response to Takagi's refusal illuminates the reciprocal nature of the award. Takagi took the honor without reproducing Bungei Shunjūsha's symbolic capital or producing sales revenue. When the award is considered in these terms, the reason for Kikuchi's anger is clear: Takagi had effectively stolen from him. Since both the committee's decision and Takagi's refusal quickly became public knowledge, he not only received the prestige of having been selected for the award, but he also gained additional prestige (in the eyes of some) for having refused it.[119] Yet from Kikuchi's perspective, Takagi vandalized the legitimacy of the committee itself.

The story for which Takagi was to receive the prize, "Uta to mon no tate" (The Defender of Poetry and Palace), illustrates an aspect of the Akutagawa Prize selection committee's conception of pure literature not yet mentioned: its attitude toward historical fiction. The story, set in eighth-century Japan, describes the life of Ōtomo no Yakamochi, the dominant poet and primary editor of the eighth-century poetry collection, the *Man'yōshū*. It begins with Ōtomo's return to Nara with his family as a child and recounts the key moments in his career through the composition of his last poem in 758. There is no doubt that the committee members considered the work a historical novel. In his selection critique Kojima Masajirō laments, "The one thing that is regrettable [about the work] is that reason, which demands the accuracy of historical facts and their criticism, has overwhelmed the artistic desire of turning those facts into a story, with the giant leap beyond those facts that novelization requires." What saved the work, for Murō Saisei at least, was that "it avoids the disagreeable pitfalls into which historical novels have a tendency to fall."[120]

The selection committee was clearly aware of the apparent contradiction in selecting the work for a prize directed at pure literature. Since many literati considered a contemporary context to be essential to literary purity, they often excluded, by tacit definition, historical fiction from the category of pure literature. As Yokomitsu Riichi declared, "My personal understanding is that an excellent contemporary work should receive the prize before an [excellent] historical work." Some committee members felt the distinction between historical fiction and pure literature was flawed to begin with and would be best ignored; others tried to rationalize their selection of the story while preserving the divide. When Sakurada Tsunehisa's "Hiraga Gennai" won the twelfth award, for example, Satō Haruo described the use of a historical persona as merely symbolic, actually representing contemporary intellectuals. "As such," Satō explained, " 'Hiraga Gennai' is neither a so-called historical novel nor a realism-centered Naturalist novel. I see it as a type of new conceptual novel that uses this sort of symbolic technique."[121] Kawabata Yasunari agreed, insisting, " 'Hiraga Gennai' is a contemporary novel that has borrowed the form of historical fiction."[122] Clearly the committee recognized that their selection of such a work might be perceived as inappropriate. Nonetheless three works of historical fiction were chosen to receive the Akutagawa Prize between 1935 and 1944. Though a boundary between historical works and literary purity was present, it remained porous.

TOPICALITY, ARTISTRY, AND CONSEQUENCES:
THE THIRTEENTH AKUTAGAWA PRIZE

As the Pacific War increased in intensity its effect on literature in general and the Akutagawa and Naoki Prizes in particular became more pronounced. For example, the censorship of literature tightened, allowing less and less implied criticism of wartime policy to be published. When Ishikawa Tatsuzō published "Ikite iru heitai" (Living Soldiers), which describes atrocities committed by Japanese soldiers, in Chūō kōron in 1938, the issue was banned. Ishikawa received a four-month sentence of imprisonment for having violated the Newspaper Law, though the sentence was reduced to a three-year suspended sentence. After this incident writers and editors became much more wary of offending the government.[123] Around the same time supplies of paper also became limited. The government began curtailing paper consumption as early as August 1938 and instituted rationing programs in July 1941.[124] Small literary coterie magazines, which were so vital to the award, were the most affected. By the end of 1941 the government had reduced the number of these magazines from ninety-seven to eight through either mergers or cancellations.[125] Since these publications had been the source of most of the works considered for the Akutagawa Prize, the pool of potential nominees was drastically reduced.

Consideration of the wartime situation (jikyoku) naturally became more prevalent in the selection critiques as well.[126] This is most apparent in the selection in 1941 of "Chōkō Deruta" (The Yangtze River Delta) for the thirteenth Akutagawa Prize.[127] The story is set in the Yangtze River Delta area, which includes both Shanghai and Nanjing, and focuses on the Japanese protagonist, Saburō, and the Chinese En siblings, Tenshi and Kōmei (using the Japanese pronunciations). The brother and sister, though close to one another, are ideologically divided over the future of China. This rift is so severe that when Tenshi is wounded by a bullet while he and Saburō are driving in the International Settlement in Shanghai, Saburō is torn over whether or not to contact Kōmei. Though Tenshi's sister would surely be concerned, Saburō realizes, she also sympathizes ideologically with the very individuals who shot her brother. This friction between the two leads Kōmei to leave Shanghai for Hong Kong. Not long after, Saburō and Tenshi receive word that Kōmei has taken her own life. Saburō attempts to comfort Tenshi by telling him that in death Kōmei has reconciled the diverse elements within her and become a "pure" Chinese woman, "an Asian" again. In death she unified the self that modernity had sundered.

As with previous prizes, the selection process began with surveys sent out to representative members of the literary establishment asking for recommendations, from which Uno, Sasaki, Takii, and Kawabata produced a short list.[128] By the end of their meeting on 19 July 1941 they had selected nine works for all of the committee members to read and consider. The second meeting, on 24 July, with eight selection committee members present, resulted in the list's being narrowed down to three works: "Chōkō Deruta" by Tada Yūkei, "Yamabiko" (Echoes) by Ainoda Toshiyuki, and "Geshoku-nin" (Workers) by Hanihara Ichijō. Nine committee members were present for the third meeting, on 29 July, but Kikuchi, Kume, and Kawabata were absent.[129]

Kawabata, however, had sent a telegram stating his position. He recommended the selection of either "Chōkō Deruta" or "Geshoku-nin." He said that he felt "Geshoku-nin" was more solid, but that "Chōkō Deruta" showed more promise and was more interesting. Satō and Uno supported "Yamabiko" and were opposed to "Chōkō Deruta" because, according to Satō, it "lost its nerve" and, according to Uno, it "had insufficient literary spirit." Kojima also voted against "Chōkō Deruta," thinking it was too journalistic and immature. Yokomitsu, who was Tada's mentor, strongly favored "Chōkō Deruta": "If the youth of China could read 'Chōkō,' I think it would make a real contribution to Sino-Japanese cooperation. Of course, if Tada hadn't really thrown himself into it, he couldn't have written this kind of work. You say the story is awkward, but that sort of awkwardness would appear in anyone's treatment of the issues because the problem that he is dealing with is very difficult. . . . Ultimately, I think that literature today has to be like this." Murō Saisei said that he thought the work sounded like a "sophomore's speech." Sasaki and Takii, while admitting that the prose was rough, supported "Chōkō." Sasaki wrote, "It is not easy to get a work that is perfect from a literary standpoint, and it seems there really aren't any works on the short list that have enduring value. If that is the case, it might be better to turn the spotlight on ['Chōkō Deruta'] rather than 'Yamabiko.' If we do that, the selection may at least be of some use." In response Satō clarified the repercussions of this position: "In that case, we would be placing more emphasis on its political efficacy than on its literary worth."[130] This left a four-four tie between "Chōkō Deruta" and "Yamabiko."

"Yamabiko" tells the story of Moriyama Sankichi, a member of the outcast class and the town cremator, explaining the key factors—including his father's madness, his uncle's compulsive gambling, and his own paralyzing shyness—that caused Sankichi to descend into this scorned position. An object of contempt in the eyes of the townspeople, Sankichi has been reduced to handling corpses in order to feed himself and his mother. The grim story comes to an end with mother and son discovered dead in their remote cabin. Throughout the story Sankichi is portrayed as an undeserving victim of others' weaknesses, misunderstandings, and malfeasance; thus his fall functions as criticism (though of the vaguest sort), particularly of Japanese society's treatment of descendants of former social outcast groups (hisabetsu burakumin). Unlike "Chōkō Deruta" the story completely ignored the fact that Japan was at war, and thus lacked topicality in that sense, but it struck most of the committee as being artistically superior. The debate revolved around this distinction. According to the notes of the deliberations, Murō Saisei suggested, "If we are talking about topicality, then it will have to be 'Chōkō Deruta,' right?" When Uno Kōji asked him which he would choose if topicality were not an issue, Murō responded, "Well I suppose, then, 'Yamabiko.'" Uno summed up: "So what you are saying is, in terms of topicality, 'Chōkō Deruta.' In terms of artistry, 'Yamabiko.'" To which Kojima responded, "If it weren't 1941, this wouldn't be a problem at all."[131]

The committee also discussed the possibility of awarding no prize, instead just publishing both "Chōkō Deruta" and "Yamabiko." Sasaki Mosaku suggested, "Since the Akutagawa Prize process is made transparent [through the publication of the selection process], it doesn't matter which one we choose in the end. If we show how we debated the decision, when people read the critiques and read the works it will be clear why we chose what we did. So it really isn't a problem at all." At this point Yokomitsu stepped in again, saying, "However, in the end, it is a question of which is the right way to go: for us to recognize the current state of affairs or not. In fact, at a time like this, it isn't even correct to refer to a [special] 'state of affairs'; it has become the everyday. That's the problem."[132] In the end even the strongest proponents of "Chōkō Deruta" recognized that, were it not 1941, this would not be a question. They remained locked in the four-four tie.

To break the tie the committee telegraphed Kikuchi and Kume, who were abroad in Sakhalin. Their responses came the next morning. Kikuchi telegraphed back, "'Chōkō Deruta' didn't impress me, but 'Yamabiko' is a problem too." Kume wrote, "'Yamabiko' is too bleak and pessimistic. I recommend 'Chōkō Deruta' because it is the first sign of a budding literature of the outer territories." With Kume's vote as the tiebreaker the prize was awarded to Tada's "Chōkō Deruta," at least in a sense. Satō said, "So, in the end, we are actually giving the award more to the author, Tada, than to the work." To this Murō added that even that was not the case, that the award had in fact "transcended even the author."[133]

The quandary faced by the selection committee (and Sasaki's proposed solution to that quandary) may have been why the thirteenth selection process alone is represented by a transcript of the debate rather than by formal critiques. While Sasaki's suggestion to publish the transcript and let readers decide seems reasonable, it betrays an underestimation of the mechanism they operated. Even if the debate suggests that both works were worthy, receipt of the award had important practical consequences: "Chōkō Deruta" has been reproduced subsequently and is readily available to readers; "Yamabiko" and its author are now practically unknown.

CENSORSHIP AND CRITICISM: THE FOURTEENTH AKUTAGAWA PRIZE

While the effect of the war on the thirteenth selection was largely indirect, by the time of the following round whatever autonomy the selection committee enjoyed had begun to be compromised. The recipient of the fourteenth Akutagawa Prize was Shibaki Yoshiko for "Seika no ichi" (The Fruit and Vegetable Market). The story chronicles the experiences of a family of fruit and vegetable wholesalers in Tokyo as they try to keep their business from going under despite the restrictions imposed by the wartime government. Yae, the eldest daughter, sets her mind on restoring the business and bringing the family back from the brink of financial ruin. Despite the regulations on profiting from speculation, Yae purchases a supply of apples on a rumor that coming snows will prevent the normal shipments from reaching the market. When the shipments are indeed delayed the family reaps a windfall. Such successes are rare, though, and the business remains tenuous. The government soon increases restrictions in an attempt to eliminate competition and excess profit, depressing the market altogether. The story closes with Yae reflecting on the sacrifices she has made for the sake of the business and the family after she hears that her childhood friend will marry.

Because the story sympathetically portrays a victim of the wartime government's price-fixing policies it can be read as implicitly criticizing those policies. Compared to "Koshamain-ki," the criticism is mild and indirect. Nonetheless in this case the selection committee immediately attempted to explain away the apparent criticism. As Kume Masao stated:

> In light of the current situation, I did feel a little sense of danger, but [I needn't have because] this is by no means a piece of social criticism. It is not a history of the regulation of produce markets that have been swept away by the times. Needless to say, it is not resistance fueled by the petty bourgeoisie against that regulation. It should be viewed as the history of a common woman's struggle. While it is a beautiful elegy for such petty bourgeois concerns, it neither regrets nor resists their passing. Therefore, the overall sense given by the work is not the least bit unwholesome, nor, therefore, is it against government policy. Rather, in times like these, an artless plea such as this one might even be what saves the individuals involved in the nation's small and middling commerce and industry. I suspect that those in charge of our wise cultural policy will read this work seriously, accepting it as the voice of the people.

Despite these attempts to control the reception of the story, "Seika no ichi" did not escape unscathed: the selection committee asked the author to change the conclusion to avoid greater controversy.[134]

The committee's concerns over the government's reactions were allayed when Kikuchi Kan reported the following to them: "I just got back from the Information Bureau. They say we are going to have some trouble with the end of the story, when the shopkeeper falls into despair. So I had the author change that last part, telling her that we want to give the revised version the award and run it in the magazine."[135] In his selection critique Uno wrote that Shibaki was asked to make the revisions because committee members felt that "the subject matter of this story, in these important times, was a problem."[136] According to the selection critiques, the committee asked for the change both to satisfy certain aesthetic concerns and to avoid difficulties that would arise due to government censorship; a reading of the two versions today suggests that the latter reason far outweighed the former. Most of what is excised from the story is Yae's frustration, indignation, and sadness over what has become of her life, thus significantly diminishing the tale's poignancy and implied criticism.[137]

The Information Bureau in the story is the Cabinet Information Bureau, which was created in 1940 as an expansion of the Cabinet Information Committee. The Committee had been established in July 1936 to augment the censorship activities of the police, and it "marked the beginning of the truly fanatical suppression of any but the most worshipful references to the imperial house."[138] *Bungei shunjū* had been under particularly intense scrutiny since 1937, when it was deemed by the military to be one of the most influential magazines. That year the military established the Four Company Society, which included Bungei Shunjūsha, Chūō Kōronsha, Kaizōsha, and Nihon Hyōronsha, and forced these companies, thought to have particular sway over the opinions of the intelligentsia, to meet with military censorship authorities each month. In response the publishing industry formed the Japan Publishing Culture Association to self-police its activities, particularly the distribution of limited paper supplies. Despite the Association's façade of self-determination, the Cabinet Information Bureau set all of its policies.[139] Thus when the Akutagawa Prize selection committee met in early 1942 to determine the award for the second half of 1941, Kikuchi Kan was careful to consider the Bureau's opinion. Awareness of external pressure was not new to the committee; the need to modify a work in reaction to that pressure was.

Why the Akutagawa Prize Succeeded

Kikuchi occasionally considered abandoning the Naoki Prize altogether.[140] From the beginning the inherent paradox of the Naoki Prize—an award for the best of the rest, from the perspective of pure literature—had limited the award's prestige within the literary field. The Akutagawa Prize, in contrast, rapidly became one of the most important awards in the literary establishment and then in Japanese society as a whole. Soon after its inception it became one of the premier goals of aspiring writers. In no small measure this success was due to Bungei Shunjūsha's recognition that the award itself required cultivation. In part Bungei Shunjūsha has done this by publishing nearly every study of the Akutagawa Prize that has appeared over the subsequent decades. This sort of cultivation has made the award a valuable asset for the publisher.

Not only did Bungei Shunjūsha make the Akutagawa Prize a success; the Akutagawa Prize helped make Bungei Shunjūsha and *Bungei shunjū* successes. By focusing on works that appeared in literary coterie magazines when choosing its nominees, the Akutagawa Prize selection committee elevated the importance of those magazines for establishing young authors. And while elevating the coterie magazines, the committee positioned *Bungei shunjū* as a transcendent judge of literary value.[141] In 1957 the magazine *Bungakukai* held a round-table discussion on the effects of the Akutagawa Prize on the literary world. The writer Niwa Fumio played down the importance of the prize to a literary career, suggesting that a writer could make it on the basis of talent alone, without the imprimatur of the prize, as proven by Dazai Osamu's case. Satō Haruo agreed that the prize was not essential but pointed out the award's tremendous influence: "Theoretically that's true, but if no one recognizes a writer's ability, editors will not feel comfortable publishing his work. That is why the Akutagawa Prize is necessary. That is why there is such demand for people who win the award."[142] Inoue Yasushi, himself a recipient of the award in 1949, also pointed out this somewhat intimidating side of winning: when an individual won the prize, requests for stories came flooding in; some writers were ready for this, but some were not.

Ultimately the Akutagawa Prize did more than become a new Dragon Gate to the literary establishment. In the aforementioned round table, the author Funahashi Seiichi commented that he felt the prize created a psychological complex for authors who failed to receive it, and that such a complex had not existed before the award. When Ishikawa Tatsuzō responded that even nominees received some prestige, Funahashi replied that in the world of up-and-coming writers there had been no such thing as prestige before the Akutagawa Prize.[143] Funahashi must have been aware that there was prestige, in the form of symbolic capital, to be had prior to the creation of the awards. He was trying to point to a different development. Soon after its creation the Akutagawa Prize became an end rather than just a means; this is why Satō's joking consolation to Dazai about an "obscure writers' society" would have been so unsatisfying. Dazai later became a writer whose manuscripts were regularly solicited. What he had been denied when he did not receive the prize was not access to the literary establishment, but access to a special prestige that only the prize imparted. The Akutagawa Prize became an end in itself because it produced a form of symbolic capital that had not previously existed: a mark of distinction that sanctified authors even as it reproduced the prize's own cultural authority and that of the literary field itself.

Preserving Works, Cultivating Prestige

The Akutagawa Prize provided a mechanism by which Kikuchi Kan and the other members of the selection committee could affect the dissemination, reception, and preservation of works they believed best met their literary criteria. Consider the Akutagawa Prize given in 1941 to Tada Yūkei for "Chōkō Deruta." As we have seen, the final decision was not easy for the committee members, nor was the best work obvious. Despite the fact that the quality of the final two works considered was sufficiently close to cause the committee members to be this divided, the subsequent lives of the works were radically different. "Chōkō Deruta" has been republished in collections and discussed in critical works.[143] "Yamabiko," however, has basically disappeared, despite having come within one vote of receiving the award. The selection committee members Satō Haruo, Uno Kōji, and Murō Saisei believed that it was the superior work. Even some of the individuals who voted for "Chōkō Deruta" conceded that, were the country not at war, "Yamabiko" would have been more deserving of the award. Without the imprimatur of the prize, however, the work did not receive the institutional attention necessary to keep it alive. Because of this decision it is difficult for us today to determine whether "Yamabiko" is indeed a valuable work, for today only a specialist would know how to find a copy of the story. The cultural authority of the Akutagawa Prize, exercised after a tenuous and contested single decision, played a large part in determining the life of the work.

At the same time that "Chōkō Deruta" received the Akutagawa Prize Kimura Sōjū received the Naoki Prize for *Un'nan shubihei* (The Yunnan Garrison). The Naoki Prize bestowed many similar benefits upon this work, including an expanded readership and reproduction in anthologies such as the *Taishū bungaku taikei* (Popular Literature Collection, 1973). At the same time, however, it relegated it into a category—popular literature—that immediately affected its reception and that often excluded it from serious consideration. The creation of the linked awards materialized a boundary produced discursively through the debates examined in chapter 4. Despite many attempts to establish parity between the Akutagawa and Naoki Prizes, they were never perceived as separate but equal. "Chōkō Deruta" and its author, though admittedly not central in the Japanese literary canon, enjoyed the prestige of literature without qualifications and were thus promoted into the imaginary of a national literature that had been reified by the *Complete Works of Contemporary Japanese Literature* (even if today that might entail only the text's reproduction and the author's inclusion in dictionaries of modern Japanese literature).[145] This special treatment was justified through claims of the work's purity, which, while ambiguous and multivalent, usually implied independence from the market and the baser desires it represented. Despite the claims to purity, and thus independence from market demand, this was not an act of resistance against the economic forces created by a new, mass market for literature. Instead it was an act fully complicit with that market, which took advantage of the unprecedented reach that market had developed in the preceding half-century. The Akutagawa Prize for literature not only became a mechanism for the perpetual elevation of literary works—a dynamic canon, in a sense—but it also reified the very problematic boundary between pure and popular literature.

EPILOGUE

● ● ●

Nation

The modern history of literary study has been bound up with the
development of cultural nationalism, whose aim was first to distinguish the national canon, then to maintain its eminence, authority,
and aesthetic autonomy.

EDWARD SAID, *CULTURE AND IMPERIALISM*

Just like the Akutagawa Prize, which is still given twice a year, collections
such as the *Complete Works of Contemporary Japanese Literature* continued
to play an important function in the dissemination, reception, and preservation of literary works well into the postwar period.[1] The largest and most
influential of these series continue to reassert the connections with the
nation and modernity, with such series in regular production from at least
1953 to 1980: the ninety-nine-volume *Gendai Nihon bungaku zenshū* (Complete Works of Contemporary Japanese Literature, Chikuma Shobō, 1953–
61); the 108-volume *Nihon gendai bungaku zenshū* (Complete Works of
Japanese Contemporary Literature, Kōdansha, 1960–71; two additional
volumes on literary history were added in 1979); the ninety-seven-volume
Gendai Nihon bungaku taikei (Collection of Contemporary Japanese Literature, Chikuma Shobō, 1968–74); the sixty-one-volume *Nihon kindai bungaku taikei* (Collection of Japanese Modern Literature, Kadokawa Shoten,
1969–74); the hundred-volume successor to Chikuma's earlier *Gendai Nihon bungaku zenshū* (Complete Works of Contemporary Japanese Literature, Chikuma Shobō, 1975); and a revised and expanded reprint of the

Kōdansha series (1980). Again editorial control of these series was largely concentrated in the hands of a few: the writer and critic Itō Sei (1905–69) was the lead editor on both the Kōdansha series and the Kadokawa series; the literary scholar Usui Yoshimi (1905–87) was the lead editor for the Chikuma *Zenshū* and likely participated in the editing of the company's *Taikei*. These series sold well; Chikuma Shobō claims to have printed a total of thirteen million volumes (not sets) from its 1953–59 series, suggesting sales comparable to those of the *Collected Works of Contemporary Japanese Literature*. The absence in recent years of a similar collection of this magnitude (smaller collections in this vein are still regularly produced) likely speaks more to market saturation and a waxing of literature's cultural centrality than to any large-scale abandonment of the concept.

Countless collections exist that group literature in other ways, of course, usually celebrating a specific author or genre. Print capital has also produced anthologies that challenge the separation between modern and premodern, absorbing recent works into a transhistorical ethnic literature. The *Shin Nihon koten bungaku taikei* (New Collection of Japanese Classical Literature, Iwanami Shoten) has recently added a *Meiji-hen* (Meiji volumes), absorbing Meiji-era works as that period recedes into the past. Also warranting mention are the collections that celebrate nonnational (or subnational) literatures, including the five-volume *Ibaraki kindai bungaku senshū* (Selected Works of Ibaraki Modern Literature, Jōyō Shinbunsha, 1977–78); the twenty-three-volume *Hokkaidō bungaku zenshū* (Complete Works of Hokkaidō Literature, Rippū Shobō, 1979–81); the twenty-volume *Okinawa bungaku zenshū* (Complete Works of Okinawan Literature, Kokusho Kankōkai, 1990–); the six-volume *Tochigi-ken kindai bungaku zenshū* (Complete Works of Tochigi Modern Literature, Shimotsuke Shinbunsha, 1990); and the thirty-three-volume *Nagano-ken bungaku zenshū* (Complete Works of Nagano Literature, Kyōdo Shuppansha, 1988–90). These have even included collections of literature from the former Japanese colonies, including the forty-seven-volume *Nihon shokuminchi bungaku seisenshū* (Selected Works of Colonial Literature, Yumani Shobō, 2000–2001). The motivations behind these series are multiple, and many are not defined in contrast to the imagined unity of modern Japanese literature. However, some, such as the four-volume *Koronia shōsetsu senshū* (Selected Fiction of the "Colonia," 1975–96), are precisely attempts to establish conceptions of literature that are not so easily assimilated into that national imaginary, in this case, the Japanese-language fiction of Japanese migrants to Brazil.

In the afterword (*kaisetsu*) to the *Koronia shōsetsu senshū* the cultural anthropologist Maeyama Takashi writes that Japanese immigrants to Brazil lack a literary history of their own.[2] His conception is not an essentialist one, nor one precipitated by a modern condition produced by capitalism. He clarifies that by "literary history" he means a sequence of causal events through which one generation of literary activity provides energy—influence—to the next, not just a sequential description of literary works. This is the fantasy of organic association that literary history often implies, stripped to its most basic manifestation. He attributes this absence of literary history to the difficulty of getting Japanese-language books published in Brazil. A given author could individually circulate his or her work, but the lack of broad distribution meant that a given piece of fiction had little impact on a whole that might be called, as Maeyama calls it, a literary history (and thus a literature) of the *colonia japonesa*. Maeyama argues that writers were instead influenced by texts from Japan, which were more easily procured, and that the writers thus partook (albeit largely unilaterally, as consumers rather than producers) of the literary history of modern Japan. What Maeyama describes as literary history is not an essential ontological category, but a contingent historical category, in which individual literary works are linked together through a web of causality.

Maeyama, a scholar from Japan, notes that the collection was paid for, compiled, edited, and put out by the Koronia Bungakukai (Gremio Literario "Colonia"), which hoped that the anthology would allow for a history of Nikkei colonial literature in Brazil.[3] The distinct literary history that Maeyama describes, the cultural entity of Nikkei colonial literature, is actually the desideratum behind the anthology's production. The anthology is hoping not to represent a unity that exists, but to create that unity: to put in motion a literary history (as defined by Maeyama) that will cause that cultural unity to come into being. These books are not mere vessels to disseminate an ontologically necessary category; they are tools by which that category is created. The constructed nature of the category "Nikkei *colonia* literature" and the dependence of that construction on the publishing industry are clearly evidenced in this liminal example. As with the case of Mizumura Minae at the beginning of this study, this example from the

Japanese diaspora is an exceptional case that brings the role of material production into extreme relief.

To a certain extent the web of influence that Maeyama describes as necessary for the existence of a colonial literary history was in existence, in the case of modern Japanese literature, prior to the creation of the *Complete Works of Contemporary Japanese Literature* and the Akutagawa Prize. The small, elite (in cultural if not socioeconomic terms) community in Tokyo that produced most of the fiction collected in the series enjoyed ready access to literary works; to that extent, the argument could be made that the series represented an organic whole. Yet the claim of the series was not that it was the literature of that community, but that it was the literature of the nation. For many readers (and future writers), particularly outside of Tokyo, the books necessary to convey the energy Maeyama describes remained inaccessible well into the twentieth century. Thinking of the literary texts that make up modern Japanese literature as a cultural unity that possesses this sort of literary history is thus an epistemological step that must be historicized; at the same time the motivations behind the call for such a unity must also be considered. Just as the Koronia Bungakukai wanted their unity to exist, so too did the Tokyo literary establishment.

This literary establishment, in conjunction with other intelligentsia and political leaders, led a project to define a national literature in the late nineteenth century and early twentieth century. It is not a coincidence that the first histories of Japanese literature, both premodern and modern, came into existence soon after individuals in Japan were exposed to histories of French and English national literary histories written by François Guizot and Hippolyte Taine, respectively.[4] Both Guizot and Taine "subscribed to the notion of national culture and civilization born of the nationalism that swept Europe in the late eighteenth century and after, as well as to the idea of 'literature' as the flower of each nation's culture."[5] The possession of a national literature became a point of pride for individuals who wanted to see Japan ranked among the greatest nations of the world. At stake was more than cultural pride; as Tomi Suzuki has written, the fate of Japan's national literature "was linked to that of Japan as a modern nation-state among Western nations."[6] When Tsubouchi Shōyō wrote "The Essence of the Novel," the text that is nearly always situated "at the originary point of modern literary reform," he began his introduction lauding the literature of *wagakuni* ("our country"): "How splendid has been the history of *monogatari* [tales] in our country!"[7] The desire to establish a national literature in a constellation of national literatures existed, even if such a literature was consciously seen as a foregone conclusion among the literary community in Tokyo.

When presented to its audience, modern Japanese literature made its claim on these consumers not only through an implied consensus on the nature of literary value, but also through this explicit connection to Japan. This was a particularly effective call in 1926, when the *Complete Works of Contemporary Japanese Literature* was launched. Only a year earlier the Universal Manhood Suffrage Law had quadrupled the number of enfranchised citizens; this helped invest even more individuals with the concept of a national literature. It must also be recognized that even as this modern national literature was being established, Japan was ceasing to be just a nation-state; it was becoming an empire. Even as modern Japanese literature made a claim on national citizens, it also made a claim on a vast array of imperial subjects who were being forced to identify themselves with the empire. This study, because of its focus on production in Tokyo, has largely avoided the impact this concept (and the books that reified it) had in the colonies and the regional periphery, merely suggesting the potential for such an impact. Much work remains to be done to explore the way these books, and the concept of modern Japanese literature, affected individual readers, especially when those readers were colonial and otherwise peripheral subjects. Work also remains to be done on the continuing impact of a conceptual framework dominated by the nation-state.[8] As Mark Driscoll has written, "The construction of the canon of Japanese literature through an exclusively cultural-national frame was one of the central catalysts leading to the deletion and forgetting of Japan's colonial imperialism."[9]

Precisely because of these links between literature and the projects of the state, Japan (as either nation or empire) has been a very useful category through which to consider these works. Valuable insights have been derived by distinguishing literary works produced in the nation-state (and at times empire) from works produced in other nation-states (and empires); similarly a legitimate difference is clarified when works written after the formation of that nation-state—and all of the cofertilization processes of so-called Westernization—are distinguished from the works that precede them. These have been summarized most clearly by James Fujii, who writes, "In the context of the twentieth century, the collectivity that canons

Epilogue

227

narrate is the nation." The "concurrent narratives of nation and empire and the construction of a 'modern' Japanese history" that were the "conditions that governed the simultaneous creation of a new literary canon" are drawn out by an emphasis on the nation as the defining collectivity.[10] Clearly both the nation-state and the empire are invaluable frames through which to interpret literary texts.

Conceiving literature through the framework of the state can also be politically expedient. Melissa Wender, writing on narratives by Koreans in Japan, argues that "Resident Korean literature" must be understood and taught "as an integrated part of Japanese literature," so that (among other positive developments) "all Japan's residents" will eventually "come to believe full citizenship should be granted to all Resident Koreans as a matter of course."[11] The grouping of literary works thus becomes part of a political and social program rather than stemming from an ontological necessity. At the same time this view highlights the problematic relationship between modern Japanese literature and Japan, particularly with regard to the concept of representativeness. Consider the Akutagawa Prize for the fall of 1999. The cowinners of the award were Gen Getsu, a resident Korean (*zainichi*) author, and Fujino Chiya, a transgender author. Neither would be considered representative of Japan's mainstream; in fact in his comments to the press Miyamoto Teru mentioned the exoticism of the two works as something that likely draws many readers to them.[12] In this way modern Japanese literature as a category is instrumentalized to change the social functioning of the state; rather than representative of what Japan is, it is representative of what Japan is *not*, but could be.

The insights (or political potential) provided by any grouping will always come at a cost, as the difference highlighted in the identification of an *other* will always elide both commonalities with that other and difference in the concomitant identification of the professedly homogeneous *self*.[13] Nor should the grouping of texts be uncritically naturalized, even when the basis of that grouping, in this case Japan, may seem unproblematic. Komori Yōichi, among others, has argued that the signifier "Japan" stems from the presumed unity of "Japan [as a state]," "Japanese [ethnicity]," "Japanese [language]," and "Japanese culture."[14] In many cases, as Naoki Sakai has pointed out, this presumed unity is defended through a circular logic: "Japanese culture is identified by referring to the Japanese language; Japanese language is then identified by referring to the national identity of the people; and finally the Japanese people are identified by their cultural and linguistic heritage."[15]

Still, this does not mean the category should be abandoned. As Fujii makes clear, Japan is not merely a discursive construct: it is a historical reality, and an abiding one at that.[16] The name captures not only a nation-state whose importance in global affairs is indisputable, but also a society and a cultural tradition—that they are "constructed" makes them no less real—with which millions of people identify. The mistake is to misrecognize this durability as permanence: to see the constructed as the natural, to see the present as the inevitable. Just as the nation-state—or the nation, for that matter—has not always existed in its current form, there is no logical necessity that it remain in its current form. A failure to historicize this current reality not only denies the contingency of the present, but also denies the potential for future change.

Purity

It is possible to close one's ears to this parochial cacophony of competing elites and focus upon the real debate, which is between those on one side who "know" what culture is and what it is not, who have a map of its fixed perimeters and a profile of the identity of its creators and its followers, who perceive culture to be something finite and fragile, which needs to be conserved and protected from the incessant Philistinism that threatens it, and those on the other side who, possessing no map and little liking for fixed and unmovable fences and boundaries, believe that worthy, enduring culture is not the possession of any single group or genre or period, who conceive of culture as neither finite nor fixed but dynamic and expansive, and who remain unconvinced that the moment an expressive form becomes accessible to large numbers of people it loses the aesthetic and intellectual criteria necessary to classify it as culture.

LAWRENCE W. LEVINE, *HIGHBROW/LOWBROW: THE EMERGENCE OF CULTURAL HIERARCHY IN AMERICA*

Despite having grown in size, the collected works listed earlier reproduce only a fraction of the tremendous amount of fiction that has been produced in the Japanese language since the Meiji Restoration of 1868, the modern period. The simplest logic of canonization argues that this is natural, for works are of different objective quality, and that, given time, the proverbial cream will inevitably rise to the surface. Such faith in the singularity of value and the resilience of texts is not justified. The criteria for determining literary value have rarely been uniform at any single point in the modern period, still less when compared over a longer historical span. Instead certain individuals and institutions have enjoyed the ability to affect the trajectory of literary works in line with their particular notions of literary value, even if their control over that trajectory was incomplete or imperfect. This power often derives from control over the physical production of literature through mechanisms of material consequence, such as these anthologies and literary awards, which have a profound impact on the dissemination, reception, and preservation of works of fiction. The texts that do not enjoy the benefits of these mechanisms may survive to be reevaluated later—the story "Yamabiko," for example, is still available, if rare—but many do not. The advantages of the reproduced works, moreover, are so overwhelming as to make a notable reappraisal nearly impossible; not the least of these advantages is the implication that the works have been carefully appraised against a consensus definition of literary value.

The key mechanism for naturalizing this illusion of consensus is the term "popular" as a category of works defined negatively, those that are not part of a "pure" category of elite literary art. The problem with the division, which I have discussed at length, resembles the problems identified by Patrick Brantlinger when he summarizes uses of the term "mass culture" in a variety of contemporary Western debates: "On the basis of the term's most frequent uses in contemporary discourse, no strict definition of 'mass culture' is possible. It is everything and anything, depending on what a particular critic most wishes to anathematize."[17] Various schools have theorized the distinction, identifying important characteristics (the divide usually involves multiple aspects of works, such as realism, complexity, innovation, intent) that those schools believe warrant a binary structure.[18] Clearly the identification of these characteristics has value, and specific works at conceptual extremes can make it seem obvious that two distinct categories exist. Without specific indication of the discourse from which the distinction is drawn, however, the terms imply that a consensus exists on which characteristics justify the divide.

The postwar history of the Akutagawa Prize suggests that the issues evident throughout the prewar and wartime functioning of the prize persist, including both shifting conceptions of what determines literary value and the resilience of the pure–popular binary structure. In 1956, when the award was given to the charismatic literary enfant terrible (and now conservative mayor of Tokyo) Ishihara Shintarō, the Akutagawa Prize grew in stature, becoming a major media event and the most prestigious literary prize in Japan.[19] That decision is particularly telling about not only shifting conceptions of literary value, but also the lack of consensus behind the concept of pure literature. Satō Haruo, one of the selection committee members in the dissenting minority, "wrote that it was the lowest type of literature [*bungei*]" and equated Ishihara with "journalists and entertainers"; the author Nakano Shigeharu captured some authors' frustration with the award when he sarcastically wrote of the decision, "It is a bad novel, therefore we should award it the Akutagawa Prize."[20] Some critics have gone so far as to suggest that it is the Naoki Prize, not the Akutagawa Prize, that truly rewards literary skill; whereas Akutagawa Prize–winning works tend to be shorter, more sensational, and written by less proven authors, the Naoki Prize–winning works tend to be more complex, more skillfully written (if more conventional), and written by more prolific authors. Though the valorization of the two categories shifts and the qualities justifying the binary are continually contested, few have recommended abandoning the binarism altogether.[21] As for the awards, even today, when the reading public has grown somewhat jaded with the vast number of prizes offered in the country—numbering in the thousands—the Akutagawa Prize still guarantees national media coverage and a significant economic and symbolic windfall for recipients.[22]

If any consensus does exist concerning the logic underpinning a distinction between pure and popular, in the Japanese context at least, it involves a fear of the market and the belief that literature within a capitalist system will result in works crafted to the tastes of the masses at the expense of art.[23] In this view "the gentlemanly author who wrote for a like-minded group of equals" is threatened by "the professional who depended for a livelihood on sales of his book to an impersonal public."[24] Rather than recognizing capitalism as the economic matrix that nearly every writer has had to contend with in the modern period—not to mention recognizing the other extraliterary forces that have always been at work on writers—a distinction is then implied between those who resisted the economic demands and those who succumbed; even when recognizing compromises elite writers made, a qualitative difference is asserted in the level of compromise. At the extreme the mildly compromised elite writer is absolved when compared with the gross commercialism of a Grub Street writer, or worse yet a fiction factory's market pseudonym, such as "Bertha M. Clay."[25]

The writers under examination in this study, however, do not fit cleanly into either half of this binary view. In almost all cases, whether or not they were classified by others as pure, the writers were writing professionally, often under a deadline, with external expectations about what they would produce; at the same time they exercised a great deal of creative freedom in their writing. Writers did have the option of avoiding the commodity form—one character in Kikuchi Kan's story "Mumei sakka no nikki" stacks his handwritten magnum opus on the floor of his room—but none of the writers studied here chose that route. Publishing has been, in almost every case, the sine qua non of serious consideration for the literature of modern Japan; even when publishing noncommercially, in such venues as coterie magazines, writers were still embroiled in an artistic field that was deeply commercial. While the effect of market forces on a writer dependent on his or her craft for a living must be considered, it cannot be used to divide works easily into two categories. Works of fiction can *be* commodities without being *reducible to* commodities.

Even when groupings, whether based on modernity, nation, or value, illuminate commonalities among works, they simultaneously elide difference.[26] As the groupings reify and are seen as inevitable they ignore historical change and forestall alternative groupings, and thus a richer understanding of variation. Similarly when the groupings are seen as natural the motivations behind those groupings are obscured. The *Complete Works of Contemporary Japanese Literature* exploited national identity and a faith in the radical newness of modernity in order to improve the dissemination, reception, and preservation of a specific group of texts; it achieved this at the cost of exaggerated commonality among those texts and denied commonality with excluded texts. The Akutagawa Prize continues to bring literary works to the attention of a wider audience than those works could ever have hoped to enjoy at the cost of perpetuating a belief in a qualitatively different field of pure literature and a singularity of literary value. Both resulted in the assertion of an economy of value autonomous from that of the market, despite occurring within that very marketplace.

Despite this assertion of autonomy from the commercial, the creation of the category of modern Japanese literature, like the creation of the Akutagawa Prize's new form of prestige, seems largely fueled by a desire to find a space for works in both a domestic and a global cultural and economic system that might not otherwise have accommodated them. Other groupings, such as those of regional literatures or ethnic subgroups that have often been overlooked by the Tokyo-centered publishing industry, are turning to similar structures to advance their causes and to garner a larger readership than they would otherwise have enjoyed. The political expediency of this solution is undeniable; it is also historically justified, to the extent that the groupings reflect real commonalities. At the same time, however, the limitations of the groupings—the limits of the works' commonalities—must be recognized, and the motivations behind the groupings must be considered.

The motivations behind groupings will always be multiple. Some of the actors behind the discursive and material mechanisms that support these groupings have cultural motivations; some have political motivations. Some have both, and often the cultural cannot be separated from the political. When the Akutagawa Prize committee nominated "Chōkō Deruta," for example, the motivations—to further the war effort by supporting a new type of literature—were a complex mix of the two. At least in the case of the mechanisms explored here, the role of capitalism cannot be ignored. Capitalism will, it would seem, support any grouping and any mechanism that results in the sale of more commodities. The ideologies behind these mechanisms cannot be reduced to the profit motive, however. Publishers regularly speak of their vocation as serving a higher purpose and point to publishing projects that do not adhere to the demands of the bottom line.

Print capital, directed as it always has been by individuals with multiple motivations, has had an enabling effect even as it has had a compromising effect on writing and reading. Even as we recognize that capitalism profited from and reified the belief in a clear distinction between national literatures, the modern and the premodern, and the popular and the pure, the enabling aspects of this change in the mode of production cannot be overlooked; vast new strata of society were given access to literary texts of all sorts, and the economic possibilities of writing, compromised as that undertaking might be, made creative activity possible for groups that could never have dedicated as much time and energy to it before. Admittedly the new writers and readers were still only a subset of the population as a whole, and these writers (and readers) should be recognized as complicit in the social system in which they participated. Even when they benefited enough from the conception of literature to become invested in its stability and profitability, however, they rarely gained control of the means of production and thus remained alienated from the majority of power in the field. The same holds true for the middlemen of this literary marketplace, academics.

Yet the recognition of this complicity need not lead to a reaction that abandons the products of the publishing industry as compromised or constructed—but then, such an option is almost impossible for anyone interested in Japanese-language literary production since the Meiji Restoration. It does, however, call upon each of us to acknowledge the nature of the system in which we operate and to admit the imperfect nature of our own proposed structures of thought, even as we work to destabilize existing structures we deem deleterious. We cannot hope to operate outside these mechanisms, from an objective viewpoint, but we can operate in fuller awareness of them. By reflecting on the construction of the groupings that underpin the literary field, we can hope not only to illuminate the historical forces that produced those specific groupings, but perhaps also to free ourselves to imagine different groupings that might reveal new commonalities that had heretofore been obscured.

The study of mechanisms of power, whether material or discursive, through which the dissemination, reception, and preservation of works are influenced suggests that the ascriptions of value that attend works are neither natural nor inevitable because they do not emanate in any simple way from the texts themselves. Whether the category of pure literature, popular literature, or modern Japanese literature itself, the epistemological frameworks we use to grasp literary events must be historicized and problematized. Literary value, the ascription of which is central to the function of these categories, cannot be thought of as singular, transhistorical, or self-evident. At the same time, however, the efficacy of these categories in allowing a host of texts that might not have survived in a fully liberalized textual marketplace to be produced, disseminated, and preserved is undeniable. While a simple return to the categories seems neither advisable nor logically supportable, the option remains—a challenge for an affirmative assertion beyond the negative critique of this study—to demonstrate perhaps a "complex normativity" that would prevent this study's deconstruction of the terms to devolve into yet another justification for a reliance on the market to determine the worth of texts.[27] One wonders if the market, readers, or academia could support an even more radical option: to remain in a state of indeterminacy and fluidity, what Gayatri Spivak has referred to as "undecidability,"[28] with regard to these epistemological categories and the calls to transcendent value upon which they are presumably erected, and thus place the burden of justification on each historically situated claim of value.

This seems consonant with the cautions laid out by David Palumbo-Liu for a "*critical* multiculturalism" that attempts to construct an "ethnic canon":

> While the traditional canon is based on a presumed set of accepted texts, each of which can be reconciled to similar aesthetic values (even as those values are modified in time yet anchored by the evocation of the same terminologies), an ethnic canon should be always in revision and contestation, its critics conscious of both its historical and ideological constructedness and their own pedagogical goals.[29]

It should be noted that, in the context of this study's articulation— primarily the Anglophonic academy in the United States, specifically in the institutional apparatus of modern Japanese literary studies—the array of texts that have been grouped together under that nationally bounded rubric is simultaneously an "ethnic canon" and a "traditional canon": it represents a dominant literary discourse in one national context and a marginal discourse in another. In either context, however, the mechanisms of power that are implied by the metaphor of the canon, as well as the value ascribed to texts by those mechanisms, must remain contested. Such contestation may then allow excluded voices to be heard without assimilating them into a celebratory narrative of a homogeneous ethnonational community.[30]

APPENDIX

● ● ●

TABLE 6   NUMBER OF TITLES PUBLISHED

Year	Newspapers	Specimens	Magazines	Official	Remainder
1919	3,423	47,254	23,940	12,761	10,553
1920	3,532	44,176	22,421	11,916	9,848
1921	3,980	45,891	21,097	12,891	11,903
1922	4,562	48,404	21,594	13,729	13,081
1923	4,592	39,950	18,409	10,576	10,945
1924	5,854	47,529	23,433	9,735	14,361
1925	6,899	56,508	25,636	12,844	18,028
1926	7,600	58,971	29,290	9,468	20,213
1927	8,350	63,258	33,715	9,576	19,967
1928	8,445	60,179	32,691	9,608	19,880
1929	9,191	68,854	37,402	10,341	21,111
1930	10,130	72,154	39,339	10,339	22,476

Source: Yayoshi Mitsunaga, *Mikan shiryō ni yoru Nihon shuppan bunka: Kindai shuppan bunka*, Shoshi shomoku shiriizu 26, vol. 5 (Tokyo: Yumani Shobō, 1988), 293.

TABLE 7 ESTIMATES OF TOTAL BOOK AND MAGAZINE SALES

Year	Total	Change (%)
1881	2,500,000	
1887	5,500,000	+20.00
1892	11,900,000	+23.27
1897	17,000,000	+8.57
1902	30,800,000	+16.24
1907	53,400,000	+14.68
1912	79,100,000	+9.63
1916	96,500,000	+5.50
1921	101,800,000	+1.10
1926	180,000,000	+15.36
1930	221,700,000	+5.79

Sources: Yayoshi Mitsunaga, *Mikan shiryō ni yoru Nihon shuppan bunka: Kindai shuppan bunka*, Shoshi shomoku shiriizu 26, vol. 5 (Tokyo: Yumani Shobō, 1988), 289, 294; Tokyo Shuppan Hanbai Kabushikigaisha, ed., *Shuppan hanbai shōshi: Tōhan sōritsu jisshūnen kinen* (Tokyo: Tokyo Shuppan Hanbai, 1959); Jonathan E. Zwicker, *Practices of the Sentimental Imagination: Melodrama, the Novel, and the Social Imaginary in Nineteenth-Century Japan* (Cambridge, Mass.: Harvard University Press, 2006).

TABLE 8 LOCATION, BY WARD, OF TOKYO NEWSPAPERS PRIOR
TO THE EARTHQUAKE

Newspaper	Ward
Chūgai shōgyō shinpō	Nihonbashi
Chūō shinbun	Kyōbashi
Hōchi shinbun	Kōjimachi
Japan Times and Mail	Kōjimachi
Kokumin shinbun	Kyōbashi
Yorozu chōhō	Kyōbashi
Miyako shinbun	Kōjimachi
Niroku shinpō	Kanda
Tōkyō asahi shinbun	Kyōbashi
Tōkyō jiji	Kyōbashi
Tōkyō maiyū shinbun	Nihonbashi?
Tōkyō nichinichi shinbun	Kōjimachi
Tōkyō ōzei shinbun	Nihonbashi
Tokyo yūkan shinbun	Kyōbashi
Yamato shinbun	Kyōbashi
Yomiuri shinbun	Kyōbashi

Source: Nagashiro Shizuo, ed., *Nihon shinbun shashi shūsei* (Tokyo: Shinbun Kenkyūjo, 1938).

TABLE 9   TOKYO NEWSPAPER MARKET SHARES (% OF TOTAL)

Year	Nichinichi	Asahi	Hōchi	Yomiuri	Jiji	Kokumin	Total
1919	7.3	4.8	6.9	3.4	9.4	4.0	35.8
1925	14.7	13.1	7.7	13.4	10.3	8.2	67.4
1930	20.6	19.8	15.0	5.9	10.4	11.5	83.2

Source: Yamamoto Taketoshi, *Kindai Nihon no shinbun dokushasō*, Sōsho gendai no shakai kagaku (Tokyo: Hōsei Daigaku Shuppankyoku, 1981), 245.

TABLE 10   CHANGES IN CIRCULATION OF *ŌSAKA ASAHI* AND *TŌKYŌ ASAHI*

Year	Ōsaka asahi	Change (%)	Tōkyō asahi	Change (%)
1920	376,032		250,088	
1921	444,552	18.22	291,957	16.74
1922	562,700	26.58	274,900	−5.84
1923	585,294	4.02	289,464	5.30
1924	689,974	17.89	410,221	41.72
1925	754,373	9.33	422,527	3.00
1926	782,709	3.76	431,811	2.20
1927	866,256	10.67	573,838	32.89
1928	922,891	6.54	553,318	−3.58
1929	966,398	4.71	587,495	6.18
1930	979,530	1.36	702,244	19.53
1931	914,355	−6.65	521,228	−25.78
1932	1,054,021	15.27	770,369	47.80
1933	1,041,115	−1.22	844,808	9.66
1934	1,138,482	9.35	885,007	4.76
1935	897,594	−21.16	913,342	3.20
1936	861,334	−4.04	1,011,190	10.71

Source: Yamamoto Taketoshi, *Kindai Nihon no shinbun dokushasō*, Sōsho gendai no shakai kagaku (Tokyo: Hōsei Daigaku Shuppankyoku, 1981), 410.

Appendix

TABLE 11   FACTORIES DESTROYED IN THE EARTHQUAKE, BY WARD

Ward	Totally Destroyed	Collapsed or Damaged	No Damage	Total	Iwasaki
Kyōbashi	87	0	0	87	85
Nihonbashi	23	0	0	23	23
Kanda	61	0	0	61	61
Ushigome	0	4	5	9	
Shitaya	20	0	1	21	20
Hongō	5	1	2	8	
Honjo	19	0	0	19	19
Kōjimachi	12	3	0	15	15
Koishikawa	1	3	1	5	1
Asakusa	19	0	0	19	19
Shiba	24	1	1	26	25
Azabu	2	4	5	11	
Yotsuya	2	1	3	6	
Fukagawa	5	0	0	5	
Total	280	17	18	315	
Iwasaki Totals	285	14			

Source: Kaizōsha, ed., Taishō daishinkasai shi (Tokyo: Kaizōsha, 1924), 76–77.

NOTES

• • •

Introduction

1. The time of this move is unclear in Mizumura's novel, though presumably it occurs in the late 1960s. The novel states that the series came out "almost immediately after" the narrator's mother was born. Mizumura, *Shishōsetsu from left to right*, 99. At the Association for Japanese Literary Studies meeting held at Princeton in November 2007, Mizumura described in a lecture how this event was drawn from her personal experience.

2. References to the "nation" throughout the manuscript are intentionally ambiguous, in an attempt to capture the blurring in the notion between the political nation-state (which during the period under consideration remained a tacit presence, even after it launched its imperial expansion and reconceptualization) and an imagined Japanese "ethnic" nation, which has often been perceived as being coterminous with the political nation-state of Japan, but which in the past has exceeded these boundaries, most notably during the period of the Great Japanese Empire. This is what Immanuel Wallerstein has called the "peoplehood construct," which presents itself as either "genetically continuous groups (races), historical socio-political groups (nations), or cultural groups (ethnic groups)," and what Etienne Balibar has called a "fictive ethnicity." See Immanuel Wallerstein, "The Construction of Peoplehood: Racism, Nationalism, Ethnicity" (71–85; quotes on 78–79) and Etienne Balibar, "The Nation Form: History and Ideology" (86–106; quote on 96), both in Balibar and Wallerstein, *Race, Nation, Class*.

3. Mizumura, *Shishōsetsu from left to right*, 110.

4. It is essential to indicate from the outset that during the period I focus on, roughly 1918–41, Japan was not a nation-state, but an empire. This fact is noted throughout the study, but is not (for reasons discussed in the conclusion) given the full attention it deserves. As Edward Said (most notably but certainly not solely) indicated in *Culture and Imperialism*, literature significantly enabled the imperialist project, cre-

ating " 'structures of feeling' that support, elaborate, and consolidate the practice of empire" and thus must be considered within that context (14).

5. Mizumura, *Shishōsetsu from left to right*, 99. I consciously conflate the usage of *gendai* (contemporary) in the title of the series with "modern" (*kindai*). For more on the distinction between *kindai* and *gendai*, see Washburn, *The Dilemma of the Modern*, 1–16, and Suzuki S., *Nihon no "bungaku" gainen*, 271, who asserts that "the use of *kindai bungaku* to designate the literature of the Meiji period and after was commonplace by the end of the 1930s." This translation comes from Royall Tyler's English translation of Suzuki's volume, *The Concept of "Literature" in Japan*, 254. See chapter 3 for a longer discussion of this issue. Though "complete works" is an accurate translation of the literal meaning of the term *zenshū*, the fact that *zenshū* have rarely been complete has led people more aware of the nature of the collections to think of them as "collected works," immediately adjusting for the advertising hyperbole of the term. I preserve the literal meaning of the term in order to highlight its implications.

6. Despite the inherent ambiguity of the term, I use "print capitalism" to facilitate dialogue with other recent studies on the connection between an economic system, capitalism, and a technology of production, print; "publishing capital," identifying a more specific mode of print production, including not only the printing of texts but their marketing and distribution, would be a more precise term. It is interesting to note that the conventional Japanese translation of "print capitalism," *shuppan shihon*, would be more accurately retranslated into English as "publishing capital."

7. Noguchi Takehiko in Karatani, *Kindai Nihon no hihyō III*, 245.

8. Similar developments were occurring in other nations at roughly the same time; comparisons, with the exception of those related to specific technical developments, are relegated to notes in this study. This is not meant to imply Japanese uniqueness nor incommensurability of any kind. I avoid comparisons of national cases partly out of a lack of expertise concerning other markets and partly out of a desire not to line up national models and thus reproduce that conceptual framework. Central to my argument in fact is the claim that Tokyo-centered, "pure" literary publishing does not even sufficiently represent the complexity of the Japanese case. Two studies that address similar questions with regard to other national literatures—Greek and German, respectively—are Jusdanis, *Belated Modernity*, and Hohendahl, *Building a National Literature*.

9. In certain uses (such as the creation of anthologies, awards, and academic fields) "modern Japanese literature," as a concept, implies a system of value, an economy, that is not based on each text's capacity for exchange, its value in the market economy, but on a text's possession of a constellation of intrinsic characteristics that make it modern, Japanese, and literature. I explore the link to "modernity" and "Japan" in subsequent chapters. When the category distinguishes a select group of works from fictional production as a whole ("pure" literature in contradistinction to the "popular" fiction of modern Japan), participation in that economy is deter-

mined merely by the presence or absence of this value, or literary significance. Hence even though the works recognized within this economy, "pure" literature, might possess greater or lesser significance (or value), the degree of significance is of less importance than the recognition that it possesses value at all. All works not recognized within this economy, "popular" literature, are marked as lacking that value. These value claims are presented (naturalized) as if they are grounded in a consensus concerning the characteristics that make a literary work consequential (not to mention modern and Japanese), despite being contingent and contested. Simultaneously this economy must declare its autonomy from the market because the presumption is that these characteristics, or the importance of these characteristics, will not naturally be recognized by the majority of readers and thus will not be appropriately recognized by the market. As I discuss later, however, this autonomy from the market is more posture than reality. For a thoroughly antifoundationalist explication of these different economic systems, see Herrnstein Smith, *Contingencies of Value*, 30–53.

10. For a collection of serious ruminations on the challenges posed by this reconceptualization of the study of literature, see Hutcheon and Valdés, *Rethinking Literary History*.

11. This is D. F. McKenzie's position, as summarized by McDonald and Suarez in McKenzie, *Making Meaning*, 6. It is worth considering how electronic distribution of texts complicates (but does not obviate) this claim, though such a consideration would be anachronistic for this study.

12. This history must also take into account the impact print has had on nonreaders, individuals with indirect access to texts. Such indirect access can be as minimal (and nonliterary) as seeing Natsume Sōseki and Higuchi Ichiyō on currency and can still give literature influence over the population's self-imagination.

13. A study such as this one in fact is merely the necessary precondition for the study of the actual impact of texts, what William St. Clair in *The Reading Nation* has described as reading's ability to shape "mentalities."

14. See English, *The Economy of Cultural Prestige*, 10. Both English's study and my own owe a profound debt to the work of the sociologist Pierre Bourdieu. Although many of the concepts in this study may be seen as aligning with those of Bourdieu, the goal of my project is far less ambitious. Whereas Bourdieu extends his study to the function of cultural power in society in general—as the concept of convertibility would imply—I maintain a much more narrow focus and do not fully embrace Bourdieu's conceptual apparatus. This study should be seen, therefore, as inspired and informed by Bourdieu's examination of power in the cultural realm rather than as an application of his model to the Japanese case.

15. In her groundbreaking essay "The Production of Literature and the Effaced Realm of the Political" Atsuko Ueda explores the ways that the new "category of literature, [which] had not gained ontological recognition" at the end of the nineteenth century, "did so by defining itself against the political" (64). My argument, which

focuses on literature's self-definition against the market, does not, I believe, contradict Ueda's claim; I would argue that both processes were working in tandem. See A. Ueda, "Meiji Literary Historiography," 167.

16. This is similar to the "new 'high literary zone'" that Janice A. Radway describes in her fascinating study, *A Feeling for Books*, 140. For those interested in similar (and partially contemporaneous) developments in the United States, Radway's book is extremely useful. The primary difference between my study and Radway's is that she focuses on the "middlebrow," which she sees as forming by "processes of literary and cultural mixing whereby forms and values associated with one form of cultural production were wed to forms and values usually connected with another" (152); middlebrow works refused "to perpetuate the distinction between two forms of value, one determined economically by the operations of particular interests in the market, the other understood to be fixed, universal, and transcendent" (153). I argue that the concept of an elevated sphere of literary production in modern Japan, as a cultural unity separate from premodern works, was formed by claims of fixed, universal, and transcendent value that remained ambiguously defined; to perpetuate the high-, middle-, and lowbrow distinction is merely to reproduce these mechanisms of power.

17. Nor should this be interpreted to mean that the works making up the category ever presented a singular voice, let alone a simple state-approved, ethnically or culturally homogeneous orthodoxy. Michael Bourdaghs's recent study of Shimazaki Tōson, *The Dawn That Never Comes*, shows how Tōson's works present a variety of perspectives, some sympathetic to the project of the nation-state but others corrosive to it.

18. This binary is intended as a heuristic device and should not be reified in the way many of the other binaries explored in this study have been. The series, for example, was not entirely static; Kaizōsha first extended the series, then produced a *Shin Nihon bungaku zenshū* (1939–43); other companies, such as Kōdansha and Chikuma Shobō, also produced similar series in the postwar. Thus while any given collection may be more or less static, the phenomenon of collections can be seen as dynamic.

19. I could also have considered a number of other mechanisms, not to mention other collected works and literary awards: literary reviews and gossip columns in newspapers; the inexpensive, soft-cover *bunkobon* form; the modern Japanese literary establishment (*bundan*); and the publication of literary histories. It is my hope that this study will prompt further examination of the various mechanisms that affect the dissemination, reception, and preservation or literary works, thereby fleshing out the sociology of literary texts. For an overview of many of the forces at work, see Marcus, "The Social Organization of Modern Japanese Literature."

20. Evidence for such reception will necessarily be circumstantial and testimonial rather than conclusive. I prefer "testimonial" to the dismissive "anecdotal" because it is hard to imagine a body of evidence that could be anything other, particularly when the question being asked focuses on changes in individuals' perceptions. Future research will be required to expand upon the specific impacts of these shifts in production on individual readers; such research will likely reveal that individual

reception differs dramatically from the modality of reception imagined by the producers. Similarly, while the centrifugal forces are the focus of this study, centripetal forces demand equal attention. The work of Richard Torrance marks an important move in this direction. See "Literacy and Modern Literature in the Izumo Region" and "Literacy and Literature in Osaka."

21. The limited nature of this reconsideration—that is, as it concerns material production—must be stressed; for a fascinating reconsideration of the boundary (and the various forms of identity, national and otherwise, enacted on either side) from the perspective of the narratives themselves, see Mertz, *Novel Japan*. For a similar study of narratives but with a much broader conception of what might constitute "the modern," see Washburn, *The Dilemma of the Modern*.

22. This continuity is of a decidedly limited type and should not be taken to imply an essentialist, transhistorical link of "Japanese" culture. See Anderson, "National Literature."

23. *Yomiuri shinbun*, 7 May 1927.

24. See Shirane and Suzuki, *Inventing the Classics*, particularly Shirane's "Curriculum and Competing Canons," 220–49; Yoda, *Gender and National Literature*, 41–80; Brownstein, "From Kokugaku to Kokubungaku." In "Bungakushi to nashonaritii" Nakayama examines how various histories written between 1890 and 1912 discuss the divide between modern Japanese literature and that which preceded it, focusing on frequently invoked clichés and the logical inconsistencies resulting from the various ways they were appropriated. In addition to illuminating the theoretical problems inherent in asserting an essential national character (evinced through literature) even as one asserts a historical view of literary development (allowing the claim that modern literature differs radically from that which precedes it), Nakayama also suggests that the timing of this sort of debate is particularly germane. As a new imperial power with colonial holdings, the nation itself was threatened by the same logical conundrum: How does a nation preserve a distinctive identity even as it incorporates elements it considers foreign?

25. Maruyama Masao, "Watashi no chūgaku jidai to bungaku," *Maruyama Masao shū*, vol. 15, 236. It should be noted that Maruyama identifies a similar, simultaneous process affecting the perception of world literature. This is a phenomenon deserving study, but one that falls outside of the purview of this book.

26. "Japanese literary history" education began in the prefectural normal schools (*jinjō shihan gakkō*) in 1892 and in the middle schools and women's upper schools in 1902 (Nakayama, "Bungakushi to nashonaritii," 88). Also see Hiraoka, "Meiji Taishō bungakushi shūsei," 1–13. Works of literature written in Japan since the Meiji Restoration were not common in Japanese literature classes, according to Yanagida Izumi (*Meiji bungaku kenkyū yobanashi*, 21–22), nor were they usually taught as a distinct group. A few universities, such as Waseda, began to offer lectures on Meiji literature around 1914 (22–23). Even at Waseda at this time, however, most teachers involved in writing literature—Tsubouchi Shōyō, Shimamura Hōgetsu, Hasegawa Tenkei, and others—taught their various specialties and did not teach contem-

porary literature at the school (53). Michael Bourdaghs sees the trend toward modern Japanese literature being made a regular part of university curricula beginning in the 1930s (*The Dawn That Never Comes*, 24–25). As Bourdaghs points out, however, the absence of the academic discipline did not equate to the absence of a literary "institution," using Peter Hohendahl's sense of this term from *Building a National Literature* (26–43).

27. A clarification concerning terms needs to be made at the outset. The *Nihon kokugo daijiten* defines *tsūzoku* as having three meanings: first, "average, common"; second, "something that someone without specialized knowledge would understand"; and third, "customary among general society." Throughout this study I explore more fully the use of the term in regard to literature and the derogatory sense that is only vaguely present in these definitions. Similarly I explore the related concept of *taishū*, which the *Nihon kokugo daijiten* defines as "a large number of people," or more specifically "the average members of the working class who hold no special position" and "the agricultural and industrial working class that makes up the majority of the population." *Taishū* is roughly homologous with the English-language concepts of "popular" and "the masses." In *Keywords* Raymond Williams explores relevant nuances of these English terms, which I argue similarly apply to the terms *tsūzoku* and *taishū*. With regard to "popular (adj.)," when used to designate cultural forms, Williams writes that the term carries two connotations: "inferior kinds of work . . . and work deliberately setting out to win favour" (237). This is to be distinguished from "popular" describing work "actually made by people for themselves," which would be related to "folk culture," and "well-liked," which might be demonstrated by bestselling status (236–37). With regard to "the masses (n.)" and "mass (adj.)," Williams notes that two distinct sets of implications exist, usually dependent upon the political position of the individual using the term: either the mob, and thus "low, ignorant, unstable" (related to the development of "vulgar" from "the vulgate"), or the same people "seen as a positive or potentially positive social force" (192–97). Since the meanings of the terms themselves shift so dramatically, translation becomes particularly challenging. I will attempt to recognize the differences in the terms despite focusing on a common logic that the terms in their derogatory senses share: the existence of a high compared to which these low categories are seen as inferior.

28. For more on the *bundan*, see Itō Sei's and Senuma Shigeki's twenty-four-volume *Nihon bundanshi*. The most concise description of the *bundan* in English appears in Fowler, *The Rhetoric of Confession*, 128–45; a lengthier study, Powell's *Writers and Society in Modern Japan*, is also available. Particularly during the period examined in this study the term is used in two senses: its broad sense, of the world of fiction as a whole, and its narrow sense, of the world of fiction that matters and the individuals with the power to define what that is. In this study I use the term in its narrow sense exclusively, in line with current usage.

29. Huyssen, *After the Great Divide*, viii.

30. Kikuchi Kan, "Taishū bungei dangi," *Tōkyō nichinichi shinbun*, 12 June 1933.

31. For an excellent rebuttal to attacks against relativism, see Rorty, *Consequences of Pragmatism*, 166–67, as cited and reinforced in Laclau and Mouffe, "Post-Marxism without Apologies," 85–86.

32. As Linda Hutcheon has written, "Writing literary historically in terms of reclaiming the repressed, the blocked out, the marginalized means openly addressing the forces that caused the repressing, the blocking, and the marginalization in the first place" (*Rethinking Literary History* 19).

1. Modernity as Rupture

1. Total sales figures are hard to establish and scholars have put forward different totals. These range from 380,000 in Suzuki Toshio, *Shuppan*, 194, to 600,000 in Okano, *Nihon shuppan bunka-shi*, 348. See chapter 3 for more detailed estimates.

2. The entrepreneur's boxcar contained books from various one-yen anthologies that were produced as a result of the boom started by the *Complete Works of Contemporary Japanese Literature*. Mack, "Marketing Japan's Literature."

3. It should be noted, however, that fiction appearing in the supposedly "disposable" print forms of newspapers and magazines had achieved comparably large readerships prior to this time. It is likely, in fact, that serial fiction in newspapers was one of the central forces leading to increased newspaper circulation itself. See Gedin, *Literature in the Marketplace*, 18.

4. Harootunian, *Overcome by Modernity*, xi–xx, x.

5. Harootunian, *History's Disquiet*, 48. In "The Invention of Edo" Carol Gluck describes this as "the originary rupture typical of the modern: an epochal threshold had been crossed, a new age now begun," in which the immediately preceding Edo period became the "mirror of modernity," "the anterior otherness against which the modern historical imagination . . . defined itself *as modern*, whether by asserting utter difference or by evoking seductively selective affinities" (265, 262).

6. The Japanese terms *tairyō seisan* (mass production) and *taishū bunka* (mass culture) preserve the semantic distinction between the two senses of "mass" (i.e., large scale and "of the masses"), though conflation often occurs in Japanese scholarship as well because of a presumed logical or causal connection between the two: large-scale production allows the masses access to identical items, even as the demands of the masses necessitate large-scale production. As for "mass literature" and "popular literature," terms which various groups have attempted to differentiate, I conflate them merely to highlight the single commonality among all the competing definitions: culture that is not elite.

7. Twyman, *Printing*, 48.

8. Dai-Nihon Insatsu Kabushiki Kaisha, *Shichijūgonen no ayumi*, 141. Satō Takumi argues persuasively that the publication of *King* magazine in 1925 actually made the one-yen book boom possible. See *Kingu no jidai*. It should be noted that the use of a rotary press to produce books was extremely exceptional; as William St. Clair has written, "The growth in books and reading brought about by the coming of print . . .

took the form of the production of more texts rather than of more copies of existing texts" (*The Reading Nation*, 22). Even today most literary books are printed in runs well within the capacity of smaller-scale technology. Christopher L. Hill focuses on the complex dialectic between discourses of continuity and rupture that was crucial to the formation of the modern nation in "Ideologies of Novelty and Agedness."

9. Jonathan Zwicker arrives at similar conclusions in *Practices of the Sentimental Imagination*, 26. Related arguments have been made about Europe; see Johns, *The Nature of the Book*, 633 (as cited in *Practices*, 28).

10. Marilyn Ivy makes a strong argument for such a break in her highly influential essay "Formations of Mass Culture"; yet simple application of this argument, which considers a wide variety of cultural forms, to the specific case of literary publishing elides significant continuities that problematize the high-low schema within that field.

11. Suzuki Toshio, *Shuppan*, 13. For more in English on the early history of the book in Japan, see Keyes, *Ehon*, and Chibbett, *The History of Japanese Printing and Book Illustration*, not to mention the work of Peter Kornicki, cited extensively below.

12. Kornicki, *The Book in Japan*, 114–17; Forrer, *Eirakuya Tōshirō*, 56–57. Four different texts are known to have been printed. The printing method remains a subject of debate, some contending that wood blocks were used, others copper plates. Hashimoto M., *Nihon shuppan hanbai-shi*, 4. Nakane Katsu considers the various theories in his *Nihon insatsu gijutsu-shi*, 52–55, and leans slightly toward the contention that wood was used.

13. Forrer, *Eirakuya Tōshirō*, 57–60; Kornicki, *The Book in Japan*, 117–25.

14. Shively, "Popular Culture," 725.

15. Kornicki (*The Book in Japan*, 125), Nagasawa (*Wakansho no insatsu to sono rekishi*, 122), and Insatsushi (*Hon to katsuji no rekishi jiten*, 11) all have the press arriving in 1590. Forrer (*Eirakuya Tōshirō*, 60) has the press arriving in the 1580s and then printing from 1591 to 1611. Altman ("Modernization of Printing," 86) has them printing until 1614. Kornicki notes church calendar production until at least 1618 (126).

16. See Boxer, *The Christian Century*, 189–98, for an overview of the Jesuits' various publications, which are known collectively as *Kirishitanban*.

17. Insatsushi, *Hon to katsuji*, 11. This was the first metal type produced in Japan (49). It was made by Japanese converts such as Constantino Dourado Augustino, who had gone to Europe to learn printing (66).

18. Kornicki, *The Book in Japan*, 125–27. Kornicki mentions the possibility that there was an impact; recent scholarship suggests the impact of the Christian press on *kokatsuji* was more profound than is often thought. Insatsushi, *Hon to katsuji*, 11–46.

19. Between 1592 and 1598, according to Forrer, *Eirakuya Tōshirō*, 60. Momose Hiroshi places the arrival at 1593 in Insatsushi, *Hon to katsuji*, 50.

20. Forrer, *Eirakuya Tōshirō*, 61.

21. Lane, "The Beginnings of the Modern Japanese Novel," 646. Most likely *Kobun kōkyō* was printed using the Korean type (Insatsushi, *Hon to katsuji*, 51). These

editions, printed by order of the emperors Go-Yōzei and Go-Mizunoo, are known collectively as the *chokuhan*.

22. Lane, "The Beginnings of the Modern Japanese Novel," 646. According to Shively, "Popular Culture," 726, the Korean type was made of copper.

23. Lane, "The Beginnings of the Modern Japanese Novel," 646.

24. Insatsushi, *Hon to katsuji*, 49. See chapter 2. Kornicki states that most of the type was wooden and was produced before 1600; the bronze type was probably existing type and "some extra type" produced by Korean immigrants (*The Book in Japan*, 130–31).

25. Lane, "The Beginnings of the Modern Japanese Novel," 646.

26. Insatsushi, *Hon to katsuji*, 64.

27. Ibid., 66.

28. See Forrer, *Eirakuya Tōshirō*, 62. Kornicki writes, the Sagabon "established the forms in which these texts were to circulate for the rest of the Tokugawa period" (*The Book in Japan*, 132).

29. Nagatomo, *Edo jidai no tosho ryūtsū*, 14.

30. Lane, "The Beginnings of the Modern Japanese Novel," 648.

31. Shively, "Popular Culture," 726–27, citing Kawase, *Kokatsuji no kenkyū*, vol. 2, appendix.

32. See Smith, "The History of the Book," 334. In addition to the reasons mentioned here, Nagatomo claims that the making of the books was easier, that a larger quantity could be produced, and that the quality was better with woodblocks (*Edo jidai no tosho ryūtsū*, 14). Hashimoto Motome names other reasons, including the high initial cost of copper type; the vulnerability of wood type, which would swell if any water got on it, causing the page to misalign; and the fact that second print runs required a complete reassembly of pages that would have been taken apart to publish other texts (*Nihon shuppan hanbai-shi*, 6).

33. Konta, *Edo no hon'ya-san*, 25–26. Smith notes that the oft-presumed greater frailty of movable type is a matter of debate and may be a myth ("The History of the Book in Edo and Paris," 334 n. 5). There is little debate, though, that woodblocks were able to produce much larger editions than many scholars originally thought; Forrer suggests that as many as twenty thousand impressions could be made from one block (*Eirakuya Tōshirō*, 75–76).

34. Smith considers this "the most important consideration" ("The History of the Book in Edo and Paris," 334).

35. Forrer, *Eirakuya Tōshirō*, 65. A closer examination of this claim seems necessary, as the cherry wood used for the blocks would have been expensive, as would storage of the blocks once produced.

36. Nakane, *Nihon insatsu gijutsu-shi*, 138.

37. Kornicki, *The Book in Japan*, 135, 165.

38. Ibid., 164.

39. The following narrative is derived from information found in Twyman, *Printing*, and other sources.

40. Altman, "Modernization of Printing," 87, citing Kawada, "Nihon ni okeru yōshiki kappan," 11–16.

41. Altman, "Modernization of Printing," 89. Altman describes these experiments as beginning with type cut in plastic clay, wood, and metal; then moving to metal plates cast from wood blocks and then cut into individual characters; and finally resulting in copper matrices formed by characters carved into steel, which was the Gutenberg method.

42. In the Gutenberg method liquefied metal is poured into a hand-casting instrument, in which the two sides close to create a casting void topped by the matrix.

43. There were more than these three experiments. See Nakane, *Nihon insatsu gijutsu-shi*, for descriptions of Ōtori Keisuke's publications (209–11), the publications of the Rikugunsho (211–12), the Hachiōji Gakuhandō (212–15), and the metal movable type experiments of Shima Kakoku (221–29).

44. Altman, "Modernization of Printing," 92–93.

45. Ibid., 93–94.

46. Kornicki, *The Book in Japan*, 164.

47. Altman, "Modernization of Printing," 96; Kornicki, *The Book in Japan*, 164.

48. Altman, "Modernization of Printing," 98, 99, describes the process. See also Richter, "Marketing the Word," 82–84. See Reed, *Gutenberg in Shanghai*, for specific information about Gamble (45–49) and for general information about the contemporary process of industrialization in China.

49. Altman, "Modernization of Printing," 102 n. 47.

50. Nakane, *Nihon insatsu gijutsu-shi*, 232.

51. The Tokyo Tsukiji Kappan Seizōsho remained a powerful company in publishing until the 1923 Earthquake, when it burned to the ground. Unable to fully recover, the company collapsed in 1938. Suzuki Toshio, *Shuppan*, 83.

52. Richter, "Marketing the Word," 88, 89–90, 91.

53. Kornicki, *The Book in Japan*, 63–65.

54. Richter, "Marketing the Word," 75. Richter discusses a number of the important calls from officials who saw advanced print cultures in Western countries (75–76).

55. Kornicki, *The Book in Japan*, 66.

56. Nakane, *Nihon insatsu gijutsu-shi*, 230; Dai-Nihon Insatsu Kabushiki Kaisha, *Shichijūgonen no ayumi* 21.

57. Takahashi, "Shuppan ryūtsū kikō no hensen," 202–3.

58. Nakane Katsu, in his *Nihon insatsu gijutsu-shi*, says this on the top of page 233, only to say on the bottom of that page that the sea change happens later, when the first true Bruce type-caster was imported in 1881. Dai-Nihon Insatsu Kabushiki Kaisha, *Shichijūgonen no ayumi*, 26–28, has a machine being imported in 1876 (not necessarily the first) and domestically produced copies appearing in 1883.

59. Nakane, *Nihon insatsu gijutsu-shi*, 248 n. 9, 255.

60. Richter, "Marketing the Word," 89.

61. Nakane, *Nihon insatsu gijutsu-shi*, 233. A stop-cylinder press functions with a flat form and sheet-fed paper; the cylinder stops after each sheet or movement of the

form, for the form to return to its original position and another sheet to be loaded. Koenig's 1812 press was a stop-cylinder.

62. Dai-Nihon Insatsu Kabushiki Kaisha, *Shichijūgonen no ayumi*, 36.

63. Nakane, *Nihon insatsu gijutsu-shi*, 234, 238.

64. In 1871 R. Hoe and Maronini's companies built web-fed rotary presses with continuous roll paper feeds; they were not the first, however. The Walter press, built in England in 1868, was the first. Ibid., 239.

65. Richter, "Marketing the Word," 105; Suzuki Toshio, *Shuppan*, 20.

66. Richter, "Marketing the Word," 105–6.

67. For growth in domestic papermaking capacity, see Suzuki H., *Gendai Nihon sangyō hattatsu shi*, appendix II-1, 15–17.

68. Richter, "Marketing the Word," 113, 119–24.

69. Suzuki Toshio, *Shuppan*, 20–21; Nakane, *Nihon insatsu gijutsu-shi*, 231; Dai-Nihon Insatsu Kabushiki Kaisha, *Shichijūgonen no ayumi*, 8.

70. Dai-Nihon Insatsu Kabushiki Kaisha, *Shichijūgonen no ayumi*, 79.

71. Ibid., 14–15.

72. Ogawa, *Shuppan kōbō gojūnen*, 351–53, 353–54.

73. Kornicki, *The Book in Japan*, 6.

74. Nakane, *Nihon insatsu gijutsu-shi*, 240–60; Toppan Insatsu Kabushiki Gaisha-shi Shashi Hensan Iinkai, *Toppan 1985*, 200–230.

75. Dai-Nihon Insatsu Kabushiki Kaisha, *Shichijūgonen no ayumi*, 135, 141.

76. Febvre and Martin, *The Coming of the Book*, 109.

77. Smith, "The History of the Book," 338–40.

78. Including *Kōshoku ichidai otoko* (1682), *Shoen ōkagami* (1684), and *Saikaku shokoku-banashi* (1685). Hibbett, "The Role of the Ukiyo-zōshi Illustrator," 69–70.

79. Hibbett, "The Role of the Ukiyo-zōshi Illustrator," 70, 76.

80. Nagatomo, *Edo jidai no tosho ryūtsū*, 11.

81. See Gedin, *Literature in the Marketplace*, 20, for more on this process of differentiation in European markets.

82. Yahagi, "Kindai ni okeru yōranki no shuppan ryūtsū," 90. This arrangement continued into the early Meiji period. Hashimoto M., *Nihon shuppan hanbai-shi*, 19.

83. Individuals involved in selling printed matter predate 1600; for example, the Surikoyomi-za (calendar printers association) in Kyoto formed in the first half of the fifteenth century. Yagi, *Zenkoku shuppanbutsu oroshi shōgyō kyōdō kumiai sanjūnen no ayumi*, 20.

84. Kornicki, *The Book in Japan*, 21–22, 174.

85. Nagatomo, *Edo jidai no tosho ryūtsū*, 14–16, 28.

86. Kornicki, *The Book in Japan*, 200.

87. Nagatomo suggests that they began to appear "from the mid-Tokugawa period," though the stores he gives as evidence appear no earlier than 1820 (*Edo jidai no tosho ryūtsū*, 60–62). The guilds of the three major cities in fact worked explicitly to prevent copying and even tried to suppress provincial publishing by vowing not to sell books produced by them. Hashimoto M., *Nihon shuppan hanbai-shi*, 11. This

continued until the early nineteenth century, when copublishing arrangements with different provincial booksellers became common. Konta, "Edo no shuppan shihon," 183–85.

88. Yahagi, "Kindai ni okeru yōranki no shuppan ryūtsū," 93–95; Hashimoto M., *Nihon shuppan hanbai-shi*, 20–22.

89. Kornicki, *The Book in Japan*, 179–80, 193.

90. Yahagi, "Kindai ni okeru yōranki no shuppan ryūtsū," 97. Recent work has found evidence that this was more common than has long been thought; see Yokota, "Santo to chihō jōkamachi no bunkateki kankei."

91. Yahagi, "Kindai ni okeru yōranki no shuppan ryūtsū," 99–104; Takahashi, "Shuppan ryūtsū," 196.

92. Takahashi, "Shuppan ryūtsū," 197.

93. Hashimoto M., *Nihon shuppan hanbai-shi*, 45–51.

94. Suzuki Toshio, *Shuppan*, 113.

95. Yahagi, "Kindai ni okeru yōranki no shuppan ryūtsū," 107–8. See also Oda, "Kindai bungaku to kindai shuppan ryūtsū shisutemu."

96. Yahagi, "Kindai ni okeru yōranki no shuppan ryūtsū," 119. For more on Hakubunkan in English, see Richter, "Marketing the Word."

97. Hokuryūkan at the time was still the Kitakuni-kumi Shutchō-sho, formed by Fukui, Ishikawa, and Toyama newspaper and magazine retailers. Takahashi, "Shuppan ryūtsū," 204.

98. Ericson, *The Sound of the Whistle*, 9.

99. Yahagi, "Kindai ni okeru yōranki no shuppan ryūtsū," 113–15, 114–19.

100. Hashimoto M., *Nihon shuppan hanbai-shi*, 176–77.

101. Ibid., 169–76.

102. Oda, "Kindai bungaku to kindai shuppan ryūtsū shisutemu," 133.

103. Hashimoto M., *Nihon shuppan hanbai-shi*, 178. At its height, around 1911–12, Hakubunkan dominated 70 to 80 percent of the publishing market (381).

104. Oda, "Kindai bungaku to kindai shuppan ryūtsū shisutemu," 133.

105. Oda, *Shoten no kindai*, 130; Hashimoto M., *Nihon shuppan hanbai-shi*, 184.

106. Hashimoto M., *Nihon shuppan hanbai-shi*, 104–5, 144–47.

107. Takahashi, "Shuppan ryūtsū," 206–13; Oda, "Kindai bungaku to kindai shuppan ryūtsū shisutemu," 133.

108. Nagatomo, *Edo jidai no tosho ryūtsū*, 4. First claimed in the *Gion monogatari*, date unclear, but thought to have been written toward the end of the Kan'ei period (1624–44).

109. Hashimoto M., *Nihon shuppan hanbai-shi*, 8.

110. Aeba, "Mukashi no sakusha no sakuryō oyobi shuppan busū," 1–3.

111. Kornicki, *The Book in Japan*, 185.

112. Fowler, *The Rhetoric of Confession*, 139 n. 21.

113. Note that this figure is not for the set as a whole, and that the sales figures are almost surely uneven, with more copies of the first volume selling than of the other volumes. Hashimoto M., *Nihon shuppan hanbai-shi*, 264. These are the figures for

Shisen presented by the publishing historian Ueda Yasuo in "Enpon zenshū ni yoru dokusha kakumei no jittai." Higher figures are often given. Matsubara Kazue claims that reprintings brought total sales rapidly to the 200,000 mark in the first year, 800,000 by the end of the next (*Kaizōsha to Yamamoto Sanehiko*, 105–6). Kimura Ki claimed in 1938 that it was the bestselling novel of the Taishō and Shōwa periods (cited in in Obi, *Shuppan to shakai*, 127). The editor of the *Kagawa Toyohiko zenshū*, Mutō Tomio, claimed that an estimated 4 million copies of the three volumes had sold by 1964, when he made the claim (cited in Obi, *Shuppan to shakai*, 125). Earlier bestsellers include Fukuzawa Yukichi's *Gakumon no susume*, which sold roughly 200,000 of each of seventeen volumes published between 1872 and 1876. As an example of how well a literary work could hope to sell at the time, Natsume Sōseki's *Wagahai wa neko de aru*, his bestselling work (at the time), sold an estimated 130,000 copies by 1927. Odagiri and Nihon Kindai Bungakukan, *Nihon kindai bungaku daijiten*, 480–81.

114. Kornicki, *The Book in Japan*, 72. Nagatomo, *Edo jidai no tosho ryūtsū*, 64–65, estimates the number of booksellers in various provincial areas. Note, however, that this is not an argument for uniform stock among these booksellers, but is merely an argument for the presence of books.

115. Konta, "Edo no shuppan shihon," 163–64.

116. Ibid., 164. Dates are noted in this format to distinguish lunar calendar dates from solar calendar dates.

117. Nagatomo, "Chihō no hon'ya-san," 103–7.

118. Nagamine Shigetoshi, "*Dokusho kokumin*" no tanjō, ii–viii. Nagamine's concept of a "reading nation" refers not only to a citizenry that can read, but one that possesses the habit of regular reading (vi). This third book of Nagamine's completes a trilogy of studies that has contributed immensely not only to my understanding of the history of books in Japan—the debt will be obvious throughout this study—but to the field as a whole.

119. See Yokota, "Santo to chihō," for one of the most detailed explanations of the ways books from China and the three capitals circulated to intellectual and economic elites in and around castle towns during the Tokugawa period. His conclusions are provided on 406–7.

120. Kornicki, *The Book in Japan*, 186.

121. Nakamura Toshihiko, "Kinsei no dokusha," 85–89.

122. Konta, "Edo no shuppan shihon," 164.

123. Hamada, *Kinsei shōsetsu*, 283–84. A *koku* of rice is traditionally thought of as the quantity necessary to feed an individual for a year.

124. Utano, "Edo jidai no hon no nedankō," 11–14.

125. Hamada, *Kinsei shōsetsu*, 276; Zwicker, "Tears of Blood," 83.

126. Konta, "Edo no shuppan shihon," 164.

127. Nagatomo, *Edo jidai no tosho ryūtsū*, 142.

128. Kornicki, *The Book in Japan*, 259.

129. When books were not rare, they seem to have ended up in hot spring resort towns,

which suggests that they might still have been serving a largely central clientele. Nagatomo, *Edo jidai no tosho ryūtsū*, 134–36.

130. Hamada, *Kinsei shōsetsu*, 286.

131. Asaoka, "Meiji-ki kashihon kashidashi daichō no naka no dokusha-tachi." The discussion of this book lender's activities comes from this essay.

132. The presence of *Tōsei shosei katagi* is particularly interesting, given that it was out of print until 1897 (according to Masamune Hakuchō), when it was reprinted in a special issue of *Taiyō* entitled, *Meiji shōsetsu kessaku-shū*. Oda, "Kindai bungaku to kindai shuppan ryūtsū shisutemu," 129.

133. It was borrowed 12 times. Asaoka, "Meiji-ki kashihon," 40. This was a relatively large number of times, given that the total number of book loans was 1,655 and the highest frequency for any book was 25 times.

134. Quoted in Torrance, *The Fiction of Tokuda Shūsei*, 26.

135. In his study of regional literatures and reading habits, Richard Torrance has shown that the rise of the magazine format was not uniform throughout the country; in Osaka, Torrance argues (following Nagamine Shigetoshi's readership data), newspapers remained dominant and Tokyo magazines made limited inroads. See Torrance, "Literacy and Literature in Osaka, 1890–1940," 43–44.

136. Zwicker, *Practices of the Sentimental Imagination*, 67.

137. While Anderson remains the most frequently cited scholar on this topic, many individuals have considered the link between a shared culture and the nation (-state). One such scholar is Gregory Jusdanis; see his *Belated Modernity* and "Beyond National Culture?"

138. Kornicki, *The Book in Japan*, 33. This claim could be further investigated to consider the *kōdan sokkibon*, which transcribed language and thus may have preserved far greater diversity. See Hyōdō, *"Koe" no kokumin kokka Nihon*.

139. Ogawa, *Shuppan kōbō gojūnen*, 184.

140. Berry, *Japan in Print*, 209, 248. See also Berry, "Was Early Modern Japan Culturally Integrated?" Haruo Shirane also approaches this issue through haikai poets in his *Traces of Dreams*, in which he describes "a new sense of communality among widely divergent commoners and samurai" that lay the groundwork for an imagined community (2). Susan L. Burns, in her book *Before the Nation*, addresses the same general question, arguing that a form of "culturalism" (she borrows Prasenjit Duara's term) formed prior to the modern period and was then deployed to support the creation of modern nationalism (224–25).

141. See, for example, Ruch, "Medieval Jongleurs."

142. Undoubtedly this is an ambiguous divide, with oral retellings showing remarkable consistency as a result of, among other things, mnemonic devices, and printed texts showing unexpected variability as a result of either rewritings or basic misprints. Nonetheless at the macro level the distinction provides insight into a significant change. See the debate between Adrian Johns and Elizabeth Eisenstein, most recently elaborated upon in "AHR Forum," for more on this divide.

143. For more on the relation of literature to the nation in Japan, see Yoda, *Gender and*

National Literature, 7–8, 41–80. The assertion of a "national subject" exemplified by a "national literature" is one that, Yoda persuasively argues, has far-reaching ramifications: "This empty ideal (the identity of national literature), in turn, becomes a convenient support for the notion of the national destiny that [the] state invokes to legitimate itself and its policies" (79).

144. Shirane and Suzuki, *Inventing the Classics*, 237.

145. My thanks to Richard Torrance for this formulation of the modern canon as an "anti-National national literature."

146. Following Prasenjit Duara, Jonathan Zwicker, in *Practices of the Sentimental Imagination*, asks a similar question concerning " 'communities with no visible presence,' other historical ideologies, other *social imaginaries*" (62) that are erased by an overdetermined focus on the nation-state in his work on the long nineteenth century. See Zwicker, *Practices of the Sentimental Imagination*, 62–64; Duara, *Rescuing History from the Nation*. As Zwicker rightfully points out, "Print capitalism, *as a form of capitalism*, is always striving to transcend the boundaries of the nation-state" (216).

2. The Stability of the Center

This chapter's epigraph is from the official translation of the Imperial Edict on Reconstruction, dated 12 September 1923, reprinted in Bureau of Social Affairs Home Office and Fujisawa, *The Great Earthquake of 1923 in Japan*. My thanks to Alex Bates for his valuable comments on this chapter. For a more in-depth examination of the junction between literature and the earthquake, see Bates, "Fractured Communities."

1. See Kōdansha Shashi Hensan Iinkai, *Kōdansha no ayunda gojūnen*, 606–13. Noma Seiji was negotiating the purchase of paper for *King* at his home when the earthquake struck. The magazine was originally scheduled for a July 1924 release. Obi, *Shuppan to shakai*, 62.

2. The primary quake on 1 September registered a magnitude of 7.9 on the Japan Meteorological Agency seismic intensity scale (an estimated 8.3 on the Richter scale); even an aftershock on 2 September registered 7.4. Based on historical records and estimates of earthquakes dating back to 799, there were only three known earthquakes of a greater estimated magnitude prior to 1923: one on 20 November 1498 (Meiō 7 VIII 25), magnitude 8.6; one on 31 December 1703 (Genroku 16 XI 23), magnitude 8.2; and one on 23 December 1854 (Kanpyō 7 XI 4) with a magnitude of 8.4. Usami, "Kantō chihō no furui jishin shin'ō ichi no han'i."

3. This shift is described by Konta Yōzō in "Edo no shuppan shihon." Konta argues that the shift in cultural center from Kamigata to Edo, when that city became the center of a broad ("national") book distribution system, is most apparent from the An'ei period, 1772–81 (139).

4. See Uchikawa et al., *Taishō nyūsu jiten*, vol. 6, 103.

5. These losses were tragically compounded by the murder of thousands of resident

Koreans and Chinese by vigilante groups in the days that followed, as malicious rumors fueled deep-seated animosities held by a portion of the Japanese population. In addition to these gruesome murders, as E. H. Norman points out, "under the cover of the confusion, the police killed numbers of socialist, labor and democratic leaders whom they were holding in prisons, hoping in this way to behead once and for all the labor and democratic movements which at this time gave promise of becoming a serious force in Japanese political life" ("Mass Hysteria in Japan," 69–70). The relationship between the absence of a functioning press and the massacre is addressed in Obi, *Shuppan to shakai*, 51–54.

6. See Iwasaki, "Kantō daishinsai no risai jōkyō, kakusho," 109. As well as for very specific damage, including parts of districts, see Uchikawa et al., *Taishō nyūsu jiten*, vol. 6, 104. These are actually conservative statistics; *Kokushi daijiten* (Tokyo: Yoshikawa Kōbunkan, 1983), vol. 3, 893–95, describes more extensive damage, claiming that two-thirds of the city was lost to the fires.

7. Iwasaki, "Kantō daishinsai no risai jōkyō, kakusho," 109.

8. Ibid., 108–9. For an example of someone who was able to flee, see Kawasaki, "Horobita Odawara yori."

9. *Kokushi daijiten*, vol. 3, 894, gives the following statistics: 99,331 dead, 103,733 injured, and 43,476 missing; recent scholarship has suggested that this total may be even higher.

10. Zen Nihon Shinbun Renmei Shuppankyoku, *Shinbun taikan*, 227.

11. *Ōsaka mainichi* special edition, 1 September 1923; Nakajima, Ōkubo, and Katō, *Shinbun shūroku Taishō shi*, 319, 478. See also Uchikawa et al., *Taishō nyūsu jiten*, vol. 6, 117, 122.

12. Zen Nihon Shinbun Renmei Shuppankyoku, *Shinbun taikan*, 228.

13. Roughly 102 miles of track and 678 trains. Iwasaki, "'Kakusho' shuppan-kai," 87–88.

14. On 4 September the *Ōsaka asahi* reported that the post office had stopped taking mail, cards, small packages, money transfers, telegraphs, and telephone calls directed at the destroyed areas. Nakajima et al., *Shinbun shūroku Taishō-shi*, 319, see also 440.

15. Telegraph lines, which were first laid in 1869, had been the primary means of long-distance communication since 1873, when a line connecting Aomori to Nagasaki, via Tokyo, was established. A nationwide system was completed in 1878. See Hunter, *Concise Dictionary of Modern Japanese History*, 224; Shibusawa, *Japanese Life and Culture in the Meiji Era*, 251–54.

16. The following restrictions were placed on messages: maximum thirty characters; business transactions and coded messages not allowed; and no messages directed at other Tokyo or Yokohama offices.

17. Telephones were introduced in 1877, but public telephones had only appeared in 1890. By the end of the Meiji period (1912) railways, police stations, and post offices throughout Japan were linked by telephones, though only a few homes, mostly upper class, had them. Apparently geisha-ya were also early adopters of the technol-

ogy. By 1923 telephones had only recently come into widespread use. According to the Ōsaka asahi article describing telegraph usage restrictions, phone usage immediately after the earthquake was restricted as follows: prices from Tokyo to Osaka were 1 yen 50 sen; to Nagoya, 1 yen; to Nagaoka, 95 sen; to Niigata, 1 yen. Calls were limited to three minutes each and could only be placed to telephone subscribers. Messages from Matsumoto to the damaged areas of Tokyo and Yokohama were possible starting at 4 P.M. on 6 September. These, however, were limited to official and newspaper-related messages.

18. Shibusawa writes that reduced telegraph rates for newspapers were "a landmark in the development of the newspaper industry" (*Japanese Life*, 254). This step was similarly important. See Mainichi Shinbunsha Shashi Hensan Iinkai, *Mainichi shinbun shichijūnen*, 244–45; Asahi Shinbun Hyakunenshi Henshū Iinkai, *Asahi shinbun shashi*, vol. 2, 241–42. Prior to the installation of the dedicated phone line between Tokyo and Ōsaka asahi shinbun, the two offices placed an average of 164 calls per day to one another: 144 made by standard reservation (*yoyaku*) and twenty made by extraordinary bulletin application (*rinji kyūhō moshikomi*), for a maximum of eight hours and twenty minutes of possible communication per day (*Asahi shinbun shashi*, 241–42). Telephone calls had time limits and reservations had to be made to place them. The installation of the dedicated line allowed for twenty-four hours of communication per day without the need for reservations. This shows the importance of communication (and thus the degree of interdependency) between the two branches.

19. Bureau of Social Affairs Home Office and Fujisawa, *The Great Earthquake of 1923 in Japan*, 561. Iwasaki makes the distinction that this was not wartime martial law (*rinsen kaigenrei*) but administrative martial law (*gyōsei kaigenrei*).

20. Iwasaki, "Taishō daishinsai daikasai," 80.

21. Bureau of Social Affairs Home Office and Fujisawa, *The Great Earthquake of 1923 in Japan*, 610–14.

22. It was not until 22 March 1925 that the first experimental broadcasts were performed in Tokyo. Seidensticker, *Tokyo Rising*, 67. Even after this time the cost of a subscription made radio prohibitively expensive for many.

23. This is not to suggest that film footage does not exist. The Ōsaka mainichi shinbun, for example, sent a film crew into the disaster area. It took footage later shown around the country by ten groups of traveling projectionists. Mainichi Shinbunsha Shashi Hensan Iinkai, *Mainichi shinbun shichijūnen*, 227.

24. Quoted in Sugimori, *Chūō Kōronsha no hachijūnen*, 195.

25. Nakajima et al., *Shinbun shūroku Taishō-shi*, vol. 11, 352–53.

26. Seidensticker, *Tokyo Rising*, 7.

27. The official translation, as quoted ibid., 7–8.

28. *Tōkyō nichinichi*, 8 September 1923; Nakajima et al., *Shinbun shūroku Taishō-shi*, vol. 11, 356.

29. *Tōkyō nichinichi*, 16 September 1923; Nakajima et al., *Shinbun shūroku Taishō-shi*, vol. 11, 376–77.

30. Katagami Noboru, "Shinsai kasai to bungaku to no kankei" in Kaizōsha, *Taishō daishinkasai shi*, 167.

31. Ibid., 169.

32. Miyamoto Mataji, "Ōsaka no shuppan-gyō to shuppan bunka no hensen," in Miyamoto, *Kamigata no kenkyū*, 147.

33. Figures from Yayoshi, *Mikan shiryō ni yoru Nihon shuppan bunka*, 293. In figure 6 and the table in the appendix "Specimens" refers to the specimen copies (*nōhon*) submitted to the Naimushō to be examined prior to publication, as per the Publications Law of 1893 and the Newspaper Law of 1909. "Official" refers to material printed by the government. The remainder of the total number of specimen copies minus the number of magazines published and the number of official publications provides a reasonably accurate estimate for the number of private publications that were submitted to the censors (i.e., books). The number is somewhat inflated by pamphlets or leaflets which were submitted. This remainder total is listed in the *Dai-Nihon Teikoku Naimushō tōkei hōkoku* simply as *tankōbon*. Some transcription errors appear in Yayoshi, *Mikan shiryō*, and the chart has been modified to reflect *Dai-Nihon Teikoku Naimushō tōkei hōkoku* statistics.

34. Figures from Yayoshi, *Mikan shiryō*, 289, 294. Percentages are mine and do not reflect actual growth per year but the total percentage of growth per number of years in order to reflect different spans of time between figures. Figures originate from Tokyo Shuppan Hanbai Kabushikigaisha, *Shuppan hanbai shōshi*. In English, see Zwicker, *Practices of the Sentimental Imagination*, for statistics on the total number of titles published between 1881 and 1926 (p. 21) and the estimated number of fiction titles published between 1750 and 1912 (p. 25).

35. Kōdansha Shashi Hensan Iinkai, *Kōdansha no ayunda gojūnen*, vol. 1, 543.

36. It was renamed the *Tokyo Zasshi Kyōkai* in 1918. See Nihon Zasshi Kyōkai Shi Henshū Iinkai, *Nihon Zasshi Kyōkai shi*, vol. 1, 58; Hashimoto M., *Nihon shuppan hanbai-shi*, 144.

37. Hashimoto M., *Nihon shuppan hanbai-shi*, 147–50.

38. Iwasaki, "Taishō daishinsai daikasai," 64.

39. Which would have been lost in the fires. Ōno Magohei, quoted in Hashimoto M., *Nihon shuppan hanbai-shi*, 285. Decisions of that meeting are listed on 286–88.

40. Hashimoto M., *Nihon shuppan hanbai-shi*, 292–93, 289–90, 291–92, 288–89.

41. Cited in Bungei Shunjū Shinsha, *Bungei Shunjū sanjūgonen shikō*, 49–50.

42. Kurita, *Shuppanjin no ibun*, 11–20. See also Shufu no Tomosha, *Shufu no Tomosha no rokujūnen*.

43. Many of the employees of *Chūō kōron* had gathered at the home of the founder, Takita Chōin, on the morning of 1 September to mourn the death of his mother and were there when the earthquake struck. Kisaki, *Kisaki nikki*, vol. 1, 325.

44. Kobayashi Ō., "Kono goro no koto," 61.

45. *Ōsaka asahi shinbun*, 7 September 1923; Nakajima et al., *Shinbun shūroku Taishō-shi*, vol. 11, 350.

46. *Ōsaka asahi shinbun*, 11 September 1923; Nakajima et al., *Shinbun shūroku Taishō-shi*, vol. 11, 365.

47. Nakajima et al., *Shinbun shūroku Taishō-shi*, vol. 11, 426.

48. Writing under the penname Kobayashi Ōri, "Bungei no fukkō," 11–12. The estimate in Kaizōsha, *Taishō daishinkasai shi* is "many tens of millions of books and magazines" (84). Kobayashi also wrote under the penname Kobayashi Shiken.

49. Okano, *Nihon shuppan bunka-shi*, 389.

50. Iwasaki, "Kantō daishinsai no risai jōkyō, kakusho," 120.

51. As noted in the anonymously written article, "Shinsaigo no furuhonkai." See also Sorimachi, *Shimi no mukashigatari*, 5–7.

52. "Shinsai to shuppan-kai," in Kaizōsha, *Taishō daishinkasai shi*, 84.

53. Tōkyō-to Koshoseki Shōgyō Kyōdō Kumiai, *Tōkyō Kosho Kumiai gojūnenshi*, 67; Sorimachi, *Shimi no mukashigatari*, 6; Edward Mack, "The Extranational Flow of Japanese-Language Texts, 1905–1945."

54. Iwasaki, "Taishō daishinsai daikasai," 73.

55. Ozaki, *Taishū bungaku no rekishi*, 116. Roughly 740,000 of a collection of 750,000. Tōkyō Daigaku Hyakunenshi Henshū Iinkai, *Tōkyō Daigaku hyakunenshi*, 393. See Obi, *Shuppan to shakai*, 58–59, for more details.

56. Tōkyō Daigaku Hyakunenshi Henshū Iinkai, *Tōkyō Daigaku hyakunenshi*, 417. J. D. Rockefeller donated 4 million yen himself in December 1924.

57. Ueda Y., "Enpon zenshū ni yoru dokusha kakumei no jittai," 42; Hashimoto Y., "Dokusho suru 'taishū,'" 46–47.

58. Kobayashi I., *Kobayashi Isamu bunshū*, vol. 9, 62–63.

59. Iwasaki, "Kudanzaka-ue kara jigoku o mita hitotachi," 46.

60. Iwasaki, "Kantō daishinsai no risai jōkyō, kakusho," 118. See also Ozaki, *Heibonsha rokujūnen-shi*, 71.

61. Kobayashi Ō., "Kono goro no koto" 61.

62. Quoted in Kōdansha Shashi Hensan Iinkai, *Kōdansha no ayunda gojūnen*, 540.

63. Kōdansha Shashi Hensan Iinkai, *Kōdansha no ayunda gojūnen*, 557, 558.

64. Ibid., 560.

65. Matsumoto, *Gyōmu nisshi yohaku*. According to Matsumoto, while magazines reached more than three thousand retailers, books normally reached only the three hundred or so bookstores that handled book consignments. At the time there were ten magazine retailers for every three book retailers, roughly 30 percent of which also handled magazines. Of these only some accepted books on consignment. As a result there were few stores where one could send books on consignment. Matsumoto adds that if one were to include stores such as stationers, dry good stores, and inns that retailed print as an ancillary business, the number of retail outlets for the *Taishō daishinsai daikasai* grew to nine thousand to ten thousand (40–41).

66. Kōdansha Shashi Hensan Iinkai, *Kōdansha no ayunda gojūnen*, 568.

67. Ibid., 565.

68. Ibid., 574.

69. Cited in Iwasaki, "Taishō daishinsai daikasai," 72. Miyatake Gaikotsu, however, estimated that, if sales were as Kōdansha claimed, they would have netted a profit of 700,000 yen on the sale of *Taishō daishinsai daikasai*, which struck him as highly unlikely. He maintained that in reality they sold fewer than 120,000 copies; later printings did not take place; and some 80,000 of the original 200,000 print run remained unsold. Cited in Iwasaki, "Taishō daishinsai daikasai," 71.

70. Kōdansha Shashi Hensan Iinkai, *Kōdansha no ayunda gojūnen*, 578.

71. Ibid., 569.

72. Hashimoto M., *Nihon shuppan hanbai-shi*, 299.

73. Hashimoto M., *Nihon shuppan hanbai-shi*, 300, 301–3.

74. Uchikawa Yoshimi, "Kantō Daishinsai to shinbun," in Uchikawa et al., *Taishō nyūsu jiten*, vol. 6, 34–37.

75. For details, see table 8 in the appendix.

76. Chiba Kameo, "Daishin tōji no shinbun no katsuyaku" in Kaizōsha, *Taishō daishinkasai shi*, 59.

77. Ōta, "Shinbun buranko," 69.

78. Nihon Shinbun Hanbai Kyōkai Shinbun Hanbai Hyakunen-shi Kankō Iinkai, *Shinbun hanbai hyakunen-shi*, 443.

79. Kaizōsha, *Taishō daishinkasai shi*, 70, 60.

80. Ibid., 62.

81. Uchikawa et al., *Taishō nyūsu jiten*, vol. 6, 35.

82. *Kodansha Encyclopedia of Japan*, vol. 5, 84.

83. In 1888 the company purchased Tokyo's *Mezamashi shinbun* and renamed it the *Tōkyō asahi shinbun*. Ibid., vol. 1, 93. A ten-point list of conditions faced by the paper, written on the second, is reprinted in Asahi Shinbun Hyakunenshi Henshū Iinkai, *Asahi Shinbunsha shi*, 231. Editors at *Tōkyō asahi* were very aware of the gravity of their situation. The surviving papers were on the brink of starting evening editions and were seizing on the earthquake as an opportunity to expand their readership.

84. Asahi Shinbun Hyakunenshi Henshū Iinkai, *Asahi Shinbunsha shi*, 235.

85. Nihon Shinbun Hanbai Kyōkai Shinbun Hanbai Hyakunen-shi Kankō Iinkai, *Shinbun hanbai hyakunen-shi*, 446. A complete chart of recovery dates is available in Kaizōsha, *Taishō daishinkasai shi*, 61.

86. Yamamoto, *Kindai Nihon no shinbun dokushasō*, 245. His figures are based on an amalgamation of four surveys and are not complete; nonetheless these estimates provide a rough sense of each paper's market share.

87. For details, see table 9 in appendix.

88. Yamamoto, *Kindai Nihon no shinbun dokushasō*, 410. The chart in figure 10 continues until the first year *Tōkyō asahi* reached a circulation of one million. Yamamoto's chart begins in 1885 and continues until 1945. The 1935 dip for the *Ōsaka asahi* reflects the split of Kyūshū and Nagoya branches; circulation of the two papers remains in rough parity through 1945 (when Yamamoto's statistics end). For details, see table 10 in appendix.

89. Asahi Shinbun Hyakunenshi Henshū Iinkai, *Asahi shinbun shashi*, 540–42.

90. Kaizōsha, *Taishō daishinkasai shi*, 76–77. In map 3 two incorrect totals have been revised. Iwasaki, "Kudanzaka-ue kara jigoku o mita hitotachi," 50. Iwasaki's figures, drawn from the *Nihon insatsu taikan*, differ slightly and thus have been included here as well. See also table 11 in appendix.

91. Iwasaki, "Kudanzaka-ue kara jigoku o mita hitotachi," 48, 125, 141.

92. Kaizōsha, *Taishō daishinkasai shi*, 76–77.

93. The figure does not include newspaper printing factories or governmental printing facilities such as the Insatsu-kyoku.

94. Kaizōsha, *Taishō daishinkasai shi*, 76. Yano was employed at the Insatsu-kyoku at the time and discusses it in detail.

95. Nakane, *Nihon insatsu gijutsu-shi*, 255–68, 263.

96. Tanaka, *Monogatari*, 163–64.

97. Hashimoto Motome claims that Seishundō was actually located in Hongō and escaped damage (*Nihon shuppan hanbai-shi*, 283).

98. Tanaka, *Monogatari*, 156–58.

99. Evidence of the book's role is listed in Iwasaki, "Taishō daishinsai daikasai," 73–75.

100. Fukuda, *Hokuryūkan gojūnen o kataru*, 85–111.

101. Tanaka, *Monogatari*, 164–68.

102. Narita and Shimoda, *Ōji Seishi shashi*, 125.

103. Togai, *Seishigyō no hyakunen*, 141. Somewhat contradictory statistics are presented in Uchikawa et al., *Taishō nyūsu jiten*, vol. 6, 114.

104. Kaizōsha, *Taishō daishinkasai shi*, 74–75.

105. Fukuda, *Hokuryūkan gojūnen o kataru*, 103.

106. Hashimoto M., *Nihon shuppan hanbai-shi*, 278–80.

107. Suzuki Toshio, *Shuppan*, 184.

3. The Static Canon

1. Nakamura Takafusa, *A History of Shōwa Japan*, 27–40. According to Nakamura, 1.6 billion yen was spent on reconstruction projects in Tokyo and Kanagawa over an eight-year period (37).

2. Suzuki Toshio, *Shuppan*, 170–89.

3. For more on *King*, see Nagamine Shigetoshi, *Zasshi to dokusha no kindai*, 203–50; Satō Takumi, *Kingu no jidai*.

4. Inagaki and Shimomura, *Nihon bungaku no rekishi*, 364. The return rate for this first issue was only 2 percent, a startlingly low rate. Published in December 1924, the issue was dated January 1925.

5. Midorikawa, *Iwanami Shoten gojūnen*, 45.

6. Kisaki, *Kisaki nikki*, vol. 2, 179. *Bungei shunjū* became a *sōgō zasshi* (general interest magazine) only in December 1926, after it paid a deposit that allowed it to carry articles on politics; until that time it had been a *bungei zasshi* (literary magazine). See Nagamine, *Modan toshi no dokusho kūkan*, 113.

7. Dai-Nihon Insatsu Kabushiki Kaisha, *Shichijūgonen no ayumi*, 135–37.

8. Though it would be forced to expand its facilities even further as a result of the boom. See ibid., 141–43, for details.

9. See Satō Takumi, *Kingu no jidai*, 39–41. In August 1935, for example, 3,500 copies of the magazine were imported into Brazil alone. See Mack, "Diasporic Markets," 163–77.

10. For more on anthologies of Anglophonic literature, see Price, *The Anthology*; Benedict, *Making the Modern Reader*; Ross, *The Making of the English Literary Canon*. For anthologies in Germany, including Reclam's Universalbibliothek, see Hohendahl, *Building a National Literature*, 329–33; Gedin, *Literature in the Marketplace*, 49–50. For more on premodern Japanese anthologies, see Burk, "Reading between the Lines."

11. Many of the larger issues of this chapter were developed through and owe much to discussions with Komori Yōichi; his position on the matter is developed in his article, "Kigen no gensetsu: Nihon kindai bungaku kenkyū to iu sotchi," in Kurihara et al., *Naiha suru chi*.

12. *Kaizō* was published from April 1919 until February 1955. Individuals involved in the magazine included Kawakami Hajime, Ōsugi Sakae, Hasegawa Nyozekan, and Kagawa Toyohiko. It strongly supported democratic thought and socialist movements. For more on Yamamoto and Kaizōsha, see Obi, *Shuppan to shakai*, 77–118.

13. Matsubara, *Kaizōsha to Yamamoto Sanehiko*, 135–37; Takashima, "Shōhin to shite no enpon," 21.

14. Seki et al., *Zasshi "Kaizō" no shijūnen*, 97.

15. Takashima, "Shōhin to shite no enpon," 21. Kobayashi Isamu makes an intriguing comment about there having been rumors that Kaizōsha continued operating despite bad business only because of connections Yamamoto had with the military and money he might have been receiving from them (*Kobayashi Isamu bunshū*, vol. 4, 307).

16. Matsubara, *Kaizōsha to Yamamoto Sanehiko*, 139–40.

17. Obi, *Shuppan to shakai*, 166.

18. Seki et al., *Zasshi "Kaizō" no shijūnen*, 101.

19. Aoyama Ki has the price of volumes at 1.30 yen (*Kaizōsha bungaku geppō*, 27); I have followed the price listed in Odagiri and Nihon Kindai Bungakukan, *Nihon kindai bungaku daijiten*, vol. 6, 65d.

20. Two amounts are given for the loan: 10,000 yen and 100,000 yen, depending on the source; 10,000 is the most frequently cited. Matsubara suggests that Ōno just knew a good thing when he saw one. According to Matsubara's (probably slightly exaggerated) figures, he was quite right: his investment was paid back dozens of times over. See Matsubara, *Kaizōsha to Yamamoto Sanehiko*, 143–45; Hashimoto M., *Nihon shuppan hanbai-shi*, 351.

21. Obi, *Shuppan to shakai*, 68.

22. Okano, *Nihon shuppan bunka-shi*, 161–64; Hashimoto M., *Nihon shuppan hanbai-shi*, 350.

23. Ogawa, *Shuppan kōbō gojūnen*, 81, 144–48.

24. Oda, *Shoten no kindai*, 117–18.

25. Kōchi, "'Nihon koten zenshū' kankō shūhen," 79, 58.

26. Hasumi Shigehiko repeats this rumor and speculates on it in Karatani, *Kindai Nihon no hihyō I*, 73. If this is the case, he continues, the expansion of book ownership through the one-yen book phenomenon would have been "connected to Fujimori's personal experience with social movements."

27. Kimura, *Watakushi no bungaku kaikoroku*, 360.

28. Seki et al., *Zasshi "Kaizō" no shijūnen*, 98.

29. Ibid., 100. Kimura Ki, who was also an author, had early received support from Tayama Katai. He graduated from the English Department of Waseda in 1917 and entered publishing. In 1924 he wrote two influential books of literary criticism, *Shōsetsu no sōsaku to kanshō* and *Shōsetsu kenkyū jūroku-kō*.

30. It is worth noting what Charles W. Eliot, the chief architect of the *Harvard Classics*, said of the selection process for the fiction portion of that series in the general introduction of its "Shelf of Fiction": "On the choice of authors, and the choice of the best available work of each author, it soon appeared that no general consent among competent judges was likely to be attained and that the ultimate decision would necessarily be more or less arbitrary, and liable to provoke dissent."

31. Kimura, *Watakushi no bungaku kaikoroku*, 360. As this express motivation suggests, Kimura Ki (much less Kaizōsha) did not purposefully skew the canon toward a specific selection of texts; rather Kimura's tastes were in constant negotiation with both professional and popular expectations about the contents, material limitations, and this desire to preserve a wide variety of works.

32. Kōno, *Shomotsu no kindai*, 227. Yanagida Izumi (1894–1969) was a Japanese and English literary scholar and translator.

33. Takashima, "Shōhin to shite no enpon," 31.

34. Kimura, *Meiji bungaku yowa*, 35, 60–63, 63–68, 87, 91. Unfortunately, Kimura relates, the nearest bookstore that carried it carried only one copy per month, so he was not always able to buy it. Issues he could not buy he was sometimes able to borrow from the relative of a schoolmate (60).

35. Yanagida, *Yobanashi*, 11, 25–34, 36–40. The magazines that especially influenced him were Ōwada Tateki's *Meiji bungaku-shi*, a special issue of *Bunshō sekai* titled *Kinpū-gō*, and a special issue of *Taiyō* dedicated to Meiji history, the seventh volume of which was on literary history (11–18).

36. Sekii, "Nihon kindai bungaku kenkyū no kigen."

37. It is interesting to speculate on Kimura's lack of interest in being involved in the collation of works of the Taishō period; perhaps he believed that the Meiji period was also fundamentally different from the present.

38. Kimura, *Watakushi no bungaku kaikoroku*, 360.

39. Sekii, "Nihon kindai bungaku kenkyū no kigen," 29.

40. In "Core, Canon, Curriculum" Harry Levin argues that a similar situation existed for Charles Eliot, whose tenure as president of Harvard University was marked by an

intellectual inclusivity that ran contrary to the exclusivity implied by the *Harvard Classics*. As Levin puts it, "The contradiction was that Eliot, having as an educator repudiated the idea of a canon . . . had returned to it as a publicist" (357).

41. Precisely why it was omitted is not clear, though likely it was due to the fact that the long essay might have been seen as having limited interest for the general reader.

42. See Suzuki S., *Nihon no "bungaku" gainen*, 211–23.

43. See A. Ueda, "The Production of Literature," 61–88, for both a recapitulation of the standard historical narrative and a compelling reconsideration of that narrative.

44. For more on the concept of paratexts, see Genette, *Paratexts*, 1–15.

45. Yamamoto M., *Gendai Nihon bungaku zenshū* (hereafter GNBZ), vol. 1 (Tokyo: Kai-zōsha, 1931), 608, 609.

46. GNBZ 51:2.

47. GNBZ 34:2.

48. GNBZ 62:174.

49. The word appears as *fuseji* (symbols used in place of suppressed characters) in the text, but was perhaps "revolution" (*kaikaku*).

50. Cited in Karatani, *Kindai Nihon no hihyō I*, 279. In focusing on this dominant genre, this study unfortunately reproduces that centrality; further studies are necessary to address the role of other genres in the larger literary field.

51. The underrepresentation of women in most conceptions of modern Japanese litera-ture is a problem that has been taken up by Rebecca L. Copeland (among others) in *Lost Leaves*, 1–6, and in her essay on Meiji women writers in Mostow, *The Columbia Companion*, 74–78. For more on the way the marginalization of literature by women works (as *joryū bungaku*, or women's literature) to reinforce a male-dominated national canon, see Bourdaghs, *The Dawn That Never Comes*, 118–24.

52. For the early history of royalties and copyrights in Japan, see Kornicki, *The Book in Japan*, 239–51.

53. Asaoka Kunio, "Chosha to shuppansha to no keizai kankei: Inzei, kaitori, chosa-kuken" (paper presented at a joint meeting of the Ōgai Kenkyūkai and the Shuppan-shi Danwakai, Tokyo, 12 March 2005).

54. The Nagai Kafū volume of the series was in fact extremely difficult for Kaizōsha to compile. For more on this saga, see Obi, *Shuppan to shakai*, 176–89.

55. For a comparison of the contents, see Yoshino Toshihiko, *"Danchōtei" no keizaigaku*, 141–42.

56. Senuma, *Hon no 100-nenshi*, 175–76. For an extended study of the two, see Taka-shima, "Shōhin to shite no enpon," 20–37.

57. Yamamoto S., "Enpon jidai," 31. The fee paid to Shun'yōdō was referred to as a *tōsai-ryō* (inclusion fee), not a royalty. See Obi, *Shuppan to shakai*, 245.

58. Cited in Obi, *Shuppan to shakai*, 246.

59. See Kimura, *Watakushi no bungaku kaikoroku*, 365. He suggests an interesting facet of the collusion when he describes Yamamoto's reaction to Satō's decision to share publishing rights to Shimazaki's *Haru* and *Arashi* sometime later. Apparently Yama-

moto took out an ad which praised Shinchōsha and said even Shinchōsha was encouraging Kaizō's project. Kimura, *Watakushi no bungaku kaikoroku*, 366.

60. Senuma, *Hon no 100-nenshi*, 176.

61. GNBZ 16: unnumbered reverse of contents page.

62. GNBZ 19:411.

63. Sakaki, "Kajin no Kigū," 98, 100.

64. Ishizuka, "Enpon o henshū shita hitobito," 37.

65. We now know who comprised the editorial staff that worked with Kimura. The editor in chief was Hirota Yoshio; the head proofreader was Taniguchi Takeshi; the editors were Tachibana Akira, Suganuma Junjirō, Fukada Kyūya, Izumi Shatei (Izumi Kyōka's younger brother), Mizorogi Masaru, Ōto Kiichirō, Shioya Jusuke, and Sekiguchi Jirō. Ibid., 34–37. See also Seki et al., *Zasshi "Kaizō" no shijūnen*, 106.

66. Satō H., "Ichienpon no hayari," 183–85.

67. I have chosen to leave the term *zenshū* untranslated throughout most of the study in order to preserve a certain ambiguity in its contemporary usage. Though strictly speaking it means "complete works," it has come to be thought of more flexibly when used for a period or a genre rather than an individual. This is likely the result of series just like the Kaizōsha series. One reason to believe that this flexible definition of the term postdated the Kaizōsha series is the criticism around its publication, some quoted in this chapter, that it was only a "selected works" after all. Thus I argue that, though no reasonable person could have thought that every work of contemporary Japanese fiction appeared in the series, the title would nonetheless have carried a rhetorical force that suggested some sort of totality.

68. Kanai et al., *Bungaku ga motto omoshiroku naru*, 255.

69. Tanizawa, *Nihon kindai shoshigaku saiken*, 108.

70. Shimamura et al., *Bungei hyakka zensho*. See entry 1150 for the conventional narrative of Tsubouchi Shōyō and Futabatei Shimei as the founders of *Nihon gendai bungaku* (664).

71. Oda and Yamamoto, "Enpon no hikari to kage," 24.

72. Okano, *Nihon shuppan bunka-shi*, 354.

73. Mizushima, *Kaizōsha no jidai*, 18. Ogawa Kikumatsu suggests that this marked a new awareness of the effectiveness of advertising, and gave publishers the courage to experiment with other innovative advertising techniques (*Shuppan kōbō gojūnen*, 139). The Okinawan Miyagi Sō, who went on to become an author, was chosen to go to Hawaii because of the large number of emigrants from Okinawa in Hawaii. Obi, *Shuppan to shakai*, 268.

74. Yamamoto S., "Enpon jidai," 31. As mentioned previously, Mitsunaga Hoshio of Dentsū covered these costs. Mizushima says that he heard the one-page ad alone cost 6,000 yen. Mizushima, *Kaizōsha no jidai*, 18.

75. Senuma, *Hon no 100-nenshi*, 173.

76. Kanbayashi, "Enpon gassen jidai," 100.

77. Obi, *Shuppan to shakai*, 271.

78. Takei, "Akutagawa no kōen ryōkō"; Shōji T., "Akutagawa Ryūnosuke no kōen ryōkō."
79. Senuma, *Hon no 100-nenshi*, 174.
80. Kōno, *Shomotsu no kindai*, 153–83. For specific references to this film, see 177–78. See also Yamagishi, "Firumu no naka no sakka-tachi."
81. For a step-by-step comparison of Kaizōsha's and Shun'yōdō's advertisements, see Obi, *Shuppan to shakai*, 247–55.
82. *Yomiuri shinbun*, 22 October 1926.
83. *Yomiuri shinbun*, 11 November 1926.
84. *Yomiuri shinbun*, 26 November 1926.
85. *Yomiuri shinbun*, 18 November 1926.
86. *Yomiuri shinbun*, 30 November 1926.
87. *Yomiuri shinbun*, 5 November 1926.
88. *Yomiuri shinbun*, 26 November 1926.
89. *Yomiuri shinbun*, 26 May 1927.
90. *Yomiuri shinbun*, 31 May 1927.
91. The use of subscription sale was entirely voluntary on the part of the publisher and was often used to minimize returns. As another example of limited sale, one might look at Iwanami's decision in 1928 to convert the magazine *Shisō* to *yoyaku-sei*. After reaching its seventieth issue that year it began to see increased return rates. To counter this a *kaikiri-sei* (no returns) system was instituted that limited publication to three thousand copies and eliminated returns. Kobayashi I., *Kobayashi Isamu bunshū*, vol. 3, 94. The magazine went on hiatus beginning with the September issue of that year. It restarted publication with a different editing staff beginning with the April 1929 issue. Midorikawa, *Iwanami Shoten gojūnen*, 53, 61.
92. Similarly the Shinchōsha system for their *Sekai bungaku zenshū* offered two methods of payment: in advance or monthly. Individuals who wished to pay in advance were asked to send 34 yen plus 10 sen per volume (26 sen if overseas) for shipping, and it was requested that this be sent separately from the one-yen application fee. Individuals who wished to pay monthly were asked to send their money by either *furikae chokin* (transfer deposit) or *kawase* (money order) so that it would arrive by the fifth of each month.
93. The distributors argued that if Kaizōsha went bankrupt, they would be required to reimburse the readers, and therefore the distributors should hold the deposit. Makino, *Kumo ka yama ka*, 26. Retailers that handled subscriptions may have kept a percentage of the one-yen deposit equal to the wholesale discount. See Matsumoto, *Gyōmu nisshi yohaku*, 67.
94. Kisaki, *Kisaki Nikki*, vol. 2, 361.
95. During the second enrollment period Kaizōsha employees visited bookstores throughout the Kantō region; they also traveled to bookstores overseas. According to Kanbayashi Akatsuki, representatives were sent to Hawaii, Manchuria, Korea, and Taiwan ("Enpon gassen jidai," 99).
96. Iwade, *Tōkyōdō no hachijūgonen*, 274. The one-yen books were sold to retailers for an

estimated 93 to 97 sen, leaving a thin but dependable margin. Obi, *Shuppan to shakai,* 294.

97. Hashimoto M., *Nihon shuppan hanbai-shi,* 362, 361, 358.

98. Makino, *Kumo ka yama ka,* 149–64. The Kinbunkai was a group of retail stores connected to Kikutake Kinbundō, a secondary distributor for Tōkyōdō based in Kurume, Fukuoka.

99. Not to mention Yamamoto's political ambitions in Kagoshima, his home prefecture.

100. The advertisement that appeared in the *Yomiuri shinbun* on 22 October 1926, the first to appear in that newspaper, listed all of the original volume titles and much of their contents, though there were some subsequent changes.

101. Seki et al., *Zasshi "Kaizō" no shijūnen,* 105; Shōji S., *Nihon no shomotsu,* 198–99. Based on Shimazaki Tōson's story "Bunpai," his volume, distributed in March 1927, sold at least 222,000 copies. He says he received 20,000 yen based on a 9 sen per volume royalty (3 sen of his royalties were held until after the distribution of the fifth volume; his volume was the fourth to be distributed). See Shimazaki, "Bunpai," *Tōson zenshū,* vol. 10, 301–25.

102. Kaizōsha first advertised the second enrollment period in the *Yomiuri shinbun* on 23 April 1926. The deadline was 31 May. Giant advertisements on 31 May declared that it was the last day, yet on 27 June 1927 an advertisement in the *Yomiuri shinbun* declared that enrollment had reopened and would continue until 31 July. No advertisement declaring a deadline appears after that time. For the role of Shun'yōdō's competition in Kaizōsha's decision, see Kanbayashi, "Enpon gassen jidai," 101.

103. We know, however, that Kaizōsha quietly abandoned subscription sales for the series and that some volumes—particularly Natsume Sōseki's, but also Kafū's—continued to sell. A recent loan of company documents from the early 1940s to the Keiō University library included records of royalty payments for newly printed copies of those specific volumes during those years. Presumably other payments, outside of the years covered by the donation, were made as well. It is unlikely, however, that these subsequent sales increased figures for many volumes in the series.

104. From his diary entry dated 8 October 1941. See Nagai K., *Kafū zenshū,* vol. 23, 214.

105. As announced in the May 1927 issue of the monthly newsletter of the series. Aoyama, *Kaizōsha bungaku geppō,* 33.

106. Based on Shimizu Kōhei's recollection. See Seki et al., *Zasshi "Kaizō" no shijūnen,* 102. The number was so great that strategies were adopted to offset the cost of the bookcases (and perhaps limit the number Kaizōsha needed to produce). See Aoyama, *Kaizōsha bungaku geppō,* 527.

107. Oda and Yamamoto, "Enpon no hikari to kage," 23, citing work by Asaoka Kunio.

108. Ueda Y., "Enpon zenshū ni yoru dokusha kakumei no jittai," 43.

109. Nagamine, *Modan toshi,* 144–45.

110. Maeda, *Kindai dokusha no seiritsu,* 155. Maeda is referring to Minami, *Taishō bunka,* 183–95, on the expanding new middle class. It should be noted that the definition

above is for the entire middle class, and not the new middle class Minami is discussing. Members of Minami's new middle class are not employed in the production of material goods; they possess a certain degree of education and intelligence; and they earn more, in most cases, than workers (*Taishō bunka*, 183). The definition of the middle class based solely on income, in contrast, originally comes from the economic historian Uchida Ginzō (184).

111. Maeda, *Kindai dokusha no seiritsu*, 156. The incomes of these three occupations averaged between 60 and 80 yen per month.

112. Ariyama, "1920, 30 nendai no media fukyū jōtai," 33–34; Nagamine, *Zasshi to dokusha*, 33.

113. Ariyama, "1920, 30 nendai no media fukyū jōtai," 36.

114. The impact of this series in the colonies (and thus the role of the series in the Japanese colonial project) can of course only be inferred from these pieces of information available in Japanese-language sources; hopefully future research will take advantage of diaries and other sources in Chinese and Korean to establish the real impact and the reaction of colonial subjects to this imperial(ist) literature.

115. Cited in Oda, *Shoten no kindai*, 148, 143–48.

116. Matsumoto, *Gyōmu nisshi yohaku*, 75.

117. Kawahara, *Taiwan shinbungaku undō to tenkai*, 250.

118. Kimura, *Watakushi no bungaku kaikoroku*, 363.

119. Nagamine, *Modan toshi*, 144–45.

120. See *Tōkyō asahi shinbun*, 3 November 1926 for the general claim, and *Tōkyō asahi*, 15 November 1926 for the list of organizations.

121. Nagamine, *Modan toshi*, 61.

122. For more on Bandō, see Mack, "Marketing Japan's Literature."

123. Ogawa, *Shuppan kōbō gojūnen*, 141.

124. Mochizuki, *Wagakuni shuppanbutsu yushutsubutsu no rekishi*, 29.

125. Matsumoto, *Gyōmu nisshi yohaku*, 75.

126. The content of this series was culled from two existing Shinchōsha *zenshū*, the *Sekai bungei zenshū* and the *Kaigai bungaku shinsen*. Okano, *Nihon shuppan bunka-shi*, 350.

127. There were 580,000 subscribers by the deadline of 1 March, according to Okano, *Nihon shuppan bunka-shi*, 351, and Senuma, *Hon no 100-nenshi*, 172. As with the *Complete Works of Contemporary Japanese Literature*, this figure is the object of some debate.

128. Three hundred different series were published, according to Okano, *Nihon shuppan bunka-shi*, 349, and more than three hundred according to Oda, *Shuppansha to shoten wa ika ni shite kiete iku ka*, 137.

129. Needless to say, the decision to increase the number of pages and decrease prices resulted in major problems for the companies. Aside from the obvious cut in margin, there were less obvious costs as well. With the larger volumes shipping costs were drastically affected. Kōdansha, for example, sold the volumes at retail

bookstores by employing the established magazine distribution routes. This resulted in problems, however, because the retail store had to pay the shipping from the *toritsugi*, and this often became too great a burden. The increased shipping costs actually led to sales boycotts of some series in Hokkaidō. Hashimoto M., *Nihon shuppan hanbai-shi*, 358–59.

130. They later added a ten-volume *Shōwa-hen* supplement.

131. Takashima actually lists five, including the use of the *geppō* to create a dialogue with readers and thus invest them in the series, and the self-destructive nature of Shun'yōdō's use of its publishing rights in the series. Takashima, "Shōhin to shite no enpon," 20–37.

132. It should be noted that rather than being an innovation, the complete gloss represents a resistance to a general movement away from glossed texts that began around this time and led to an almost complete absence of glosses after the Second World War. For more on syllabic glosses in Japanese literature, see Ariga, "The Playful Gloss."

133. Hashimoto M., *Nihon shuppan hanbai-shi*, 361–62.

134. To this one must add advertising costs, which were also rising into the tens and hundreds of thousands of yen. Okano, *Nihon shuppan bunka-shi*, 350–51.

135. Ogawa, *Shuppan kōbō gojūnen*, 139. Tokyo's *Hōchi shinbun*, 31 March 1927, quoted a bookseller in Hongō saying, "The *zenshū* [sales] are fine, but the drying up of magazine and *tankōbon* sales is a big problem [*yarikiremasen*]." Quoted in Uchikawa et al., *Shōwa nyūsu jiten*, vol. 1, 274.

136. Hashimoto M., *Nihon shuppan hanbai-shi*, 362.

137. Matsumoto, *Gyōmu nisshi yohaku*, 133.

138. Some publishers even purchased their own trucks to distribute books. Hashimoto M., *Nihon shuppan hanbai-shi*, 361–62.

139. Iwade, *Tōkyōdō no hachijūgonen*, 269–71.

140. Matsumoto, *Gyōmu nisshi yohaku*, 71–72.

141. The entire pamphlet is reprinted in Yoshino Takao, *Miyatake Gaikotsu kono naka ni ari*, vol. 23, 167–231. See 177 for the list. After listing the negative repercussions of one-yen books, Miyatake warns that one-yen books are "an uncommon torrent of poison flowing into ports and inlets in every part of the country."

142. Hashimoto M., *Nihon shuppan hanbai-shi*, 363.

143. Senuma, *Hon no 100-nenshi*, 195.

144. Fukuda, *Hokuryūkan gojūnen o kataru*, 122.

145. This series was consciously modeled on Reclam's Universal-Bibliothek series in Germany, which began in 1867. See King, "Reclam's Universal-Bibliothek," for more on the history of this series. For the relationship between the two series, see Mathias, " 'Reading for Culture.' "

146. With the introduction of this series the term *bunkobon* comes to refer to smaller, inexpensive books and is used in contrast to the traditional hardcover book, the *tankōbon*. *Bunkobon*, in name, existed prior to the Iwanami series, but they were

not what we think of today as *bunkobon*. In 1893, for example, Hakubunkan began publishing their *Teikoku bunko* series, which was made up of larger books. For a history of *bunkobon* to Iwanami, see Ogawa, *Shuppan kōbō gojūnen*, 144–48.

147. When Kōda Rohan received his royalties of 30,000 yen he asked, "Can I really have this? [*Konna ni moratte mo ii no ka?*]." Quoted in Suzuki Toshio, *Shuppan*, 195.

148. *Kokumin Shinbun*, 27 November 1927, quoted in the Uchikawa et al., *Shōwa nyūsu jiten*, vol. 1, 275. Needless to say, these projected figures were never achieved, as cancellations reduced the total number of subscribers.

149. Yamamura, "Enpon narikin no narikin-buri."

150. Ogawa, *Shuppan kōbō gojūnen*, 80.

151. See Hirotsu, "Shōwa shoki no interi sakka," *Hirotsu Kazuo zenshū*, vol. 2, 181. This was also the rate Tōson stated in "Bunpai"; see Shimazaki, *Tōson zenshū*, vol. 10, 308, 315.

152. See Satō Haruo, *Bungeika no seikatsu o ronzu* (September 1926), *Satō Haruo zenshū*, vol. 11, 374–88, for more information about writers' incomes just two months before the introduction of one-yen books. This piece is a key resource in re-creating a picture of the occupation of writer at the end of the Taishō period.

153. Shōji S., *Nihon no shomotsu*, 200, 334.

154. Senuma, *Gendai bungaku no jōken*, 126.

155. Kimura, *Watakushi no bungaku kaikoroku*, 368.

156. Kobayashi I., *Kobayashi Isamu bunshū*, vol. 3, 75. A certain accessibility of style was also preferred. Satō talks about the need to translate into "unwarped Japanese [*hōgo*]." Satō Toshio, *Shinchōsha shichijūnen*, 97.

157. Kanō, "Kanbatsu-toki no jumoku," 88–89.

158. Yamamoto Y., *Bungakusha wa tsukurareru*, 280–81, 300–301. See 291–98 for quotes from various writers about how hard the period was for them. See Kanō, "Kanbatsu-ji no jumoku," 89, for the source of the "golden age" quote.

159. Shiobara, "Shozō sareru shomotsu," 4–6. See Sand, *House and Home*, for more on the *bunka jutaku* movement.

160. Ōya, "Sarariiman no seikatsu to shisō," *Ōya Sōichi zenshū*, vol. 2. Cited in Shiobara, "Shozō sareru shomotsu," 10 n. 26.

161. Shiobara, "Shozō sareru shomotsu," 6, 10 n. 29.

162. Ueda Y., "Enpon zenshū ni yoru dokusha kakumei no jittai," 51, 56, 57. Ueda cites the authors and critics on 58, 59, 55, 52, 49, 52, 55, 56.

163. Ōshima, *Rekishi no naka no "jihi shuppan" to "zokki-bon,"* 187.

164. As an example of the instability of the term *kindai* at the time, one can consider another series released the same year, 1926, by the publishing company Kokumin Tosho. This series, the *Kindai Nihon bungaku taikei*, contained works written solely in the Tokugawa period.

165. Havens, "Japan's Enigmatic Election of 1928," 543.

166. Komori, *Nihongo no kindai*, 225.

167. Tanizawa, *Nihon kindai shoshigaku saiken*, 108.

168. In English this issue has begun to be addressed by such scholars as Mark Driscoll, in his translation of Yuasa Katsuei, *Kannani and Document of Flames*.

169. Maruyama, "Watashi no chūgaku jidai to bungaku," 235. My thanks to Professor Matsuzawa Hiroaki for bringing this article to my attention.

170. Ōshima, *Rekishi no naka*, 185–86.

171. The partial exception to this is in their use as models for composition training. Selections by modern Tokyo authors were part of the writing education process described by Haruo Shirane in Shirane and Suzuki, *Inventing the Classics*, 220–49. As Tasaka's *Kyūsei chūtō kyōiku kokugaku kyōkasho naiyō sakuin* shows, some short works and selections by modern authors were incorporated into textbooks, but it was "not until 1908–10 that [*genbun itchi* texts] began entering into textbooks in significant form, and [they] did not become dominant until the late Taishō period" (Shirane and Suzuki, *Inventing the Classics*, 239–40). Texts included were often short segments provided as models for composition rather than objects of aesthetic contemplation.

172. The use of the word "mandarin" is meant to be partially ironic, though also to connect this discussion with that of Fritz K. Ringer in his book, *The Decline of the German Mandarins*.

173. The mass production even went beyond Tokyo's capacity. According to an article in Tokyo's *Hōchi shinbun* on 31 March 1927, "One problem has been . . . that the extent of this mass production is such that Tokyo does not have the printing and book-making capacity to publish everything. As a result, a portion of *Taishū* [*Gendai taishū bungaku zenshū*, which was already collecting subscriptions though it had not yet been delivered] is already being published in Osaka." Quoted in Uchikawa et al., *Shōwa nyūsu jiten*, vol. 1, 274.

174. Senuma, *Hon no 100-nenshi*, 194. See Suzuki Toshio, *Shuppan*, 206, for a quote from a printing historian on the specific effect on a few factories. It also attributes the creation of a domestic (thread) binding (*ito-tsuzuri*) industry and the lowering of prices of all publishing to the *enpon*. As for the structure of book and magazine selling, which changed dramatically in response to the mass production of books, see Suzuki Toshio, *Shuppan*, 207–10.

4. Literary Value

1. On the history of the term "popular" in Japan, see Torrance, "Pre–World War Two Concepts of Japanese Popular Culture." On the use of these terms in the early postwar, see Seidensticker, "The 'Pure' and the 'in-Between'"; Strecher, "Purely Mass or Massively Pure?" The most complete treatment appears in Suzuki S., *Nihon no "bungaku" o kangaeru*.

2. I read the debates narrowly in order to maintain focus on the use of specific rhetorical devices and on the absence of aesthetic consensus. These debates have been written about extensively elsewhere. Key relevant works in English include

(in order of their original appearance) Hijiya-Kirschnereit, *Rituals of Self-Revelation*; Fowler, *The Rhetoric of Confession*; Doak, *Dreams of Difference*; Tomi Suzuki, *Narrating the Self*; Suzuki S., *The Concept of "Literature" in Japan*; Lippit, *Topographies of Japanese Modernism*.

3. For a study of the use of similar (and sometimes identical) terms with regard to modern Spanish literature, see Sieburth, *Inventing High and Low*.

4. A great deal has been written on this distinction, including Iwanami Shoten Bungaku Henshū-bu, *Meiji bungaku no ga to zoku*, a special issue of *Bungaku*, and Sekine, *Ga/Zoku Dynamics*. The continuity between *ga/zoku* and *tsūzoku*, not to mention among uses of *ga/zoku* itself, should not be overstated. On the adoption of the terms during the Meiji period, Kamei Hideo writes, "They were borrowed as vocabulary that structured discourse, ranking one thing as superior to another, unrelated to the normative consciousness implied by the use of *ga/zoku* during the Edo period." Iwanami Shoten Bungaku Henshū-bu, *Meiji bungaku no ga to zoku*, 17.

5. Komori, *Yuragi no Nihon bungaku*, 15.

6. Suzuki S., *Nihon no "bungaku" o kangaeru*, 239–40.

7. The *Complete Works of Contemporary Japanese Literature* was only one such manifestation of the influence of the market and the commercialization of literary texts; on women's magazines, another form that wielded tremendous economic influence, see Frederick, *Turning Pages*. The fascinating element introduced by these magazines is the simultaneous fear that female demand would determine literary value.

8. Kikuchi Kan (1888–1948) was born in Kagawa prefecture. Beginning in September 1910 he attended the First Higher School, where he met his classmates Akutagawa Ryūnosuke, Kume Masao, Naruse Seiichi, and Matsuoka Yuzuru. In his same grade were also Yamamoto Yūzō, Tsuchiya Bunmei, Kurata Hyakuzō, Fujimori Seikichi, and Hata Toyokichi. Just prior to graduation, in April 1913, he was accused of theft and left the school. With the help of Naruse's father he entered Kyoto University, where he studied under Ueda Bin and Kuriyagawa Hakuson. When the third series of the literary coterie magazine *Shinshichō* was started in February 1914 at Tokyo Imperial University, Akutagawa and the others invited him (then twenty-five) to be part of it. Although he contributed many plays and stories, he did not gain as much recognition as some of his colleagues, particularly Akutagawa. Kikuchi graduated from Kyoto University in July 1916. In October of that year he became a reporter for the newspaper *Jiji shinpō*. Starting in June 1918 he began to publish regularly in *Shinchō* and *Chūō kōron* and established his reputation within the *bundan*. He published "Ōshima ga dekiru hanashi" in June (*Shinchō*), "Mumei sakka no nikki" in July (*Chūō kōron*), "Tadanao-kei gyōjōki" in September (*Chūō kōron*), and "Onshū no kanata ni" in January 1919. His *Shinju fujin* (The Woman in Pearls, 1920–23) was serialized in the *Ōsaka mainichi* and the *Tōkyō nichinichi* from June to December 1920. It was with this work that he began to be characterized as a *tsūzoku* writer.

9. Kikuchi, *Kikuchi Kan zenshū*, vol. 22, 404–6. The collected works reports that the source and original publication date of the essay are unclear, but situates it among

essays written in March 1919. It appears in a book published in June 1920: Kikuchi, *Bungei ōrai*, 164–67, though this might not be its first time in print.

10. Kikuchi, *Kikuchi Kan zenshū*, vol. 22, 404. Note that the original meaning of the ancient Greek root of "canon" meant a measuring rod, and therefore a yardstick (or a law, or a principle) by which things could be judged. See Ross, *The Making of the English Literary Canon*, 23.

11. Satō Giryō (1878–1951) began publishing the literary magazine *Shinchō* in May 1904. It was the successor of *Shinsei*, a magazine Satō had begun in July 1896 as a contribution magazine (*tōsho zasshi*). After business difficulties forced him to relinquish *Shinsei* in May 1903, he began *Shinchōsha*. The magazine was closely affiliated with the naturalist movement, including Kunikida Doppo. By the beginning of the Taishō period *Shinchō* arguably had become the single most important literary magazine. As proletarian literature became more and more influential at the end of the Taishō period and the beginning of the Shōwa period, the magazine focused on *Shinkankaku-ha* and *Geijutsu-ha* literature.

12. Kikuchi, *Kikuchi Kan zenshū*, vol. 22, 413, 414. The Saintsbury quote is a retranslation of Kikuchi's translation. I have not been able to find the original. The only full work of Saintsbury's that had been translated at the time of Kikuchi's essay was his *Short History of French Literature*, which appeared in Japanese as *Furansu bungakushi*. The closest I have found to a statement of how criticism should be practiced comes in Saintsbury's discussion of Charles Augustin Sainte-Beuve (525–28). There Saintsbury repeats Victor Hugo's principle of criticism, that "the critic has only to judge of the intrinsic goodness of the book, and not of its conformity to certain pre-established ideas" (526).

13. As an example, he lists Nanbu Shūtarō, who had made a statement to similar effect in the June 1919 issue of *Bunshō sekai*, from which Kikuchi quotes.

14. Kikuchi, *Kikuchi Kan zenshū*, vol. 22, 415.

15. Ibid., 416.

16. The literary magazine *Bunshō sekai* was published by Hakubunkan from September 1906 until December 1920, and then was published from January 1921 until December 1921 under the name *Shin-bungaku*. Circulation for the first issue was eighteen thousand and then leveled off to around twelve thousand beginning with the third issue. Affiliated with Tayama Katai, the magazine was seen as a bastion of naturalist thought, along with *Waseda bungaku*, *Shumi*, and *Yomiuri shinbun*. It too started out as a *tōsho zasshi*. Contributors to the magazine who went on to some fame include Murō Saisei, Uchida Hyakken, Nakamura Murao, Kimura Ki, and Yokomitsu Riichi.

17. Kikuchi, *Kikuchi Kan zenshū*, vol. 22, 429, 431.

18. Yamamoto Y., *Bungakusha wa tsukurareru*, 140–44.

19. For more on this debate in the context of Kikuchi's career, see Maeda Ai, "The Development of Popular Fiction in the Late Taishō Era: Increasing Readership of Women's Magazines," in Fujii, *Text and the City*, 184–90.

20. Hirano, Odagiri, and Yamamoto, *Gendai Nihon bungaku ronsō shi* (hereafter RSS), vol. 1, 49. I have used the versions of many of the following essays in this three-

volume anthology of literary criticism, often limiting myself to the essays that he selected to comprise the debates. This has inevitably led to the omission of other articles that may have been written in response to the articles cited here; however, I believe that these essays sufficiently represent the most important statements in each debate. Note that the anthology, despite its name, merely reproduces the original essays and does not provide analysis, apart from short *kaisetsu* in each volume.

21. Benedetto Croce (1866–1952) was an extremely influential Italian aesthetician at the turn of the century. René Wellek argues that though Croce did say that "the aesthetic fact is form and nothing but form," he was not a formalist. Wellek writes, "There is, of course, no distinction between content and form. Content to Croce would be, at most, brute matter preceding the art of intuition" (*Four Critics*, 6–7). Joel E. Spingarn (1875–1939), a white author and critic and one of founders of the NAACP, was, according to Wellek, "a propounder of a simplified Croceanism" (3). Croce's ideas later influenced the New Criticism school.

22. He also cites Kagawa Toyohiko's *Shisen o koete* and Fujimori Seikichi's *Kyū-sensei*. RSS 1:49–50.

23. Ibid., 49.

24. Ibid., 51. In this he later suggests that he is more lenient than G. B. Shaw, who said (in a reverse translation from Kikuchi's), "Anyone who writes even one line for the sake of art is an unsalvageable fool" (64).

25. Ibid., 52.

26. Satomi Ton (1888–1983) was the younger brother of the writers Arishima Takeo and Arishima Ikuma, though Satomi was adopted into and raised by his mother's family. Like so many other members of the Shirakaba-ha, he had an aristocratic, wealthy family and attended both the Peers' School and Tokyo Imperial University (though he left without a degree in 1908). Donald Keene distances Satomi's motivations from those of the other Shirakaba-ha members, however, calling him "an immoralist in a group of earnest men" (*Dawn to the West*, 499).

27. RSS 1:54.

28. Ibid., 50, 55.

29. The fact that he published his essay in a journal that was consumed primarily by the literary establishment suggests, perhaps, that he wanted to address the direction of literature, as he suggested in earlier writings that critics should.

30. RSS 1:56.

31. The original quote from Kikuchi is "Bungei wa keikoku no daiji" (ibid., 52). This is probably a reference to an almost identical line ("Bunshō wa keikoku no daigyō") in *Lun-wen* by Ts'ao P'i (197–226), which Stephen Owen translates as "Literary works are the supreme achievement in the business of state." Owen, *Readings in Chinese Literary Thought*, 68. In Japan the same line (as in the *Lun-wen*) appeared in the preface of the *Ryōunshū*, the first imperial anthology of *kanshi*, completed in 814.

32. He also is concerned with contemporary works that do not confront the bigger issues of life, for example, how the protagonist in Shiga's *A Dark Night's Passing* never thinks about money.

33. The first series of the literary magazine *Shinshōsetsu* was published from January 1889 until June 1890; this essay appeared during its second series, from July 1896 until November 1926. Akutagawa and Kikuchi joined the magazine as editors in January 1924, probably after that month's issue was already completed. *Shinshōsetsu* was the site of publication for many important works, including *Kusamakura*, *Kōya hijiri*, *Futon*, *Sumidagawa*, and *Kain no matsuei*. In January 1927 it changed its name to *Kuroshio* and stopped publication that March.

34. For the gist of Nakamura's argument as it fits into the larger I-novel debate, see Fowler, *The Rhetoric of Confession*, 44–46. The first distinction that Nakamura makes that is relevant to our discussion is that for the *shinkyō shōsetsu*, "who" wrote it is more significant than the fact that "it was written" (*RSS* 1:93). Factors about the writer come into the evaluation of works for the Akutagawa Prize as well. Unlike later Akutagawa Prize *senpyō*, which would take into consideration what was known about the artistic integrity or sincerity of the writer, however, Nakamura is describing the fact that the reading audience was expected to bring certain knowledge about the writer to their reading of a work.

35. As an interesting exception, Nakamura points out that Kikuchi Kan seems to be producing both: the works that use the facts of his life as material lean toward the *shinkyō shōsetsu* side, while his works that use old materials and are seen as *tsūzoku shōsetsu* lean toward the *honkaku shōsetsu* side. In Nakamura's schema the authentic novel is the primary alternative to the I-novel.

36. *RSS* 1:94.

37. Fear of following the herd is one step away from fearing the herd itself. Scorn for the tastes of the masses is an essential component to many of the debates that follow. Such scorn is not unrelated to a fear of the political power of the masses, which was being agitated for when this essay was written and which was broadly expanded with the 1925 Universal Male Suffrage Act.

38. *RSS* 1:94–95.

39. Ibid., 96.

40. I leave *tsūzoku* untranslated for the reasons given in the introduction.

41. Ikuta Chōkō (1882–1936) was born in Tottori prefecture. In 1896 he went to Osaka, and in 1899 he went to Tokyo. He entered the First Higher School in 1900 and formed the *kairan zasshi Tabufu* with his classmates Kuribara Kojō, Nakamura Ko-kyō, and Morita Sōhei, among others. His first work published outside *Tabufu* was in *Shinsei* (the precursor to *Shinchō*, mentioned above). He entered Tokyo Imperial University in 1903. He first gained the attention of the *bundan* for his essay "Oguri Fūyō-ron," which appeared in the March 1906 issue of *Geien*. He graduated from Tokyo Imperial University in July of that year. He became known for a series of essays on literary issues, most of which were published in *Shinchō* or the *Yomiuri shinbun*. In 1914 he started the literary journal *Hankyō* with Morita Sōhei. Around that time he became friends with Sakai Toshihiko and Ōsugi Sakae, leading to his involvement in social issues.

42. *RSS* 1:99.

43. Ibid.

44. Ibid., 101.

45. As an aside, Ikuta raises Saikaku as an example, conceding that some might think that Saikaku is not of the same caliber as Shakespeare, but "in the history of modern [*kindai*] Japanese literature, it is not easy to think of another literary master as great as he." This speaks to the issue of how contemporaries conceived of the "modern" period versus "contemporary" times. RSS 1:103.

46. The two parts of the essay appeared in *Bungei kōza* no. 7, published in January 1925, and *Bungei kōza* no. 8, published the following month, respectively. They appear in RSS 1:108–14. For more on Kume's argument as it relates to the I-novel debate, see Fowler, *The Rhetoric of Confession*, 46–48. Kume Masao (1891–1952) was born in Nagano prefecture and later moved to Fukushima. In 1910 he entered the First Higher School on recommendation; in 1913 he entered Tokyo Imperial University's English Literature Department. In December 1915 he and Akutagawa visited Sōseki and became his disciples. In 1916 he was graduated from the university. The first work he received pay for, "Ginka," was published that year in *Shinchō*. In March 1917 he published "Kengi" in *Chūō kōron* and was thus recognized by the *bundan*. In 1919 he founded the literary magazine *Ningen* with Satomi Ton, Yoshii Isamu, and Tanaka Jun. It continued publication until June 1922.

47. RSS 1:108.

48. Ibid., 110.

49. Ibid., 111.

50. Ibid., 112.

51. Ibid., 113.

52. Lippit, *Topographies of Japanese Modernism*, 26. See 26–31 on this debate as it relates to the concept of interiority.

53. Uno Kōji (1891–1961) was born in Fukuoka prefecture. Because of his father's death, at the age of three he moved to Kobe and then Osaka. In 1910 he entered Waseda's English Department. In 1915, unable to get the sufficient number of credits, he left school prior to graduation. He worked as an assistant translator under Shimamura Hōgetsu on Tolstoy's *War and Peace*, a job which he received through a recommendation by Hirotsu Kazuo. It was also through Hirotsu that Uno's first piece at the *bundan* level, "Kura no naka," was published in *Bunshō sekai* (April 1919).

54. These are likely references to Tolstoy, Zola, Kafū, Akutagawa, and Kikuchi, respectively. RSS 1:118.

55. Ibid., 119–24. Hirano gives the source as *Rajio kōen hikki*. Satō Haruo (1892–1964) was born in Wakayama prefecture. A writer from an early age, starting in 1907 Satō had poems published in *Myōjō*, *Shumi*, *Bunko*, and *Shinsei*. When *Subaru* began in 1909, he published ten poems in its early issues. In 1910 Satō went to Tokyo, where he entered Keio University's preparatory department, which he left in 1913. He published his first prose works in 1917, including *Yameru bara*, which was the first part of *Den'en no yūutsu*. He was close friends with Tanizaki at this time. With these

and other works, he entered the *bundan* around 1918. In 1919 he began an affair with Tanizaki's wife, Chiyo. He published *Tokai no yūutsu* in 1922. In June 1925 he began serializing a book about his triangular relationship in *Kaizō*. He cut it off, unfinished, in October 1926. During these last years of Taishō he was known both for his relationship with Tanizaki and his rivalry with Akutagawa.

56. *RSS* 1:121–22.

57. Ibid., 122.

58. Ibid., 127.

59. Hirabayashi Hatsunosuke (1892–1931) was born in Kyoto. In 1910 he entered the Kyoto normal school, where he met Sakai Toshihiko, with whom he corresponded. In 1913 he went to Tokyo to enter Waseda's English Department. In 1918 he joined Yamato Shinbunsha, writing the literary review column for that newspaper beginning in 1919. In 1920 he left the company and joined Kokusai Tsūshinsha, where he translated English telegrams. During this time he became very interested in Marxism and socialism. Around 1921 he was writing literary reviews for *Shinchō* and *Yomiuri shinbun*, with many of his reviews based in socialist theory. He had a materialist view of literature and began publishing *Musan kaikyū* with friends. He joined the Communist Party in 1922. In 1923 he became a Waseda lecturer in French literature on Yoshie Takamatsu's recommendation. Despite being a socialist, he escaped persecution after the Great Kantō Earthquake because he had been on a lecture tour in Nagano at the time. When *Bungei sensen* was founded in 1924 he became a member. In 1925 he became a member of the resurrected magazine *Kaihō*, though he did not rejoin the Communist Party when it re-formed in 1926. In December of that year he joined Hakubunkan to become the head editor of *Taiyō*. In April 1927, when the Nihon Puroretaria Geijutsu Renmei divided into the two camps of "Puro-gei" and "Rōgei," he cut ties with both factions.

60. Kobayashi Hideo's essay, "Watakushi-shōsetsu ron" (Discourse on Fiction of the Self), which is often seen as central to this debate as a whole, is not considered here because of his limited use of the terminology being examined. The essay is translated in full in Kobayashi H. and Anderer, *Literature of the Lost Home*, 67–93. While Kobayashi does argue that "all literature longs for purity" (by which he seems to imply writing that "unfolds as though all artifice were invisible"), he goes on to caution that "one must not fixate on words such as 'pure' that are ambiguous by nature" (85). (Note that the final phrase is my translation of the original "Tada junsui nado to iu ganrai ga mōrō to shita kotoba ni kodawaru no ga yoku nai dake da.")

61. Yokomitsu Riichi (1898–1947) was born in Fukushima, but his family moved a number of times. In 1916 he entered the preparatory course of Waseda high school; he remained affiliated with Waseda until 1921, but rarely attended classes. During this time he became friends with Kikuchi Kan and, through him, Kawabata Yasunari. In 1923 he became an editor for Kikuchi's magazine, *Bungei shunjū*. That year he published *Nichirin* and "Hae," which got him attention within the *bundan*, and positioned himself as anti-Marxist. In 1924 he founded the literary magazine *Bungei jidai* along with Kawabata Yasunari, Kataoka Teppei, Nakagawa Yoichi, and others.

Between 1928 and 1929 Yokomitsu was in charge of *Bungei shunjū*'s *jihyō* column (he was succeeded in this by Kobayashi Hideo, who was a supporter of Yokomitsu's work). *Bungei jidai* stopped publication in May 1927. In 1929 he started the literary magazine *Bungaku* with Hori Tatsuo. At the time he wrote "Junsui shōsetsu-ron," his work was being praised not only by Kobayashi Hideo, but also by Kawakami Tetsutarō (both of whom contributed to the debate). Yokomitsu had also been called, echoing praise originally directed at Shiga Naoya, the "god of the novel" (*shōsetsu no kamisama*).

62. *RSS* 3:71.

63. The specificity of the reference to the "Japanese" literary establishment should not be overlooked. See Doak, *Dreams of Difference*, 111–12, for more on the centrality of the concept of an ethnic people (*minzoku*) to Yokomitsu's argument.

64. Suzuki Sadami suggests that by *junbungaku*, Yokomitsu meant an essay-like style written as one would write a diary, therefore the I-novel and the mental state novel; by *geijutsu bungaku* he meant the Shinkō Geijutsu-ha; by *taishū bungaku* he meant primarily historical novels; by *tsūzoku bungaku* he meant contemporary novels of manners, such as those written by Kikuchi Kan (*Nihon no "bungaku" gainen*, 228). *Junsui shōsetsu* refers to Yokomitsu's proposed syncretic genre.

65. *RSS* 3:73.

66. Ibid., 76.

67. Ibid., 79. Yokomitsu (perhaps because of a typographical error) refers to Tom Jones as a novelist; I have taken the liberty of correcting this mistake.

68. Ibid., 72.

69. Nakamura Mitsuo (1911–88) was born in Tokyo. In 1928 he entered the First Higher School, specializing in French; three years later he entered Tokyo Imperial University's Law Department, dropped out temporarily, and then reenrolled in 1932 in the French Literature Department. That year he joined Takami Jun's literary coterie magazine, *Jūka*, in which he published his first novel and criticism that year. In 1934 he published essays on Maupassant and Nagai Kafū in *Bungakukai*. Because of the praise for these he received from (his high school acquaintance) Kobayashi Hideo and Hayashi Fusao, he made an impressive entrance as a critic despite his young age. In 1935 he graduated from the university; by January of that year he had already begun to write a regular literary review column in *Bungakukai*. The series of *Bungakukai* in which this essay appeared (the second series) was established in October 1933 by Hayashi Fusao, Takeda Rintarō, Kobayashi Hideo, Kawabata Yasunari, and others. It continued publication until April 1944.

70. *RSS* 3:80.

71. It should be noted that the production of literary works and theoretical works were closely interrelated, thereby complicating any assertions of cause and effect.

72. *RSS* 3:81.

73. Ibid., 82, 83, 84.

74. Ibid., 85.

75. In this Nakamura is strongly influenced by Lev Shestov's writings about Dostoyevsky, which were very influential at the time. Lev Shestov, "Dostoevsky and Nietzsche: The Philosophy of Tragedy," *Dostoevsky, Tolstoy and Nietzsche*, 141–322.

76. *RSS* 3:87.

77. Ibid., 93.

78. Moriyama Kei (1904–89) was a novelist, poet, and critic. Through involvement in left-wing literary groups he became close to Nakano Shigeharu, who attended the same junior high school as Moriyama. He joined the All-Japan Federation of Proletarian Arts (NAPF) in 1928 and remained involved in proletarian journals into the 1930s. He began publishing books of literary criticism in 1933 and released a volume titled *Bungaku-ron* the same month this essay appeared.

79. *RSS* 3:95.

80. Ibid.

81. Ibid., 97, 98.

82. At the time that he was writing the essay he was also participating in the selection process for the first Akutagawa Prize. The selection committee met between 14 June and 10 August.

83. *RSS* 3:107, 107–8.

84. Kataoka Teppei, "Gūzen—nichijō-sei—bi no mondai," *Mita bungaku*, May 1935, quoted in *RSS* 3:108.

85. Ikumi Kiyoharu, "Tsūzoku shōsetsu to junsui shōsetsu," *Mita bungaku*, May 1935, quoted in *RSS* 3:109.

86. *RSS* 3:109.

87. Ibid., 110.

88. *RSS* 1:132.

89. Ibid., 134. Karatani Kōjin suggests that Kume's implication is that mental state novels (*shinkyō shōsetsu*) will soon disappear, since their writing requires this sort of free time. Karatani, *Kindai Nihon no hihyō III*, 216.

90. Hirotsu Kazuo, " 'Junbungaku yogi-setsu' ni kotau," as quoted in *RSS* 1:137. "Journalism," as it is used here, closely resembles what I have been referring to as print capitalism.

91. *RSS* 1:137.

5. The Dynamic Canon

1. For more on literary awards, see *Booker* 30; English, *The Economy of Cultural Prestige* and "The Prize Phenomenon in Context," in Schaffer, *A Companion to the British and Irish Novel*, 160–77; Cabanès, Kopp, and Mollier, *Les Goncourt dans leur siècle*.

2. It is often argued that few Akutagawa Prize–winning works, particularly from the period under consideration, are considered classics today; Ishikawa Jun's *Fugen* (The Bodhisattva) is often proposed as one of the few. The claim here is not to the uppermost strata of the canon, access to which requires more support than any single

mechanism can hope to bring to bear on the reception of a work. Receipt of the Akutagawa Prize is beneficial in attaining that status, but is not sufficient. This does not, however, negate the benefits that the prize does provide and which are listed here. The subsequent disappearance of winning authors is not limited to the Akutagawa Prize; see Gedin, *Literature in the Marketplace*, 188, on the situation in France.

3. Komori Yōichi takes this argument a step further, suggesting that "modern Japan" is celebrated through such events (he is discussing the one-yen collections, but it is relevant here as well). Komori, "Kigen no gensetsu," 170–71.

4. Committee members and the year they received the Akutagawa Prize: Ikezawa Natsuki (1988), Miura Tetsuo (1960), Ishihara Shintarō (1955), Miyamoto Teru (1977), Kuroi Senji (short-listed 1968), Kōno Taeko (1963), Takubo Hideo (1969), and Furui Yoshikichi (1970). Furui was absent from this selection.

5. Quote based on notes I took at the event.

6. The winning works were Gen Getsu's "Kage no sumika" and Fujino Sen'ya's "Natsu no yakusoku." Although no specific voting results are made available to the public, one can make educated guesses about how individuals voted by reading the selection critiques (*senpyō*) each member writes after the selection. Based on these published comments it is likely Ishihara voted against both works, Miura voted against Gen, and Takubo voted against Fujino. Takubo and Ikezawa also disagreed with the selection of Gen and Fujino, respectively, but did not reject their selection.

7. At first glance Miyamoto's claim might seem to be a clear confession of subjectivity; the implication of his statement, however, is that anyone as discerning as Miyamoto would readily identify the literary value inherent in the works, not that we would merely see why the works suited his personal tastes. Thus the claim is that the value he identified and that would be obvious at a glance is universal, or at least shared by those with the ability to recognize it. The concepts of misrecognition, symbolic capital, and the literary field are drawn from the work of Pierre Bourdieu. Disinterestedness in the act of aesthetic judgment, which is essential to Immanuel Kant (see *Critique of Judgment*, 45–46), is a central object of Bourdieu's criticism. See Bourdieu, *Distinction* and *The Rules of Art*. For a clear overview of Bourdieu's concepts, see Swartz, *Culture and Power*, particularly 88–94 (symbolic capital and misrecognition) and 117–42 (fields).

8. Though the Akutagawa Prize did not reach its contemporary levels of national celebrity until 1956, when Ishihara Shintarō received the award, it possessed authority within the literary establishment from the time of its announcement. Even before the first awards were bestowed, for example, their importance was evident in an article on the authority of the prizes entitled "Akutagawa, Naoki ryōshō no 'ken'i,'" *Yomiuri shinbun*, 19 December 1934, which welcomed the "long-rumored" awards.

9. The winner was Nakanishi Rei. For the most comprehensive examination of the construction of the discourses surrounding modern Japanese literature, including that of purity, see Suzuki S., *Nihon no "bungaku" o kangaeru* and *Nihon no "bungaku" gainen*.

10. Though the use of the category "pure" has declined in recent years, the use of the term "popular" continues to reproduce and reinforce this elevated sphere.

11. Examples of the first category are Fowler, *The Rhetoric of Confession*, xviii, 128–29, and, to a certain extent, Hijiya-Kirschnereit, *Rituals of Self-Revelation*, x, 136–37. It should be noted that Hijiya-Kirschnereit admits ambiguity when she writes of the term that its "varying connotations arose from the context of its use" (156). Examples of the second category are Seidensticker, "The 'Pure' and the 'in-Between' " and Strecher, "Purely Mass or Massively Pure?"

12. Bourdieu, *The Rules of Art*, 122. "Distinction" refers to the establishing and marking of difference, and elevation through an implication of quality and rarity.

13. Because the central issue is the construction of pure literature, this study focuses primarily on the Akutagawa Prize, referencing the Naoki Prize only to highlight differences. Future studies of the Naoki Prize will, I hope, address this imbalance and help to dissolve the absolute boundary between purity and popularity. For those interested in comparisons with other central prizes, Kjell Espmark's study of the Nobel Prize, *The Nobel Prize in Literature*, reveals many similarities. These include "thoroughly and constantly revised" evaluative criteria (3), a desire to use the award to direct the course of literature (26), a pragmatic and instrumentalized view of the award (88), cultivation of the award's prestige and impact (125), and widespread criticisms of the award's relevance to literary value (145–68).

14. The primary source for this historical overview is Senuma, "Bungakushō: Sono shurui to seikaku," 1721–24.

15. By the close of the Taishō period in 1926 the journal *Bungei shijō* was able to compile a list of 164 coterie magazines active throughout the country. The list, which initially appeared in the April 1926 issue, is reproduced in Takami, *Shōwa bungaku seisui-shi*, 60–63.

16. For a look at how these awards functioned and the discourse they created, see Kōno, "Sensō hōdō to 'sakka sagashi' no monogatari."

17. Apparently he requested the alternate prize of 50 yen instead. Odagiri, "Akutagawa-shō no hanseiki," *Akutagawa-shō shōjiten*, 8.

18. An award's prestige could be overspent; the *Yorozu chōhō* award for short stories (*tanpen shōsetsu*), created in 1897, was given 1,720 times between 1897 and 1924. Because the award was given with such frequency, the wager of cultural prestige made by *Yorozu chōhō* on a specific work was minimal. If *Yorozu chōhō*'s audience disagreed with one selection, they might be appeased the following week.

19. Odagiri, *Akutagawa-shō shōjiten*, 11.

20. An early example is Prime Minister Saionji's "Gatherings in the Murmuring Rain" (Useikai), beginning in 1907, for which he gathered famous writers to discuss literature. For similar interactions between literary and governmental figures, see Rubin, *Injurious to Public Morals*, 110–14.

21. For more on the High Treason Incident (*Taigyaku jiken*), see Rubin, *Injurious to Public Morals*, 145–219.

22. This reciprocal connection between the government and authors was also pivotal in

Natsume Sōseki's refusal of an honorary doctorate on February 1911. For a detailed description of the committee's and writers' reactions to it, see ibid., 195–219.

23. "Dragon Gate" is the standard metaphor used to speak of the barrier between dominated and dominant. According to the Chinese legend from which the term comes, there once existed a section of the Yellow River where the current was so strong that it was nearly impossible for carp to swim upstream. Any carp able to ascend the rapids, it was said, would become a dragon. While this metaphor for cultural authority was used consistently throughout much of the twentieth century, the actual site of that authority (as it pertains to modern Japanese literature) has shifted a number of times over the past century.

Writing in 1924, Takita Choin, the editor of *Chūō kōron*, acknowledged that *Kaizō* had become another "dragon's gate" alongside *Chūō kōron*, which had performed that function for some time. Quoted in Obi, *Shuppan to shakai*, 116–17.

24. By the early 1920s women's magazines were paying the highest prices for manuscripts. See Maeda, *Kindai dokusha no seiritsu*, 162–63.

25. The *Kaizō* award bestowed in 1929 was particularly famous: that year Kobayashi Hideo's "Samazama naru ishō" was awarded second place after Miyamoto Kenji's "Haiboku no bungaku." As that decision suggests, *Kaizō* showed a strong predilection toward works with a connection to the proletarian movement. With the announcement in June 1934 of the *Kaizō* award, the editors lamented that few works were proletarian in nature and that most of them instead seemed to "depict the unrelieved anguish and unrest of petit-bourgeois lives." Quoted in Senuma, "Bungaku-shō o meguru shomondai (jō)," 158.

26. It did not begin to accept fiction for consideration until 1934.

27. Odagiri, *Akutagawa-shō shōjiten*, 7, 10.

28. The *Chūō kōron* award was given only three more times before it was canceled. The *Kaizō* award lasted slightly longer; it was awarded ten more times before finally being discontinued in 1939. Ibid., 16.

29. The writer and publisher Kikuchi Kan (1888–1948) was a central figure (known as the *ōgyosho*, or tycoon, of the *bundan*) in the prewar and wartime Tokyo literary establishment. After he initially established himself as a writer of pure literature, his literary reputation suffered with the great success of the so-called popular novel, *Shinju fujin* (1920). Despite a compromised reputation as a pure writer, Kikuchi assumed a central role in its production when he established the literary journal *Bungei shunjū* in 1923. *Bungei shunjū* rapidly gained importance in Tokyo letters, increasing Kikuchi's influence in the world of letters.

30. Reprinted in Kikuchi, *Hanashi no kuzukago to hanjijoden*, 79.

31. Apparently Kikuchi was convinced by Sasaki Mosaku and a group of reporters he had assembled for a discussion about the new awards. Nagai T. et al., *Akutagawa-shō no kenkyū*, 8–9.

32. According to the author Funahashi Seiichi, who became a selection committee member when the award was restored after the war, an unwritten rule existed that

works that had appeared in commercial magazines would not be considered for the award. Satō H. et al., "Akutagawa-shō to bundan," 16.

33. Kikuchi, "Akutagawa-Naoki-shō sengen." Nominally the watch was the primary prize and the money the secondary prize. The watch was added because there was concern that a mere cash award would be too crude. Sasaki Mosaku, "Akutagawa-shō no umareru made," in Nagai T. et al., *Akutagawa-shō no kenkyū*, 17. Kikuchi had wanted the money to be the only prize; only through Sasaki's urging was the watch added. See Dekune, "Akutagawa-shō no nedan," 289. Five hundred yen was a substantial but not tremendous amount of money for a prize; in fact Yokoyama Michiko, the winner in 1934 of the *Tōkyō asahi kenshō shōsetsu* award, apparently received 10,000 yen as her prize. See Senuma, "Bungaku-shō o meguru shomondai (jō)," 153. Kikuchi actually responded in his column to criticisms that the Akutagawa Prize money was insufficient. In March 1935 he wrote, "The two awards bestow a total of 2,000 yen per year, which is roughly the same as the amount given the runner-up for the Asahi Prize. I wish people would give us credit, Bungei Shunjūsha being the small company it is" (*Hanashi no kuzukago to hanjijoden*, 104).

Nagai Tatsuo states that he has no memory of Tanizaki's having attended, and he believes that there was probably an agreement allowing Kikuchi to use his name even though he would not actually participate. Nagai T., *Kaisō no Akutagawa*, 16. He speculates that Tanizaki might have agreed to this out of feelings of guilt after he briefly married and then divorced a member of the Bungei Shunjūsha staff, Furukawa Tomiko. Most of the other members of the committee will be familiar to readers as authors of varying degrees of fame. Sasaki Mosaku (1894–1966) was a writer who became general editor at Bungei Shunjūsha in 1929 and was made president of the company when it was reconstituted after the war. Takii Kōsaku (1894–1984) was a writer, poet, and close friend of Shiga Naoya; he worked as an editor at both the *Jiji shinpō* and *Kaizō* before leaving the publishing business to focus on his writing.

34. The "Hyōron-kabe" column of the *Yomiuri shinbun* that day expresses concern that neither professional critics nor left-wing writers are represented.

35. For an elaboration of the various links between the committee members, see Mack, "The Value of Literature," 317–21. The Naoki committee members had comparable connections and similarities.

36. In fact most of them were sufficiently established in the decade preceding the establishment of the Akutagawa Prize to be included in the *Complete Works of Contemporary Japanese Literature*. Tanizaki, Satō, Kikuchi, Kume, Murō, Yamamoto, Yokomitsu, Kawabata, and Takii were all included in the sixty-three-volume collection. Given their current fame, it is worth noting that Kawabata and Yokomitsu, who were younger than the other members, barely made it into the series. Their works were finally included in volumes 50 and 61, the *Shinkō bungaku-shū* and the *Shinkō geijutsu-ha bungaku-shū*, respectively.

37. Osaragi, "Naoki-shō ni tsuite," 178–79.

38. Uno, "Ku to raku no omoide," 199.

39. *Ōru yomimono* began as a special issue of *Bungei shunjū* in July 1930. Because it was so well received, Bungei Shunjūsha began publishing it monthly in April 1931. By January of the following year *Ōru yomimono* had a circulation of approximately 300,000.

40. Uno Kōji lists nineteen authors who submitted recommendations. See Uno, "Kaisō no Akutagawa-shō," 243. Thirty-eight authors are listed in Bungei Shunjū Kabushiki Kaisha, *Akutagawa-shō zenshū* [hereafter ASZ], 1:340.

41. "Akutagawa-shō no kaado kaikyū," *Yomiuri shinbun*, 3 March 1935.

42. "Hansei" by Ōtani Fujiko (1901–77) was selected in August 1934 to become a *Kaizō kenshō shōsetsu*, marking her as a rising author.

43. Uno Kōji states that Kawabata and Takii shared the responsibility for the first five awards. See Uno, "Kaisō no Akutagawa-shō," 245. Based on the selection critiques it appears that Takii's opinion dominated this process. Around the time that Uno Kōji joined the selection committee (in 1937, for the sixth awarded, to be decided in February 1938), Uno began assisting Kawabata and Takii with this responsibility. Satō H. et al., "Akutagawa-shō to bundan," 10.

44. By 1940 it had become standard for the committees to meet only three times.

45. Translated as "The Emigrants," the novel appeared in *The East* 21, nos. 4–6 (1985) and 22, no. 1 (1986). No translator is credited. This is actually a translation of the first part only, which was the portion that received the Akutagawa Prize. A second part was published between April and July 1946, and a third in July 1946.

46. Kawamura, " 'Gaichi' to bungaku-shō," *Ikyō no Shōwa bungaku*, 143.

47. In a March 1969 article titled "Shusse-saku no koro," Kawaguchi wrote that, though everyone thought he was awarded the prize for *Tsuruhachi Tsurujirō*—his first major work—in fact he received it for "Fūryū Fukagawa-uta." As Mawatari Kenzaburō points out, he is right, strictly speaking, as *Tsuruhachi Tsurujirō* did not appear during the period specified by the prize's regulations, January to June 1935. Hasegawa, *Naoki-shō jiten*, 233.

48. Ibid., 232.

49. The two awards were announced together, though it should be noted that the Akutagawa Prize appeared first, with Ishikawa's serious picture placed above Kawaguchi's more playful image. The formats, wording, and prizes were nearly identical, but the hierarchy of the two awards—as manifested in the order of their presentation—was never inverted. The order of presentation was the same for the selection critiques as well: the Akutagawa committee's preceded those of the Naoki committee.

50. Quoted in Nagai T., *Kaisō no Akutagawa*, 23, 25.

51. Quoted ibid., 23.

52. Quoted ibid., 24.

53. Quoted ibid., 25, 25–26.

54. Osaragi, "Naoki-shō ni tsuite," 178.

55. In at least one case the committee rewarded potential and overall achievement

instead of a specific work. When Ozaki Kazuo won (the fifth award, spring 1937) the selection committee wrote that the prize rewarded his previous writings and his years of hard work rather than the inferior *Nonki megane*. Uno, "Senkō iin no kansō," 128.

56. *ASZ* 1:338, 335.

57. Ibid., 335.

58. This is of course contrary to what one might have expected had pure literature been tantamount to the I-novel, and had the novel truly dominated the modern Japanese literary tradition at this point. Hence Suzuki Sadami's statement, " 'I-fiction' was never the mainstream of 'modern Japanese literature'; there existed only a historical view that interpreted 'modern Japanese literature' in terms of 'I-fiction' " (*The Concept of "Literature" in Japan*, 267).

59. *Hijiya-Kirschnereit*, 179–92. See Suzuki Tomi, *Narrating the Self*, 1–12, for a concise rendering of the discourse on the I-novel. Hibi Yoshitaka provides a similar overview that divides the I-novel discourse into periods. See Hibi, *"Jiko hyōshō" no bungaku-shi*, 12–15.

60. Kume Masao, "Shishōsetsu to shinkyō shōsetsu." The essay appeared in two parts, the first in *Bungei kōza*, January 1925, 7, and the second in *Bungei kōza*, February 1925, 8. They appear in *RSS* 1:108–14. The translation here is quoted from Suzuki Tomi, *Narrating the Self*, 1.

61. Though Ishikawa did migrate to Brazil for a number of months in 1930, no character readily recognizable as the author dominates the narrative.

62. Kikuchi, *Hanashi no kuzukago to hanjijoden*, 118.

63. *ASZ* 1:336.

64. Nagai T., *Kaisō no Akutagawa*, 30–31.

65. Part was also due to the reception of the award by the public, which tended to interpret it as an award for achievement rather than potential.

66. *ASZ* 1:335–36.

67. Kikuchi, *Hanashi no kuzukago to hanjijoden*, 119.

68. Quoted in Nagai T., *Kaisō no Akutagawa*, 27.

69. *ASZ* 1:336. "Dark clouds," according to Nagai T. (*Kaisō no Akutagawa*, 214 n. 3), probably refers to Dazai's failed attempt to pass the employment examination for *Miyako shinbun* in 1935, his failed attempt to take his own life, and his subsequent hospitalization for appendicitis.

70. Quoted in Nagai T., *Akutagawa-shō no kenkyū*, 53–54; first published in *Bungei tsūshin*, October 1935. The translation comes from Keene, *Dawn to the West*, 1043, with one exception: I have replaced "flannellike" with "Nelly-esque" for *Neruri no yō na*, presuming that Dazai is referring to the character Nelly from Dostoyevsky's *The Insulted and Injured*, to whom he also refers in the story "Ha." The sentence after the ellipsis is my own translation. Dazai is referring to Kawabata's "Kinjū," published in the July 1933 issue of *Kaizō*.

71. Nagai T., *Akutagawa-shō no kenkyū*, 54–55.

72. Ibid., 55.

73. Satō H. et al., "Akutagawa-shō to bundan," 12.
74. For the public statements at the time on the matter, see Yamanouchi, *Dazai Osamu ronshū*, 1:57–88, 115–40.
75. It was referred to this way as early as 8 December 1934, in an article titled "Shinshin sakka yorokobe: Hiraketa tōryūmon" in *Yomiuri shinbun*.
76. Quoted in Odagiri, *Akutagawa-shō shōjiten*, 27.
77. Nagai T., *Kaisō no Akutagawa*, 14–15. It is not clear what Kikuchi was expecting, because articles did run in a number of newspapers, some as early as 8 December 1934 (both the *Asahi* and *Yomiuri* ran articles on it that day). The papers dutifully announced the recipients on 11 August, and on 13 August *Tōkyō asahi* ran an article on the Akutagawa Prize's success, "Akutagawa-shō wa seikō."
78. From the October 1935 issue of *Bungei shunjū*, reprinted in Kikuchi, *Hanashi no kuzukago to hanjijoden*, 120–21. For more on the Literary Chat Society and its awards, see Rubin, *Injurious to Public Morals*, 246–55. Despite Kikuchi's nationalist leanings, from its announcement he resisted this pro-fascist group, which had been formed by the chief of the Police Bureau, Matsumoto Gaku. Akutagawa Prize selection committee members had different attitudes about the group; Satō Haruo resigned when it became clear that left-wing writers were being excluded from consideration for prizes, while Kawabata Yasunari felt that Matsumoto did not control the group's political agenda.
79. From the October 1936 *Bungei shunjū*, quoted in Nagai T., *Kaisō no Akutagawa*, 50.
80. Satō H. et al., "Akutagawa-shō to bundan," 10.
81. Nagai T., *Akutagawa-shō no kenkyū*, 11.
82. Even Dazai, because he had been one of the short-listed authors, was commissioned to write a new story for the October 1935 issue of *Bungei shunjū*. As a result of his subsequent behavior, however, he was not published by *Bungei shunjū* again, but was instead picked up by *Shinchō*.
83. Quoted in Nagai T., *Kaisō no Akutagawa*, 50.
84. Akutagawa and Naoki Prizes are dated according to the half-year period from which eligible works are drawn. Thus the second competition, which took place in early 1936, examined works published between July and December 1935. I have labeled these half-years spring and fall. In my translation the selection process that occurred in early 1936 would be "the second competition (fall 1935)."
85. For a detailed analysis of the changing political situation as it impinged upon publishing and writing, see Rubin, *Injurious to Public Morals*.
86. Despite the name of the main character, the story is not based on the Koshamain who led a rebellion against the Japanese in 1457.
87. "Goki" in an earlier *Akutagawa-shō zenshū* (not to be confused with the ASZ), vol. 1 (Tokyo: Koyama Shoten, 1949), quoted in Hasegawa, *Akutagawa-shō jiten*, 237.
88. In a personal interview Komori Yōichi suggested the possibility that censors were primarily concerned with criticism of the imperial system (*tennō-sei*) in the second half of the 1930s after activist Marxism had been largely suppressed. "Koshamain-

ki," which is set during the Tokugawa period, portrays actions directed by the Tokugawa *Bakufu*. Since the Meiji imperial system overturned the *Bakufu*, the story could be read as implicitly supporting (or at least not criticizing) the imperial system. Komori added that Tsuruta Tomoya was a member of the Rōnō-ha, which was generally not perceived as a threat to the imperial system.

89. As far as I can tell, Tsuruta was not arrested as a part of this crackdown.

90. *ASZ* 1:350.

91. Hasegawa, *Akutagawa-shō jiten*, 237.

92. Itō Sei, "Akutagawa-shō no futa sakuhin," *Asahi shinbun*, 2 September 1936.

93. *Yomiuri shinbun*, 25 August 1936.

94. "Sōbō," "Koshamain-ki," "Jōgai," "Chichūkai," "Fun'nyō-tan," "Noriai basha," "Niwatori sōdō," "Mitsuryōsha," "Chōkō Deruta," "Renraku-in," "Tensoku no goro," "Ryūkanfuku," "Tōhan," and "Karitachi."

95. See Kawamura, *Ikyō no Shōwa bungaku*, 143–46, for a list of the Akutagawa Prize–winning stories in the prewar period that deal with *gaichi*, including relevant details from each of the works. Kawamura also discusses how colonial literature took advantage of the awards.

96. Kawamura, "Akutagawa-shō senpyō o yomitoku," 204–5.

97. Nagai T., *Akutagawa-shō no kenkyū*, 87.

98. *ASZ* 1:346, 2:393, 394.

99. *ASZ* 3:352, 343, 354.

100. Hino had come to Tokyo from Kyūshū to study English at Waseda University. While there he started the literary coterie magazine *Machi* with Nakayama Seizaburō and others. In 1928 he enlisted in the army but was soon discharged. He then returned to Kyūshū to become more active in the labor movement. After being arrested and performing *tenkō* in 1932, he returned to writing, submitting works to the Kyūshū literary coterie magazines. Hino published *Fun'nyō-tan* in the September 1937, around the time he reentered the army and was sent to the mainland.

101. According to Uno, Kume Masao dismissed the number of votes any given work received as simply being what he called "a multiplicity of one" (*hitori ga tasū*). He explained that if one person liked a work, that individual could often convince a number of others to submit votes for it as well; therefore a large number of votes often reflected the opinion of only one person. See Uno, "Kaisō no Akutagawa-shō," 245.

102. Tsuruta was recommended by Hayashi Fusao. Nagai T., *Akutagawa-shō no kenkyū*, 68. This was also the case for Ibuse Masuji's selection for the Naoki Prize: Ozaki Kazuo cast the only vote nominating his work. See Uno, "Kaisō no Akutagawa-shō," 245.

103. Uno, "Kaisō no Akutagawa-shō," 235–52.

104. *ASZ* 2:347–8.

105. Uno suggests that length—whether it was too long to publish in the magazine—was a serious consideration. When one member of the selection committee, who

was also on the Shinchō Prize committee, told them "Yokudo" would receive the Shinchō Prize, they all breathed a sigh of relief. Uno, "Kaisō no Akutagawa-shō," 246.

106. A parenthetical remark in Uno's comment elaborates on the meaning of a "*tsūzoku feel*" by saying they both dealt with love. In another aside, this time glossing *tsūzoku shōsetsu*, Uno equates it with a *shinbun shōsetsu*, or newspaper novel. Uno, "Kaisō no Akutagawa-shō," 246. By the time he wrote his selection critique Kume had tempered this sentiment (ASZ 2:349).

107. Uno, "Kaisō no Akutagawa-shō," 247.

108. Nagai T., *Akutagawa-shō no kenkyū*, 65–67.

109. Kobayashi Hideo (1902–83) was a central critic of modern Japanese literature who has been called everything from the "first critic" of modern Japan to the "god of criticism." See Kobayashi H. and Anderer, *Literature of the Lost Home*, 14.

110. From *Bungei shunjū*, May 1938, within the column "Kōshū," reprinted in Nagai T., *Kaisō no Akutagawa*, 52.

111. In "Jon Manjirō hyōryū-ki," the work that received the Naoki Prize, Ibuse retells the famous story of John Manjiro, the Japanese fisherman who in 1841, at the age of fourteen, was stranded on a deserted island, only to be rescued by an American ship. He traveled throughout the world for the next twelve years, mastering the English language and being introduced to nineteenth-century American culture before returning to Japan. Soon after his return the Tokugawa shogunate ordered him to Edo, where he served a vital role as an interpreter in the government's negotiations with Admiral Perry.

112. Osaragi Jirō claims he pushed for this work because he thought that the Akutagawa committee, which considered only novels to be literature, would not have considered it. He wanted to use the Naoki Prize to reward all forms of writing, including nonfiction, which is what he considered Ibuse's story of John Manjirō to be. Osaragi, "Naoki-shō ni tsuite," 179.

113. Nagai T., *Kaisō no Akutagawa*, 52.

114. Quoted in Odagiri, *Akutagawa-shō shōjiten*, 151–52. In 1952 Uno wrote that he thought, if forced to choose, he would say that Ibuse's "Jon Manjirō" was more pure than Hino's "Fun'nyōtan." Uno, "Kaisō no Akutagawa-shō," 248.

115. The incidents depicted in this and the next paragraph come from Ibuse's own account, "Tokei to Naoki-shō," which appeared in the October 1963 issue of *Ōru yomimono*, reprinted in Ibuse, *Ibuse Masuji zenshū*, 22:440–42.

116. The Naoki Prize was also refused once, by Yamamoto Shūgorō in 1943. He felt that it should be given to someone who was more of a newcomer, thus fulfilling the expressed purpose of the award more closely. Nagai T., "Naoki-shō shitabatara-ki," 114.

117. Nagai T., *Akutagawa-shō no kenkyū*, 76–79. Although "Kairo no shō" is not among the officially short-listed texts, it was clearly considered (see ASZ 2:407); apparently it was even ranked second, after "Uta to mon no tate," but was removed from

consideration when Takii pointed out that an identical story existed in Chinese (Nagai T., *Akutagawa-shō no kenkyū*, 76; the story is "The Tale of Li Wa").

118. *Bungei shunjū*, September 1940, quoted in Kikuchi, *Hanashi no kuzukago to hanji-joden*, 257.

119. Satō Haruo wrote, "When I heard the news that Takagi had refused the award, I was impressed by his self-knowledge and admired his self-respect more, even, than that of a recipient" (ASZ 2:410).

120. ASZ 2:408, 408–9.

121. Ibid., 3:337, 336. Satō also wrote, "Had he made even the slightest misstep, it would have been a Naoki Prize work." Clarifying what he meant, he added, "[The work's] interesting plot was not constructed solely in order to be interesting; instead, it was born out of the writer's essential desire to express certain ideas and feelings" (335).

122. Ibid., 343.

123. Nagai T., *Akutagawa-shō no kenkyū*, 82–83.

124. Rubin, *Injurious to Public Morals*, 233.

125. Hashimoto M., *Nihon shuppan hanbaishi*, 560. It is likely that far more than ninety-seven existed; as cited previously, more than one hundred and sixty existed in 1926. Fewer than ninety-seven, however, were probably regularly combed for potential award recipients. Uno notes the existence of about twenty or thirty in Tokyo and another twenty or so in the countryside in one source (Satō H. et al., "Akutagawa-shō to bundan," 10) and over ten in Tokyo and seven to eight in the countryside in another (Uno, "Kaisō no Akutagawa-shō," 250).

126. Takami Jun makes an interesting point when he writes, in the 1950s, that the concept of *jikyoku* already seems as though it is a thing of the past, but, he adds, "if one thinks of it in terms of problematic [or perhaps "subject matter"; *mondai-sei*] versus artistry in the novel, the concept remains as one of the two ways to evaluate a work." Takami, *Shōwa bungaku seisui-shi*, 361.

127. Senuma, "Bungaku-shō o meguru shomondai (jō)," 164. See also Nagai T., *Akutagawa-shō no kenkyū*, 83. Arguably it was already visible in the selection of the twelfth prize, which came down to two works: Shirakawa Atsushi's "Gake" and Ushijima Haruko's "Shuku to iu otoko." In the end the selection committee avoided "Gake," which dealt with the problem of war widows' remarrying and thus could be read as critical of the war effort. Senuma reads this decision as the first to show a prejudice for works that were in line with the dominant ideology. Senuma, "Bungaku-shō o meguru shomondai (jō)," 163–64.

128. Thirty-six recommendations were received for this Akutagawa Prize. For a complete list of individuals who submitted recommendations, see ASZ 3:362.

129. A transcript of this third meeting appears ibid., 349–62.

130. Ibid., 350, 351, 358, 356, 352.

131. Ibid., 356, 358.

132. Ibid., 359, 361.

133. Ibid., 362, 361.

134. Ibid., 363, 367. Satō Haruo wrote that Shibaki had shown great care not to "cross that subtle line" between acceptability and unacceptability. Satō pointed out that the central problem for the committee was not its rather *tsūzoku* character, but the danger of handling this sort of material "at times like these" (367).

135. Quoted in Uno, "Ku to raku no omoide," 202.

136. *ASZ* 3:367.

137. The story originally appeared in the October 1941 issue of *Bungei shuto*. Substantial excised portions can be found in this original version on pp. 6–7 (references to an undercover police inspector), 33 (Yae as a "sacrifice" to the market changes and her sadness over the pending dissolution of the market), 35 (Yae's emotional declaration that her twenty-eight years of life thus far have been "wasted"; that she had mistakenly thought that all her efforts would result in something—anything— good, and that she wanted to die), and 36–37 (almost entirely changed).

138. Rubin, *Injurious to Public Morals*, 256.

139. For a detailed account of the expansion of the Cabinet Information Committee and its activities, see ibid., 256–78.

140. Uno, "Ku to raku no omoide," 200.

141. As the place of publication for the award-winning works and the selection critiques, this remained true even after the independent Nihon Shinkō-kai foundation was formed in 1937 to administer the awards.

142. Satō H. et al., "Akutagawa-shō to bundan," 15.

143. Ibid., 14.

144. Such as the *Akutagawa-shō zenshū* and Kawamura Minato's *Ikyō no Shōwa bungaku*.

145. Though this certainly does not amount to canonical centrality, these factors should not be underestimated. One can be certain, for example, that any study of Tada Yūkei will begin—partly as a justification—with a reference to the author's receipt of the prize. The importance of preservation, even for texts that originally appeared in large-circulation magazines, is even greater when one recognizes the historical paradox identified by William St. Clair, that "the more common and less expensive a printed text when it was produced . . . the poorer its survival rate to the present day" (*The Reading Nation*, 28).

Epilogue

1. It should not be presumed that these anthologies and the Akutagawa Prize functioned in precisely the same way in the postwar period; that remains to be studied. These concluding references to postwar developments are merely meant to show that the prewar mechanisms were not entirely isolated cases.

2. Maeyama, "Kaisetsu," 308.

3. Ibid., 307. Gremio Literario "Colonia" ("Colonia" Literary Society) is the Portuguese name of the group. Note that the quotations are used in the group's name

itself (see the colophon for the *Koronia shōsetsu senshū*), suggesting self-awareness of the unconventional use of the term.

4. François Guizot, *Histoire de la civilisation en Europe* (1828–30), translated in 1874–75, and Hippolyte Taine, *Histoire de la littérature anglaise* (1863). See Suzuki S., *The Concept of "Literature" in Japan*, 113, 177.

5. Suzuki S., *The Concept of "Literature" in Japan*, 177.

6. Tomi Suzuki, "Gender and Genre: Modern Literary Histories and Women's Diary Literature" in Shirane and Suzuki, *Inventing the Classics*, 78.

7. The first quote comes from A. Ueda, "The Production of Literature," 61; the second comes (in slightly modified form) from Nanette Twine's translation of Tsubouchi, *The Essence of the Novel*, 1.

8. In his study of the link between the disciplinary boundaries in the humanities and nationalism, David Shumway writes, "No condition of knowledge production is so fundamental and yet remains so little recognized as nationalism" ("Nationalist Knowledges," 357).

9. Driscoll, in the introduction to Yuasa, *Kannani and Document of Flames*, 174.

10. James A. Fujii, "Writing Out Asia," in Barlow, *Formations of Colonial Modernity*, 176, 193. Note Fujii's hesitations about the term "canon" (195 n. 18).

11. Wender, *Lamentation as History*, 201. Citizenship is only one part of a larger social transformation to which Wender believes literature can contribute, a transformation dedicated to "liberation and dignity" for *zainichi* (201). She also makes the invaluable point that the literary fame that accompanies the Akutagawa Prize can make *zainichi* works "big sellers, literary commodities marketed at least in part as testament to Japan's multiculturalism" (92). The interweaving of these conceptual groupings and political praxis is also central to queer studies. See Keith Vincent's introduction to the special collection of *Gendai shisō*, "Resubian/gei sutadiizu."

12. Homogeneity should not be presumed among these "minority" groups either; a number of *zainichi* writers, for example, consciously avoid that identification and the politics accompanying it. Perhaps coincidentally one of the Naoki Prize cowinners during the very next prize period, the first half of 2000, Kaneshiro Kazuki, also avoided the *zainichi* classification, despite dealing with many of the issues usually considered characteristic of that category. Sonia Ryang argues that, as a result, "the sub-genre itself becomes obsolete" ("Diaspora and Beyond," 67–68). Many would argue in fact that many of the works celebrated as the greatest of modern Japan are similarly unrepresentative of the mainstream, and perhaps are powerful for precisely that reason.

13. A problem that Fujii identifies as well: "Viewed paradigmatically in relation to other (national) canons, a particular literary canon will *appear* unified and even stable" ("Writing Out Asia," 177, emphasis added). This is not unique to this case in Japan; see Ross, *The Making of the English Literary Canon*, 24–25.

14. Komori, *Yuragi no Nihon bungaku*, 8–9. In English, see Tai, "Rethinking Culture."

15. Naoki Sakai, "Modernity and Its Critique: The Problem of Universalism and Particularism," in Miyoshi and Harootunian, *Postmodernism and Japan*, 101.

16. As Fredric Jameson, following Tom Nairn, points out, "All nationalism is both healthy and morbid. . . . A Left which cannot grasp the immense Utopian appeal of nationalism . . . can scarcely hope to 'reappropriate' such collective energies and must effectively doom itself to political impotence" (*The Political Unconscious*, 298).

17. Brantlinger, *Bread and Circuses*, 33.

18. In *An Introduction to Theories of Popular Culture* Strinati provides a clear overview of many of these schools. In his introduction he writes, "The various conceptual attempts to define popular culture [included in this book] . . . inevitably [involve] its analysis and evaluation. It therefore seems difficult to define popular culture independently of the theory which is designed to explain it" (xvii).

19. For more on this fascinating decision, see Sherif, "The Aesthetics of Speed."

20. Quoted ibid., 204, 206; translations are Sherif's.

21. More persuasive divisions have been proposed by individuals such as Charles Altieri and Kuwabara Takeo. Altieri argues that a distinction exists between works that present "possible worlds" that we consider superior to the one we know—"the modes of agency" that these works "can make available and desirable for us"—and those works that do not. For Altieri, however, there must be an "active principle" underlying this distinction, one that "guides selection of meanings from a range of semantic and cultural possibilities" (*Canons and Consequences*, 47, 79, 13). This is what makes Altieri's argument inapplicable to the pure-*tsūzoku* distinction studied here. As both the debates and the selection critiques reveal, the distinction was invoked as if a shared "active principle" existed, despite the absence of consensus concerning what the principle might be. Altieri's challenge to antifoundationalist aesthetics, however, must be taken seriously, particularly when one is concerned with the role of the humanities in education. This study, in illuminating the role of material production in the transmission of texts—reminding us that no abstract canon ever exists, only physical manifestations of those canons—addresses Altieri's position dialectically, without any presumption that the issue of literary value is resolved. Kuwabara has written that literary works can be divided into two types: those that participate in the production of value and those that participate in the reproduction of value (Kuwabara Takeo, *Bungaku nyūmon*, cited in Suzuki S., *Nihon no "bungaku" o kangaeru*, 279–80). Problems arise when Kuwabara forces this concept into the existing pure-popular frame, reproducing problematic insinuations concerning both purity and the masses. More subtle distinctions such as these seem to have largely replaced—in analytical studies, if not in general attitudes—earlier distinctions such as that between "novels that attack the established society" and those "whose intention was to provide relaxation, entertainment and escapism" (Gedin, *Literature in the Marketplace*, 47), though the question behind each of these formulations, that of literature's capacity within the system described here to effectively perform what Herbert Marcuse termed "the Great Refusal—the protest against that which is," remains (Marcuse, *One-Dimensional Man*, 63).

22. For an interesting insight into the award, as well as specific details about the economics of writing in contemporary Japan, see Greenfeld, "Prizefighting in Japan." Greenfeld's mother, Kometani Fumiko, received the prize for the fall of 1985.

23. Trevor Ross sees a similar mechanism in the English literary canon: "The commodification of literature that print entailed was a threat [producers desiring distinction] could exaggerate to reinforce the binarism of high and low" (*The Making of the English Literary Canon*, 73–74).

24. Gilmore, *American Romanticism*, 1.

25. Janice Radway explores this "new form of cultural production" in *A Feeling for Books*, 133–34. By contrasting the extreme differences between this group of writers and the "single writer who thought of himself or herself as an individual communicating in a unique fashion with a series of discrete individuals" through "more unified volume[s that they] conceived, penned, and edited" (135), Radway unfortunately leaves the binarism functioning. For more on "Bertha M. Clay," see Denning, *Mechanic Accents*, 23–24, an important reconsideration of these marginalized works.

26. As Zwicker and Duara have both argued, the modern–premodern divide, with its attendant focus on the nation, obscures other "social imaginaries" (Zwicker, *Practices of the Sentimental Imagination*, 62) and reinforces "the assumption of modern consciousness as a unified episteme marked by an epistemological break with past forms of consciousness" (Duara, *Rescuing History*, 54).

27. Zuidervaart, "The Social Significance of Autonomous Art," 74–75.

28. Spivak, *Death of a Discipline*, 26.

29. Palumbo-Liu, *The Ethnic Canon*, 14.

30. See Lowe, *Immigrant Acts*, 37–59.

WORKS CITED

Adorno, Theodor W. *The Culture Industry: Selected Essays on Mass Culture*. London: Routledge, 1991.

Aeba Kōson. "Mukashi no sakusha no sakuryō oyobi shuppan busū." *Aoi* 4 (1910): 1–3.

Altieri, Charles. *Canons and Consequences: Reflections on the Ethical Force of Imaginative Ideals*. Evanston, Ill.: Northwestern University Press, 1990.

Altman, Albert Avraham. "Modernization of Printing in Mid-Nineteenth Century Japan." *Asian and African Studies* (Jerusalem) 4 (1968): 85–105.

Anderson, Mark. "National Literature as Cultural Monument: Instituting Japanese National Community." *New Directions in the Study of Meiji Japan*, ed. by Helen Hardacre and Adam L. Kern. Leiden: Brill, 1997.

Aoyama Ki, ed. *Kaizōsha bungaku geppō*. Shōwa-ki bungaku shisō bunken shiryō shūsei 5. Tokyo: Gogatsu Shobō, 1990.

Appadurai, Arjun. *The Social Life of Things*. Cambridge: Cambridge University Press, 1986.

Ariga, Chieko. "The Playful Gloss: *Rubi* in Japanese Literature." *Monumenta Nipponica* 44, no. 3 (1989): 309–35.

Ariyama Teruo. "1920, 30 nendai no media fukyū jōtai: Kyūryō seikatsu-sha, rōdō-sha o chūshin ni." *Shuppan kenkyū* 15 (1984): 30–58.

Asahi Shinbun Hyakunenshi Henshū Iinkai. *Asahi shinbunsha shi*. Tokyo: Asahi Shinbunsha, 1990.

Asaoka Kunio. "Meiji-ki kashihon kashidashi daichō no naka no dokusha-tachi." *Nihon shuppan shiryō* 4 (1999): 1–46.

Balibar, Etienne, and Immanuel Wallerstein. *Race, Nation, Class: Ambiguous Identities*. London: Verso, 1991.

Barlow, Tani E., ed. *Formations of Colonial Modernity in East Asia*. Durham, N.C.: Duke University Press, 1997.

Bates, Peter Alexander. "Fractured Communities: Class and Ethnicity in Representations of the Great Kanto Earthquake." Ph.D. diss., University of Michigan, 2006.

Benedict, Barbara. *Making the Modern Reader: Cultural Mediation in Early Modern Anthologies.* Princeton: Princeton University Press, 1996.

Berry, Mary Elizabeth. *Japan in Print: Information and Nation in the Early Modern Period.* Berkeley: University of California Press, 2006.

———. "Was Early Modern Japan Culturally Integrated?" *Modern Asian Studies* 31, no. 3 (July 1997): 547–81.

Booker 30: A Celebration of 30 Years of the Booker Prize for Fiction. London: Booker PLC, 1998.

Bourdaghs, Michael. *The Dawn That Never Comes: Shimazaki Tōson and Japanese Nationalism.* New York: Columbia University Press, 2003.

Bourdieu, Pierre. *Distinction: A Social Critique of the Judgement of Taste.* Cambridge, Mass.: Harvard University Press, 1984.

———. *The Rules of Art: Genesis and Structure of the Literary Field.* Stanford: Stanford University Press, 1996.

Boxer, C. R. *The Christian Century in Japan: 1549–1650.* Berkeley: University of California Press, 1951.

Brantlinger, Patrick. *Bread and Circuses: Theories of Mass Culture as Social Decay.* Ithaca, N.Y.: Cornell University Press, 1983.

Brownstein, Michael C. "From Kokugaku to Kokubungaku: Canon-Formation in the Meiji Period." *Harvard Journal of Asiatic Studies* 47, no. 2 (1987): 435–60.

Bungei Shunjū Kabushiki Kaisha, ed. *Akutagawa-shō zenshū.* 19 vols. Tokyo: Bungei Shunjūsha, 1982–2002.

Bungei Shunjū Shinsha, ed. *Bungei Shunjū sanjūgonen shikō.* Tokyo: Bungei Shunjū Shinsha, 1959.

Bureau of Social Affairs Home Office and Morihiko Fujisawa, eds. *The Great Earthquake of 1923 in Japan.* Tokyo: Naimushō Shakaikyoku, 1926.

Burk, Stefania Eliza. "Reading between the Lines: Poetry and Politics in the Imperial Anthologies of the Late Kamakura Period (1185–1333)." Ph.D. diss., University of California, Berkeley, 2002.

Burns, Susan L. *Before the Nation: Kokugaku and the Imagining of Community in Early Modern Japan.* Durham, N.C.: Duke University Press, 2003.

Cabanès, Jean-Louis, Robert Kopp, and Jean-Yves Mollier, eds. *Les Goncourt dans leur siècle: Un siècle de "Goncourt."* Villeneuve d'Ascq, France: Presses universitaires du Septentrion, 2005.

Chibbett, D. G. *The History of Japanese Printing and Book Illustration.* Tokyo: Kodansha International, 1977.

Copeland, Rebecca L. *Lost Leaves: Women Writers of Meiji Japan.* Honolulu: University of Hawai'i Press, 2000.

Dai-Nihon Insatsu Kabushiki Kaisha, ed. *Shichijūgonen no ayumi: Dai-Nihon Insatsu Kabushiki Kaisha-shi.* Tokyo: Dai-Nihon Insatsu Kabushiki Kaisha, 1952.

Dekune Tatsurō. "Akutagawa-shō no nedan." *Bungei shunjū*, September 1995, 288–95.

Denning, Michael. *Mechanic Accents: Dime Novels and Working-Class Culture in America.* London: Verso, 1998.

Doak, Kevin Michael. *Dreams of Difference: The Japan Romantic School and the Crisis of Modernity.* Berkeley: University of California Press, 1994.

Duara, Prasenjit. *Rescuing History from the Nation.* Chicago: University of Chicago Press, 1995.

English, James F. *The Economy of Cultural Prestige: Prizes, Awards, and the Circulation of Cultural Value.* Cambridge, Mass.: Harvard University Press, 2005.

Ericson, Steven J. *The Sound of the Whistle: Railroads and the State in Meiji Japan.* Cambridge, Mass.: Council on East Asian Studies, Harvard University, 1996.

Espmark, Kjell. *The Nobel Prize in Literature: A Study of the Criteria behind the Choices.* Boston: G. K. Hall, 1986.

Febvre, Lucien, and Henri-Jean Martin, *The Coming of the Book: The Impact of Printing 1450–1800.* London: Verso, 1976.

Forrer, Matthi. *Eirakuya Tōshirō, Publisher in Nagoya: A Contribution to the History of Publishing in 19th Century Japan.* Amsterdam: J. C. Gieben, 1985.

Fowler, Edward. *The Rhetoric of Confession.* Berkeley: University of California Press, 1988.

Frederick, Sarah. *Turning Pages: Reading and Writing Women's Magazines in Interwar Japan.* Honolulu: University of Hawai'i Press, 2006.

Fujii, James, ed. *Text and the City: Essays on Japanese Modernity.* Durham, N.C.: Duke University Press, 2004.

Fukuda Ryōtarō. *Hokuryūkan gojūnen o kataru.* Tokyo: Hokuryūkan, 1940.

Gedin, Per. *Literature in the Marketplace.* Trans. George Bisset. Woodstock, N.Y.: Overlook Press, 1977.

Genette, Gérard. *Paratexts: Thresholds of Interpretation.* Cambridge: Cambridge University Press, 1997.

Gilmore, Michael T. *American Romanticism and the Marketplace.* Chicago: University of Chicago Press, 1985.

Gluck, Carol. "The Invention of Edo." *Mirror of Modernity: Invented Traditions of Modern Japan,* ed. by Stephen Vlastos. Berkeley: University of California Press, 1998.

Greenfeld, Karl Taro. "Prizefighting in Japan." *The Nation,* 20 May 1991, 669.

Hamada Keisuke. *Kinsei shōsetsu: Eii to yōshiki ni kansuru shiken.* Kyoto: Kyōto Daigaku Gakujutsu Shuppankai, 1993.

Harootunian, Harry. *History's Disquiet: Modernity, Cultural Practice, and the Question of Everyday Life.* New York: Columbia University Press, 2000.

——. *Overcome by Modernity: History, Culture, and Community in Interwar Japan.* Princeton: Princeton University Press, 2000.

Hasegawa Izumi, ed. *Akutagawa-shō jiten.* Tokyo: Shibundō, 1977.

——, ed. *Naoki-shō jiten.* Tokyo: Shibundō, 1977.

Hashimoto Motome. *Nihon shuppan hanbai-shi.* Tokyo: Kōdansha, 1964.

Hashimoto Yukiko. "Dokusho suru 'taishū': Enpon būmu ni arawareta 'taishū' no imeeji." *Tōkyō-to Edo Tōkyō Hakubutsukan kenkyū hōkoku* 9 (October 2003): 41–58.

Havens, Thomas. "Japan's Enigmatic Election of 1928." *Modern Asian Studies* 11, no. 4 (1977): 543–55.

Herrnstein Smith, Barbara. *Contingencies of Value: Alternative Perspectives for Critical Theory.* Cambridge, Mass.: Harvard University Press, 1988.

Hibbett, Howard. "The Role of the Ukiyo-zōshi Illustrator." *Monumenta Nipponica* 13, nos. 1–2 (1957): 67–82.

Hibi Yoshitaka. *"Jiko hyōshō" no bungaku-shi: Jibun o kaku shōsetsu no tōjō.* Tokyo: Kanrin Shobō, 2002.

Hijiya-Kirschnereit, Irmela. *Rituals of Self-Revelation: Shishōsetsu as Literary Genre and Socio-Cultural Phenomenon.* Cambridge, Mass.: Council on East Asian Studies, Harvard University, 1996.

Hill, Christopher L. "Ideologies of Novelty and Agedness: Narrating the Origins of the Meiji Nation." *New Directions in the Study of Meiji Japan,* ed. by Helen Hardacre and Adam Kern. Leiden: Brill, 1997.

Hirano Ken, Odagiri Hideo, and Yamamoto Kenkichi, eds. *Gendai Nihon bungaku ronsō shi.* 3 vols. Tokyo: Miraisha, 1956–57.

Hiraoka Toshio. "Meiji Taishō bungakushi shūsei: Kaisetsu." *Meiji Taishō bungakushi shūsei* 12. Tokyo: Nihon Tosho Sentaa, 1999.

Hirotsu Kazuo. *Hirotsu Kazuo zenshū.* 13 vols. Tokyo: Chūō Kōronsha, 1973–74.

Hohendahl, Peter Uwe. *Building a National Literature: The Case of Germany, 1830–1870.* Trans. Renate Baron Franciscono. Ithaca, N.Y.: Cornell University Press, 1989.

Hunter, Janet. *Concise Dictionary of Modern Japanese History.* Berkeley: University of California Press, 1984.

Hutcheon, Linda, and Mario J. Valdés, eds. *Rethinking Literary History: A Dialogue on Theory.* Oxford: Oxford University Press, 2002.

Huyssen, Andreas. *After the Great Divide: Modernism, Mass Culture, Postmodernism.* Bloomington: Indiana University Press, 1986.

Hyōdō Hiromi. *"Koe" no kokumin kokka Nihon.* Tokyo: Nihon Hōsō Shuppan Kyōkai, 2000.

Ibuse Masuji. *Ibuse Masuji zenshū.* 30 vols. Tokyo: Chikuma Shobō, 1996–2000.

Inagaki Tatsurō and Shimomura Fujio, eds. *Nihon bungaku no rekishi.* Vol. 11. Tokyo: Kadokawa Shoten, 1968.

Insatsushi Kenkyūkai, ed. *Hon to katsuji no rekishi jiten.* Tokyo: Kashiwa Shobō, 2000.

Ishikawa Tatsuzō. "The Emigrants." *The East* 21, no. 4 (1985): 62–70; no. 5 (1985): 64–70; no. 6 (1985): 62–70; and 22, no. 1 (1986): 58–65.

Ishizuka Jun'ichi. "Enpon o henshū shita hitobito: Kaizōsha-ban 'Gendai Nihon bungaku zenshū' to gendai." *Shuppan kenkyū* 29 (1998): 29–48.

Itō Sei and Senuma Shigeki, eds. *Nihon bundanshi.* 24 vols. Tokyo: Kōdansha, 1953–78.

Ivy, Marilyn. "Formations of Mass Culture." *Postwar Japan as History,* ed. by Andrew Gordon. Berkeley: University of California Press, 1993.

Iwade Sadao. *Tōkyōdō no hachijūgonen.* Tokyo: Tōkyōdō, 1976.

Iwanami Shoten Bungaku Henshū-bu, ed. *Meiji bungaku no ga to zoku.* Tokyo: Iwanami Shoten, 2001.

Iwasaki Katsumi. " 'Kakusho' shuppan-kai, Kantō daishinsai zengo." *Nihon shuppan shiryō* 2 (1996): 86–108.

——. "Kantō daishinsai no risai jōkyō, kakusho." *Nihon shuppan shiryō* 1 (1995): 108–47.

——. "Kudanzaka-ue kara jigoku o mita hitotachi." *20c.–21c.: Masukomi, jaanarizumu ronshū.* Vol. 3. Tokyo: Komaesukūru Dōjin, 1996.

——. "Taishō daishinsai daikasai." *20c.–21c.: Masukomi, jaanarizumu ronshū.* Vol. 4. Tokyo: Komaesukūru Dōjin, 1996.

Jameson, Fredric. *The Political Unconscious: Narrative as a Socially Symbolic Act.* Ithaca, N.Y.: Cornell University Press, 1981.

Johns, Adrian. *The Nature of the Book: Print and Knowledge in the Making.* Chicago: University of Chicago Press, 1998.

Johns, Adrian, and Elizabeth Eisenstein. "AHR Forum: How Revolutionary Was the Print Revolution?" *American Historical Review* 107, no. 1 (2002): 84–128.

Jusdanis, Gregory. *Belated Modernity and Aesthetic Culture: Inventing National Literature.* Minneapolis: University of Minnesota Press, 1991.

——. "Beyond National Culture?" *Boundary 2* 22, no. 1 (1995): 23–60.

Kaizōsha, ed. *Taishō daishinkasai shi.* Tokyo: Kaizōsha, 1924.

Kanai Keiko et al. *Bungaku ga motto omoshiroku naru: Kindai Nihon bungaku o yomitoku 33 no tobira.* Tokyo: Daiyamondo-sha, 1998.

Kanbayashi Akatsuki. "Enpon gassen jidai." *Shinshōsetsu,* April 1950, 98–101.

Kanō Sakujirō. "Kanbatsu-ji no jumoku." *Shinchō,* August 1928, 86–90.

Kant, Immanuel. *Critique of Judgment.* Indianapolis: Hackett, 1987.

Karatani Kōjin, ed. *Kindai Nihon no hihyō I: Shōwa-hen. jō.* Tokyo: Kōdansha, 1997.

——, ed. *Kindai Nihon no hihyō III: Meiji-Taishō-hen.* Tokyo: Kōdansha, 1998.

Kawada Hisanaga. *Kappan insatsushi: Nihon kappan insatsushi no kenkyū.* Tokyo: Tōkyō Insatsu Gakkai Shuppanbu, 1949.

——. "Nihon ni okeru yōshiki kappan, enkatsuji narabi ni dentaihō ni kansuru saishō no bunken." *Insatsu jōhō* 157 (October 1938): 11–16.

Kawahara Isao. *Taiwan shinbungaku undō to tenkai: Nihon bungaku to no setten.* Tokyo: Kenbun Shuppan, 1997.

Kawamura Minato. "Akutagawa-shō senpyō o yomitoku." *Bungakukai,* July 1999, 1923.

Kawase Kazuma. *Kokatsuji no kenkyū.* Tokyo: Nihon Koshosekishō Kyōkai, 1967.

Keene, Donald. *Dawn to the West: Japanese Literature in the Modern Era, Fiction.* New York: Holt Rinehart and Winston, 1984.

Keyes, Roger S. *Ehon: The Artist and the Book in Japan.* Seattle: University of Washington Press, 2006.

Kikuchi Kan. "Akutagawa-Naoki-shō sengen." *Bungei shunjū,* January 1935, 110–13.

——. *Bungei ōrai.* Tokyo: Arusu, 1920.

——. *Hanashi no kuzukago to hanjijoden.* Tokyo: Bungei Shunjūsha, 1988.

——. *Kikuchi Kan zenshū.* 24 vols. Tokyo: Bungei Shunjūsha, 1993–95.

Kimura Ki. *Meiji bungaku yowa.* Tokyo: Rikiesuta no Kai, 2001.

——. *Watakushi no bungaku kaikoroku.* Tokyo: Seiabō, 1979.

King, Lynda. "Reclam's Universal-Bibliothek: A German Success Story." *Die Unterrichtspraxis/Teaching German* 28, no. 1 (1995): 1–6.

Kisaki Masaru. *Kisaki nikki.* 4 vols. Tokyo: Gendaishi Shuppan-kai, 1975–76.

Kobayashi Hideo and Paul Anderer. *Literature of the Lost Home: Kobayashi Hideo—Literary Criticism, 1924–1939*. Stanford: Stanford University Press, 1995.

Kobayashi Isamu. *Kobayashi Isamu bunshū*. 11 vols. Tokyo: Chikuma Shobō, 1982–83.

Kobayashi Ōri [Zenpachi]. "Bungei no fukkō." *Tosho geppō* 22, no. 3 (1924): 11–12.

———. "Kono goro no koto." *Tosho geppō* 22, no. 5 (1924): 60–62.

Kōchi Nobuko. " 'Nihon koten zenshū' kankō shūhen: 1920 nendai kōhan no shuppan 'taishūka' to shōshuppan-sha/insatsu-jo no ichi." *Shuppan kenkyū* 21 (1990): 56–84.

Kodansha Encyclopedia of Japan. Tokyo: Kodansha, 1983.

Kōdansha Shashi Hensan Iinkai, ed. *Kōdansha no ayunda gojūnen*. Tokyo: Kōdansha, 1959.

Komori Yōichi. *Nihongo no kindai*. Tokyo: Iwanami Shoten, 2000.

———. *Yuragi no Nihon bungaku*. Tokyo: Nihon Hōsō Shuppan Kyōkai, 1998.

Kōno Kensuke. "Sensō hōdō to 'sakka sagashi' no monogatari." *Bungaku* 5, no. 3 (1994): 2–15.

———. *Shomotsu no kindai: Media no bungakushi*. Tokyo: Chikuma Shobō, 1992.

Konta Yōzō. *Edo no hon'ya-san*. NHK bukkusu 299. Tokyo: Nippon Hōsō Shuppan Kyōkai, 1977.

———. "Edo no shuppan shihon." *Edo chonin no kenkyū*, vol. 3, ed. Nishiyama Matsunosuke. Tokyo: Yoshikawa Kōbunkan, 1974.

Kornicki, Peter. *The Book in Japan: A Cultural History from the Beginnings to the Nineteenth Century*. Honolulu: University of Hawai'i Press, 2001.

Kurihara Akira et al., eds. *Naiha suru chi: Shintai, kotoba, kenryoku o aminaosu*. Tokyo: Tōkyō Daigaku Shuppan-kyoku, 2000.

Kurita Kakuya, ed. *Shuppanjin no ibun: Shufu no tomosha. Ishikawa Takemi*. Tokyo: Kurita Shoten, 1968.

Laclau, Ernesto, and Chantal Mouffe. "Post-Marxism without Apologies." *New Left Review* 166 (November–December, 1987): 79–106.

Lane, Richard. "The Beginnings of the Modern Japanese Novel: Kana-zoshi, 1600–1682." *Harvard Journal of Asiatic Studies* 20, nos. 3–4 (1957): 644–701.

Levin, Harry. "Core, Canon, Curriculum." *College English* 43, no. 4 (1981): 352–62.

Levine, Lawrence W. *Highbrow/Lowbrow: The Emergence of Cultural Hierarchy in America*. Cambridge, Mass.: Harvard University Press, 1988.

Lippit, Seiji M. *Topographies of Japanese Modernism*. New York: Columbia University Press, 2002.

Liu, Lydia H. *The Clash of Empires: The Invention of China in Modern World Making*. Cambridge, Mass.: Harvard University Press, 2004.

Lowe, Lisa. *Immigrant Acts: On Asian American Cultural Politics*. Durham, N.C.: Duke University Press, 1996.

Mack, Edward. "Diasporic Markets: Japanese Print and Migration in São Paulo, 1908–1935." *Script and Print: Bulletin of the Bibliographical Society of Australia and New Zealand* 29 (2006): 163–77.

———. "Marketing Japan's Literature in Its 1930s Colonies." *Books and Empire: Bibliographical Society of Australia and New Zealand Bulletin* 28, nos. 1–2 (2004): 134–41.

——. "The Extranational Flow of Japanese-Language Texts, 1905–1945," *Sai: Kan* (Seoul: Kukche Han'guk Munhwa Hakhoe) 6 (May 2009): 147–76.

——. "The Value of Literature: Cultural Authority in Interwar Japan." Ph.D. diss., Harvard University, 2002.

Maeda Ai. *Kindai dokusha no seiritsu.* Tokyo: Chikuma Shobō, 1989.

Maeyama Takashi. "Kaisetsu: Imin bungaku kara mainoritii bungaku e." *Koronia shōsetsu senshū,* vol. 1, ed. Koronia Bungakukai. São Paulo: Koronia Bungakukai, 1975.

Mainichi Shinbunsha Shashi Hensan Iinkai, ed. *Mainichi shinbun shichijūnen.* Tokyo: Mainichi Shinbunsha, 1952.

Makino Takeo. *Kumo ka yama ka.* Tokyo: Gakufū Shoin, 1956.

Makita Inagi. *Nihon shuppan taikan.* 2 vols. Osaka: Shuppan Taimususha, 1928.

Marcus, Marvin. "The Social Organization of Modern Japanese Literature." *The Columbia Companion to Modern East Asian Literature,* ed. by Joshua Mostow. New York: Columbia University Press, 2003.

Marcuse, Herbert. *One-Dimensional Man: Studies in the Ideology of Advanced Industrial Society.* Boston: Beacon Press, 1964.

Maruyama Masao. *Maruyama Masao shū.* 17 vols. Tokyo: Iwanami Shoten, 1995–97.

Mathias, Regine, " 'Reading for Culture' and the Dawn of Mass Produced Literature in Germany and Japan: Case Studies of Reclams Universal-Bibliothek and Iwanami Bunko." *Japanese Civilization in the Modern World V: Culturedness,* ed. by Tadao Umesao, Catherine C. Lewis, and Yasuyuki Kurita. Osaka: National Museum of Ethnology, 1990.

Matsubara Kazue. *Kaizōsha to Yamamoto Sanehiko: Yamamoto Sanehiko's Kaizosya.* Kagoshima-shi: Nanpō Shinsha, 2000.

Matsumoto Shōhei. *Gyōmu nisshi yohaku: Waga shuppan hanbai no gojūnen.* Tokyo: Shinbunka Tsūshinsha, 1981.

McKenzie, D. F. *Making Meaning: "Printers of the Mind" and Other Essays.* Ed. by Peter D. McDonald and Michael F. Suarez. Amherst: University of Massachusetts Press, 2002.

Mertz, John Pierre. *Novel Japan: Spaces of Nationhood in Early Meiji Narrative, 1870–80.* Ann Arbor: Center for Japanese Studies, University of Michigan, 2003.

Midorikawa Tōru, ed. *Iwanami Shoten gojūnen.* Tokyo: Iwanami Shoten, 1963.

Minami Hiroshi. *Taishō bunka.* Tokyo: Keisō Shobō, 1965.

Miyamoto Mataji, ed. *Kamigata no kenkyū.* Vol. 4. Osaka: Seibundō Shuppan, 1972.

Miyoshi, Masao, and H. D. Harootunian, eds. *Postmodernism and Japan.* Durham, N.C.: Duke University Press, 1989.

Mizumura Minae. *Shishōsetsu from left to right.* Tokyo: Shinchōsha, 1995.

Mizushima Haruo. *Kaizōsha no jidai.* Tokyo: Tosho Shuppansha, 1976.

Mochizuki Masaji. *Wagakuni shuppanbutsu yushutsubutsu no rekishi.* Tokyo: Nihon Shuppan Bōeki Kabushiki Kaisha, 1971.

Mostow, Joshua, ed. *The Columbia Companion to Modern East Asian Literature.* New York: Columbia University Press, 2003.

Nagai Kafū. *Kafū zenshū.* 29 vols. Tokyo: Iwanami Shoten, 1963–74.

Nagai Tatsuo. *Kaisō no Akutagawa—Naoki-shō*. Tokyo: Bungei Shunjūsha, 1979.

———. "Naoki-shō shitabatara-ki." *Bessatsu Bungei shunjū*, October 1952, 109–15.

Nagai Tatsuo et al. *Akutagawa-shō no kenkyū*. Tokyo: Nihon Jaanarisuto Senmon Gakuin Shuppanbu, 1970.

Nagamine Shigetoshi. *"Dokusho kokumin" no tanjō*. Tokyo: Nihon Editaa Sukūru Shuppanbu, 2004.

———. *Modan toshi no dokusho kūkan*. Tokyo: Nihon Editaa Sukūru Shuppanbu, 2001.

———. *Zasshi to dokusha no kindai*. Tokyo: Nihon Editaa Sukūru Shuppanbu, 1997.

Nagasawa Kikuya. *Wakansho no insatsu to sono rekishi* (1952). Reprinted in *Nagasawa Kikuya chosakushū*. Vol. 2. Tokyo: Kyūko Shoin, 1982.

Nagashiro Shizuo, ed. *Nihon shinbun shashi shūsei*. Tokyo: Shinbun Kenkyūjo, 1938.

Nagatomo Chiyoji. "Chihō no hon'ya-san." *Kokubungaku kaishaku to kyōzai no kenkyū* 42, no. 11 (1997): 103–7.

———. *Edo jidai no tosho ryūtsū*. Kyoto: Bukkyō Daigaku Tsūshin Kyōikubu, 2002.

Naimushō Daijin Kanbō Bunshoka, ed. *Dai-Nihon Teikoku Naimushō tōkei hōkoku*. Tokyo: Insatsu-kyoku, 1925.

Nakajima Kenzō, Ōkubo Toshiaki, and Katō Hidetoshi. *Shinbun shūroku Taishō shi*. Vol. 11. Tokyo: Taishō Shuppan, 1978.

Nakamura Takafusa. *A History of Shōwa Japan, 1926–1989*. Trans. Edwin Whenmouth. Tokyo: University of Tokyo Press, 1998.

Nakamura Toshihiko. "Kinsei no dokusha." *Ōsaka furitsu toshokan kiyō* 9 (1973): 80–98.

Nakane Katsu. *Nihon insatsu gijutsu-shi*. Tokyo: Yagi Shoten, 1999.

Nakayama Akihiko. "Bungakushi to nashonaritii: Waisetsu, Nihonjin, bunka bōei-ron." *Kindaichi no seiritsu: Iwanami kōza Kindai Nihon no bunka-shi*, vol. 3, ed. by Narita Ryūichi. Tokyo: Iwanami Shoten, 2002.

Narita Kiyofusa and Shimoda Masami. *Ōji Seishi shashi*. Vol. 3. Tokyo: Ōji Seishi Kōgyō Kabushiki Kaisha, 1958.

Nihon Shinbun Hanbai Kyōkai Shinbun Hanbai Hyakunen-shi Kankō Iinkai, ed. *Shinbun hanbai hyakunen-shi*. Tokyo: Nihon Shinbun Hanbai Kyōkai, 1969.

Nihon Zasshi Kyōkai Shi Henshū Iinkai, ed. *Nihon Zasshi Kyōkai shi*. Vol. 1. Tokyo: Nihon Zasshi Kyōkai, 1968.

Norman, E. H. "Mass Hysteria in Japan." *Far Eastern Survey* 14, no. 6 (1945): 65–70.

Obi Toshito. *Shuppan to shakai*. Tokyo: Genki Shobō, 2007.

Oda Mitsuo. "Kindai bungaku to kindai shuppan ryūtsū shisutemu." *Nihon kindai bungaku* 65 (October 2001): 116–35.

———. *Shoten no kindai: Hon ga kagayaite ita jidai*. Tokyo: Heibonsha, 2003.

———. *Shuppansha to shoten wa ika ni shite kiete iku ka*. Tokyo: Paru Shuppan, 1999.

Oda Mitsuo and Yamamoto Yoshiaki. "Enpon no hikari to kage." *Bungaku* 4, no. 2 (2003): 21–34.

Odagiri Susumu, ed. *Akutagawa-shō shōjiten*. Tokyo: Bungei Shunjūsha, 1983.

Odagiri Susumu and Nihon Kindai Bungakukan, eds. *Nihon kindai bungaku daijiten*. Vol. 4. Tokyo: Kōdansha, 1977.

Ogawa Kikumatsu. *Shuppan kōbō gojūnen*. Tokyo: Seibundō Shinkōsha, 1953.

Okano Takeo. *Nihon shuppan bunka-shi.* Tokyo: Hara Shobō, 1981.

Osaragi Jirō. "Naoki-shō ni tsuite." *Bessatsu Bungei shunjū,* December 1955, 178–79.

Ōshima Kazuo. *Rekishi no naka no "jihi shuppan" to "zokki-bon."* Tokyo: Haga Shoten, 2002.

Owen, Stephen. *Readings in Chinese Literary Thought.* Cambridge, Mass.: Harvard University Press, 1992.

Ōya Sōichi. *Ōya Sōichi zenshū.* 31 vols. Tokyo: Sōyōsha, 1980–82.

Ozaki Hotsuki. *Heibonsha rokujūnen-shi.* Tokyo: Heibonsha, 1974.

———. *Taishū bungaku no rekishi.* Vol. 1. Tokyo: Kōdansha, 1989.

Palumbo-Liu, David, ed., *The Ethnic Canon: Histories, Institutions, and Interventions.* Minneapolis: University of Minnesota Press, 1995.

Powell, Irena. *Writers and Society in Modern Japan.* Tokyo: Kodansha International, 1983.

Price, Leah. *The Anthology and the Rise of the Novel: From Richardson to George Eliot.* Cambridge: Cambridge University Press, 2000.

Radway, Janice A. *A Feeling for Books: The Book-of-the-Month Club, Literary Taste, and Middle-Class Desire.* Chapel Hill: University of North Carolina Press, 1997.

Reed, Christopher A. *Gutenberg in Shanghai: Chinese Print Capitalism, 1876–1937.* Vancouver: University of British Columbia Press, 2004.

Richter, Giles. "Marketing the Word: Publishing Entrepreneurs in Meiji Japan, 1870–1912." Ph.D. diss., Columbia University, 1999.

Ringer, Fritz K. *The Decline of the German Mandarins: The German Academic Community, 1890–1933.* Cambridge, Mass.: Harvard University Press, 1969.

Rorty, Richard. *Consequences of Pragmatism: Essays, 1972–1980.* Minneapolis: University of Minnesota Press, 1982.

Ross, Trevor. *The Making of the English Literary Canon: From the Middle Ages to the Late Eighteenth Century.* Montreal: McGill-Queen's University Press, 1998.

Rubin, Jay. *Injurious to Public Morals: Writers and the Meiji State.* Seattle: University of Washington Press, 1984.

Ruch, Barbara. "Medieval Jongleurs and the Making of a National Literature." *Japan in the Muromachi Age,* ed. by John W. Hall and Toyoda Takeshi. Berkeley: University of California Press, 1977.

Ryang, Sonia. "Diaspora and Beyond: There Is No Home for Koreans in Japan." *Review of Korean Studies* 4, no. 2 (2001): 55–86.

Said, Edward. *Culture and Imperialism.* New York: Vintage Books, 1994.

Saintsbury, George. *Furansu bungakushi.* Trans. Kubo Masao. Tokyo: Kōryōsha, 1916.

———. *A Short History of French Literature.* Oxford: Clarendon Press, 1882.

Sakaki, Atsuko. "Kajin no Kigū: The Meiji Political Novel and the Boundaries of Literature." *Monumenta Nipponica* 55, no. 1 (2000): 83–108.

Sand, Jordan. *House and Home in Modern Japan: Architecture, Domestic Space, and Bourgeois Culture, 1880–1930.* Cambridge, Mass.: Harvard University Asia Center, 2004.

Satō Haruo. "Ichienpon no hayari." *Chūō kōron,* April 1927, 183–85.

———. *Satō Haruo zenshū.* 11 vols. Tokyo: Kōdansha, 1967–69.

Satō Haruo et al. "Akutagawa-shō to bundan." *Bungakukai* 11, no. 9 (1957): 8–16.

Satō Takumi. *Kingu no jidai: Kokumin taishū zasshi no kōkyōsei.* Tokyo: Iwanami Shoten, 2002.

Satō Toshio, ed. *Shinchōsha shichijūnen.* Tokyo: Shinchōsha, 1966.

Schaffer, Brian, ed. *A Companion to the British and Irish Novel, 1945–2000.* Oxford: Blackwell, 2004.

Seidensticker, Edward. "The 'Pure' and the 'In-between' in Modern Japanese Theories of the Novel." *Harvard Journal of Asiatic Studies* 26 (1966): 174–86.

———. *Tokyo Rising: The City Since the Great Earthquake.* New York: Knopf, 1990.

Seki Chūka et al., eds. *Zasshi "Kaizō" no shijūnen.* Tokyo: Kōwadō, 1977.

Sekii Mitsuo. "Nihon kindai bungaku kenkyū no kigen: Meiji Bunka Kenkyūkai to enpon." *Nihon bungaku* 43, no. 3 (1994): 26–32.

Sekine, Eiji, ed. *Ga/Zoku Dynamics in Japanese Literature.* West Lafayette, Ind.: Midwest Association for Japanese Literary Studies, 1997.

Senuma Shigeki. "Bungaku-shō o meguru shomondai (jō)." *Bungaku* 28, no. 2 (1960): 151–64.

———. "Bungakushō: Sono shurui to seikaku." *Nihon kindai bungaku daijiten kijōban.* Tokyo: Kodansha, 1984.

———. *Gendai bungaku no jōken.* Tokyo: Kawade Shobō Shinsha, 1960.

———. *Hon no 100-nenshi: Besuto seraa no konjaku.* Tokyo: Shuppan Nyūsusha, 1965.

Sherif, Ann. "The Aesthetics of Speed and the Illogicality of Politics: Ishihara Shintarō's Literary Debut." *Japan Forum* 17, no. 2 (2005): 185–211.

Shestov, Lev. *Dostoevsky, Tolstoy, and Nietzsche.* Athens: Ohio University Press, 1969.

Shibusawa Keizō. *Japanese Life and Culture in the Meiji Era.* Trans. Charles Terry. Tokyo: Ōbunsha, 1958.

Shimamura Takitarō [Hōgetsu] et al., eds. *Bungei hyakka zensho.* Tokyo: Waseda Bungakusha, 1909. Reprinted in *Bungei shiryō jiten.* Tokyo: Nihon Tosho Sentaa, 2002.

Shimazaki Tōson. *Tōson zenshū.* 18 vols. Tokyo: Chikuma Shobō, 1966–71.

"Shinsaigo no furuhonkai." *Shomotsu ōrai* 1, no. 1 (1924): 40–42, and 1, no. 2 (June 1924): 105–8.

Shiobara Aki. "Shozō sareru shomotsu: Enpon būmu to kyōyō-shugi." *Yokohama Kokudai kokugo kenkyū* 20 (March 2003): 1–10.

Shirane, Haruo. *Traces of Dreams: Landscape, Cultural Memory, and the Poetry of Bashō.* Stanford: Stanford University Press, 1998.

Shirane, Haruo, and Tomi Suzuki, eds. *Inventing the Classics: Modernity, National Identity, and Japanese Literature.* Stanford: Stanford University Press, 2000.

Shively, Donald. "Popular Culture." *Cambridge History of Japan,* vol. 4, ed.by John W. Hall et al. Cambridge: Cambridge University Press, 1991.

Shōji Sensui. *Nihon no shomotsu: Kodai kara gendai made.* Tokyo: Bijutsu Shuppansha, 1978.

Shōji Tatsuya. "Akutagawa Ryūnosuke no kōen ryōkō." *Shōnan bungaku* 24 (1990): 80–93.

Shufu no Tomosha, ed. *Shufu no Tomosha no rokujūnen: Shufu no Tomosha kanren gosha, zaidan*. Tokyo: Shufu no Tomosha, 1977.

Shumway, David R. "Nationalist Knowledges: The Humanities and Nationality." *Poetics Today* 19, no. 3 (1998): 357–73.

Sieburth, Stephanie. *Inventing High and Low: Literature, Mass Culture, and Uneven Modernity in Spain*. Durham, N.C.: Duke University Press, 1994.

Smith, Henry D., II. "The History of the Book in Edo and Paris." *Edo and Paris: Urban Life and the State in the Early Modern Era*, ed. by James L. McClain, John M. Merriman, and Ugawa Kaoru. Ithaca, N.Y.: Cornell University Press, 1994.

Sorimachi Shigeo. *Shimi no mukashigatari*. Tokyo: Yagi Shoten, 1987.

Spivak, Gayatri Chakravorty. *Death of a Discipline*. New York: Columbia University Press, 2003.

St. Clair, William. *The Reading Nation*. Cambridge: Cambridge University Press, 2004.

Strecher, Matthew. "Purely Mass or Massively Pure?" *Monumenta Nipponica* 51, no. 3 (1996): 357–74.

Strinati, Dominic. *An Introduction to Theories of Popular Culture*. London: Routledge, 1995.

Sugimori Hisahide. *Chūō Kōronsha no hachijūnen*. Tokyo: Chūō Kōronsha, 1965.

Suzuki Hisao. *Gendai Nihon sangyō hattatsu shi: Kami/parupu*. Tokyo: Kōjunsha shuppankyoku, 1968.

Suzuki Sadami. *The Concept of "Literature" in Japan*. Trans. Royall Tyler. Kyoto: Nichibunken, 2006.

———. *Nihon no "bungaku" gainen*. Tokyo: Sakuhinsha, 1998.

———. *Nihon no "bungaku" o kangaeru*. Tokyo: Kadokawa Shoten, 1994.

Suzuki, Tomi. *Narrating the Self: Fictions of Japanese Modernity*. Stanford: Stanford University Press, 1996.

Suzuki Toshio. *Shuppan: Kōfukyō-ka no kōbō no isseiki*. Tokyo: Shuppan Nyūsusha, 1970.

Swartz, David. *Culture and Power*. Chicago: University of Chicago Press, 1997.

Tai, Eika. "Rethinking Culture, National Culture, and Japanese Culture." *Japanese Language and Literature* 37, no. 1 (2003): 1–26.

Takahashi Masami. "Shuppan ryūtsū kikō no hensen: 1603–1945." *Shuppan kenkyū* 13 (1982): 188–228.

Takami Jun. *Shōwa bungaku seisui-shi*. Tokyo: Kōdansha, 1965.

Takashima Ken'ichirō. "Shōhin to shite no enpon: Kaizōsha to Shun'yōdō no hikaku o tōshite." *Nihon shuppan shiryō* 9 (2004): 20–37.

Takei Shizuo. "Akutagawa no kōen ryōkō." *Hoppō bungei* 11, nos. 6–8 (1978).

Tanaka Haruo. *Monogatari: Tōkyōdō-shi*. Tokyo: Tōhan Shōji, 1975.

Tanizawa Eiichi. *Nihon kindai shoshigaku saiken*. Osaka: Izumi Shoin, 2003.

Tasaka Fumio, ed. *Kyūsei chūtō kyōiku kokugaku kyōkasho naiyō sakuin*. Tokyo: Kyōkasho Kenyū Sentaa, 1984.

Togai Yoshio and Nihon Keieishi Kenkyūjo. *Seishigyō no hyakunen: Kami no bunka to sangyō*. Tokyo: Ōji Seishi, 1973.

Tōkyō Daigaku Hyakunenshi Henshū Iinkai, ed. *Tōkyō Daigaku hyakunenshi: Tsūshi.* Vol. 2. Tokyo: Tōkyō Daigaku Shuppankai, 1985.

Tōkyō Insatsu Dōgyō Kumiai. *Nihon insatsu taikan, sōgyō nijūgo-shū-nen kinen.* Tokyo: Tōkyō Insatsu Dōgyō Kumiai, 1938.

Tōkyō Shuppan Hanbai Kabushikigaisha, ed. *Shuppan hanbai shōshi: Tōhan sōritsu jisshūnen kinen.* Tokyo: Tōkyō Shuppan Hanbai, 1959.

Tōkyō-to Koshoseki Shōgyō Kyōdō Kumiai. *Tōkyō Kosho Kumiai gojūnenshi.* Tokyo: Tōkyō-to Koshoseki Shōgyō Kyōdō Kumiai, 1974.

Toppan Insatsu Kabushiki Gaisha-shi Shashi Hensan Iinkai, ed. *Toppan 1985: Toppan Insatsu Kabushiki Gaisha-shi.* Tokyo: Toppan Insatsu, 1985.

Torrance, Richard. *The Fiction of Tokuda Shūsei and the Emergence of Japan's New Middle Class.* Seattle: University of Washington Press, 1994.

———. "Literacy and Literature in Osaka, 1890–1940." *Journal of Japanese Studies* 31, no. 1 (2005): 27–60.

———. "Literacy and Modern Literature in the Izumo Region, 1880–1930." *Journal of Japanese Studies* 22, no. 2 (1996): 327–62.

———. "Pre–World War Two Concepts of Japanese Popular Culture and Takeda Rintarō's 'Japan's Three Penny Opera.'" *A Century of Popular Culture in Japan,* ed. by Douglas Slaymaker. Lewiston, Maine: Edwin Mellon Press, 2000.

Tsubouchi Shōyō. *The Essence of the Novel.* Occasional Papers no. 11. Trans. Nanette Twine. University of Queensland, Department of Japanese, 1981.

Twyman, Michael. *Printing 1770–1970: An Illustrated History of Its Development and Uses in England.* London: British Library, 1998.

Uchikawa Yoshimi et al., eds. *Shōwa nyūsu jiten.* 9 vols. Tokyo: Mainichi Komyunikeeshonzu, 1990–94.

Uchikawa Yoshimi et al., eds. *Taishō nyūsu jiten.* 8 vols. Tokyo: Mainichi Komyunikeeshonzu, 1986–89.

Ueda, Atsuko. "Meiji Literary Historiography: The Production of 'Modern Japanese Literature.'" Ph.D. diss., University of Michigan, 1999.

———. "The Production of Literature and the Effaced Realm of the Political." *Journal of Japanese Studies* 31, no. 1 (2005): 61–88.

Ueda Yasuo. "Enpon zenshū ni yoru dokusha kakumei no jittai: Shoka no dokusho henreki ni miru." *Shuppan kenkyū* 14 (1983): 40–65.

Uno Kōji. "Kaisō no Akutagawa-shō." *Bessatsu Bungei shunjū,* September 1952, 235–52.

———. "Ku to raku no omoide." *Bessatsu Bungei shunjū,* December 1955, 196–206.

———. "Senkō iin no kansō." *Bessatsu Bungei shunjū,* October 1952, 126–34.

Usami Tatsuo. "Kantō chihō no furui jishin shin'ō ichi no han'i." *Kantō daijishin 50-shūnen ronbunshū.* Tokyo: Tōkyō Daigaku Jishin Kenkyūjo, 1973.

Utano Hiroshi. "Edo jidai no hon no nedankō." *Nihon kosho tsūshin* 772 (November 1993): 11–14.

Vincent, Keith. "Resubian/gei sutadiizu." *Gendai shisō* 25, no. 6 (1997): 8–17.

Washburn, Dennis. *The Dilemma of the Modern in Japanese Fiction.* New Haven: Yale University Press, 1995.

Wellek, René. *Four Critics: Croce, Valéry, Lukács, and Ingarden.* Seattle: University of Washington Press, 1981.

Wender, Melissa L. *Lamentation as History: Narratives by Koreans in Japan, 1965–2000.* Stanford: Stanford University Press, 2005.

Williams, Raymond. *Culture and Society: 1780–1950.* New York: Columbia University Press, 1983.

———. *Keywords: A Vocabulary of Culture and Society.* Revised ed. New York: Oxford University Press, 1983.

Yagi Toshio, ed. *Zenkoku shuppanbutsu oroshi shōgyō kyōdō kumiai sanjūnen no ayumi.* Tokyo: Zenkoku Shuppanbutsu Oroshi Shōgyō Kyōdō Kumiai, 1981.

Yahagi Katsumi. "Kindai ni okeru yōranki no shuppan ryūtsū: Meiji shonen—Meiji 20 nendai e." *Shuppan kenkyū* 12 (1981): 89–123.

Yamagishi Ikuko. "Firumu no naka no sakka-tachi: Senden tsuuru to shite no 'Gendai Nihon bungaku junrei.'" *Bungaku* 3, no. 6 (2002): 101–22.

Yamamoto Mitsuo et al., eds. *Gendai Nihon bungaku zenshū.* 63 vols. Tokyo: Kaizōsha, 1926–31.

Yamamoto Sanehiko. "Enpon jidai." *Shomotsu tenbō* 5, no. 5 (1935): 29–32.

Yamamoto Taketoshi. *Kindai Nihon no shinbun dokushasō.* Sōsho gendai no shakai kagaku. Tokyo: Hōsei Daigaku Shuppankyoku, 1981.

Yamamoto Yoshiaki. *Bungakusha wa tsukurareru.* Mihatsu sensho 9. Tokyo: Hitsuji Shobō, 2000.

Yamamura Miyoshi. "Enpon narikin no narikin-buri." *Fujin kōron,* December 1928, 52–56.

Yamanouchi Shōshi, ed. *Dazai Osamu ronshū: Dōjidai hen.* 11 vols. Tokyo: Yumani Shobō, 1992–93.

Yanagida Izumi. *Meiji bungaku kenkyū yobanashi.* Tokyo: Rikiesuta no Kai, 2001.

Yayoshi Mitsunaga. *Mikan shiryō ni yoru Nihon shuppan bunka: Kindai shuppan bunka.* Shoshi shomoku shiriizu 26. Vol. 5. Tokyo: Yumani Shobō, 1988.

Yoda, Tomiko. *Gender and National Literature: Heian Texts in the Construction of Japanese Modernity.* Durham, N.C.: Duke University Press, 2004.

Yokota Fuyuhiko. "Santo to chihō jōkamachi no bunkateki kankei: Shomotsu no ryūtsū o sozai ni." *Kokuritsu Rekishi Minzoku Hakubutsukan kenkyū hōkoku* 103 (March 2003): 389–408.

Yoshino Takao, ed. *Miyatake Gaikotsu kono naka ni ari.* 33 vols. Tokyo: Yumani Shobō, 1993–95.

Yoshino Toshihiko. *"Danchōtei" no keizaigaku.* Tokyo: Nihon Hōsō Shuppan Kyōkai, 1999.

Yuasa Katsuei. *Kannani and Document of Flames: Two Japanese Colonial Novels.* Trans. Mark Driscoll. Durham, N.C.: Duke University Press, 2005.

Zen Nihon Shinbun Renmei Shuppankyoku, ed. *Shinbun taikan.* Vol. 1. Tokyo: Zen Nihon Shinbun Renmei, 1978.

Zuidervaart, Lambert. "The Social Significance of Autonomous Art: Adorno and Bürger." *Journal of Aesthetics and Art Criticism* 48, no. 1 (1990): 61–77.

Zwicker, Jonathan E. *Practices of the Sentimental Imagination: Melodrama, the Novel, and the Social Imaginary in Nineteenth-Century Japan.* Cambridge, Mass.: Harvard University Press, 2006.

———. "Tears of Blood: Melodrama, the Novel, and the Social Imaginary in Nineteenth-Century Japan." Ph.D. diss., Columbia University, 2003.

INDEX

• • •

Page numbers in italics refer to illustrations.

block printing, 22–23. *See also* printing technology

book distribution, 37–38, 42, 44–45. *See also* distribution companies

book exchange (*hongae*), 35

book lending, 45

book production, print technologies in, 30

book publishing industry, effect of earthquake on, 70–73

bookselling business: consignment sales in, 38–39; effect of earthquake on, 71–72; estimated sales in, 238; historical developments in, 34–36; Maruzen bookstore and, 58; sales statistics of, 254–55n113

Bourdaghs, Michael, 246n17, 248n26

Bourdieu, Pierre, 245n14, 282n7

Brantlinger, Patrick, 230

Bruce pivotal caster, 24. *See also* printing technology

bundan, as term, 248n28

Bungakukai (magazine), 220

"Bungakushi to nashonaritii" (Nakayama Akihiko), 247n24

bungei fukkō, 166

Bungei shunjū (magazine), 13, 188–90, 200–201

Bungei Shunjūsha, 219, 220

bunkobon, as term, 271–72n146

Bunshō sekai (literary magazine), 275n16

Burns, Susan L., 256n140

Cabinet Printing Bureau, 28

canon, concept of, 7

capital intraconversion and alternate economy of value, 5

capital investment for printing, 32–33

censorship, 214

"Chōkō Deruta" (The Yangtze River Delta) (Tada Yūkei), 206, 214–17

chosaku-ken (authorial rights), 107

Chūō Kōronsha, 69

collections. *See* anthologies

colonialism, 203–6

commercialization of print, 31–36, 33, 39

commonness and mental state novels, 155–57, 156

community and literary marketplace, 40–49

Complete Works of Contemporary Japanese Literature: accessibility of, 102; acquisition of rights for, 106–9; advertising of, 112–18, 113, 116, 117; bookshelf for subscribers of, 11, 120; decision to produce, 93–96; editorial intervention in, 109–12; gender bias in, 106; impact of, on readers, 131–36; limitations of, 136–38; market for, 124–26, 134; predecessors of, 94–96; role of, in national literature, 133–36; schools of literature included in, 103–4; subscription sales of, 118–20; success of, 120–24, 121–22; title of, 133

complete works (*zenshū*), as term, 244n5, 267n67

consignment, 38–39. *See also* bookselling business

content value of literary works, 148

contribution magazines, 185. *See also* magazines; periodicals

Copeland, Rebecca L., 266n51

copublishing (*aiaiban*) texts, 36

coterie magazines (*dōjin zasshi*), 185–86, 214. *See also* magazines; periodicals

Crime and Punishment (Dostoyevsky), 170

critics, criticism, 143–46, 153–54

Croce, Benedetto, 276n21

cultural authority and canon, 7

cultural integration, 47

Dazai Osamu, 196–99, 221

distribution companies, 37–38, 85, 85–87. *See also* book distribution

Dostoyevsky, Fyodor, 170

"Dragon Gate," 284n23

Driscoll, Mark, 227

Meiji period, technological revolution in, 20

Meiji Taishō bungaku zenshū, 126

mental state novels, 152, 157–59. *See also* I-novels

metal type, 21–22. *See also* printing technology

middle class, as term, 269–70n110

Minakami Tsutomu, 132

Ministry of Education, concept of national literature and, 48

Mitarai Tatsuo, 77–78

Miyako shinbun (newspaper), 76

Miyatake Gaikotsu, 128

Mizumura Minae, 137

"Modern Japanese literature," concept of, 244–45n9

monotype machines, 24

Moriyama Kei, 171–72

Motoki Shōzō, 25–26

movable type (*kokatsuji*), 21–23, 25, 27. *See also* printing technology

Murō Saisei, 208, 213, 216

Nagai Kafū, 120

Nagai Tatsuo, 196

Nagamine Shigetoshi, 42, 122–23, 255n118

Nagata Shin'nojō, 76

Nagatomo Chiyoji, 42, 251n32

Nakamura Mitsuo, 169–71

Nakamura Murao, 151–55

Nakane Katsu, 23

Nakano Shigeharu, 231

Nakayama Akihiko, 247n24

Naoki Prize: Akutagawa Prize vs., 184; criticism of press coverage of, 199–200; early years of, 201–19; establishment of, 188–90; "Jon Manjirō hyōryū-ki" (John Manjiro, a Castaway's Chronicle) (Ibuse Masuji) and, 210–12; reconsideration of, by Kikuchi, 219; refusal of, 290n116; selection process for, 190–202; *Tsuruhachi Tsurujirō* (Kawaguchi Matsutarō) and, 191–92; *Un'nan shubihei* (The Yunnan Garrison) (Kimura Sōjū) and, 222

Naoki Sakai, 228–29

nation, as term, 243n2

national language, 46

National League of Book Associations (Zenkoku Shoseki-shō Kumiai Rengōkai), 39

national literature, 226–29

national marketplace, 41–45

"Natsu no yakusoku" (Fujino Sen'ya), 282n6

Natsume Sōseki, 109, 117

newspapers: circulation statistics of, 240; *Hōchi shinbun*, 76–78; lending of, 46; locations of, prior to earthquake, 239; market shares of, 240; number of titles published, 237; *Ōsaka asahi*, 79; recovery of, after earthquake, 76–81, 77, 80; *Tōkyō asahi*, 78–79; *Tōkyō nichinichi*, 27, 76, 78; *Yomiuri*, 78, 186. *See also* periodicals

"Nichijō seikatsu o henchō suru akukeikō" (The Negative Tendency to Prioritize Daily Life) (Ikuta Chōkō), 155–57

Nietzsche, Friedrich Wilhelm, 156

Nisshin Insatsu printing company, 69

Niwa Fumio, 220

Noma Seiji, 66–68, 72–73. *See also* Kōdansha publishing house

nonreaders, impact of print on, 245n12

Norman, E. H., 258n5

Oda Takeo, 204–6

Ōji Seishi, 74

one-yen books: accessibility of, 17; publishing industry vs., 126–31; royalties from, 129–31; sales of, 125

Ōno Magohei, 94

Osaka, cultural shift toward, 57–65, 58, 63, 64

Tōkyōdō, aid to Kaizōsha and, 94
Tokyo Magazine Association Secretariat
    (*rinji kanji-kai*), 67–68
Tokyo Magazine Marketing Cooperative
    (Tōkyō Zasshi Hanbai-gyō Kumiai), 68
Tōkyō nichinichi (newspaper), 78
Tōkyō nichinichi shinbun (newspaper), 76
Tokyo Publishing Association (Tōkyō
    Shuppan Kyōkai), 68
Tokyo Shoseki-shō Kumiai (Tokyo Book
    Association), 39, 68
Tokyo Shoseki Shuppan Eigyōsha Kumiai
    (Tokyo Book Publishing Businessmen's
    Association), 36–37
Tomi Suzuki, 226
Tōri Sanjin, "Takarabune kogane no
    hobashira," 33
Torrance, Richard, 256n135
Tōson, Shimazaki, 108
translators, one-yen books and, 129–31
trends, 152–53
Tsubouchi Shōyō, 226–27
Tsuruhachi Tsurujirō (Kawaguchi Mat-
    sutarō), 191–92
Tsuruta Tomoya, 202–4
tsūzoku, as term, 142, 248n27
tsūzoku novels: description of, 158–59;
    Hirabayashi on, 164–65; as term, 178.
    See also *junbungaku* (pure literature or
    fiction)
type-casting, 27–28
typesetting, historical developments in,
    24

Uchiyama Kanzō, 124
Uchiyama Shoten, 124
Ueda Yasuo, 132
uncommonness, mental state novels and,
    155–57, 156
Un'nan shubihei (The Yunnan Garrison)
    (Kimura Sōjū), 222
Uno Kōji: on "Chōkō Deruta" (The

Yangtze River Delta), 215; on Hino,
    208; I-novel debate and, 160–61; on
    "Seika no ichi" (The Fruit and Vegeta-
    ble Market), 219
Urisabakijo (authorized retailers), 37
Ushijima Haruko, 206
Utano Hiroshi, 43
"Uta to mon no tate" (The Defender of
    Poetry and Palace) (Takagi Taku), 213

Wada Toshihiko, 108. *See also* Shun'yōdō
    publishing company
Wallerstein, Immanuel, 243n2
Walter press, 24
wartime situation (*jikyoku*), 214–17, 218
Waseda bungaku (Waseda Literature; mag-
    azine), 186–87
Watashi no hansei (The First Half of My
    Life) (Noma Seiji), 72–73
Wellek, René, 276n21
Wender, Melissa, 228, 293n11
Wicks rotary caster, 24. *See also* printing
    technology
Williams, Raymond, 248n27
Women's World (*Fujin sekai*; magazine),
    38
woodblock printing, 22–23. *See also* print-
    ing technology

"Yamabiko" (Echoes) (Ainoda Toshiyuki),
    216–17
Yamamoto Sanehiko, 93, 96. *See also* Kai-
    zōsha
Yamamoto Shūgorō, refusal of Naoki Prize
    by, 290n116
Yanagida Izumi, *Complete Works of Con-
    temporary Japanese Literature* and, 97–
    106
Yokohama mainichi (newspaper), 27
Yokomitsu Riichi: on "Chōkō Deruta"
    (The Yangtze River Delta), 215–16; on
    historical fiction, 213; on prize selec-

Edward Mack is an associate professor of Japanese at the University of Washington.

Library of Congress Cataloging-in-Publication Data
Mack, Edward Thomas.
Manufacturing modern Japanese literature : publishing, prizes, and
the ascription of literary value / Edward Mack.
p. cm. — (Asia-Pacific : culture, politics, and society)
Includes bibliographical references and index.
ISBN 978-0-8223-4660-9 (cloth : alk. paper)
ISBN 978-0-8223-4672-2 (pbk. : alk. paper)
1. Literature publishing—Japan. 2. Japanese literature—Publishing.
3. Literary prizes—Japan. 4. Canon (Literature) I. Title. II. Series: Asia-Pacific.
Z463.4.M33 2010
070.50952—dc22
2010005177